Environment and Behavior Studies

Emergence of Intellectual Traditions

Human Behavior and Environment

ADVANCES IN THEORY AND RESEARCH

Environment and Behavior Studies

Emergence of Intellectual Traditions

Edited by

IRWIN ALTMAN
University of Utah
Salt Lake City, Utah

and

KATHLEEN CHRISTENSEN
The Graduate School and University Center
City University of New York
New York, New York

PLENUM PRESS • NEW YORK AND LONDON

Library of Congress Cataloging-in-Publication Data

Environment and behavior studies : emergence of intellectual
  traditions / edited by Irwin Altman and Kathleen Christensen.
      p.   cm. -- (Human behavior and environment ; v. 11)
  Includes bibliographical references.
  ISBN 0-306-43468-7
  1. Environmental psychology--History.   I. Altman, Irwin.
II. Christensen, Kathleen.   III. Series.
BF353.H85 vol. 11
155.9 s--dc20
[159]   90-7098
                                                                 CIP

© 1990 Plenum Press, New York
A Division of Plenum Publishing Corporation
233 Spring Street, New York, N.Y. 10013

Printed in the United States of America

This volume is dedicated
to the Environmental Design Research Association
in honor of its twentieth anniversary, 1969–1989

Articles Planned for Volume 12

PLACE ATTACHMENT
Editors: Irwin Altman and Setha Low

Home as a Workplace in the Lives of Women
SHERRY BOLAND AHRENTZEN

Attachment to Possessions
RUSSELL W. BELK

Disruptions in Attachment
BARBARA B. BROWN

Childhood Place Attachments
LOUISE CHAWLA

Thresholds to an Alternate Realm: Mapping
the Chaseworld in Lebanon State Forest
MARY HUFFORD

Community Attachment
DAVID M. HUMMON

Transcendence of Place: The Role of La Placeta
in Valencia's Las Fallas
DENISE L. LAWRENCE

Symbolic Theories of Place Attachment:
Cultural Meaning in the Costa Rican Plaza
SETHA M. LOW

Attachment to Home
CLARE COOPER MARCUS

Space Talks: Neighboring in Africa
DEBORAH PELLOW

Roots, Views and Bonds: Attachment to the Larger Landscape
ROBERT B. RILEY

Place Attachment among the Elderly
ROBERT RUBINSTEIN AND PATRICIA PARMELEE

Home Gardens, Place Attachment and the Experience of Time
JONATHAN D. SIME

Contributors

IRWIN ALTMAN • Department of Psychology, University of Utah, Salt Lake City, Utah 84112

ROGER G. BARKER • Department of Psychology, University of Kansas, Lawrence, Kansas 66045

MICHAEL BRILL • The Buffalo Organization for Social and Technological Innovation, 1479 Hertel Avenue, Buffalo, New York 14216, and School of Architecture, State University of New York at Buffalo, Buffalo, New York 14214

DAVID CANTER • Department of Psychology, University of Surrey, Guildford, Surrey GU2 5XH, England

KENNETH H. CRAIK • Institute of Personality Assessment and Research, University of California at Berkeley, Berkeley, California 94720

M. POWELL LAWTON • Philadelphia Geriatric Center, 5301 Old York Road, Philadelphia, Pennsylvania 19141

CLARE COOPER MARCUS • Department of Architecture and Department of Landscape Architecture, University of California at Berkeley, Berkeley, California 94720

HAROLD M. PROSHANSKY • Environmental Psychology Program, The Graduate School and University Center of the City University of New York, 33 West 42nd Street, New York, New York 10036

AMOS RAPOPORT • School of Architecture and Urban Planning, University of Wisconsin–Milwaukee, Milwaukee, Wisconsin 53201

LEANNE G. RIVLIN • Environmental Psychology Program, The Graduate School and University Center of the City University of New York, 33 West 42nd Street, New York, New York 10036

ROBERT SOMMER • Department of Psychology and Center for Consumer Research, University of California at Davis, Davis, California 95616

SEYMOUR WAPNER • Heinz Werner Institute for Developmental Analysis, Frances L. Hiatt School of Psychology, Clark University, Worcester, Massachusetts 01610-1477

ERVIN H. ZUBE • School of Renewable Natural Resources, University of Arizona, Tucson, Arizona 85721

Preface

This eleventh volume in the series departs from the pattern of earlier volumes. Some of those volumes addressed research, design, and policy topics in terms of environmental settings, for example, homes, communities, neighborhoods, and public places. Others focused on environmental users, for example, children and the elderly. The present volume examines the field of environment and behavior studies itself in the form of intellectual histories of some of its most productive and still visible senior participants. In so doing we hope to provide readers with a grand sweep of the field—its research and design content, methodology, institutions, and past and future trajectories—through the experiences and intellectual histories of its participants.

Why intellectual histories? Several factors led to the decision to launch this project. For one, 1989 was an anniversary and commemorative year for the Environmental Design Research Association, perhaps the major and most long-standing interdisciplinary organization of environment and behavior researchers and practitioners. Established in 1969, this organization has been the vehicle for generations of researchers and practitioners from many disciplines to come together annually to exchange ideas, present papers, and develop professional and personal relationships. It held its first and twentieth meetings in North Carolina, with the twentieth conference substantially devoted to discussions of the past, present, and future of the field—a taking stock, so to speak. Thus it seemed appropriate to launch a volume on intellectual histories at this significant juncture in the life of the field.

Moreover, the field of environment and behavior studies has matured, with many of its participants having achieved a sophisticated perspective on their own work and on the field as a whole. Many of them come from different disciplines and have diverse backgrounds and values. As a result, peers, juniors, and emerging generations can profit from the experiences and varying perspectives of those who contributed in significant and sustained ways to environment and behavior studies. In addition, it is likely that newer generations will have less and less opportunity to interact directly with senior participants, to learn about the opportunities and challenges they faced, and to share in those experiences. Those intellectual experiences need to be recorded—not only for archival and historical reasons, but for the promise and potential those careers illustrate, and for newer generations to capitalize on as they set their own future course.

The focus of the chapters in the volume is on the intellectual histories of a diverse, still active, and intellectually influential and alive group of early contributors to the field of environment and behavior studies. Although some of the accounts of the researchers, theorists, and practitioners who wrote essays for this volume are chronological, the emphasis is nevertheless on the development of their ideas and work; the twists and turns of their professional careers; and the people, places, and settings within which they worked. The chapters are diverse in format and writing style, but we hope that they illustrate the vast diversity of perspectives, content, and intellectual interests of environment and behavior participants. And, most important, the intellectual histories illustrate the challenges, opportunities, and breadth of subject matter in the environment and behavior field, as well as the need for all people to learn about and act upon environmental problems. The environmental issues that will face us in the 1990s and in the soon-to-be twenty-first century need the work and commitment of the best minds that we can attract to environment and behavior studies. The essays in this volume are a testimonial to what a handful of people began and accomplished—men and women who can serve as beacons and role models for future generations as they face their own unique problems.

Volume 12 in the series, *Place Attachment*, now in preparation, will address people's attachment to an array of environmental places and settings, varying from small-scale objects to homes, communities, and neighborhoods, and beyond to larger-scale urban and regional settings. Setha Low, City University of New York, joins me in editing this next volume in the *Human Behavior and Environment* series.

Because of its two-decade commitment to environment and behavior studies, its nurturing of the free expression of a diversity of views, and its egalitarian and supportive values for all environment and behavior researchers and practitioners, this volume is dedicated to the Environmental Design Research Association. May it prosper in the next twenty years of its life.

IRWIN ALTMAN

Contents

CHAPTER 3

SETTINGS OF A PROFESSIONAL LIFETIME   49

ROGER G. BARKER

CHAPTER 4

SCIENCE AND THE FAILURE OF ARCHITECTURE:
AN INTELLECTUAL HISTORY   79

AMOS RAPOPORT

CHAPTER 5

FROM THE PRAGMATIC TO THE SPIRITUAL:
AN INTELLECTUAL AUTOBIOGRAPHY   111

CLARE COOPER MARCUS

CHAPTER 6

ENVIRONMENTAL AND PERSONALITY PSYCHOLOGY: TWO
COLLECTIVE NARRATIVES AND FOUR INDIVIDUAL STORY LINES 141

KENNETH H. CRAIK

Chapter 7

Paths toward Environmental Consciousness   169

LEANNE G. RIVLIN

Chapter 8

Thinking . . . As Much Fun as Sex, Drugs, and Rock 'n Roll 187

MICHAEL BRILL

CHAPTER 9

TOWARD A TRANSACTIONAL PERSPECTIVE:
A PERSONAL JOURNEY   225

IRWIN ALTMAN

CHAPTER 10

ONE PERSON-IN-HIS-ENVIRONMENTS   257

SEYMOUR WAPNER

Chapter 11

Landscape Research: Planned and Serendipitous   291

ERVIN H. ZUBE

Chapter 12

In Search of Objectives   315

DAVID CANTER

CHAPTER 13

AN ENVIRONMENTAL PSYCHOLOGIST AGES   339

M. POWELL LAWTON

Environment and
Behavior Studies

Introduction

The field of environment and behavior studies occupies a special niche on the intellectual scene. Interdisciplinary by nature, and spanning several social science and environmental design fields, this problem-focused discipline emerged, partially by intent and partially by accident, in the 1960s and 1970s. Its sources were many. At the societal level, an array of social and political problems focused attention on the physical environment and human affairs. Ferment surrounded issues such as war and peace, civil rights, sexual liberation, education, and the environment. In fact, the first Earth Day in the spring of 1970 galvanized public activity on environmental concerns as diverse as air, water and land pollution, toxic waste disposal, desecration of the natural landscape, urban decay, crime, suburban sprawl, unsatisfactory housing for the poor and elderly, and so on.

On the intellectual scene during those years, a handful of social scientists and environmental designers criticized their parent disciplines for ignoring social and environmental problems. Environmental designers from architecture, interior design, landscape architecture, and related fields called for an intellectual approach capable of studying the psychological, social, and cultural needs of the users of physical places, with less attention to traditional emphases on self-expression, intuition, and esthetic formalism.

At the same time, some social scientists were expressing discontent with their disciplines. Cultural and behavioral geographers, urban sociologists, planners, and psychologists criticized their parent fields for ignoring aspects of complex, molar physical settings in relation to psychological and social phenomena.

It was within this social, political, and intellectual maelstrom of the late 1960s and early 1970s that a cross-pollination of ideas occurred as thinkers and practitioners in disparate fields influenced and incorporated ideas from one another into their own work. Born of separate disciplines, many of these social scientists, designers, and planners forged a collective identity as members of the environment and behavior field.

This book presents the intellectual histories of 13 of these first-generation thinkers and designers. Although aspects of the history of the environment

1

and behavior field have been well documented by others,[1] this book comprises the first collective effort on the part of leading thinkers in the field to trace their own intellectual development.

THE EMERGING FIELD

As scientists and designers in different disciplines began to learn of one another's individual efforts, the need for a formalization of the field became apparent. In a first meeting in North Carolina in 1969, what had been a loose affiliation of scholars and practitioners coalesced into a professional organization—the Environmental Design Research Association (EDRA). This organization has held annual meetings ever since and celebrated its twentieth anniversary in 1989, meeting again in North Carolina. The environment and behavior field also became institutionalized in several major universities in the United States and abroad. Interdisciplinary educational programs were established, including the Environmental Psychology Program, at the Graduate School of the City University of New York, the Social Ecology Program at the University of California–Irvine, the Man–Environment Program at The Pennsylvania State University, and the program in Environmental Psychology at the University of Surrey, England. In 1970, the journal *Environment and Behavior* was begun. Over a short period of time, additional journals, book series, conferences, and other degree-granting programs appeared, thereby providing an institutional grounding for the environment and behavior field.

Although it has had its fair share of intellectual and organizational ferment, the field of environment and behavior studies has matured and achieved stability, although its continued diversity and openness to new directions makes predictions about its future trajectory somewhat uncertain.

Several consistent themes have guided the research and practice of many who joined the environment and behavior field. These themes include the study of holistic and complex units of analysis, an interdisciplinary perspective, an eclectic and broad-based methodological approach to research, and a focus on the solution of environmental problems directly or through theory and research-based analyses.

ABOUT THE BOOK

With the field now established and entering its third decade, and with many of its leading figures professionally mature, we decided to tap their wisdom through the vehicle of intellectual histories. Our goal was to have authors put their intellectual histories at the forefront, not their strict chronological and autobiographical histories. As such, we intended that authors make

---

[1] Aspects of the history of the environment and behavior field have been well documented by Moore (1987), Proshansky and Altman (1979), Stokols (1977), and in 10 chapters on international developments in *The Handbook of Environmental Psychology* (Stokols & Altman, 1987).

salient the development of their ideas, the streams of their thinking and work over the years, and the twists and turns in their intellectual development, with strict autobiographical facts and figures, places, and people serving as background and context. In a field with so many intellectual lines of thought and diverse disciplines and traditions, we encouraged authors to make their intellectual histories the "figure" of the chapters, with people, places, and strict chronology as the background or "ground."

Although the audience for this volume will include seasoned researchers and practitioners from diverse fields, the most important audience may well be the junior generation of researchers and practitioners and the cohorts of students and neophytes who are interested in environment and behavior issues. In a world of increasing complexity, uncertain economics, and intellectual and institutional retrenchments, younger generations may profit by seeing the diversity of intellectual and personal histories of those whose work is visible to them, as well as the perseverance, struggles, and pressures faced by their predecessors. In so doing, they may come to appreciate the fact that there are many exciting possibilities, opportunities, and challenges in the environment and behavior field.

The intellectual histories reported in this volume demonstrate that, in spite of obstacles, one can succeed and grow and make significant contributions in unique and sustained ways. This fact is all the more salient in view of the reality that environment and behavior problems of the 1960s, 1970s, and 1980s are still with us today, perhaps even exacerbated, and that they will continue to call for creative solutions, energy, good sense, and sophisticated intellectual and professional advances in the last decade of this century.

THE AUTHORS

The 13 authors in this volume provide a broad-ranging perspective on the environment and behavior field. Yet, we realize that any attempt to characterize the whole of a field by means of the particulars of a small sample of individuals is always fraught with difficulty. No matter how varied and rich individual careers may be, it is impossible to capture the complete intellectual flavor and life of a field by focusing on the development of a handful of men and women. Yet, many of the major themes, issues, and tensions that have characterized the field since its inception and that will continue to be relevant issues in the future are embedded in the essays that follow.

Selecting authors for this volume was at once easy and difficult. Those finally invited had to be included because of the richness and continuity of their contributions to the field. Those selected are, we believe, representative of the large number of important contributors to the field over the past decades and illustrate its diversity and richness. Yet, there are many other participants in the environment and behavior field who deserved inclusion but were necessarily omitted because of limited space.

The 13 authors were either originally trained or still identify themselves as affiliated with the fields of anthropology, geography, psychology, architecture, regional planning, urban planning, landscape architecture, gerontology, and others. Some continue to identify with their disciplinary field of training; others identify with one or more different fields. They are, therefore, difficult to categorize and type in any particular way. Moreover, most of the authors have now or have previously been associated with one or more of the following types of organizations: traditional departments in universities, interdisciplinary research centers, public or private research, consulting or design organizations, federal, state, or local governmental agencies, and so on. Many of them maintain primary identities as either researchers and scholars, or practitioners and consultants; some are active in legislation and policy formulation and in organizational management and administration. And most of the authors have had involvement with or presently engage in one or more of these professional activities. So they are a diverse lot in terms of theory, research, design, practice, policy, and organizational activities and affiliations.

The authors in this volume have also played critical roles in the development of the environment and behavior field and, most important, have made major and visible contributions on a sustained basis, and continue to be active in their careers and in the field. Their work and commitments have been steady and long term.

The authors also come from a diversity of backgrounds, with the voices of women and men represented in the volume, some having grown up in Europe and Australia, and some representing urban and rural backgrounds, different ethnic and religious heritages, and the like. Although we would have been pleased to have had even more diversity of representation, the range of perspectives offered by the authors is a good sample of the heterogeneity of the environment and behavior field.

The order of presentation of chapters in the volume is essentially random, with the exception that the first several chapters are those of senior members of the field, who are among the earliest pioneers of environment and behavior studies.

SOME EDITORIAL IMPRESSIONS

The histories that follow are unique contributions and reflections and also collectively offer a profile of the environment and behavior field. The individual chapters neither need nor deserve editorial comment, for they speak clearly and with unique and diverse voices. Yet we also came away with several impressions about the collection of histories, based on our reading and commentaries on successive drafts, and from conversations and discussions with authors over the 3 years of the project. Perhaps some of our impressions and observations may add an additional perspective beyond those provided by the individual intellectual histories.

Every author welcomed the opportunity to join the project, felt that it was an appropriate time to reflect on his or her career trajectory, and looked forward to the task. Soon thereafter, and often throughout the project, however, they struggled, fussed, procrastinated, had self-doubts, and wondered how to cast their personal histories. How to make sense out of so many accidental twists and turns in their lives? How to account for a particular conceptual or pragmatic turn in their work? How to figure out why they had done what they did at a particular juncture? Many told us, and sometimes wrote in their essays, how they had often made the description of their choices and career paths coherent and orderly when, in fact, chance, accident, and serendipity had often played a most important role. This theme appeared over and over in their accounts, intermingled with order and planning of their work.

It may be that the lives of our authors reflect a dialectic of order and disorder, or coherent planning and accident. Most authors did pursue consistent themes throughout their careers, but they did not always do so in a completely systematic or always orderly fashion. And their creativity and success may have resulted from the simultaneous qualities of order and chance in their lives, allowing them to be open to unanticipated alternatives, opportunities, and people and places, while they still followed a broadly defined path. This dialectic interplay may underlay their oftstated concerns about trying to make their lives sound sensible and coherent when, in fact, accident and unpredictability played an important role.

A related theme is that chance and serendipity in their lives did not follow a consistent pattern from author to author, or even within a particular author's career. Accidental encounters with people, places, issues, readings, singly or in combination, and at different times propelled them in directions that seemed promising. They seemed to follow a path that "felt" right at the time, often without a great deal of lengthy professional decision making.

Another consistent theme in many chapters is a sense of dissatisfaction by authors with the status quo, often reflected in unhappiness and a sense of disappointment with their parent disciplines. Their dissatisfaction took the form of feelings that the norms, methods, or practices of their parent discipline simply did not always work when applied to environment and behavior problems. They often felt intellectually constrained by the paradigms and perceived restrictions of their fields of training. They wanted to go beyond the limits of their disciplines, in order to uncover new ideas, methods, and perspectives and to achieve knowledge and design concepts that were missing or beyond the borders of their fields. For many, this meant trying out and incorporating the perspectives of other disciplines in their research and practice, joining interdisciplinary organizations and job settings, searching for new people, places, and opportunities. Some authors were able to maintain comfortable ties with their parent disciplines; others felt that this was not possible and rejected identification with their parent fields.

For most authors, their dissatisfaction proved to be an impetus to gamble—with methods, topics, projects, and at times even with their careers. Often equipped with more understanding of what was not working than what would work authors were willing to reach out on their own, taking risks with what they did and how they went about doing it. This gambling instinct symptomizes the fact that these were not people who were content to simmer over their discontent but rather converted their energies into productive ends. They each reflect an incredibly high level of scholarly energy and, indeed, their energy and consistent output of scholarly and practical products is unusual and unabated. They are working, thinking, and doing all the time, constantly taking on more than they can handle, but still doing the job, searching out or welcoming new opportunities beyond a time when most others have peaked in their careers or slowed their pace of professional activity. This group of environment and behavior scholars continues to be active and are able easily to project what they want to do next, or the kinds of opportunities to which they will be receptive.

The intellectual energy they exhibit is not only cognitive and rational; there is passion and emotion in their work. They care deeply and personally about the issues they address—whether they be oriented to research and theory, action and problem solving, social justice and humanitarian causes, or some combination of these. They fret and worry about environment and behavior questions; they want to achieve change in their own and others' thinking or in the real world, and they are passionate about what they do. Although they may approach problems in a detached, cool, and rational way, there is simultaneously in their work and presence strong emotional underpinnings that appear in between the lines of their writing, and more directly, when they speak about and discuss their work.

Thus their commitment to their work is not detached from their personal lives, goals, and experiences. Some have revealed more than others about their personal lives and the ways in which their personal and professional lives are intertwined. However, if one reads between the lines of their histories and if one reflects on aspects of their statements, one will sense that their lives are represented in their work. They "do their own work" in that their research or practice is closely linked in one way or another with their qualities as humans beings—their values, perspectives, past experiences, childhood, and so on. It is perhaps this bonding of work and personal life, above all, that is associated with an endless search, quest for knowing, high level of commitment, boundless energy, sustained work, discomfort with the status quo, and never "knowing" enough about a subject or being comfortable with what one does that underlies the intellectual histories of authors in this volume.

There is also an air of confidence and certainty in the past, present, and projected work of these authors. They are strong willed and established in their thinking, even though most are open to opportunities and challenges. Their views and values are reasonably clear and consistently stated, reflecting a strength of commitment, direction, and character that has evolved over long and productive careers. At the same time, however, and not always reflected directly in their intellectual histories, their self-confidence is often accompanied by uncertainty, anxiety, insecurity, and hesitation. Authors sometimes wondered about the value of their work, probable success of projects they were working on, whether or not they had anything "new" to say, and they often displayed a modesty that concealed uncertainty about their work. They reflect, therefore, a mixture of confidence and hesitation, intellectual security and anxiety, brashness and timidity, flexibility and stubbornness. It may well be that the synthesis of these dialectic opposites—confidence and uncertainty—drives these authors to pursue their work, seek new opportunities, and put themselves and their ideas on the line.

Yet, for all of their similarities, authors differ widely in several ways. Some are research and theory oriented, focusing on development of basic knowledge and concepts in the environment and behavior field. Others translate basic research into applied studies. Others are practice oriented, drawing on research and theory but focusing on problem solving and design solutions to environment and behavior issues. Still others are geared to communicating with large public audiences through their efforts in formulating public policy and participating in governmental settings.

And, as one might have anticipated, authors differ widely in the subject matter of their work, philosophical perspectives regarding the nature of science, the linkages of research and practice, how to engage in practice and environmental design, and where they think environment and behavior studies should proceed in the future.

Having reflected on what we know personally about authors, having lived with them through the process of writing and reviewing their histories, and having them react to our comments left us with a sense that we had provided our colleagues with a giant Rorschach card—an ambiguous stimulus or even a blank canvas—on which they could project themselves in unique and idiosyncratic ways. And, they did exactly that, each speaking with his or her own voice, style of self-presentation, and providing a rich and varied fabric to the volume as a whole. The organization and structure of their chapters, their different styles of writing, the form of self-disclosure they selected, all portray them as distinctive individuals, with each chapter revealing the unique persona of authors. The consequence is what we had hoped to achieve—personally crafted intellectual histories, not mechanically written pieces following a common format. But this leads to considerable variation in style, content, and organization that may be initially disconcerting. On reflection, however, readers have an opportunity to see each person in a distinctive way. The Rorschach-like quality of the contributions should encourage readers to realize that there are diverse paths to success and that they have before them 13 models who have disclosed their unique personalities and intellectual styles.

We also came away with a mixture of surprise and pleasure about what we learned about our colleagues over the 3 years of this project. On the one hand, we originally felt that we "knew" the authors pretty well on personal and professional grounds. After all, we had read their writings, participated in meetings with them for years, socialized and held long conversations with them on many occasions, and felt that we knew who they were and what they believed in. Yet, we were surprised and pleased to learn about aspects of their lives and work that we hadn't previously known. Their chapters filled in many gaps about them. How often it is that we know so little about one another as human beings and colleagues and that having known more earlier would have helped us understand one another as persons and as intellectuals and scholars because, after all, so much of our scholarly lives are intertwined and guided by our personal lives. So, although gratified to learn a great deal more about the lives of these colleagues, we regret that we did not know them better sooner.

If readers, especially students and young researchers and practitioners, are to come away with any singular principle from the contributions to this volume, it is that the field of environment and behavior studies is rich, laden with opportunity, and permits multiple paths to scholarship and practice. The field welcomes a diversity of perspectives and individuals who are free to explore, challenge, alter their directions of effort, and who can expect surprises and serendipity as they mingle and exchange ideas, values, and the approaches of many disciplines and points of view. In so doing, the opportunities for intellectual, practical, and personal growth are enormous, although one cannot easily specify in advance the exact path for progress. That is the responsibility and freedom of each individual to determine. The authors in this volume collectively illustrate these principles and provide encouragement and stimulation for new generations of environment and behavior scholars and practitioners to find their own way in the 1990s and beyond.

IRWIN ALTMAN
KATHLEEN CHRISTENSEN

REFERENCES

Moore, G. T. (1987). Environment and behavior research in North America: History, developments and unsolved issues. In D. Stokols & I. Altman (Eds.), *Handbook of environmental psychology* (pp. 1259–1410). New York: Wiley.

Proshansky, H. M., & Altman, I. (1979). Overview of the field. In W. P. White (Ed.), *Resources in environment and behavior* (pp. 3–36) Washington, DC: American Psychological Association.

Stokols, D. (Ed.). (1977). *Perspectives on environment and behavior.* New York: Plenum Press.

Stokols, D., & Altman, I. (Eds.). (1987). *Handbook of environmental psychology.* New York: Wiley.

1

The Pursuit of Understanding

AN INTELLECTUAL HISTORY

HAROLD M. PROSHANSKY

I WAS BORN IN NEW YORK IN 1920 and was educated in public schools from kindergarten to City College, where I received my BS in 1941. In June 1942 I received my master's degree in social psychology from Columbia University; that fall I was married to Etta Weissman.

I entered the U.S. Army Air Corps in October 1942 and was assigned to Psychological Research Unit #1, which was responsible for the classification of aircrew cadets as navigators, pilots, or bombardiers. After 3½ years in the service and then 2 years as an adjunct faculty member and experimental laboratory researcher in a private research laboratory, I returned to graduate school and received my PhD in social psychology from New York University under Morton Deutsch in 1952 (I was his first PhD student). I also worked with Marie Jahoda, Stuart Cook, Gerhardt Saenger, and others. I received an interim appointment and then a full-time appointment at Brooklyn College, teaching courses in social psychology and personality but doing most of my research in such social psychology areas as impression formation, attitude measurement, and ethnic prejudice.

From September 1959 to August 1961 I spent a sabbatical and a leave at the Research Center for Group Dynamics (Institute for Social Research) and the Department of Psychology at the University of Michigan. By the time I returned to Brooklyn College, I had decided not to do more psychological research of the laboratory type; my increasing association with William H. Ittelson and Leanne G. Rivlin had turned my attention to the real-world physical environment and its effect on the behavior of the individual. By 1966, I was identifying myself as an environmental psychologist. My interests were focused on developing appropriate methodology and theory for environmental psychology and on conceptualizing place identity, environmental security, and human privacy in the context of urban places and spaces.

In the mid-1960s I began teaching at CUNY's Graduate School. In 1968 I became dean of the Graduate School and in time its provost, acting president, and then presi-

HAROLD M. PROSHANSKY • Environmental Psychology Program, The Graduate School and University Center of the City University of New York, 33 West 42nd Street, New York, New York 10036.

dent. For the last 17 years, during my presidency, I have also spent time thinking and writing as an environmental psychologist. From the 1950s to the present, I have served the American Psychological Association (APA), the Society for the Psychological Study of Social Issues (SPSSI), and Division 8 of the APA in many ways.

Leaving my field of interest and my once considerable involvement as a social psychologist and environmental psychologist to become a full-time administrator was a wrenching experience. I have no regrets, however, because building CUNY's Graduate School and University Center has provided me with extraordinary experiences and satisfactions that more than made up for my losses.

I have had a remarkably rewarding professional career, and if I owe anyone anything, it is my wife. Her good sense, her perception, and her acute intelligence have helped me immeasurably when I have confronted difficult problems as a research psychologist and as an administrator. I dedicate this chapter to my wife, Etta Proshansky.

INTRODUCTION

When the editors of this volume first approached me and asked that I write the intellectual history of my career as a social and then environmental psychologist, I readily agreed, despite the fact that as a full-time administrator I have little if any time to pursue scholarly interests. I assume my eagerness to participate was in part due to the fact that I would be in the distinguished company of the other contributors. The ego can be inexorable in its pursuits and quite sneaky about getting its way.

Ego satisfaction alone, however, could not have gotten me to consent so quickly to write a so-called intellectual autobiography. As a seasoned administrator with some very painful deadline experiences, I had learned to tame the ego and say no to scholarly commitments. What really moved me was curiosity about my own intellectual development—where my ideas came from, who influenced me and how, and what caused me at first to accept a particular theoretical position and then give it up in favor of another. The very fact that my thinking and approach as a social psychologist changed quite radically over the years, leading me to switch my specialization from social to environmental psychology, was reason enough for me to want to take a look back. Perhaps the ego is even sneakier than I thought.

One final introductory comment is in order. Curious or not, I still had a problem with available time. However, because this was to be a chapter written by me about me, I had the naive idea that it would be a relatively easy thing to do. It turned out not to be. On the contrary, it was the most arduous and time-consuming writing task I have ever undertaken. Not only is it very difficult to retrace one's intellectual steps in any detail over a 50-year period, but one can never be sure how much is true and accurate recollection and how much is plausible and logically consistent reconstruction. Subtle but significant experiences and influences are inevitably lost to memory, never to be recaptured again. Yet for all these limitations, the effort did end up providing a substantial amount of "hard data" about the sources of my ideas and their intellectual consequences. It also proved addictive: Besides remembering many satisfying experiences and activities that I had forgotten, I truly learned a great deal about who and what pushed me and pulled me intellectually. Nevertheless, what the reader will encounter here probably falls somewhere between "true and accurate recollections" and "plausible and logically consistent reconstructions."

HOW IT ALL BEGAN: PEOPLE, PLACES, AND EVENTS

My formal training as a psychologist began at the City College of New York, where I did my undergraduate work in the late 1930s. My significant psychology mentors during that time were Gardner Murphy and the brilliant although less known member of the psychology department, Max Hertzman. The influence on my thinking exerted by Murphy and Hertzman, and later by Otto Klineberg, can only be understood, however, in the context of my background long before I was a student in their courses. Briefly, I was born into a Jewish family that moved from lower class to lower middle class and then back again during the Great Depression years. It was a family that prided itself on being intellectual, cultured, and above all liberal and humanistic in its views. My mother and father were labor union members with a strong socialistic orientation who voted the Democratic ticket in all elections and openly espoused racial equality, intergroup harmony, compassion for the downtrodden, the essential goodness of all human beings, and the sublimity of American democracy. They strongly identified with their left, liberal working-class roots, but at the same time saw their children doing better by becoming educated and entering a high-status profession, with medicine clearly having the highest priority. It was thus my highest priority when I entered City College in 1937.

That did not last long, though. During my freshman year I began painfully to realize that my career commitment was tied more to potential economic and social satisfactions than to intellectual ones. I found myself being excited and challenged far more by courses I was taking in history, art history, philosophy, and introductory psychology than by my biology and other physical science courses—understandably enough, given my cultural upbringing. By the end of my sophomore year I knew that medicine was out, and I began to suspect that psychology might be the major for me. With my strong science background, I found the introductory psychology course and the methodological courses in statistics and experimental psychology quite absorbing in the laboratory as well as the lecture hall. My readings and tutorial experiences left me ecstatic about the potential of the experimental laboratory approach for the study of such psychological processes as motivation, learning, perception, and emotion.

As I moved from biology and the "hard sciences" to psychology, it was fascination with the nature of human experience and conduct that drove me, not dissatisfaction with what I was leaving behind. The sheer interest value for me lay more in people and their manifest behavior than in the physiological or even distinct psychological processes underlying this behavior. Indeed, it was

Gardner Murphy's almost legendary course in personality that clinched my decision to change my major to psychology.

My training with Murphy and the other faculty members led me to view the person as a dynamic organism in which the interaction of psychological processes—influenced by inner biological and enduring social factors on the one hand and the situational context on the other—determined human behavior and experience; the challenge was to somehow put all those sources of influence together. The impact of Gestalt theorists such as Kohler (1929), Koffka (1935), and Lewin (1935) was evident in Murphy's thinking and therefore in mine. Our approach moved away from stimulus–response conceptions of how individuals felt, thought, learned, saw, and comprehended. Not unlike the Freudian paradigm, it readily accepted biological as well as social input into the dynamics of human behavior. Moreover, contrary to the reductionistic model of complex human behavior, it hypothesized levels of organization of greater and greater complexity as one moved up the phylogenetic scale, in which unique biological and psychological properties emerged that could not be explained at simpler levels.

What intrigued me initially about Murphy's dynamic biosocial approach was his persistent concern with the way psychological processes interacted with one another, and in particular his discussion of *autism*, or how needs and other motivational states affected perception (Murphy, 1947). It was his lectures and the many tutorial conversations I had with him that led me to devote my Senior Honors research project to studying the influence of human needs—in this case the gratifications of rewards—on perception under experimental laboratory conditions (Proshansky & Murphy, 1942).

Max Hertzman's theoretical orientation had much in common with Murphy's. He, too, was drawn to Lewinian field theory and to Lewin's dynamic conception of human behavior and experience (1951). Hertzman, far better than anyone else, introduced me to the mathematical/conceptual basis of statistical measurement ("understand," he said, "don't memorize or mimic") and to the nature and meaning of qualitative data—whether in the form of a Rorschach test, a diary, or an interview.

Murphy and Hertzman were eclectics, it must be emphasized, not narrow ideologues. They in no way rejected the experimental laboratory approach and the conceptions of learning, thinking, and motivation that went along with it. Hertzman, in particular, constantly stressed to his students the importance of both the quantitative laboratory approach and qualitative ideographic analyses, insisting that the choice of a methodology depended on the problem to be studied and the manner in which it was formulated. Both men felt that although some problems of human behavior and experience required ideographic and qualitative approaches (Allport, 1940), others could be experimentally studied and quantified. What they did reject was the commitment to a stimulus–response analysis of complex psychological processes rooted in operational methodology and a theoretical reductionistic conception (Bridgeman, 1927); and above all the assumption made by traditional psychologists of the time that *only* those human problems that could be studied through the model of controlled laboratory research were worthy of the designation "scientific."

I received my BS in June of 1941. The intellectual orientation with which I left City College reflected the thinking of Murphy in many ways, especially in its eclecticism about psychological theory and methodology. I was at the time an ideologue only in my strong distaste for stimulus–response models of behavior and the use of animal research as a basis for understanding human behavior. I was attracted to Lewinian field theory, yet I also saw great promise in psychoanalytic theories, particularly of the social kind (e.g., Horney, 1939), and in the thinking of major sociologists and anthropologists. I was truly an eclectic, and perhaps this was why I wasn't sure in June of 1941 whether I would become a clinical psychologist, a social psychologist, or an experimental cognitive psychologist. With service in World War II imminent, I decided to take a master's in social psychology at Columbia University with Otto Klineberg, whose work on racial intelligence impressed and interested me a great deal.

At Columbia I found myself in a department of psychology that was traditional in every sense of the word and therefore heavily weighted toward the experimental laboratory study of learning, perception, emotion, motivation, and other psychological processes. The courses I had taken at City College to obtain a proper grounding in the field were now repeated in most instances at an advanced level. Although this certainly added to my knowledge and research expertise, my real interest was in Otto Klineberg's courses, and he was indeed the major influence on my thinking in the 1 year I spent at Columbia getting an MA degree in psychology.

Klineberg's courses in social psychology and race relations first revealed to me that the view of the individual as a social being I had encountered in my courses at City College was a narrow one. With the exception of Murphy's personality course, the emphasis at City College was always on the psychological level of analysis—that is, on the individual—with no more than lip service given to social organization, historical change, and more complex levels of analysis. Klineberg, by contrast, focused on culture, society, and broad social groupings as well as on the individual. He was problem oriented, as is suggested by his now classic research on intelligence and race differences (Klineberg et al., 1957). At Columbia my own thinking became directed to some small degree on problems in the real world and not simply on psychological processes. I came into contact with Mamie and Kenneth Clark, Goodwin Watson, Herbert Hyman, Isidore Chein, and others who were very concerned with the sociopsychological analysis of human social problems. This helped me not only with defining my approach to social psychology but also with the thorny issue of how it was to be implemented methodologically.

In particular, I came to have misgivings about applying the method of scale measurement to social attitudes. In my master's research I tried to develop a *projective* test to study attitudes toward labor (Proshansky, 1943). If needs, values, and feelings influenced perception and cognition, I reasoned, then a person's descriptions of what was happening in newspaper pictures having to do with social class problems and conflicts—photos depicting strikes or pover-ty-stricken families, for instance—could be quite revealing. The original idea for this kind of projective test of attitudes came from Allan Fromme's early work (1941). My own research (Harding, Kutner, Proshansky, & Chein, 1954) revealed the existence of what Murphy called "shared autism" in social class attitudes (Murphy, 1947), in that the individual perceived and thought about what was going on in the pictures in attitudinally selective ways. Because the respondents couched the descriptions they gave in their own language instead of responding to attitude scale items, there was a greater likelihood that they were expressing enduring attitudes; moreover, I was able to derive a quan-titative measure from their verbal accounts.

By the time I left Columbia in June 1942 with my MA in hand, my doubts about what kind of psychology I wished to pursue had disappeared. I saw myself as a social psychologist interested in establishing concepts and princi-ples of social behavior and experience, especially as they related to the issues of racial and ethnic prejudice, poverty, and social class conflict.

Four months later I was drafted into the armed services and assigned to Psychological Research Unit #1, in what was then known as the United States Army Air Corps. I spent the next years working with the many academic and applied psychologists in this unit. My activities consisted of individual and group aptitude testing, test-development research, clinical evaluation of nor-mal populations, program evaluation, and even some teaching. The mission of the Psychological Research Unit was to predict aircrew success for Air Corps cadets who wanted to serve as either pilots, navigators, or bombardiers. Be-cause our attention was focused on improving predictions of success in these aircrew functions, methodological and theoretical differences among us did not loom as a significant problem inasmuch as classic psychometric approaches dominated the thinking of those who established the units and their purposes. Yet in a unit that included experimental, clinical, social, and psychoanalytically Lewinian-oriented psychologists among others, such differences did emerge in informal discussions about what would work best in evaluating cadets for aircrew success.

Although I learned a great deal during my stint as an Air Corps psychol-ogist, there was no shift in my theoretical viewpoint; indeed, it was preserved and even reinforced by the highly practical nature of the applied tasks that confronted us (the presence of other psychologists in the unit with theoretical orientations similar to mine also contributed to this stability). Still, by the time I was discharged from service I had begun to have some doubts about the field of social psychology, even in regard to the work of researchers whose approach was very close to my own. These doubts were not derived from any sophisticated epistemological notion of the role of theory and data in social psychology. Rather, they arose from my having spent a substantial amount of time as an applied psychologist in the real world. I simply could not ignore the difficulties in the approach I had embraced as a social psychologist. Two of these I remember particularly well because they were the subjects of dis-cussions I had with a number of other psychologists in the Air Corps unit.

First, there was the apparent and incontrovertible fact that much of the field of psychology was far more empirical than theoretical. In fact, the emphasis given to the "hard science" model of research made the field seem almost atheoretical, as methodology became supreme. Second, when psychologists did invoke theory in formulating problems, the level of abstraction was so far removed from the reality of the problem that the empirical research subsequently undertaken had little real consequence for the theory itself. This was even true for the kind of dynamic social psychology with which I so strongly identified.

Perhaps this explains why, upon returning to civilian life in January 1946, I decided not to take up graduate training toward a doctorate. Instead, I landed a job as a research associate at Haskins Laboratories, a privately endowed and government-supported organization engaged in psychological (as well as medical) research relevant to overcoming reading and mobility problems in the newly blind by the development of "speech machines" and light-sensitive guidance systems, respectively. My return to the experimental laboratory was by no means reluctant, given my growing conviction that applied research that focused directly on solving human problems and improving the quality of life was a worthy career in its own right. Within a year, however, I realized that laboratory research into these kinds of human problems could never be of sufficient interest or satisfaction for me over any lengthy period of time. I therefore applied and was accepted as a doctoral student in social psychology at New York University in the fall of 1947.

The years I spent at NYU as a student, research assistant, and undergraduate instructor greatly influenced my professional development. My involvement in the Research Center for Human Relations with Morton Deutsch, Stuart Cook, Marie Jahoda, and others not only strengthened my field-theoretical orientation but also added to my methodological skills, particularly with respect to field research and opinion-attitude surveys. Deutsch, who was my thesis advisor, is a brilliant theoretician and research practitioner; his integration of theory and method was the best I had encountered. By the time I finished my PhD any doubts I might have entertained about the *dynamic* or field-theoretical approach to human problems had vanished.

For a year during my doctoral studies I worked full-time for the Commission on Community Interrelations (CCI) of the American Jewish Congress. Our research was concerned with techniques of diagnosing, describing, and changing negative racial and ethnic attitudes—particularly anti-Semitism—in given community settings. The overarching view that guided us was Lewinian field theory. This "action research" was the sort of real-life, problem-oriented inquiry that Lewin (1946) believed could be theoretically meaningful as well as socially useful.

In the summer of 1952, CCI was more or less phased out by the American Jewish Congress because of a sharp decline in financial support. I was fortunate enough to get an interim appointment in the Brooklyn College psychology department, where I taught mainly advanced social psychology and personality courses while carrying out my own research and writing projects.

GROWING DISENCHANTMENT

My first 6 years at Brooklyn College (1952–1958) marked the beginning of my disenchantment with the field of social psychology. The rather innocuous origin of this attitude lay in an earlier study by Asch (1946) of how impressions of personality were formed. This study was often cited in support of the Gestalt principle that the individual's percepts made up a unified whole even in the face of contradictory information. Given a list of traits and asked to describe a person who possessed them, the college students Asch used as subjects reconciled those that were inconsistent. Some of the traits, moreover, showed a greater influence on the final impressions they formed than others.

Asch's findings had a considerable impact on social-perception theory and on my own thinking—that is, until my graduate students and I attempted to replicate his study some 12 years after it was originally done. Some startling facts emerged in interviews we held with our student subjects after they had written their impressions based on the list of traits presented to them. Some of the students offhandedly pointed out that this was not the typical way that people formed first impressions of others in their day-to-day social interactions: Not only did such impression formation usually take place with the other person present, but the time of "exposure" varied considerably. In those instances where the other person is not present and someone else is describing him or her, that description may include anecdotes and behavior examples in addition to personality traits, and the information is presented successively rather than simultaneously as is the case with a list. Perhaps even more disturbing were the remarks of several of the subjects that they were aware of inconsistencies in the traits presented but felt compelled to present "an impression that made sense," that is, that was consistent—even though people often do indeed act in inconsistent ways.

In Asch's study, the Gestalt principle of perceptual wholeness or integration was tested in the laboratory setting in what seemed to be a very simple and direct way. Owing to assumptions about the universality of the principle and the "inexorable" validity of the experimental method, neither the reality of the impression-formation process nor its meaning for the student subjects was considered. Like so many of the complexities inherent in social behavior, they were treated as "error factors." This troubled me a great deal, as did the reliance on undergraduate students as subjects in most departments of psychology with active research faculties. Although work by Rosenthal (1966), Orne and Holland (1968), and others showing the vitiating influence of "student culture" on contrived studies of social behavior did not appear until somewhat later, the anecdotal evidence for this had been growing steadily. Like the laboratory rat in comparison with rats in their natural habitat, undergraduates were providing us with findings based on a social world far removed from the one we believed we were studying.

Also falling by the wayside around the same time was the once classic study of Bruner and Goodman (1947) on the influence of social needs on perception; subsequent replications (McClelland & Atkinson, 1948) not only failed to verify the original findings but also revealed that psychophysical factors rather than the students' economic need produced their increasing overestimations of the size of coins with increased value. Then there was the body of research on social attitude formation and change initiated by Hoveland in collaboration with Kelman (1953), and continued by Feshbach and Singer (1957), McGuire (1957), and others. These studies dominated the field of attitude research and were treated as the "best data" we had on how to change undesirable social attitudes. Space limitations do not permit me to describe in any detail the reservations I was developing about these studies. Suffice it to say that over time their validity began to dim as serious doubts arose about the contrived attitudes used for the research (e.g., toward brushing one's teeth in McGuire [1969]) and the deceptive instructions employed. Above all, as Hoveland himself acknowledged, the university laboratory findings could not be corroborated by studies on individuals in nonuniversity settings.

While my doubts about contrived experimental research continued to mount, another very different concern emerged as a result of quite accidental circumstances. First, I was asked to teach a 1-year interdisciplinary social science course to freshmen, the purpose of which was to present and analyze major human problems and issues in terms of concepts taken from psychology, sociology, anthropology, economics, and political science. A while later, I team-taught a yearlong seminar for 3 consecutive years with an anthropologist and a political scientist; here the audience consisted of much older students who had achieved professional success without a college degree. Both my freshman students and these older students were called upon to grasp the essential concepts of the various behavioral sciences to explain human behavior and events. From teaching these courses it became apparent that my training in undergraduate and graduate departments of psychology had been quite isolated from related behavioral science disciplines—even though I had come out of the dynamic, field-theoretical camp. Talk about the social context of behavior and the need for an interdisciplinary approach had been mostly lip service. It was as if the individual level of analysis were the only one that mattered.

I decided to pursue my growing interest in interdisciplinary integration by joining with Bill Ittelson, a perception psychologist, and Martin Landau, a distinguished political scientist (and one of the seminar team teachers) in preparing a book chapter on the topic. This was done at an Interdisciplinary Behavioral Sciences Research Conference organized at the University of New Mexico for 2 months during the summer of 1958 and sponsored by the U.S. Air Force. There were some 20 other behavioral and social scientists participating in the conference from the fields of economics, political science, sociology, anthropology, philosophy, social psychology, experimental psychology, and linguistics. The brief but very intense nature of the experience reinforced my view—almost painfully—that traditional social psychology, including my own brand, was due for an overhaul. Its concepts, its definitions of social problems, its methodology, and certainly its self-image as a science that seeks to establish a verifiable body of knowledge all needed revision.

Taking this view, of course, put me in limbo at Brooklyn College, where I was the exception rather than the rule in a traditional department of psychology. What I could do at the conference was simply not possible there. I felt that a change in the field of psychology, and more particularly in social psychology, was not possible in my lifetime. After all, the social structure that defined the role and separation of the various behavioral and social sciences both within the university and without presented a formidable obstacle to an interdisciplinary approach. The thought also crossed my mind that I was being premature. Although the full understanding of human behavior might indeed require conceptual linkages among the various behavioral and social sciences, such linkages might be impossible until theoretically fruitful concepts in these disciplines were found.

Still, back at Brooklyn in the fall of 1958, my doubts about the approach I had adopted as a social psychologist began to seem less pressing, perhaps because of my decision to take my first sabbatical leave the following year at the Research Center for Group Dynamics and in the Department of Psychology at the University of Michigan. The research center, as part of the Institute for Social Research, was interdisciplinary in its concerns, despite being dominated by Lewinian social psychologists. Moreover, both at the institute and in the psychology department there were individuals doing research in real-life settings, research that was by no means experimental in its methodological thrust. Besides honing my research skills, I would have a chance to discuss and rethink the qualms I had about the value of "my kind" of social psychology.

I spent 2 rewarding years at Michigan, enjoying both the teaching I did and the research I was involved in with other faculty. The trouble was that all my doubts concerning how social psychologists went about developing and testing their theoretical insights came surging back. Some of my students in an advanced graduate seminar on attitude structure and change that I gave in the spring of 1960 may remember how, in an informal discussion at the end of one class session, I remarked: "I no longer believe in the research on attitudes that we have discussed, and I am not sure I can continue to teach it." That statement is etched in my memory. The moment I said it, I knew that my doubts had become certainties and that I could no longer teach and do research in the framework of traditional social psychology.

What prompted this realization is simple enough to describe. At Michigan the overwhelming majority of investigations into small group structure and process, social attitudes and their changes, conflict resolution, and so on were experimental laboratory studies with undergraduate psychology students as subjects. There could be no question but that the outcomes of these investigations were inextricably tied to an "underground" student culture. It was also clear that much of the essence of social phenomena like group leadership, group structure, and interpersonal conflict was left out in the contrived experimental situations used to study them.

At Michigan's famed Institute for Social Research, which was staffed by social and behavioral scientists, community and organizational studies having to do with the real world were rooted in interdisciplinary collaboration. Still, there was no meaningful conceptual integration. The methodology employed, that of large-scale survey studies, did little more than specify and later relate findings at different levels of social analysis. Generally speaking, the theoretical and even methodological isolation of social psychology from other behavioral science approaches was no less evident at Michigan than elsewhere, despite the cooperation among social psychologists, sociologists, political scientists, and economists.

What also seemed clear to me during my stay at Michigan, particularly in the Research Center for Group Dynamics, was that Lewin's belief in "action research" was honored more in the breach than in the observance. Undertaking the kind of research on major social issues in the day-to-day world that Lewin advocated is, of course, expensive and difficult. Yet the real obstacle to action research was undoubtedly a commitment on the part of the psychologists there to the experimental laboratory paradigm. It was more than a decade later that Daniel Katz (1972) said what had to be said about experimental laboratory studies in social psychology:

> Of the thousands of experimental studies published in social psychology in the past twenty years, the number that supplies new information to a cumulative body of knowledge is surprisingly small. A great deal of the experimental effort has been without impact not because of poor method but because of the lack of ideas behind the work. (p. 557)

As I pointed out around the same time (Proshansky, 1972), this lack of ideas "reflects the almost obsessive desire to achieve scientific respectability by the use of the experimental method in the narrowly defined context of the college laboratory" (p. viii). In effect, method was defining the problem instead of the other way around. The moral is not that the experimental paradigm in social psychology should be discarded but rather that it ought not to be misused.

THE MAKING OF AN ENVIRONMENTAL PSYCHOLOGIST

I returned to Brooklyn College in the fall of 1961 with no real plan about what I would do as a "dissident" social psychologist. This was not an easy time for me. Strongly identified by others as a modern experimental social psychologist, I was approached about writing and/or research by colleagues and students who did not know about or consider important my concerns about the field. If I was scared to death about changing my ways as a social psychologist—and I was—the fundamental reason was that although I could wax eloquent on what was *wrong* with the contemporary approach in experimental social psychology, I had little to offer in the way of specifics on what would make it right.

Serendipity came to my rescue. Late in the spring of 1959, some months before my sabbatical departure for the University of Michigan, Bill Ittelson, a colleague of mine in the Brooklyn psychology department, had asked me if I would be interested in doing a review of the research literature on the physical design of mental hospitals and psychiatric ward facilities in relation to patient and staff behavior. Ittelson had been requested by one of the hospital divisions of the National Institute of Mental Health (NIMH) to think about formulating a research project that would address the broad question of how psychiatric facilities could be better designed to enhance patient treatment. I had agreed to undertake this review during the summer before I left for Ann Arbor because it seemed to be a better way of spending my time than once again teaching undergraduate summer courses.

Ittelson had subsequently been funded by NIMH to study the relationships between patient and staff behavior and the design features of psychiatric environments. Previous research in this area was meager. It is fair to say that we began at the beginning, driven by the need to develop some kind of conceptual orientation and research methodology for a problem in a real-life natural setting. Here was something that obviously could not be studied in the college laboratory or manipulated to fit the experimental paradigm. The first task we set for ourselves was simply to find out what was going on: who the patients, doctors, and nurses were, and how they used the space they occupied, both at specific times and over longer periods. I should stress that in no sense did I, Ittelson, or our other colleagues who joined the research team (Daniel Rosenblatt, Leanne Rivlin, and Gary Winkel) conceive of ourselves as *environmental psychologists* in this initial 2-year period; only over the next decade (1961–1971) did the challenge of carrying out this kind of systematic research lead us to shift our professional identities as social, experimental, or developmental psychologists in that direction.

During our exploratory foray into the nature of psychiatric wards and hospitals as physical settings, basic issues had to be resolved at every step of the way. It would be no exaggeration to say that we incrementally hammered out an approach rather than intellectually designing one via some rational group process. We knew from the very beginning that we had to be guided by the problem itself and not by preconceived conceptions or traditional methodologies. After all, we were working in a real-world milieu where the well-being of patients and those responsible for them took precedence over any and all research considerations. Ethical concerns must, we felt, dictate our methodological thrust. Existing social psychology methodology was not to be cast aside but rather selectively modified and used (if indeed it were possible) in ways that would not violate the integrity of the events we were studying.

Confronted with this project, my colleagues and I could no longer simply proclaim the importance of an interdisciplinary, multilevel approach; we now had to practice and implement it. We realized the importance of involving architects and designers in our research, even in the preliminary stages. Sociologists and organizational psychologists were needed as well, because, as we learned very early on, physical and social spaces are inextricably tied to each other. It is not only the physical properties of the setting that determine why and how space is used; the fact that there is an administrative social structure, with certain individuals in authority, is also critical.

Various events during the 1960s, when the environmental psychology approach began to take shape, both reinforced and directed our thinking. I have already commented on how university-based experimental laboratory research, in which college students were used to study complex human problems, came under severe attack. At the same time, the social revolution of the 1960s, especially prominent on college and university campuses, was raising questions about the purposes and validity of behavioral science courses and research. The hue and cry from many students and some faculty was for *relevance*, particularly with respect to the fields of psychology and sociology. The essence of the criticism was that academic psychology was removed from the real-world problems of poverty, ethnic prejudice, intergroup conflict, crime, and the like. Thus the true issue was not relevance but *reality*.

Near the end of the 1960s, no doubt in response to "setbacks" experienced by social psychology during these years, a "malaise" developed among a goodly number of its practitioners (Caplan & Nelson, 1973; Elms, 1975; Silverman, 1971). In the words of Katz (1972), "The development of experimental social psychology has been costly if the energy output is compared to the significant output" (p. 557). Although my own malaise had long since passed, I was troubled by the fact that the unhappiness of some social psychologists over the state of theory and research on campus led to scant change in the training of graduate students in social psychology. This was true on my own campus—which was now CUNY's Graduate Center—as well as in most other major doctoral training programs in the country. In our PhD specialization in environmental psychology, which was established early on—in 1967–1968—the pattern of training departed quite radically from what was traditional for PhD programs in social psychology.

When I and my colleagues (William Ittelson, Daniel Rosenblatt, Leanne Rivlin, and Gary Winkel) moved to the Graduate Center in the mid-1960s it was not for the purpose of setting up the PhD specialization in environmental psychology. In the years that all of us were active in research with the Department of Psychology at Brooklyn College, there were few if any graduate courses given in environmental psychology, and certainly there were none at the undergraduate level. A number of us were already involved in the doctoral specializations in social psychology, developmental psychology, and others. What brought us to the Graduate Center was our need for space and the desire to involve doctoral students in our research.

It soon became apparent that students were drawn to doing our kind of environmental research, both from interest and from the practical considerations of the many research assistantships we had available (we were extremely well-funded at the time). A specialization of environmental psychology had to be developed if we were to serve the interests of the doctoral students within the university and those outside the university who heard about the nature of our research.

Yet, for all our interest and desire to develop the specialization in environmental psychology, if it were not for the serendipitous factors that altered my own research career I am not certain we would have succeeded. For one thing, I had never held a significant administrative position of any kind in my academic career. In 1966 as a temporary measure I agreed to become the executive officer of the PhD program in psychology (which at that time had some nine fields of specialization). Before I finished that term, I was asked to serve as dean of the

Graduate School. There can be little question that my role as an administrator was important in getting final approval for the specialization in environmental psychology. (Over the next few years, except for the time I spent on sabbatical at the Bartlett School of Architecture in London, I became provost and then president of the Graduate School and University Center.) Yet I must stress, and our colleagues in a variety of fields would agree, that the significance of our work, the strong interest of many students seeking training at the Graduate School, and our capacity to provide a great deal of outside funding also provided the important ingredients for establishing the environmental psychology specialization.

The curriculum we designed and the demands that were made of our doctoral students were in many ways a reflection of the conceptions we had about the kind of theory and methodology that was appropriate to studying people and places in real-life settings. We deemphasized laboratory research and urged the students not to conform to the need for experimental paradigms. In my judgment we have done this quite successfully and have maintained and preserved our original assumptions in training our students to be environmental psychologists. We are concerned with the fact that although the field of environmental psychology has grown, that growth is not evidenced in other departments of psychology except for a few schools of architecture in this country. We continue to worry whether our students will have job opportunities in the university and beyond over the next decade.

CONCEPTS AND ASSUMPTIONS
OF AN ENVIRONMENTAL PSYCHOLOGIST

I view environmental psychology as a science. However, it is to be distinguished from the model of science that characterizes the physical and natural sciences. Although there can be no dispute concerning the significant achievements of the hard sciences in establishing generalized principles derived from the use of controlled experimental investigations, the model they are based on is quite inappropriate for understanding complex human behavior and experience.

Let me at this point redefine environmental psychology as the science that studies the interactions and relationships between people and their environments. In all my previous discussions, the definition was far more specific, in that it made environmental psychology out to be the study of the behavior and experience of people in relation to their physical settings. The focus on *physical settings* was misleading, though, because every physical environment is also a social environment and conversely. With the new definition, it is important to stress that neither the individual nor the environment is the unit of analysis but rather the *interactions and relationships* between the two. To speak of a person's need for privacy or personal space, for example, implies such interactions. But it must also be understood that in defining environmental psychology this way, we are *not* defining another specialization within the broader traditional conception of psychology, with an emphasis on the physical environment instead of on the child or social behavior.

Understanding the interaction between individual and environment requires the development of *interactional concepts* in place of merely psychological ones. (Environmental psychologists view privacy, for instance, as an interactional concept rather than simply characterizing it as another psychological need.) Furthermore, the interactions between people and environments involve at least three levels of human behavior/experience: First, there is the interaction of the person and his or her environment—and that environment can be one room, a house, a neighborhood, or even a city; second, there are the interactions of small groups with any of these environments; and third, there are the interactions among larger numbers of persons, constituted as organizations, with these environments. Which of these categories will concern the environmental psychologist depends on the kind of problem being addressed. Human privacy, for example, is a phenomenon that exists and can be conceptualized at each of these levels: How an individual achieves visual privacy in an open crowded space is related to, yet different from, how a group or organization would achieve privacy in the same setting.

Environmental psychology, as I have defined and explicated it here, requires interdisciplinary analysis. This means far more than "lining up and matching" concepts and data from each kind of behavioral-science and environmental-design specialty so that a full answer is achieved. That approach has never worked, nor can it, because it begins with discipline-isolated conceptions that are often limited, if not spurious. For environmental psychology to succeed, conceptual linkages are required among the various levels of human organization. Perhaps this is the reason that some researchers in the field feel uncomfortable with it being designated *environmental psychology*. It has been suggested that it would be better to call the field "environmental behavior," although it must be admitted that this designation was put forward as a way of giving recognition to psychologists doing experimental research on the effects of the physical environment on behavior (Wohlwill & Carson, 1972).

By now it should be evident that the broad theoretical approach in which my definition of the field is rooted is a *systems* conception. People, environments, and the interactions that bind them together make up dynamically organized systems in which causal influences in one part ramify throughout. Indeed, an event that provokes change may very likely bring about a chain of consequences that affects that event itself. The unit of analysis in this systems approach to person–environment interactions is the relationship between the two at all levels of social organization. It follows that both the behaving person or persons and the manifest environment must be the starting points for any interactional conceptions we employ to describe these relationships. Therefore, our research concerning these interactions must be in the real world.

There is no way that the integrity of the complex behaviors and events that concern us as researchers can be maintained in a laboratory setting that involves experimental manipulation. Such contrived situations are simply too far from the reality of the behaviors being studied. The broad context of a person's day-to-day existence is left out in the experimental approach because it cannot be reproduced in the laboratory. Traditional psychology, including social psychology, was never too concerned with this shortcoming because it focused not on content but on *process*. Its practitioners ignore the content involved in learning, perception, motivation, emotion, and cognition in their quest for a small number of universal or highly generalizable principles that will explain their operation. Essentially, the experimental-laboratory paradigm in psychology is a search for relatively simple cause-and-effect relationships.

The systems approach, by contrast, deals with behavior that is rooted in a pattern of other dynamically related events at various levels of human organization. To single out particular variables as "causes" because they can be isolated, manipulated, and measured is just as much an affront to the integrity of the phenomenon being studied—even in a field experiment—as directly attempting to reproduce reality in the laboratory. In the dynamic system that characterizes person–environment interactions there are no specific causes and effects but only events, behaviors, objects, activities, and so forth that at times produce changes and at other times are themselves changed.

To recapitulate, I see environmental psychology as a systems approach in which the theoretical complexity of the interactions of people and their environments is taken for granted; because the unit of analysis is the interaction itself, the integrity of the interaction's context must be maintained. It should be pointed out that however momentary the interaction, part of this context is the *time* dimension. Places, spaces, and people endure in some ways and change in others over time; as the temporal horizon is lengthened, the "permanents" and "temporaries" may exchange status. Time as a variable can play a greater or lesser role depending on the nature of the questions being asked in the research, but it should never be disregarded in the name of "basic conceptions" that transcend temporal considerations. To do so is to assume erroneously a universality of lawful relationships in person–environment interactions in a form that emulates the physical and natural sciences.

Taking account of historical context is also essential to the study of the interactions between persons and environments. Early on, I found myself in agreement with Gergen's view that social psychology and the other behavioral sciences had to be historical sciences in the sense that their concepts and principles were necessarily grounded in the social context of given times and places (Gergen, 1982). This view, of course, is quite alien to traditional psychology's quest for a set of basic universal principles of human behavior and experience that would permit us to understand *all* human phenomena regardless of time or place. The laws I seek are specific to particular places at particular times. To the extent that they solve problems in the context they were intended for, I have been successful in establishing a bit of knowledge. That "bit of knowledge," however, may be applicable to overlapping or similar person–environment arenas, leading in incremental steps toward generalizations. Yet asking how far our generalizations extend or whether they are universal at this stage of our understanding is neither a significant nor a useful approach. What is important is to recognize that our theory and research efforts are bound by a relatively enduring time–place–culture context. If that context changes, then the knowledge we have will need to be reconsidered and indeed revised.

The reader may well ask at this point, perhaps with some exasperation, what kind of methodology will characterize my approach, given my commitment to studying only the real world and focusing on substantive meanings, activities, and behaviors in particular settings at particular times. Let me respond in the broadest terms (a more extensive and detailed answer would require a chapter in its own right). First, to be consistent with the approach I have espoused here, the methodology must be, at least at the beginning stages of study, an *empirical-exploratory* one—"search and learn," if you will. There is no question that the real world is complex. Deciding where and how to begin looking into it often seems to be an insuperable obstacle to inquiry. Yet that is only because researchers in the behavioral sciences have virtually no experience, patience, or even belief in such an approach. William Whyte's recent book, *City* (1988), is a good example of how to proceed. By attempting to show how the people of New York City use their metropolis, relate to it, and change it, Whyte provides a wealth of knowledge.

A second dimension of the broad methodology I have in mind has to do with how to carry out this search-and-learn approach. Those who do the research and those being researched must become almost interchangeable. The environmental psychologist cannot just appear on the scene "up front," even if he or she has been asked to do the research. She or he must be a behind-the-scenes player and start by becoming immersed in the environment to the point of knowing everything possible about it. This process begins long before the research itself. It means talking to those who experience and therefore know about and are part of the problem. The researcher must also involve those in other disciplines who define the problem from analytical vantage points different from his or her own. This interdisciplinary integration should be continued throughout the research process.

If, as I have suggested, researchers ought to become part of the real-world setting they are studying, then it is also true that some of the people in that setting should participate in the research process. Scientific objectivity must defer to the fact that they know best what is going on and how to describe it. Not only must researchers be participants, but some of those being studied must play the role of observers and recorders to the extent that they can be called *participant–researchers*. Besides furnishing and helping to gather information, they must—with guidance—be conceptualizers, theorizers, and indeed interpreters of the data as well.

There is much that I have left out in describing the broad theoretical and methodological approach that has guided my thinking as an environmental psychologist during the last two decades. That it is an approach fraught with difficulties and extraordinary demands—including the demand for time and money—I would not deny. But this has been true in the past for sciences in various stages of development and undoubtedly will always be true. Some 25 years after I became wrapped up in the study of problems involving the relation of persons to their physical environment, I am more firmly convinced than ever that the approach I have outlined here is the only way to go.

The real problem confronting environmental psychologists is the fact that they have stood, and will continue to stand, in the very deep shadow of traditional psychology. Like any other science, psychology is a social institution in which certain dominant approaches, dressed in the concepts and methods of the hard sciences, determine the distribution of resources and rewards. This in turn determines how students shall be trained, how and what kind of research shall be done, and, as a result, how and by whom professional societies, relevant government offices and programs, and private-sector research departments shall be constituted and directed. It matters little that over some 75 years, the accumulation of knowledge in the field of social psychology has been trivial, to say the least. The traditional experimental-laboratory approach continues to prevail because it is consistent with the broader traditional field of psychology wherein the power and discretion over resources continue to reside.

TODAY AND TOMORROW

The editors of this volume asked that all the authors describe their present or projected work in environmental psychology and where they think the field is and ought to go. I should confess to the reader that during the last 15 years my involvement in research and teaching as an environmental psychologist has been minimal compared to my colleagues. Holding a primary administrative position in CUNY's Graduate School and University Center during this period has made it next to impossible for me to play an active role in the field without compromising the quality of my efforts. However, with the aid of advanced graduate students who have served in successive periods as my research assistants and collaborators, I have been able to keep up with the relevant literature, develop theoretical conceptions, participate in some national conferences, and, on a biweekly basis, talk about research if not do it.

Currently my special interest is the urban metropolis, and New York City in particular. At the core of this interest is my concern with the environmental psychologist's conception of *place identity*. Although this is usually defined as a kind of place belongingness consisting in a person's strong emotional attachment to the home or other milieus associated with growing up, I see it as a far more complex conception closely tied to the self-identity of each individual (Proshansky, Fabian, & Kaminoff, 1983). My contention is that if it is the social contexts and the people in them who minister to our needs that determine our social identity, then the same must be true of the significant places and spaces as the basis of a corresponding place identity. Together, social identity and place identity are the foundation of a person's self-identity.

Place identity can be seen as a substructure of self-identity that defines an individual's personal identity in relation to the physical world through memories, ideas, feelings, attitudes, values, preferences, meanings, and conceptions about behavior relevant to the physical settings in his or her daily life. These attitudes, beliefs, and other cognitions emerge from the individual's personal experiences, good and bad, in relation to the physical world. However, because any physical setting is also clearly a social one, other people and their attitudes about the physical world, as well as the social meanings associated with particular places, influence an individual's place identity.

Cognitions about disparate physical settings do not exist in isolation from each other. Indeed, because a person's place identity reflects to some extent the pattern of settings in his or her daily world, these cognitions are interrelated in the same way that physical settings in day-to-day activities are interrelated. Furthermore, because both individuals and the everyday environments they encounter change over time, place identity must be an enduring yet changing structure. This does not simply mean that the actual physical places in the daily life of an individual change but that types of physical settings may change over the course of the life cycle and thereby no longer correspond to the existing place-related cognitions. For example, the nature of the workplace (as well as the nature of work) is continuing to change dramatically, particularly as we approach the next century. Satellite and neighborhood work centers and home-based work may alter the ways in which some people think about "workplace," which would be reflected in their place identities. Changes in school settings, family household, and indeed the nature and organization of cities themselves have corresponding consequences in the place identity of the individual.

Theory is always a matter not only of thought and reflection but of strong conviction as well. I am absolutely convinced that the urban physical world of the individual, as he or she experiences it, lives it, and learns it, becomes integral to the way in which the person defines himself or herself in relation to others as well as to the day-to-day physical settings that are a part of his or her existence.

Of particular interest to me is the way in which place identity is manifested for the urban dweller. The primary urban settings for establishing the individual's place identity are the home, the school, and the workplace; also involved but less significant are a variety of secondary public spaces (e.g., parks and libraries). The physical properties of these primary settings, the way they are normatively defined and used, and the individual's experiences over time in and with them all underlie what we commonly refer to as the socialization of the person. Urban place identity arises from the physical socialization or—for want of a better term—the *physicalization* of the urban dweller (Proshansky, 1978).

It is my intention over the next few years to try to make sense of what is going on in urban settings by making use of such concepts as personal space, privacy, environmental control, crowding, place belongingness, territoriality, environmental security, and place personalization. Fleshing out the notion of place identity, as I have defined it here, is my main aim. As a participant in ongoing real-life events, I have already collected an abundance of anecdotal and observational data in ways that minimized my role as a researcher. I mean to continue my research using just this kind of methodological approach, exploring almost at random a variety of urban environments. The next step will be to take a detailed look at a smaller number of these with the aid of graduate students.

Briefly now, let me comment on the editors' question about the future of environmental psychology. If, over time, a scientific field attracts more and more researchers and produces more and more journals and books as outlets for their findings, then one can say that it is a growing field. However, there is another more demanding and meaningful criterion of growth, and that is the extent to which research efforts in a scientific field lead to the accumulation of knowledge. In the behavioral sciences these two kinds of growth are by no means correlated.

As I look at the field of environmental psychology today, I am concerned about its future. It has not, since its emergence in the early 1960s, grown to the point where it can match the fields of social, personality, learning, or cognitive psychology. To be sure, it has increased in membership, in the number of journals devoted to it, and even in the amount of professional organizational support it enjoys, but not enough so that one could look at any major university and find it to be a field of specialization in a department of psychology, or, more importantly, in an interdisciplinary center or institute. If it were not for environmental psychology's growth in Europe and, to a lesser extent, on other continents, its practitioners would be few indeed. Here in the United States only the fact that architects, geographers, designers, and social planners as well as psychologists now identify themselves as environmental psychologists ensures that their numbers stay respectable.

Can environmental psychology flourish as a specialized program within an academic setting? Only, I would argue, if it is ceded a fair degree of autonomy. Departments or programs in environmental psychology at the graduate level, such as CUNY's PhD specialization or the interdisciplinary program in social ecology at the University of California, Irvine, have been productive precisely because they have been given the requisite autonomy. So have a number of programs within schools of architecture—the Environment–Behavior Studies Program in the School of Architecture at the University of Wisconsin at Milwaukee, for one. Typically, however, in order to survive as a specialization in departments of psychology, environmental psychology must conform in a variety of ways to the traditional curricular and research-related requirements. In the end, this vitiates the approach I have presented here. To study complex person–environment problems in real-life settings, conceptualized in interdisciplinary terms, really requires an interdisciplinary autonomy of structure and effort that is quite antithetical to the traditional department of psychology.

The way environmental psychologists are organized is only part of the problem that confronts the field. There is still the issue of the approach they are to take, even when they have a degree of autonomy. An examination of the major journals of environmental psychology over the last decade and a half reveals research whose approach reflects the thinking of traditional social, cognitive, and learning psychologies. As the field has grown, newer generations of environmental psychologists are making more and more use of the experimental model in their research and are relying on a variety of measurement techniques whose value was limited to begin with (e.g., semantic differential and questionnaires). This is not a good sign.

Some years back I took the view that environmental psychologists should scrupulously avoid the theoretical conceptions and empirical findings of social psychology because the latter's research efforts and findings had little relationship to the real-world nature of the problems being studied (Proshansky, 1976). Irwin Altman, an esteemed colleague, disagreed with me (Altman, 1976), arguing that at least some of these conceptions and findings could be useful. I would concede that ideas of social perception, small-group structure and process, and social interactions might provide a basis for understanding the more complex aspects of personal space, territoriality, crowding, and human privacy. These latter, after all, are not likely to be understood very fully if we leave them in their pristine state, viewed simply as a matter of the person in relation to his or her environment. At the nexus of the individual's interaction with given spaces are his or her interactions with other people who are potentially relevant to these spaces. The very fact that every human environment is a sociophysical system, in which physical and social properties are inextricably bound up with each other, makes this evident.

Over time my stringent view that environmental psychologists should turn away from existing conceptions of social psychology has softened considerably. In the matter of methodology, however, my attitude has not changed. The traditional methodology of social psychology created its own world of phenomena, one having little if any bearing on the real-world behaviors and experiences that were presumably being studied. That is why so much of the data and research accumulated by social psychologists have been "packed away" and forgotten. If environmental psychologists succumb to the aura of the "respectable science" methodology that has borrowed so heavily and indiscriminately from the physical and natural sciences, their efforts will bear little fruit in understanding how humans interact with their environment. I hope they can resist the temptation.

REFERENCES

Allport, G. W. (1940). The psychologist's frame of reference. *Psychological Bulletin, 37,* 1–28.
Altman, I. (1976). Environmental psychology and social psychology. *Personality and Social Psychology Bulletin,* 2(2), 96–113.
Asch, S. E. (1946). Forming impressions of personality. *Journal of Abnormal and Social Psychology, 41,* 258–290.
Bridgeman, P. (1927). *The logic of modern physics.* New York: Macmillan.
Bruner, J. S., & Goodman, C. C. (1947). Value and need as organizing factors in perception. *Journal of Abnormal and Social Psychology, 42,* 33–44.
Caplan, N., & Nelson, S. D. (1973). On being useful: The nature and consequences of psychological research on social problems. *American Psychologist,* 28(3), 199–211.

Elms, A. C. (1975). The crisis of confidence in social psychology. *American Psychologist, 30*(10), 967–976.

Feshbach, S., & Singer, R. (1957). The effects of fear arousal and suppression of fear upon social perception. *Journal of Abnormal and Social Psychology, 55,* 283–288.

Fromme, A. (1941). On the use of certain qualitative methods of attitude research: A study of opinions on the methods of preventing war. *Journal of Social Psychology, 13,* 429–459.

Gergen, K. J. (1982). *Toward transformation in social knowledge.* New York: Springer-Verlag.

Harding, J. S., Kutner, B., Proshansky, H. M., & Chein, I. (1954). Prejudice and ethnic relations. In G. Lindzey (Ed.), *Handbook of social psychology* (1st ed., Vol. II, Chapter 28, pp. 1021–1061). Cambridge, MA: Addison-Wesley.

Horney, K. (1939). *New ways in psychoanalysis.* New York: W. W. Norton & Co., Inc.

Katz, D. (1972). Some final considerations about experimentation in social psychology. In C. McClintock (Ed.), *Experimental social psychology* (pp. 549–561). New York: Holt, Rinehart & Winston.

Kelman, H. C., & Hoveland, C. I. (1953). "Reinstatement" of the communicator in delayed measurement of opinion change. *Journal of Abnormal and Social Psychology, 48,* 327–335.

Klineberg, O. *et al.* (1957). On race and intelligence. *World mental health, 9,* 87–89.

Koffka, K. (1935). *Principles of gestalt psychology.* New York: Harcourt, Brace & World.

Kohler, W. (1929). *Gestalt psychology.* New York: Liveright.

Lewin, K. (1935). *A dynamic theory of personality.* New York: McGraw-Hill.

Lewin, K. (1946). Action research and minority problems. *Journal of Social Issues, 2,* 34–46.

Lewin, K. (1951). *Field theory in social science.* New York: Harper.

McClelland, D. C., & Atkinson, J. A. (1948). The projective expression of needs: The effect of different intensities of the hunger drive on perception. *Journal of Psychology, 25,* 205–222.

McGuire, W. J. (1957). Order of presentation as a factor in "conditioning" persuasiveness. In C. I. Hoveland (Ed.), *Order of presentation of persuasion* (pp. 98–114). New Haven, CT: Yale University Press.

McGuire, W. J. (1969). Nature of attitudes and attitude change. In G. Lindzey, & E. Aronson (Eds.), *Handbook of social psychology* (2nd ed., pp. 136–314). Cambridge, MA: Addison-Wesley.

Murphy, G. (1947). *Personality: A biosocial approach to origin and structure.* New York: Harper & Row.

Orne, M. T., & Holland, C. C. (1968). On the ecological validity of laboratory deceptions. *International Journal of Psychiatry, 6,* 282–293.

Proshansky, H. M. (1943). A projective method for the study of attitudes. *Journal of Abnormal and Social Psychology, 38,* 393–395.

Proshansky, H. M. (1972). Foreword. In C. McClintock (Ed.), *Experimental social psychology* (pp. vii–ix). New York: Holt, Rinehart & Winston.

Proshansky, H. M. (1976). Environmental psychology and the real world. *American Psychologist, 3*(4), 303–310.

Proshansky, H. M. (1978). The city and self-identity. *Environment and Behavior, 10*(2), 147–169.

Proshansky, H. M., & Murphy, G. (1942). The effects of reward and punishment on perception. *Journal of Psychology, 13,* 295–305.

Proshansky, H. M., Fabian, A. K., & Kaminoff, R. (1983). Place-identity: Physical world socialization of the self. *Journal of Environmental Psychology, 3,* 57–83.

Rosenthal, R. (1966). *Experimenter effects in behavioral research.* New York: Appleton.

Silverman, I. (1971). Crisis in social psychology: The relevance of relevance. *American Psychologist, 26*(6), 583–584.

Whyte, W. H. (1988). *City: Rediscovering the center.* New York: Doubleday.

Wohlwill, J., & Carson, D. H. (1972). Environment and behavioral science: retrospect and prospect. In J. Wohlwill and D. H. Carson (Eds.), *Environment and the social sciences: Perspectives and applications* (pp. 293–300). Washington, DC: American Psychological Association.

2

A Fish Who Studies Water

ROBERT SOMMER

I WAS BORN IN NEW YORK CITY and attended public schools there. We spent our summers in Stroudsburg, Pennsylvania, where my father worked. These summers helped me develop an appreciation for nature that has remained with me. After graduating from high school, I attended Hobart College in Geneva, New York, and then became what the Germans called a *Wandervogel* (wandering bird). I lived in Greenwich Village and took courses at Columbia, New York University, and the New School for Social Research. Later I attended Penn State and the University of Oklahoma, before encountering Gardner Murphy who brought me to the Menninger Foundation in Topeka, Kansas, where I completed my PhD at nearby Lawrence. Coincidentally, my grandmother had attended Kansas University where she had grown up. My great-grandfather had a large clothing store in Lawrence (he hid under the bed dressed in women's clothing during Quantril's Raid), and his store is now an historical landmark.

After completing my PhD in the area of perception in 1956, I spent a summer teaching in Sweden before beginning a postdoctoral fellowship in social psychology at Southeast Louisiana Hospital. This launched me upon a succession of research positions in state mental hospitals. I was part of the 1950s reform wave that laid the basis for subsequent deinstitutionalization programs. In 1957 while working in Saskatchewan, I developed an interest in environmental influences on behavior that led to the personal space studies and various consultation projects with designers. From 1961 to 1963 I was assistant professor of psychology and director of the Psychological Clinic at the University of Alberta at Edmonton. In 1963 I came to the young psychology department at the University of California, Davis, where I have remained.

I chaired the psychology department from 1965 to 1971 and during that time was a visiting professor in the Departments of Architecture at Berkeley and the University of Washington. For a while I had a part-time appointment in environmental studies. In 1978 I became director of the Center for Consumer Research in the College of Agricultural and Environmental Sciences.

ROBERT SOMMER • Department of Psychology and Center for Consumer Research, University of California at Davis, Davis, California 95616.

I have three children: Ted (age 31), who is an aquaculturist raising algae in Perth, Australia; Ken (29), who is in the development department of the San Francisco Conservatory; and Margaret (27), who works in a bakery in Berkeley, California. The most significant influence in my life is my partner, Barbara A. Sommer, a noted menstrual cycle researcher and developmental researcher, with special interests in puberty and adolescence. Barbara has a profoundly practical view of the world and keeps me from becoming unduly autistic as I am wont to do if left to my own proclivities. My hobbies are mushrooming, watercolor painting, gardening, cross-country skiing, and bicycling. Because all the aspects of my life blend, these are activities shared with Barbara and are the subjects of my research.

INTRODUCTION

I have known for a long time that my interests in psychology are "different" from the mainstream without spending much time trying to understand the source or nature of this. My mentor, Gardner Murphy, devoted his life to a search for *plus ultra*, the something more than the world appeared to be, which led him to the farthest reaches of philosophy, evolutionary biology, cultural anthropology, depth psychology, and parapsychology. My verbal guideposts are more prosaic, ranking among the more undistinguished words in the English language—both/and. I believe it is possible and often necessary to combine viewpoints and activities that others see as disparate, such as art and science, science and philosophy, research and implementation, doing good and doing right, being respectable and going far out.

I am most interested in things within my immediate environment. Some of this can be credited to serious nearsightedness. In school I always had the worst eyesight in the class. Things nearby were clear, whereas distant items were a blur. This may also have favored a tendency toward introspection. In contrast, the congenital farsightedness of the eminent developmental psychologist, Lois Murphy, created a lifelong difficulty in seeing things close. In a letter to me she described how her ability to see things at a distance that other people could not see had important consequences for her research career. It created a feeling of confidence that her perceptions were correct no matter what others said (corollary: unassailable confidence that the topics she wanted to research were important, no matter how much others ridiculed the ideas, e.g., children's sympathy, coping, etc.). Farsightedness also gave her an interest in vistas, long distance views ahead and behind (corollary: orientation toward long-range planning and historical roots).

Within my immediate environment, I like to keep things whole and see them in their larger environmental context. I do not have the temperament or inclination for molecular analysis. When I sketch fungus (a current hobby), I do not cut them up or examine them under a microscope. I am content with their visual appearance and knowledge about their place in the larger scheme of things, that is, the role of fungi in breaking down organic matter and how this influences their form and structure. When I conducted research on seating arrangement, I focused upon functional relationships between the participants rather than the microelements of chair and table design or head-and-eye orientation. I have never had much interest in reductionistic approaches or in soaring to so lofty a perch as to lose contact with the world below.

I rarely do things deliberately to be different; they just turn out that way. This can be credited to a unique way of seeing the world. I am one of Colin Wilson's (1956) outsiders who "sees too much and thinks too much." I do not assume that others see the world as I do or even that the world is as I see it. I believe only that there is sufficient validity in my explication of phenomena to interest others, pay the bills, and allow me to continue. The alchemy of converting an unusual mode of perception into published articles and books is the achievement of an efficient writer. The "me" who invades people's space bubbles, moves around chairs in airports, and studies the personality of vegetables may be strange, but I who write these lines am not. The combination of unusual perceptions and a conventional intellectual superstructure has allowed me to approach mundane issues in novel ways and unusual topics using conventional methods.

CHAPTER PLAN

So that all the careers in this volume do not seem cast from the same mold, I will devote most attention to those activities in environmental psychology that set my career apart from my colleagues, in such areas as consultation, public service, writing for practitioners and the public, and expert witness testimony. The chapter begins with my undergraduate years at a liberal arts college with a strong Western Civilization program, proceeds to a peripatetic predoctoral search for questions and answers, doctoral work under an erudite and generous mentor, a succession of research positions that focused my attention on the importance of environmental influences on behavior, culminating in remarkably stable academic employment with frequent forays into the outside world to carry the fruits of collaborative intellectual labor to practitioners, policymakers, and the public. To avoid creating the false impression that this has been a clear, consistent, and logical progression from baccalaureate to graduate school, postdoctoral fellowship, research employment, and an academic career, I will discuss activities orthogonal to a straight-line life projection, including interests in art, humor, natural history, and ecology.

EARLY ACADEMIC INFLUENCES

Three periods of college/university can be identified: undergraduate, predoctoral, and doctoral. Each one is associated with places and names, of which only a few can be mentioned.

My undergraduate years from 1946 to 1949 were spent at Hobart College, a small liberal arts college in upstate New York. World War II had just ended with firebombing of Dresden and the atomic bombs dropped on Hiroshima and Nagasaki. Revelations of the holocaust were documented in the press. The United Nations had been created, weapons of war were being turned into scrap, and a period of great economic expansion was on the horizon. Amid all the returning veterans, I was one of the youngest students on campus, which had a profound effect on my social life. A woman student was unlikely to go out with a 17-year-old with so many mature men available. The lack of sexual experience (other than in my fantasies) contributed to my intellectual development.

The two psychologists at Hobart when I arrived, F. L. and R. Dimmick, were perceptual structuralists trained by Titchener. Their replacement, Neil Bartlett, had spent the war years at the New London Submarine Base doing research on camouflage patterns seen through a periscope. Hobart gave me a lifelong interest in perception. I was also influenced by a sociology instructor, Martin Allwood, whose interests spanned community studies, popular culture, and psychoanalysis.

When I left Hobart in December 1949, I tried the business world, didn't like it, dropped out, and rented a furnished room in Greenwich Village to write. Eight months of unpublished essays, talking politics, and eating in dingy cafeterias was unsatisfying. I applied to several graduate schools and took the first acceptance that arrived. I spent portions of 1951–1952 at the University of Oklahoma where I was influenced by Sociologist Lewis Killian whose fields were race relations and collective behavior. This was a time of segregation and other forms of institutionalized discrimination. I collaborated with Lewis on studies of attitudes and racial stereotypes. I also took classes with Social Psychologist Muzafer Sherif who introduced me to field experimentation.

I continued my peregrinations, first to Penn State, and later to New York City in part-time study at three universities. I met Gardner Murphy when he came to New York to lecture and decided to work with him in perception research at the Menninger Foundation while concurrently doing doctoral studies at nearby Kansas University. Kansas was a hotbed of Gestalt psychology. Most significant from my standpoint was the presence of Roger Barker, who had studied with Lewin, and Martin Scheerer and Fritz Heider, who had worked with Wertheimer. I was also an occasional participant in an underworld of clinical phenomenology. The person who had most influence upon me during this period was Gardner Murphy, a successor to William James with his broad interests, lucid writing style, and ability to integrate psychology with literature, philosophy, evolutionary theory, culture study, physical science, and the arts. His books on personality, experimental social psychology, and the history of psychology remain classics.

I discovered at this time that I could *get paid* for doing research. As an undergraduate and predoctoral student, I had done studies and published papers without external support. At the Menninger Foundation, I realized this could become a livelihood. Since then, I have managed to convert even the most mundane activities, such as riding a bicycle to work, collecting mushrooms in the forest, and waiting in airports into research projects. I feel less compelled to explain this alchemy then to ask why others do not possess the formula.

Following graduate work at Kansas and a summer teaching English in Sweden at a school run by my former sociology teacher from Hobart, I took a postdoctoral fellowship in social psychology at Southeast Louisiana Hospital, across Lake Ponchatrain from New Orleans. I did not endear myself to the research director whose major interest was lobotomy, so I departed the day after Mardi Gras for a research position at Larned (Kansas) State Hospital where I came across an article by Psychiatrist Humphry Osmond (1957) on psychiatric architecture. The ideas were exciting, so I wrote Osmond, who was then superintendent of a mental hospital in Western Canada, to ask if he wanted a creative psychologist on his research staff. He replied affirmatively, and once the immigration hurdles were passed, I crossed the border into Canada where I remained for 6 years.

Osmond coined the term *psychedelic* and turned on his friend Aldous Huxley, resulting in Huxley's (1954) *The Doors of Perception.* Under Osmond's leadership, the hospital was a testing ground for new ideas. I have never seen a place come as close to Robert Hutchins's (1968) *learning society.* I had unlimited access to subjects, something that has never occurred before or since, including several thousand patients, hundreds of employees, and a continuing stream of visitors touring the hospital. I struck an agreement with the volunteer coordinator to give a brief talk on mental illness to all visiting groups who would subsequently hold brief discussions in furniture groupings that I had created according to an experimental plan. This quid pro quo provided hundreds of participants for the personal space studies (Sommer, 1959a). I learned more than I ever wanted to know about how people sat at tables of various sizes and shapes.

With Osmond's support, our research findings became the basis of ward renovations. Walls were repainted, corridors shortened, and outside areas made less institutional. After 4 years, I had largely played out my options in mental hospital research. Deinstitutionalization loomed, and mental health programs were moving into the community. I became assistant professor of psychology at the University of Alberta in Edmonton, where I remained for 2 years before joining the young psychology department at the University of California, Davis. I have taught at Davis since 1963, apart from brief stints as a visiting professor in the Departments of Architecture at Berkeley and the University of Washington, and in the Department of Design at the University of Nevada, Reno.

ORTHOGONAL LINES

I have a long-standing interest in the visual arts. I was art editor of my high-school yearbook and invented several reversible figures during my perception studies. Later I was to document murals around the country and write a book on public art (Sommer, 1975a). Anyone who has sat next to me at a lecture can attest to my marginal drawings. My last published cartoons were done for the Menninger Foundation newsletter on psychoanalytic themes, for example, a theater stage shaped like a mouth titled "acting out on the oral stage" and a fellow on a bicycle declaiming heatedly to another man, "No, I want the cycle path, not the psychopath." Drawing led to an interest in photography and to a current passion for watercolor, a medium that is quick, clean, appropriately low-tech, and veridical.

My sketches reflect aspects of my surroundings. I have numerous drawings of apartment and house interiors. There are sketches of offices going back as far as the Menninger Foundation in 1957. Drawing is a way to become familiar with a setting. Psychologists might profitably follow the example of designers who often sketch a location at the outset of a project. The field artist is part of the setting, experiences the ground, sounds, and the play of traffic and people, some of whom will stop and chat. Unlike the photographer who is often perceived as exploitive and alienated from the action, everyone loves artists or at least is interested in seeing them work.

I also have a professional interest in abnormal psychology. I have taught an abnormal psychology course more than 30 times, served on my county mental health board, and am active in local mental health programs, most often as a research advisor. My research on the architecture of mental hospitals was motivated by complementary interests in environments and psychopathology.

Some people know me primarily as a past contributor to the *Worm Runner's Digest*, the *Journal of Irreproducible Results*, and other small periodicals at the margins of science. When I couldn't change things, I could at least satirize them. My first recognition for humor came with Sommer's law (1960) that one secretary equals two scientists. When Novelist Arthur Koestler came across this gem in the *Worm Runner's Digest*, he reported it in a news column that was picked up by *Newsweek* and the wire services. I went on to greater heights with additional laws and a tradebook (*Expertland*) published in 1963, and subsequently translated into German. In Canada I did occasional nonserious commentaries for CBC. When I moved to California I wrote articles for Sunday supplements. Most of these pieces were devoted to aspects of my immediate surroundings. As a researcher, it was cathartic to take a nonserious view of grants and consultants; as a mental hospital employee to note the extraordinary symbolic power of keys; as a teacher to use humor to demystify examinations, and in my personal life, to focus on unnoticed aspects of home and neighborhood, for example, sidewalks, snails, moving to a new house, and so on. Humor has been a coping device, a relaxing literary form, and a valued part of my teaching and lecture style.

UNIVERSITY OF CALIFORNIA–DAVIS

The Davis campus has been a center of environmental activism. This represents a blend of the traditions of a land grant university with the liberal political climate of northern California. Because my work on institutional environment had been inspired by the ethology of Hediger (1950) and Tinbergen (1953), it was very satisfying to find that my writings helped to sensitize students in the animal behavior program to the effects of confinement. Terry Maple, who took his degree in comparative psychology at Davis, became an advocate for humane conditions in zoos, and subsequently became director of the Atlanta Zoo, the first time that a psychologist has ever directed a major zoo.

A land grant institution also provides numerous opportunities for interdisciplinary collaboration. Our College of Agriculture changed its name 20 years ago to the College of Agricultural and Environmental Sciences, to indicate that the environmental sciences are not a stepchild but an integral part of teaching and research. My research and public service interests came together during the mid-1970s when Sim van der Ryn was appointed state architect. His office was located in Sacramento, only a 20-minute drive from Davis, which allowed for easy contact. As one of the first practicing architects interested in environment–behavior research, Sim was very interested in bringing behavioral scientists into state building projects. I became part of a task force examining mental hospital architecture and another to plan the future of downtown Sacramento. At the same time I was appointed to a federal task force on correctional architecture. This period in the mid-1970s was for me a golden age of environmental psychology.

A DIFFERENT APPROACH

My divergence from the mainstream can be seen in topic, method, writing style, and approach to dissemination. Each of these factors is sufficiently unusual to warrant discussion and taken together represent a singular package. I tend to select topics and settings taken for granted or ignored by others, employ nonexperimental methods appropriate for these unusual topics, use a writing style that permits me to range widely and learn while I write, and follow a dissemination strategy capable of reaching multiple audiences.

CHOICE OF TOPIC

My first research in environmental psychology had the practical objective of improving drab institutional environments. Before making any renovations, I felt we should obtain systematic information about the way patients used space. At the time there was more information about the spatial needs of captive animals than about people's spatial needs. I recorded the spacing of people in different settings and undertook experiments in which people were randomly assigned to different kinds of spaces. No psychological journal would publish the findings. It was not until Dick Hill, editor of *Sociometry*, published the papers that the work reached a social science audience. This line of research subsequently became fashionable and appeared in mainstream journals. A half-dozen editors identified me as the person to review papers on this topic. Sometimes I reviewed the same paper (unrevised) for three journals. My interest in this research waned as people correlated paper-and-pencil measures of personal space with authoritarianism, Machiavellianism, and androgyny. I was eager to apply the personal space concept to real-world settings to learn its external validity and generalizability.

Other settings that have become our research sites, such as the salad bar and the pub, were equally immediate and unstudied. When I became acting director of research at the Alcoholism Foundation of Alberta in the summer of 1962, it seemed natural for me to investigate the natural occurrence of drinking in the community. My students and I embarked on a systematic observational study of all 32 beer parlors in Edmonton, Canada (Sommer, 1965). The study was one of only a handful of systematic observational studies of alcohol consumption in a natural setting. Unlike the mental hospital ward that was a sociofugal setting, the pub was a sociopetal setting designed to support interaction, which linked the research to the earlier studies of small-group ecology. It also provided the opportunity to test the social facilitation hypotheses in determining if people in groups drank faster or more than did lone individuals.

An obvious choice for applying concepts of spatial behavior, at least for me, was bicycle transportation. I rode a bicycle to work and did most of my shopping on a bike. I was not pleased with motorists who drove as if I did not exist and gave me no space on the road. Every other means of transportation had specially designed facilities (freeways for automobiles, tracks for railroads, sidewalks for pedestrians, and equestrian paths for horses), but in the early 1960s there was not a single traffic lane on an American street dedicated to bicycles. I examined the standards for bicycle paths in other nations, but conditions were so different that it seemed inappropriate to generalize to the United States. I became part of an interdisciplinary team to design a bicycle path system. My portion of the research drew heavily upon the personal space studies except that now the people were on bikes. To determine the optimal width of a bicycle lane, we measured the distances that riders kept from one another and from parked cars and the "shy distance" that cars traveling at different speeds kept from bicycles (Sommer, 1975b).

We had to fight to use part of the street for a bicycle lane. I had been vaguely aware of the politics of space during the mental hospital studies when custodians and nurses resisted the attempts to create more sociopetal ward arrangements, but the cloistered hierarchical structure of the mental hospital (in which we had the support of the superintendent) provided little guidance for dealing with opposition from motorists, neighborhood residents, and merchants. Space was a valued resource, and numerous constituencies would be in competition for it. Involvement in real-world issues like this broadened my understanding of concepts like territoriality and personal space.

A few years later the appearance of murals and graffiti on city walls provided the opportunity to study real-world manifestations of territorial markings. These could be seen in the themes expressed, the relationship of the work to buildings and neighborhoods, and the cooperative nature of the work. At one point I photographed murals around the country, occasionally exchanging lectures at architectural schools for a guided tour of public art, and wrote a book on the subject (Sommer, 1975a). Graffiti represented vandalism and debasement of city walls but also had elements of territorial marking. There are a host of questions associated with graffiti that have implications for theories of territoriality and group action, for example, whether graffiti is more prevalent at the center of territories or at the borders, what symbols are used, to what degree the symbols are meaningful to outsiders, and so on.

When I became director of the Center for Consumer Research, the farmers' market seemed an interesting research site. This was not only a setting where small farmers sold fruits and vegetables to consumers, although that was its economic function, it was also an anasocial institution that helped to build community. It represented the multiuse of public space, a mechanism for downtown revival, and a tool for environmental education. At the outset I was alone among my fellow psychologists in documenting what had become a national revival in farmers' markets (Sommer, 1980), but in the next decade, other environmental researchers began to include the markets in theories of city life (Lennard & Lennard, 1987) and Whyte (1988).

The consumer center also brought me into contact with people in the cooperative movement. There are 350 million people worldwide in organizations affiliated with the International Cooperative Alliance. Although there are sociologists and economists who have done research on cooperatives, there is virtually nothing in the psychological literature. This is surprising in view of the importance of cooperation in social psychological theory, going back at least as far as the classic investigations of Triplett (1897) and F. Allport (1924), and the thousands of prisoners' dilemma studies.

Little would be gained by adding to the list of unusual topics or settings studied. The quality of immediacy runs through the list. There are very few locations on my campus, for example, that my students and I have *not* investigated. If our work was not always driven by theory, it was at least enriched by theory and made a modest contribution by showing how genotypic laws are modified by local circumstances. Privacy on a mental hospital ward is not the same as privacy in an airport or at an automatic teller machine. The same is true of territoriality, crowding, personalization, and the other important concepts in environmental psychology. There are similarities, of course, but there are also important differences. I cannot say that I studied these diverse settings only because they were there. That they existed and the form they took were interesting to me both from a theoretical and a practical standpoint. If we could identify environmental problems through research, it should be possible to design more suitable settings in the future.

CHOICE OF METHOD

Consistent with a background in experimental psychology, my dissertation was a laboratory study of perception (Sommer, 1959a). College students in a darkened room peered into a tachistoscope to view ambiguous figures. Hypotheses were stated in advance, and the experimental design included random assignment of subjects to treatment conditions. The research built on a body of previous studies that I could recite as a litany. Investigators at other laboratories were testing the same hypotheses. Meetings, conferences, and consultants provided information on current studies.

With only a few minor exceptions, this was my last significant involvement with laboratory research. There was nothing about it that I actively disliked; I wasn't satisfied with the external validity of the findings. It was difficult to explain to my grandmother, for example, what I was doing and why it was important. For the rest of my life, I have called this the grandmother question, that is, why is a grown person like you spending time doing something like this? It was a good question at the time and it remains so. However, I did not renounce laboratory experimentation because my grandmother did not understand what I was doing. My post-PhD jobs were at mental hospitals as a research psychologist. Laboratory research could not touch the important behavioral and administrative issues around me.

It was fortunate that my academic background had included work in social psychology. When I completed my PhD, my publications were equally divided between those on perception and those on intergroup relations. Questionnaires and interviews seemed more appropriate than a tachistoscope for conducting research in a mental hospital, so I surveyed patients, staff, and visitors in a variety of issues connected with hospital environment and programs. It was not until the ward renovation studies (Sommer & Ross, 1958) that I used natural observation. Because similar wards could be found throughout North America, I could publish my findings on furniture arrangements with the expectation that other mental hospitals could increase interaction in this same manner. The ability to do research that improved conditions appealed to my altruistic impulses.

We needed to conduct basic studies of the human use of space because there was neither a theoretical nor an experimental literature on human spatial behavior. We began observing people in the staff cafeteria and lounge areas. I spent my lunch hours diagramming the spatial locations of conversations at nearby tables. The method was quick, inexpensive, and fun. I discovered that I liked to watch people. The findings appeared to have a high degree of external validity, and the use of multiple observers established the reliability of the data. The approach followed the dictum laid down by Barker (1965) to study nature while disturbing it as little as possible. The method opened up the world for further study. All that was needed was a researcher willing to spend time in the setting recording behavior unobtrusively. Later, as a college instructor, access to student observers expanded my observational range. The emphasis was always on public spaces in which observer and observed could remain anonymous.

In 1979, when Barbara Sommer and I were writing an introductory research methods textbook (Sommer & Sommer, 1986), I became aware of my preference for a multimethod approach. This had been something I had done unself-consciously. Several methods were superior to one, especially if the methods were independent and came out with similar results. Studying airports, we observed passengers' spatial behavior and followed this with interviews. At farmers' markets we made observations, conducted interviews, employed double-blind flavor comparisons, contracted with the state laboratory to analyze pesticide residues, undertook price comparisons, and made extensive use of photography. Each procedure improved our understanding of environment–behavior relationships.

WRITING STYLE

I rise at 5 every morning, feed the cat, perform a few warm-up exercises, make a pot of coffee, and talk into a dictaphone for the next 2 hours. Tapes and drafts are dropped off in my psychology office where they are picked up by my secretary at 9:30 A.M. and returned typed at 4:00 P.M. This has been my schedule for the past 25 years.

Everything I write starts out as the spoken word. Articles are dictated numerous times before there is a proper first draft to be typed on a word processor. From that point on, revisions are made on paper copy and redictated as needed. I don't know any colleagues who use this approach. I call it "writing," although it is literally talking. On any single day, dictation can include field notes, a first draft, correspondence, memos, and reviews. The technique is responsible for a free-ranging conversational style.

I started using a dictaphone early in my academic career. As a research assistant at the Menninger Foundation, I was assigned an office previously used for therapy. All the equipment needed for clinical practice was there, including a couch and a dictating machine for case records. Because Gardner Murphy used a dictaphone, I tried my hand at "writing by talking," and the advantages of this procedure became apparent. Dictation allows me to think out loud about topics, pursue issues that seem significant even when I cannot explain why, and reflect on current activities. The method makes it easy to record field notes and maintain a written record of events, meetings, and conversations. The dated notes are placed in topical file boxes in my office along with reprints, clippings, and brochures. This open-ended system facilitates the easy addition or removal of materials from file boxes with subject headings like "airports," "peace research," and "recycling." The system seems especially suitable for environment and behavior research (EBR) where archival materials come in many different forms and purely electronic storage would not be sufficient. Stored materials on a current project include interviewer's field notes, dictated memos, grant applications, correspondence, several versions of a survey instrument, reprints, newspaper clippings, brochures, slides, photographs, and floppy disks.

DUAL DISSEMINATION

For as long as I can remember, environment–behavior researchers have wrung their hands and loudly lamented the applications gap. Architects, they complained, were not using the findings of environment and behavior results.

One explanation was that the studies had not originated from practical problems facing architects but from issues of interest to academics. Furthermore, the articles were written in a style that architects could not understand and published in journals that architects did not read. At the same time, it was necessary for researchers to share information with each other through technical journals.

Considered as a design problem, the question can be asked whether it is possible to "design" a paper that can convey technical information to other behavioral scientists and also present information to architects that will be useful in their professional practice. The answer, it seems to me, is no; the same article or book cannot successfully fulfill both objectives. The solution lies in dual dissemination of research findings; different articles in different outlets for different audiences.

This recognition has led me to write articles for refereed technical journals, while at the same time seeking other outlets to reach designers. The latter include periodicals published by design societies and glossy trade magazines catering to designers and space managers. There is a periodical devoted to almost any behavior setting one can conceive of, from day care centers to convalescent homes, beauty parlors to zoos, bowling alleys to mortuaries. For common settings such as offices or schools, there may be glossy periodicals that design researchers can use to bring their work to the attention of practitioners. I have written articles for these periodicals from the earliest days of doing environment and behavior research. This writing was not done at the expense of technical articles but in addition to them.

My first personal space papers appeared in *Sociometry*, a journal directed exclusively to a social science audience (Sommer, 1959a). Because the research also had practical implications, I wrote separate articles for hospital architects and administrators who would not be reading social science journals (Sommer, 1966a). The research on invasions of personal space was done in a university library. The findings of theoretical significance were published in a technical social science journal (Felipe & Sommer, 1966), whereas information of primary interest to librarians was published in library journals (Sommer, 1966b). I do *not* refer here to writing pop psychology. I am very uninterested in writing this type of article. I qualify too many things, avoid the vivid adjectives, glittering generalities, glitzy fast-paced prose and one-liners desired by the mass media. However, I do a reasonably good job writing articles for practitioners.

Employment at a land grant university has made me aware of the role of the Cooperative Extension Service in disseminating research findings to the public. Extension specialists based at the university go out into the community and identify problems that are brought back to campus researchers for answers and also disseminate the findings of university research. It would be splendid if we had a cadre of individuals in EBR to identify important issues facing designers and bring these issues to the attention of researchers. These individuals could also disseminate the findings of EBR in a form understandable to practitioners. Lacking people specifically mandated to bridge the applications gap, I feel a personal responsibility not only to write for my colleagues but also to bring our findings to the attention of practitioners in a form that they can understand.

CONSULTATION

An enticing dream in EBR has been that design firms would routinely hire social science consultants. This would provide employment opportunities for the graduates of the new programs and realistic experience on actual projects. In the early 1970s, the dream appeared reasonable and attainable. Architectural offices recruited consultants in specialty areas related to the nature of a complex project. Because buildings necessarily affected people and behavioral scientists were experts on human behavior, there seemed a probable niche for behavioral science consultants.

My experience in consulting with architects began at the Saskatchewan Hospital in Weyburn, Canada. The superintendent, Humphry Osmond, collaborated with Kyo Izumi, an architect who was the principal of a small firm with a specialty in mental health facilities. Osmond (1957) and Izumi drew up plans for a small sociopetal community mental hospital whose interior spaces emphasized circular patterns. Prototypes were constructed in Yorkton, Canada, and in New Jersey. At the same time, Osmond and Izumi were involved in renovation projects at the Saskatchewan Hospital. The supervising architect on these projects was Arthur Allen, with whom I collaborated. This seemed a good opportunity to apply my long-standing interests in perception and environmental influences to the improvement of the hospital where I worked. When the architects inquired about the best colors for the endless corridors or the optimal number of beds in a sleeping area, there were no solid data that could provide answers. All that was available in the 1950s was the zoo research of Hediger and a few isolated case studies whose results could be generalized only with caution. From my standpoint, the most effective strategy was to embark on research to find the answers rather than provide consultation based upon sketchy or nonexistent data.

This absence of valid information in the technical literature continues to trouble social scientists asked direct questions by architects who want on-the-spot answers rather than to wait years for further research. If I were interested in consulting, the choice was clear: either I would have to provide answers based on whatever information already existed plus my experiences and intuitions or refrain from giving advice. The combination of curiosity about the inner workings of architectural practice and the desire to have a direct impact on the outcome encouraged me to continue.

The renovation projects provided real-world tests of laboratory-based principles. To break up the endless corridors, we divided them into colored segments. The outcome proved successful for paradoxical reasons. We had imagined that division into colored segments would reduce the apparent length of a corridor. The division into colored areas filled the intermediate spaces and thereby *increased* the apparent length of the entire corridor according to the filled space illusion. However, because the long area was now divided, people who occupied one segment (e.g., the green area) no longer felt compelled to look down the entire corridor. We accomplished the superordinate objective of humanizing the corridor, not as we had planned by reducing its overall apparent length, but by creating smaller divisions in which people could feel more comfortable.

The dream of routine, significant social science consultation on major projects remains to be realized. Most projects, major and minor, are completed without direct input from social scientists. To the degree that we have had an effect, it is through research, writing, and teaching. Most consultation remains sporadic and variable in outcome. My subjective impression (I have not done a survey on this) is that it has occurred less often with large firms and superstar architects than with small firms where a behavioral scientist has established a relationship with one of the principals. Superstar architects seem more interested in formalism (exterior appearance) than in user satisfaction that receives little recognition in architectural awards.

Specialization appears the wave of the future in consultation. I refer here to colleagues like Powell Lawton on senior citizen housing, Frank Becker on offices, and Terry Maple on zoo design. There will be niches in consultation for new graduates willing to specialize in a building type. This requires getting to know the history, jargon, and economics of the industry and making contact with potential clients to identify their needs for behavioral science information. I could have become a specialist but declined to do so. It was much more fun to shift topics than become typed in psychiatric hospitals, airports, bicycle paths, jails, or anything else. I think my eclecticism represents the wave of the past *in consultation*. There will still be a place for generalists in research, teaching, and theory construction, but when a design firm has a specific building in mind, it is probably more effective for them to hire a consultant who has specialized in that field than to hire a generalist and pay for that person to come up to speed on the project.

Consultation did not prove to be an appropriate vehicle for undertaking research. The time constraints, funding, and expectations on all sides were too different. However, there was an obvious *indirect* relationship between my research and consultation. Publishing in journals directed to design professions, I received calls from architects requesting my services as a consultant. As a full-time university professor, I looked upon these invitations less from the standpoint of monetary gain than as new learning and opportunities to test methods and concepts. I saw myself in a vanguard of social scientists who might someday be employed by architectural offices on a regular basis. My students benefited most from this exposure to real-world projects. I became sensitized to the realities of design, in terms of personal, political, and economic factors, as contrasted with theoretical discussions of how things should be done.

PROBLEMS AND FRUSTRATIONS

Consultation could be heady and exciting but also frustrating and unsatisfying. It is not an activity for the faint-hearted or cautious. Consultation requires "winging it" on tight deadlines, in the sense of going beyond available data through a combination of prior experience, sketchy prior information, metaphor, and intuition. The obstacles to successful advice-giving are manifold.

Sometimes I was not provided with accurate, complete, or current information. During the morning of a one-day consultancy on the design of a university library, I assumed that the project involved a general library. After several hours, I realized that the building was to be a specialized undergraduate library. The difference was significant in terms of items such as journal storage and usage. The architects' belief that they would have to pay me extra if I were sent materials in advance induced them to send me nothing.

Sometimes I was hired after all the major decisions had been made and it was too late to change anything. The plans had to be in Washington on Tuesday and could not be altered without great expense and inconvenience. Jargon terms, both governmental and architectural, were difficult to decipher. There would be cryptic telegraphic numbers and acronyms for building codes, state standards, and agency regulations. On a hospital project, most of the discussion concerned differences between SNH, IMF, and B and C. There were times when I concluded a consulting day still unsure of the meaning of the squiggly little lines or symbols at the rear entrance of the building but had been reluctant to inquire to avoid holding up the discussion.

Communication problems were especially likely during the first session, when there might be unrealistic expectations among one or both parties on the nature of the consultant's role, the time to be committed to the project, and conditions of remuneration. My best experiences involved a second or third project with the same office. This happened only a few times, and the continuity was appreciated by everyone. I envy those colleagues who have durable relationships with designers. Most of my relationships have been one-night stands. I would advise a young environmental psychologist who wants to do consulting to establish relationships with one or two offices that do quality work on interesting projects. This means getting a foot in the door before becoming a fixture.

Because the consultant's per diem is likely to come from the architect's fee, the architect has a stake in reducing time to a minimum. Architectural consultants are typically hired to answer specific questions in known areas of expertise. This is more realistic for technical questions (e.g., psychoacoustics, human factors, or seating arrangements) than for social design. For example, I provided a half-day consultation on seating arrangements for the San Francisco Bay Area Rapid Transit. Four hours were sufficient to draw implications from personal space research for the distance and orientation of seats. However, the hit-and-run quality of such brief consultation is intellectually and emotionally unsatisfying.

EXPERT WITNESS AS HIRED GUN

Among my least favorite professional activities is service as an expert witness. One lawyer described expert witnesses as "hired guns" who do the client's bidding for a fee; another calls them less charitably, "ladies of the night." My first experience in this role came in 1958 as a research psychologist in Saskatchewan (Sommer, 1959b). The case involved a hunting accident in which the authorities had charged the shooter with negligence. I was requested by the defense to testify on color perception under low illumination and the effects of mental set on perception. I felt comfortable testifying on both issues because my doctorate and much of my graduate training was in visual perception.

Several features of the case distinguished it from the ordinary hunting accident. This was the third time that the victim had been shot while hunting and survived. The accident took place just as it was getting dark and both victim and defendant had been drinking. Finally, and most relevant from my standpoint, was that the victim had dyed his hunting jacket an off-red hue, rather than the more common scarlet. I was able to testify that this off-red would become darker and brownish (deerlike) under low illumination. I could also testify that under low illumination, a hunter set to see a deer could easily misinterpret a distant moving reddish-brown pattern. This latter point helped to counter the government's charge of gross negligence. The shooter was acquitted, although I heard that he and the victim were no longer on speaking terms.

I was not comfortable on the witness stand. Although I could testify about perception in general, I had no direct knowledge of the accident other than what others told me. Nor did I feel positive about seeming to condone hunting accidents, especially when they involved the bad combination of guns and alcohol and the further violation of shooting in low illumination. No one asked my opinion on these issues.

I have been an expert witness a dozen times since then. The largest number of cases concerned prison conditions. My research on mental hospital environments brought me into contact with individuals concerned with prison environment. I had hoped these contacts would result in research opportunities. This proved not to be the case, due to the antipathy of most prison administrators to behavioral research.

I have provided consultation on other types of cases. Often this amounted to no more than a telephone conversation with an attorney (privacy vs. solar access) or visiting an accident scene to examine conditions from the standpoint of user perception. I was uncomfortable in an adversarial system in which one or the other side hired me to support its case. I would like to see the system changed to one in which experts presented testimony for the court rather than for opposing sides. This would eliminate a great deal of inconsistency among expert opinions. Until the system changes, I prefer to keep off the witness stand. If one is to play the lawyers' game, it is better to be a lawyer. Being a psychologist in a lawyers' game is not an enviable position. At one time, this seemed one way among several in which a psychologist could influence public policy, but the risks of corrupting the rational scientific model through participation in an adversarial system are not worth the gains.

FUTURE DIRECTIONS

I am obsessed with one of the oldest issues in our young field, the closing of the implementation gap. This has generally been stated as how we (researchers) can produce information that they (practitioners) will use. I have come to see that this conceptualization is an impediment to a solution. Researchers work largely at universities and study issues of interest to them, whereas practitioners work in the community on projects funded by clients. Bridging the implementation gap can take place only when researchers, designers, and clients work together on projects of mutual interest. I believe that the action research pioneered by Lewin (1946) is one of the most promising ways to accomplish this integration. Involving potential users of the information (in this case clients and practitioners) in the research will alter the questions asked, increase their involvement in the information collected, and create a constituency for utilization. I have been using this approach successfully at the Center for Consumer Research for the past 11 years.

I would like to package action research in a form understandable to other psychologists. When I try to explain the method to colleagues who think in traditional terms, the result has been similar to explaining user participation to a formalistic designer. It is possible that a traditional psychology department is not the most congenial setting for teaching action research.

I would also like to encourage more use of natural observation in psychology. A century ago, psychology shifted from philosophical speculation to laboratory experimentation without passing through an observational stage. Although it is not possible to return to those early days on a metaphorical couch and correct the misshapen psychosocial development of our field, we can at least become acquainted with the potential of observational techniques in our present stage. I have found that experimentation, with random assignment of subjects to groups, is perhaps the least useful of all techniques in EBR. For most projects, there will be more utility in interviews, questionnaires, and natural observation than in experimentation. I say this not to disparage the work of earlier psychologists but to emphasize the need for broadened research training. Although environmental psychology has been ahead of most other branches of the field in this respect, we need to train students in methods of observation, recording, and taxonomy.

My contact with the correctional system has left a strong *Zeigarnik* effect. Part of me would prefer to leave alone this lugubrious topic and concentrate on more pleasant issues. Yet the problems in the correctional system are so vast and urgent that my social conscience cries out for further involvement.

I am also likely to become more heavily involved in gerontology in teaching and research. This will bring me full circle in research topics. My first work on seating arrangements was done on a geriatric ward (Sommer & Ross, 1959), and this interest has persisted. As the years proceed, I can see the fish who studies water writing more articles about settings containing older people.

I am ready to try out different things but probably in the old style. These would probably not be the big ticket issues of world hunger, international tension, or population control, although I would not deny their critical importance; I happen to work most efficiently and creatively on things within my immediate experience. This could include the debased quality of city life, the despoliation of the natural environment, inadequate schools, and other medium-sized problems that a researcher can get a handle on with modest resources and access. Any of these topics could provide the opportunity to try out action research, employ natural observation, sketch and photograph, and write articles for colleagues and practitioners.

REFERENCES

Allport, F. H. (1924). *Social psychology*. Boston: Houghton Mifflin.
Barker, R. G. (1965). Explorations in ecological psychology. *American Psychologist, 20*, 1–14.
Felipe, N. J., & Sommer, R. (1966). Invasions of personal space. *Social Problems, 14*, 206–214.
Hediger, H. (1950). *Wild animals in captivity*. London: Butterworths.
Hutchins, R. M. (1968). *The learning society*. New York: Praeger.
Huxley, A. (1954). *The doors of perception*. New York: Harper.
Lennard, S. H. C., & Lennard, H. L. (1987). *Liveable cities*. Southampton, NY: Gondolier Press.
Lewin, K. (1946). Action research and minority problems. *Journal of Social Issues, 2*, 34–46.
Osmond, H. (1957). Function as the basis of psychiatric ward design. *Mental Hospitals, 8*, 23–29.
Sommer, R. (1957). Effects of rewards and punishments during perceptual organization. *Journal of Personality, 25*, 550–558.
Sommer, R. (1959a). Studies in personal space. *Sociometry, 22*, 247–260.
Sommer, R. (1959b). The new look on the witness stand. *Canadian Psychologist, 8*, 94–99.
Sommer, R. (1960). Einstein's girl Friday. *The Worm Runner's Digest, 2*, 98–100.
Sommer, R. (1963). *Expertland*. Garden City, NY: Doubleday.
Sommer, R. (1965). The isolated drinker in the Edmonton beer parlor. *Quarterly Journal of Studies on Alcohol, 26*, 95–110.
Sommer, R. (1966a). The physical environment of the ward. *Hospitals, 40*, 71–74.
Sommer, R. (1966b). The ecology of privacy. *The Library Quarterly, 36*, 234–248.
Sommer, R. (1975a). *Street art*. New York: Links.
Sommer, R. (1975b). Guide to better bikeways. *Design and Environment, 6*, 28–29.
Sommer, R. (1980). *Farmers' markets of America*. Santa Barbara, CA: Capra.
Sommer, R. (1983). *Social design*. Englewood Cliffs, NJ: Prentice-Hall.
Sommer, R. (1987). Consumer behavior in self-service food outlets. *Journal of Environmental Health, 49*, 277–281.
Sommer, R., & Ross, H. F. (1958). Social interaction on a geriatrics ward. *International Journal of Social Psychiatry, 4*, 128–133.
Sommer, R., & Sommer, B. B. (1986). *A practical guide to behavioral research* (2nd ed.). New York: Oxford.
Tinbergen, N. (1953). *Social behavior in animals*. London: Methuen.
Triplett, N. (1897). The dynamogenic factors in pacemaking and competition. *American Journal of Psychology, 9*, 507–533.
Whyte, W. H. (1988). *The city*. Garden City, NY: Doubleday.
Wilson, C. (1956). *The outsider*. London: Gollancz.

---- 3 ----

Settings of a
Professional Lifetime

ROGER G. BARKER

I WAS BORN IN IOWA IN 1903. My forbearers came from Western Europe in the seventeenth century and were pioneers in the westward movement. At the time of my birth, they were businessmen and government officials in the small communities of Western Iowa. The first 7 years of my life were spent in one of these small towns where my father ran the general store. I had a happy early childhood in our family of five children.

My second 5 years were lived in Des Moines, Iowa. I attended public school and went to the First Baptist Church on Sundays with my family. Life for a middle-class boy in the city brought me new situations and problems, but I survived and became a regular fellow.

In the next 7 years my family had a rough passage. First my father lost his job in Des Moines and, following his ancestors, he went west to Alberta, Canada, to become a farmer. The first year the crops were good, but there followed 5 years of dry weather. During those years I was ill with a serious debilitating illness, so I received little formal schooling. In spite of the harsh aspects of this time, there were many rewarding experiences, such as acquaintance with another settler who farmed with oxen, a one-room one-teacher high school, and the buffalo skull collection I made.

In 1922 we moved to California, taking with us an appreciation of frontier life. I was able to enter Stanford University soon thereafter and thus begin my career in psychology that I describe later and elsewhere.

Here I will tell of some of my pleasures. Two started in my childhood—travel and shared reading. We traveled by train to California in 1908, and as long as trains ran I continued to enjoy train travel. In 1915 with father driving, mother navigating, the five children in the back of the 1909 Pierce Arrow, and the trailer of camping gear, we set out

ROGER G. BARKER • Department of Psychology, University of Kansas, Lawrence, Kansas 66045.
This chapter originally appeared in *The Journal of Personality and Social Psychology, 37*(12), 2137–2157 (1979). Copyright 1979 by the American Psychological Association. Reprinted, with minor modifications, by permission.

from Des Moines to arrive 6 weeks later in Palo Alto, California. With this trip, my interest in car travel started and continued through Model T and Model A Fords, and finally a motor home that gave us special enjoyment after retirement.

Father had read aloud to the family as long as I can remember and later my wife Louise read to our family. We shared the adventures of Peter Rabbit, Laura and Mary in the Little House books, *The Swallows and Amazons*, and finally *Kon Tiki*. When Louise and I were on our own, we read many books from Pepys Diaries and Bernard Shaw's letters to novels by Henry James and Trollope. Again a shared experience.

As for my own reading it has been confined to professional papers, books, and news reports of world events. I have been a newspaper buff for many years. *The Oskaloosa Independent*, *The New York Times*, *The Weekly Manchester Guardian*, and *The Darlington* and *Stockton Times* have followed me in our travels.

An important travel experience was connected with the establishment of a satellite field station in Leyburn, Yorkshire, England. Altogether we spent 3½ years in Leyburn collecting data for comparison with Oskaloosa. This venture provided not only data, but new friends and, as a family, the shared experiencing of a new culture. We observed the schools and our children attended them.

We have been fortunate with our three children, Celia, Jonathan, and Lucy, and their families with whom we share many interests, and in our six grandchildren each of whom we admire as well as love. Not many psychologists have been privileged to have lived happily in the communities they know well through research as well as daily living. Oskaloosa and Leyburn have been good to us.

INTRODUCTION

I was Professor of Psychology and Department chairman at the University of Kansas in Lawrence in 1948. On a particular day of that year, I worked on a research report in my Study at Home, answered correspondence, and made some phone calls at my desk in the Chairman's Office, met my Graduate Class in Experimental Social Psychology for 2 hours, conferred with the Dean of the College of Arts and Sciences in the Dean's Office, chaired a meeting of the Department Faculty, and attended a Departmental Colloquium; these six behavior settings made up my professional environment. During my life in psychology, which began, I shall presume, when I entered upon graduate study at Stanford University in 1928, and has continued to this day, the stream of my behavior as a psychologist has meandered through thousands of behavior settings. These settings have constituted the environment of my professional life, and in this chapter I shall describe some of their features and consequences for me.

The settings of my environment have had widely varying attributes; I have entered some of them by my own choice and have been coerced in varying degrees to inhabit others; in some settings I have had considerable influence, in others little power. The Chairman's Office differed greatly in these respects from the Experimental Social Psychology Class: In the Office there was great diversity of both human and nonhuman components (secretaries, faculty, students, typewriters, telephones, files, people conversing, dictating, typewriting, and more), and all of these were incorporated into a relatively stable, multiform pattern of office activities. In the class there was less diversity (no secretaries, telephones, typewriters, files, people conversing or dictating) and a radically different, less complex standing pattern of lecturing, listening, and note taking. I entered the Chairman's Office by my own choice, but I was under strong compulsion to turn up for the class at the scheduled time. I was powerless to change the program of activities of the Dean's Office, but I was able to alter the program of the Class, although my power was by no means unlimited. This setting had been a part of the College and the University before I joined the faculty, and they imposed certain features upon it that I was powerless to alter: I had to teach experimental social psychology, the setting's raison d'être (not ecology, a great interest of mine at the time), and I had to give grades (objectionable to me, but a policy of the University). Still, within these and other limits, I was in command of the program of activities.

When I have inhabited a behavior setting—whatever its attributes, the conditions of my entrance, and my power—I have become one of its component parts, and my behavior and experience have been formed by its ongoing program; these, therefore, have changed appropriately as I have moved from setting to setting. I did not pick up my mail or dictate letters in the Experimental Social Psychology Class or give lectures or quizzes in the Chairman's Office. The impress of some settings upon me has not extended beyond their boundaries; the stamp of others has been long-lasting. The influence of the Chairman's Office ceased abruptly at the door, whereas some attributes of my behavior and experience first occurring in response to forces within the Class have remained with me. In this account, I shall pay special attention to behavior settings that had long-continuing consequences for me.

Unfortunately the data I have to work with are poor. Few contemporaneous accounts of any setting are available, and still fewer are by independent observers. Most of what I am able to report is the fallible memory of how settings appeared to one inhabitant. In an attempt to mitigate the faults of the data, I shall confine my account to those settings for which there are contemporary data or very clear memories and that appear to have been crucial to my scientific activity. Fifteen behavior settings or clusters of settings most adequately meet these requirements. Here they are listed in temporal order of their occurrence and with their institutional connections: Stanford University, 1929–1935 (Terman's Seminar, Miles's Later Maturity Facility, Stone's Animal Laboratory); University of Iowa, 1935–1937 (Lewin's Offices, Nursery School Laboratory, Topology Meetings); Harvard University, 1937–1938 (Murray's Clinic, Child Psychology Class, Boring's Sack Lunch); University of Illinois, 1938–1942 (Study at Home, Extension Classes); Stanford University, 1942–1945 (Office of Disability Survey); Clark University, 1946–1947 (Office at the University); University of Kansas, 1947–1972 (Office of Department Chairman, Field Station in Oskaloosa).

I shall introduce each of these settings with its specifications under six rubrics: program, physical attributes, temporal characteristics, human components, powers of human components, and boundary properties. Then I shall report the forces and circumstances that brought me into them, the actions and experiences they elicited from me when I inhabited them and after I left them, and my power within them.

But first I must describe the 1928 person who was to make the trip through these behavior settings.

THE 1928 PERSON

He was unsound physically, his intellectual powers were unknown, his financial resources were meager, his motivation was strong but unfocused.

An osteomyelitis infection of the left hip and right knee had had many acute phases since its beginning 12 years before. In 1928 the disease was quiescent, but acute episodes were a threat; a flare-up kept him out of school during 1929–1930. In its quiescent periods, the disease was mildly debilitative, and its destruction of joints caused some locomotor impairment.

The 1928 person was 25 years old and 3 years behind academically. He attributed this to missing school because of illness, but he did not know what it signified for a career in science. Perhaps his isolation in sickrooms and his 6 instead of 8 years of secondary and college education handicapped him for advanced study; he was poorly grounded in mathematics and languages; he had studied no physics and had had only elementary courses in chemistry and biology. He remembered many evidences of intellectual marginality and inadequacy. There was his experience in the fourth grade, when the teacher could not decide if he belonged with the A group or the B group, so she had him sit alone between the elect and the scrubs. And he could not forget failing the first course in high school algebra, having to repeat it, and edging through the second go by memorizing the answers to likely problems, ending with the unanswered question: "How can it be possible to add, subtract, multiply, and divide letters, and why do it in any case?" Years later, too late to be of any comfort to him, he discovered that George Bernard Shaw had also had trouble with algebra, "mistaking the a, b, n and x for goods" such as eggs and cheese "with the result that I rejected algebra as nonsense" (Shaw, 1949, p. 41). Shaw blamed the instruction; "I had been made a fool of"; the 1928 person blamed himself. And there was his mother's aunt, an intelligent and insightful person, who was devoted to him during his adolescence and greatly worried about his future; she summed up her impressions of his assets and liabilities with the advice that he should prepare himself to be a short-order cook in a country restaurant. There was some evidence on the other side. There was the occasional, ambiguous remark about him by partisan adults: Still water runs deep. But this was less convincing than his great aunt's explicit evaluation. There was the thrilling time in the eighth grade when he was called upon to stand before the class and explain how to point off decimals in the quotient of a long division problem, and the teacher praised him. Having graduated from Stanford University with sufficient promise for the psychology department to accept him for graduate study would have been reassuring had there been entrance requirements; at least he was not discouraged by Professor Terman, the chairman. By far the most persuasive evidence, which tipped the scale in his self-evaluation, was the engagement between him and Louise Dawes Shedd. Louise Shedd knew him well, she herself had high scholarly credentials and bright goals for a life in the classroom and laboratory, and she was not about to link her life with that of a short-order cook. He was willing, in fact, relieved, to accept her evaluation, and he hoped to justify it.

His financial resources were less than zero, for during his undergraduate years he had accumulated hundreds of dollars in tuition loans that became due to the university in years immediately ahead.

Psychology for him was a means, not an end. His undergraduate introduction to the subject matter and methods of the science had no special appeal to him, but he believed it to be the least onerous route to his goal of "doing good" for mankind. He was a thoroughgoing, naive idealist and ardent reformer. He considered medicine but was sure he would not be accepted as a student, and his long, discouraging experience as a consumer of medical services had alienated him from the profession. He found economics too remote from particular people, and sociology too speculative and wordy. He tried to get a handle on demography but could discover no people or publications to inform him sufficiently about it. He did not consider literature, art, or the physical and biological sciences of any relevance to his goals. Psychology seemed to be a promising route, but even as he began graduate study he did not foreclose other routes, and within psychology's varied and vast domain, he had no preference. Although the zeal of the 1928 person was great, there were clouds on the horizon. He anticipated that the psychology route to good works would have difficult and unpleasant stretches, and he was keenly aware of the likelihood of recurring acute phases of his illness. His prescience in the latter respect was verified by the flare-up in 1929–1930, and he hesitated about persisting, but for reasons impossible for him to comprehend to this day, his fiancee stood fast, encouraged him, and even married him in the summer of 1930. So in the autumn of 1930 he made a second start and became an anxious, vigilant, expectant psychologist in the making.

STANFORD UNIVERSITY, 1929–1935

I was a graduate and postgraduate student at Stanford University for 6 years. For 4 years I attended classes, did research under supervision, led "quiz sections" of elementary psychology, did various departmental chores (mimeographed class notes and exams, scored Strong Vocational Interest Tests, and cared for the animal colony), passed examinations, and received the MA degree (1930) and the PhD degree (1934). Being unable to find a regular position in the depression year of 1934, I was fortunate in being kept on as a research associate for 2 more years. The work was rewarding, and the salary of $100 a month was satisfactory; with Louise's $1,800 a year as high-school biology teacher we were able to pay my tuition loan debts to the university and save some money. Three behavior settings were crucial to me during these Stanford years.

TERMAN'S SEMINAR

Program: Report by seminar member, usually a student, with interruptions by others discussing or questioning points made. *Physical attributes:* Locus, Terman's home on the Stanford University campus, in an attractive living room of sufficient size for a single-row circle of 25 persons. *Temporal characteristics:* Weekly meetings (with occasional skips) for about 2 hours during most autumn, winter, and spring terms; approximately 20 meetings most years. *Human components:* Dr. Lewis M. Terman, one or two other faculty members, occasional guests, 10 to 20 graduate psychology students. *Powers of human components:* Program determined at three levels of power. Terman's power extended over the entire setting (he selected the speaker, approved the topic, opened and closed the meeting); the speaker's power was supreme over the content and method of his report; the power of the other inhabitants was limited to supplementing, correcting, criticizing, and approving the speaker's presentation. *Boundary properties:* Admission at the invitation or urging (in the case of students) of Dr. Terman.

Reports usually described completed research or plans for research; occasionally books or monographs were reviewed. Almost all reports were concerned with research, emphasizing methods; theories or general issues were very rarely seminar topics. Interchanges between reporters and other members were usually for more information about procedures. The Seminar was eminently civilized and controlled, the occasional disagreements and arguments being muted. Terman set the tone, being quietly attentive, making few contributions himself other than introducing the speaker, and ending the session with general remarks. Despite its appearance of tranquility, many students reported, outside the Seminar, that it was a tense, even traumatic experience for them. Many of the controlled interactions were undoubtedly reactions to the Seminar as a dangerous place for students; they were on trial before powerful present and future evaluators.

When Terman opened the Seminar to me, I eagerly attended. The name of the game for me was to learn as much as possible, to discover if I was likely to make the grade in scientific work, and to improve my chances of doing so by demonstrating what strength I had to Terman, the other faculty members, and my peers. The first and last intentions were not congruent. Optimal learning requires acknowledgment of ignorance, whereas putting one's best foot forward requires masking ignorance. And to walk on thin ice, as I did in the Seminar, always on the brink of both disaster and improved footing, is not conducive to a wide perspective and clear thinking; it is inhibiting. Still, one must act; to remain motionless on the ice, or dumb in the seminar, is a sure way to disaster. Alert caution is essential. Under these circumstances motives and abilities and disabilities are not openly revealed, and valid judgments of persons are not possible, though reputations are made. I never knew my reputation among the members of the Seminar, but I did know my self-estimate. I placed myself near the median of the student seminarians, I was uncertain of passing the examinations, and I was quite sure my destiny was at best to become a journeyman psychologist, perhaps in a junior college where, after all, there was plenty of scope for good works. Considering the people against whom I was judging myself, this self-estimation is not surprising; during the years of my attendance they included six who became president of the American Psychological Association and a number of others who were honored by the association for their scientific contributions.

My immediate reaction after the Seminar was frequently one of great dismay: at my ignorance of what seemed to be common knowledge, at my failure to contribute what afterward appeared to me to be a valuable input, and at my espousal of weak, foolish, or irrelevant ideas. Louise came to dread the late-night aftermath of the Seminar.

I cannot now remember what I learned; I am quite sure that I encountered no mountain peaks of new understanding. But the Seminar provided a regular update of what was happening in psychology, especially with respect to methods of investigation. More than this, I became acculturated into the language, the mores, the ethos of the psychology tribe. And I made acquaintances who have continued to be valued personal friends and influential connections within the profession. On the negative side, I first encountered an aspect of academic life that has continued to be distasteful to me: the ubiquity of judging others (passing and failing students, approving and not approving candidates, promoting and not promoting colleagues, accepting and not accepting research proposals, and so forth) and of being judged by others. The fact that most interpersonal relations within Terman's Seminar involved, explicitly or implicitly, judgments of personal worth reduced its attraction as a social occasion and eroded its educational benefits.

Miles's Later Maturity Facility

Program: To study change in abilities from middle to later years of life. *Physical attributes:* Located near the central business district of Palo Alto in a one-time residence. The former reception hall, parlor, living room, dining room, and bedrooms were modified for use as offices and for administering tests and experiments; office furnishings and equipment for tests and experiments. *Temporal characteristics:* Operated weekdays for several months during academic year 1931–1932 from 9:00 A.M. to 5:00 P.M. *Human components:* Walter R. Miles, graduate student research assistants, secretary, subjects. *Boundary properties:* Free access by staff; subjects admitted by appointment. *Distribution of power:* The power of Miles extended over the entire setting and program; he planned the research, secured the financing, selected the staff, recruited the subjects, approved the methods of testing and experimentation. The power of each research assistant was dominant within his laboratory room. The only power of subjects was to refuse to participate in a particular procedure; to my knowledge this did not occur.

I had completed my master's degree work under Miles with a thesis on finger maze learning, and it was now time to undertake research for the PhD degree. So when Miles returned from a trip East, bringing the news of a grant for the magnificent sum of $10,000 to support a study of old age, I eagerly embraced the opportunity to participate. For reasons I cannot recall, I chose to study muscular fatigue. Miles gave me complete freedom to devise a muscle fatigue test suitable for both robust 50-year-olds and frail centenarians, and I took considerable satisfaction in adapting a spirometer to determine hand and arm fatigue quickly. Other graduate students investigated changes in intelligence, learning, memory, motor skills, and sensory acuity. Subjects were recruited from clubs, churches, and living groups by paying the organization for each member who became a subject. They were brought to our experimental rooms by the secretary. At the time, I did not appreciate the luxury of having subjects provided to me with no effort on my part; many times since, I have appreciated Miles's efficient logistics.

I greatly enjoyed working within the Later Maturity Facility; the freedom within my own domain, and the straightforward problem were agreeable. I went home most nights feeling I was making progress toward providing some potentially useful new knowledge.

The more enduring consequences of this setting for me were, first, increased confidence in my ability to engage in research on my own; after approving the area of my contribution, Miles took no part in my project; it became my own. Second, I learned something about the possibilities and difficulties of a kind of field study; I observed the extensive public relations activities required to secure subjects, and I was especially impressed with the effectiveness of approaching citizens by way of the organizations to which they were devoted. I also noted that the demands of public relations, at which Miles was very effective, divorced him from the details of the research. Because of this experience, I believe it was easier for me, when I later engaged in field studies myself, to realize that they require staffing different from that of laboratory investigations with captive or hired subjects and that community experts are as essential as observers, interviewers, testers, and so forth.

Stone's Animal Laboratory

Program: To investigate motivation in animals, chiefly rats, with emphasis on sexual behavior. *Physical attributes:* Locus, third-floor attic of the building housing the psychology department in an area partitioned into a sky-lighted animal room for about 100 animal cages, perhaps 10 small rooms for assistants and equipment, and Stone's large office. The equipment was primitive by present standards: student-made mazes, jumping apparatus, activity drums, Monroe hand calculators, simple shop equipment. *Temporal characteristics:* Functioned at some time every day. *Human components:* Calvin P. Stone, one or two postdoctoral fellows, two graduate assistants, several thesis students, a few students doing class projects, visitors. *Powers of human components:* Stone's power extended over the entire laboratory; he approved the fellows, selected the assistants, admitted the students and approved their research, set rules and standards. Fellows had complete power over their own research; assistants controlled their particular segment of the total program of the laboratory after consultation with Stone. Visitors' power was limited to viewing approved areas and asking questions. *Boundary properties:* Fellows, assistants, and students admitted by Stone personally; visitors were tolerated, but except for professionals, they were not welcomed.

As in 1931 (the opportunity to participate in the Later Maturity Facility came at a crucial time), I was fortunate in 1933 to be able to work in Stone's

Animal Laboratory when I could not find a regular job. I did not choose to spend 2 years in this setting, but neither did I object; it was inevitable.

I found work in the setting even more satisfying than in the Later Maturity Facility. I had passed all examinations and written my thesis; that tension was gone. The intellectual comaraderie was congenial; postdoctoral fellows brought news and innovations from other laboratories; the pace of activities was not determined by tightly scheduled subject appointments. But there was a vigorous, steady program of activities; almost all the animal work required regular cleaning, feeding, observing, testing, and examining; Stone was a hard, regular worker himself, and everyone knew that he valued industriousness right along with honesty and intelligence. He was known to disapprove strongly of the policy of another university that reportedly provided technicians to do such detail work for graduate students as sectioning and preparing tissues for examination and running rats in mazes. In Stone's Laboratory, students cared for their own animals and spent the boring hours putting them through the necessary procedures. Inasmuch as Stone was in and out of the laboratory many times most days, beginning at 7:30 A.M., his power and reputation were sufficient to maintain a fairly tight ship without many definite rules and regulations.

Special emphasis during this period was on variation in the age of sexual maturity of rats, its genetic basis, and its relation to other behavior and somatic characteristics. Parallel investigations were conducted of the age of maturity of human females and its relation to their size and their interests and attitudes. I came to find much of the work interesting, and some of it had a permanent influence upon me. Even the evening after evening of testing young male rats for age of first copulation became enjoyable when Louise came along and read aloud from a high stool in the center of the animal room. (Conrad, Tolstoy, and Galsworthy in no way diverted the rat subjects from their putative activities.)

It was here that I first became aware of the potential value of archival data for psychological science. Stone was interested in the intellectual level of children of abnormally early sexual maturity, and he had previously reviewed and summarized the literature. He set me to updating the survey, and I was impressed to find that although most evidence was in the form of reports of single or a very few cases, and none were adequate methodologically in terms of number and selection of cases and methods of testing, still, en masse, these data, reported by many independent investigators at widely varying times, in diverse situations and cultures, provided overwhelming evidence that early intellectual maturation does not accompany abnormally early sexual maturation. I noted that almost no cases were reported in the psychological literature, whereas medical journals served as valuable archives for these rare cases. I began to see that the insistence of academic psychology that every publication conform to all current canons of scientific adequacy was depriving the science of data on important issues. Years later I discovered a pair of identical adolescent twins, one of whom had been seriously crippled since childhood, and I saw this as an exceptional opportunity to obtain data from a very rare natural experiment on the effects of physique on personality; I studied them extensively. But I was advised not to attempt to get the material published because "one case means nothing." I wondered: Would a paleontological journal reject a study of 1 dinosaur egg because the investigator did not present data on 50 eggs? The lesson I began to learn in Stone's Laboratory has stayed with me, and I and my colleagues have not hesitated to collect "inadequate" data under certain circumstances, namely when the problem to which the data refer is important, when fully acceptable data cannot be obtained due to their temporal or physical dispersion or their rarity, and when the data are such that investigators at other times and in other places can add to them.

It was in Stone's Laboratory that I first encountered a set of problems that have occupied me ever since, namely environmental influences on behavior. At the time, however, I did not see the particular problem in this context. It arose from our studies of relations between age at menarche and physical and social development in girls. We discovered that in the early adolescent years, early maturing girls are more similar to older females in measurements of physique than are late maturing girls of the same chronological ages, and when we asked if this same relation holds for social interests and attitudes, we found that it does: Postmenarcheal girls 12, 13, and 14 years of age are more similar to older females in their responses to interest and attitude test items than are premenarcheal girls of the same ages. So we faced this question: To what degree are the differences in attitudes and interests due to direct hormone influences, and to what degree to the fact that the physiques of the early and late maturing girls provide the girls and their associates with stimuli with different social significances, thereby imposing different social environments upon them? We could not answer this question with the data at hand. Five years later, at the University of Illinois, I returned to this problem and found evidence that powerful adults (parents, teachers) bring greater pressure upon physically mature girls to engage in mature behavior than upon physically immature girls. And 10 years later, when I was back at Stanford, I returned to the problem in connection with studies with my students of the psychological consequences of physical crippling.

In addition to initiating this particular continuing interest, Stone's Animal Laboratory further strengthened an attitude I carried with me from other Stanford settings, namely that strong and persisting but rather narrow programs of activities are productive. There were no brilliant performances at Stanford. The research of Terman on the gifted, of Stone on animal motivation, and of E. K. Strong on interests yielded no remarkable breakthroughs, but they were and have continued to be recognized as substantial achievements. This was not an "Aha!" experience for me; but as I look back I can see that it became a deeply rooted conviction that this was to be my way of doing science. Along with this vaguely developing insight there was increased self-assurance. At the end of my 6 years at Stanford, I was more sure that my aspirations for a productive career in science were not hopeless. However, I did not have a strong commitment to any problem. I had worked on a rather wide range of problems via a considerable number of methodologies, but I had become devoted to none. I was still unfocused, at the beck and call of almost any opening that would allow me to earn a living as a psychologist. In the spring of 1935 an opening came that radically altered my intellectual life-style and threw me again into uncertainty about myself.

I took part in many behavior settings at Stanford other than the three I have described: classes, lectures, seminars, laboratories, projects, examinations. They enriched my intellectual life and widened my perspective, but only one of them had particular, identifiable consequences for me. This setting channeled the stream of my behavior as a psychologist into its first great bend. Kurt Lewin came as a visiting professor for the year 1932–1933. I was very busy during this year finishing my doctoral thesis so I was able to attend Lewin's class only as a visitor. He attracted me greatly as a person, but his psychology confused me or, perhaps more correctly, it was incomprehensible to me. Fairies and ectoplasm would have been more comprehensible than life space, valence, psychological force, inner-personal regions, substitute value, psychological satiation, and so forth. Stanford students knew something about Gestalt psychology experiments and theories of perception from the writings of Wertheimer and Köhler, and of development from the works of Koffka, but Lewin's so-called Gestalt psychology seemed to have nothing to do with these, as we expected. And equally disconcerting, Lewin seriously reported experiments with seven subjects, and instead of replicating the experiments, he changed the conditions; even worse, if the results from the altered conditions were in accord with his predictions on the basis of theory, he took this as a verification of the findings and the theory. I suppose Stanford University in those days was among the least auspicious places in the United States for an understanding of Lewin; theory was almost a nonword in the psychology department, although we did use it in connection with Spearman's interpretation of intelligence test intercorrelations (theory of general intelligence), and we read about psychoanalytic theory. But most of us had no background in the philosophy of science, and the place of theory in science. So Lewin's *Dynamic Theory of Personality*, which I reviewed (with Terman) and which he taught in his course, was a transient foreign body, a UFO, to most of us. I cannot recall that any of the students who attended his class took and retained a serious interest in his viewpoint unless they had later association with him. The gulf was too wide to be bridged quickly, and the dissonance was so great that some rejected his ideas out of hand. I was not negative; I was tolerantly baffled.

So when the opportunity arose to join Lewin as a General Education Board Fellow at the University of Iowa for the year 1935–1936 I was intrigued; here was a chance to learn a different kind of psychology, to earn a full living for Louise and me for the first time, and to have the prestige of the fellowship. Indeed, I had no choice; circumstances beyond my knowledge and control were turning the stream of my professional behavior, indeed my whole life, in a new direction. I have no idea to this day how my nomination to this fellowship came about, but I am sure that an important factor on the Stanford side must have been: It is really time for Barker to push off the home place. I thought so, too.

UNIVERSITY OF IOWA, 1935–1937

Kurt Lewin went to the Iowa Child Welfare Station in the autumn of 1935 on a grant from the General Education Board, with provision for three research assistants. The first assistants were Tamara Dembo (who had been a student of Lewin in Berlin), Herbert F. Wright (who had been a student of Donald K. Adams at Duke University; Adams had studied with Lewin in Berlin), and me. My fellowship was extended in the spring of 1936 for 1 more year. Three behavior settings were of primary importance to me at Iowa.

Lewin's Offices

Program: To plan the research project we would undertake, and to discuss and make decisions about procedures and problems when it was underway; to analyze data from the project and write up reports; to read the writing Lewin was doing, to listen to his proposals for reformulations and additions, and to criticize and make suggestions. *Physical attributes:* Located in four adjacent office rooms on an upper floor of East Hall, University of Iowa campus; the building had been a hospital, and the rooms were former single-patient rooms; they were a little crowded with a desk, a bookshelf, a blackboard (in Lewin's office), and four chairs when we were all present in a single office. *Temporal characteristics:* In operation at some time almost every day, with one or more participants; sessions with Lewin occurred whenever the project needed his attention and whenever he had something to discuss. *Human components:* Lewin, the three assistants, frequent visitors. *Boundary properties:* Assistants selected and admitted by Lewin; free entrance for visitors. *Powers of human components:* Lewin established the program of the setting; he decided that the research would be upon frustration, but the details of procedure were worked out in group consultation, where he was first among equals; he was, of course, in total control of his own writing, the assistants serving more as persons upon whom he could try out his ideas than as consultants or collaborators, although he took seriously all criticisms and suggestions.

It is difficult to imagine more different climates for scientific work than those obtaining at Stanford and at Iowa. At Stanford, science gathered facts about behavior via experiments and tests, determined their central tendencies, and analyzed their interrelations; in Lewin's setup, science explored ideas about behavior via experiments and observations. At Stanford, conclusions were in terms of the means, dispersions, and correlations of samples of *facts* about behavior; my own work discovered that the rate at which 80-year-olds pump air into a spirometer declines faster during a work period than the rate at which 50-year-olds pump air. At Iowa, conclusions were in terms of verified or altered *ideas* about behavior; in our work there we found (in accordance with a theory) that in psychological frustration, inner-personal systems can be considered to be in a state of blocked tension that amounts to functional dedifferentiation, one expression of which is lowered level of intellectual activity, that is, intellectual regression.

In the beginning, the sessions in Lewin's Office were an ordeal for me; they were bewildering and tiring. The ideas we were to explore and clarify in connection with the frustration study were too unfamiliar for me to make many contributions; as for the monograph Lewin was working on, *The Concep-*

tual Representation and Measurement of Psychological Forces (1938), the ideas were utterly baffling. Lewin's eagerness and the energy to back it up seemed boundless, whereas the tension and alertness of the 2-hour sessions of Terman's seminar left me dog-tired; after meeting with Lewin, Dembo, and Wright from 2:00 to 7:00 in the afternoon (with Lewin reading aloud what he had dictated the day before, interlining new sentences, rearranging the order, violently objecting to a criticism by Dembo, turning to Wright—"Herbert, is she right?"—accepting Dembo's criticism, diagramming a relation on the blackboard, crossing the whole page out, dictating a new version to Dembo and so forth), I was ready to drop. After 5 o'clock I would hope beyond hope that my dear, pregnant wife, lonesome at home, would telephone that I was urgently needed. Sometimes she did. A frequent concluding remark by Lewin was "We must think about this," and that after 3, 4, 5 hours of nothing else. Did this add up, perhaps, to a kind of brainwashing? In any case, as the months went by, I began to understand Lewin, and his ideas have remained at the center of all my subsequent work. But equally important to me has been the new, higher level of intellectual effort to which I became adapted. I could never come close to Lewin's intensity; I had to take it much slower, but his refrain, "We must think about this," has stayed with me. Although no one could have been more subordinate to Lewin in terms of knowledge, I was always treated as a colleague, never as a pupil. My contributions, however naive, were always taken seriously, Lewin often seeing in them more than I had intended.

Nursery School Laboratory

Program: To carry out the research on frustration, we planned in the offices in East Hall. *Physical attributes:* Two ground-floor rooms in a remodeled residence across the street from the station's nursery school equipped with a one-way observation booth, child-sized chairs and tables, toys, and a movable barrier in accordance with the research design. *Temporal characteristics:* Setting occurred intermittently during winter and spring of 1936–1937, according to a schedule of appointments. *Human components:* Tamara Dembo and myself, alternating as observer and experimenter, and a single child from the nursery school at each occurrence. *Boundary properties:* Free access to Dembo and me; child subjects, a different one on each occasion, selected and required to attend in accordance with decisions made by us and nursery school staff. *Powers of human components:* Dembo and I had joint authority over the entire setting, although, according to the experimental design, we did not intrude into regions designated for free play; child subjects had no power except in designated free play regions.

Basic to much of the early research Lewin initiated is the theory that psychological tension systems correspond to intentions to engage in molar actions. The studies of interrupted and substitute tasks issued from this theory. Lewin came to Iowa with the intention of investigating this idea further; he thought that the undischarged tensions that occur in frustration result, via increased rigidity and spread of tension to adjacent regions of the person, in functional dedifferentiation, and that one manifestation of this is intellectual regression to a state normal for an earlier age. The problems for the assistants were to devise a frustrating situation and methods of assessing intellectual level inside and outside this situation. The nursery-school setting in which we worked on these problems elicited from me two insights that have remained with me. I discovered the value, for studies of molar actions, of situations where the investigator intrudes not at all or very little, and the value of detailed narrative records of behavior. The frustration study involved, for the most part, a continuation of the child's usual nursery-school day, and in his free situation, we were able by means of nonintrusive narrative records to assess intellectual level as accurately as formal intelligence tests do. In later work, my colleagues and I have come to depend very extensively on narrative records of behavior in situations that are completely free of our influence, and we continue to be impressed with the value of ordinary language as a coding system for the subtleties and complexities of behavior. The Nursery School Laboratory was a welcome refuge for me from the conferences in Lewin's office. Here I found a kind of therapy in applying my Stanford expertise to the gathering and analyzing of masses of data.

Topology Meetings

Program: To discuss Lewinian theory and research findings. *Physical attributes:* Occurred in academic conference rooms of various universities. *Temporal characteristics:* Took place during Christmas vacation for two or three full-day and evening sessions. *Human components:* Lewin and invited guests; the latter were former and present students and colleagues, and a few others interested in Lewin's ideas. *Boundary properties:* Invitations issued by Lewin and by people at host school. *Powers of human components:* Designated persons at host institution controlled local arrangements, Lewin arranged program of papers; free discussion.

The topology meetings were as much a part of my Iowa experience as were Lewin's office and the Nursery School Laboratory, even though the meetings were held at Cornell University and Bryn Mawr College in those years. They agitated me somewhat as Terman's seminar had, although the testing aspect was less pervasive and the learning aspect more pervasive; still these settings were new and strange, and I was alert and cautious. In them my world expanded greatly, to encompass many new friends and acquaintances, many new concepts applied to new problems, and many new locales and institutions (I had not previously been east of the Mississippi).

The adjustments I made to the three crucial behavior settings at Iowa were only part of the intellectual turmoil I experienced. There were other upsettings settings. In some of them Herbert Feigl expounded physicialism and the views of the Vienna Circle; in others, Spence's kind of Hullian behaviorism was expounded. Iowa, for that brief time, at least, was a bubbling cauldron of antagonistic ideas. With my nontheoretical background, I was severely buffeted by the strongly asserted convictions of these sophisticated advocates. Lewin's handling of these disturbances impressed me and has been a model for me since. Although he defended his viewpoints strongly, he was not rigidly partisan. An early remark he made to a student objector at Stanford, when his English was poor, expressed his position: "Con be, but I sink absolute uzzer."

He did not think current controversy would settle basic issues, that only empirical evidence would in the long run sift the true from the false, and that the business of science was to get ahead with empirical tests. He strongly deplored the disruptive partisanship within German psychology.

Before the end of my second fellowship year a new opportunity arose that I could not decline: an instructorship at Harvard University to teach a course in child psychology. As with the General Education Board Fellowship, I have no knowledge of the forces that brought this opportunity to me. But again, after 9 years, the stream of my professional behavior was to flow in a ready-made channel. Previously, the Later Maturity Faculty, the Animal Laboratory, and the General Education Board Fellowship had taken charge of my life in psychology, and now the Harvard Psychology Department took over with no effort by me. But there was a difference: Whereas previously I had been in the role of pupil (to Terman, to Miles, to Stone, to Lewin), now I was to be on my own in my teaching and in my research.

HARVARD UNIVERSITY, 1937–1938

I arrived at Harvard under the cloud of an illness, not my old familiar trouble, but suspected appendicitis. I presume now, more than I admitted then, that the symptoms were of psychosomatic origin. And why not? I was confronted with the task of teaching a subject new both to me and to the Harvard Psychology Department (child psychology had not been in its curriculum before) to hypercritical Harvard students (Boring warned me of them in a letter in which he also expressed the concern of the department about its reputation among undergraduates for good teaching) before the eyes of some of psychology's top brass (Boring, Allport, Murray, Lashley) and its brightest lieutenant colonels (S. S. Stevens, B. F. Skinner, Robert W. White).

Murray's Clinic

Program: To carry out studies of personality; the program was minimal this year, however, as Murray was on sabbatical leave. *Physical attributes:* Located in a converted residence on Plimpton Street, a block and a half from Emerson Hall, headquarters for the department; clinic office, staff offices, library, experimental rooms, shop, kitchen; the library and several offices were elegantly furnished with fine rugs and period furniture. *Temporal characteristics:* In regular operation weekdays and at any time for particular staff members. *Human components:* Acting director, three or four staff and/or psychology department members, a postdoctoral fellow, several students, clients and subjects, secretary, shop man. *Boundary properties:* Free access to official personnel, clients and subjects by appointment. *Powers of human components:* The acting director was Robert W. White, who had final control of the entire setting, although staff members and the fellow were quite independent; the secretary and shop man were semiautonomous within their areas; powers of clients and students were limited by the staff members with whom they were associated.

Murray's clinic was my salvation: It was leisurely and quiet; my office was large, with comfortable chairs and a couch; after the hectic pace at Iowa, it was a refuge. Here I could sit and think about where I had been and where I was going, emerging only at intervals to grapple with my one class. Part of where I had been was with me in the form of a partially completed manuscript about the Iowa frustration experiment; sitting on my desk in a big box, it was a continual irritant, but it did not claim or oppress me. I tested where I was going by doing an experiment on conflict resolution; it was a Lewinian experiment, and it was congenial to me, but I did not see it as a channel to a lifetime of research; I did only one other study of conflict. I believe I became dimly aware, then, that further investigation of conflict resolution would lead to finer grained and more complex theories and more detailed and precise experimental procedures that did not suit me. This may have been the beginning of my aversion to the reduction of theoretical explanations of molar events to theories of their more molecular components, with the implication that the latter are the more fundamental. Murray's clinic was my first experience of a behavior setting without a coercive program. Whereas the settings at Stanford and Iowa took me in hand and put me through their paces, Murray's clinic protected me from impositions. Settings of this kind have fortunately occurred at regular intervals in my career.

Child Psychology Class

Program: To teach child psychology to undergraduate students. *Physical attributes:* Classroom for about 40 students in the basement of the Clinic; chairs, podium, blackboard; furnishings and decorations somewhat shabby. *Temporal characteristics:* One hour's duration, three times weekly for one semester. *Human components:* Instructor and 35 students. *Boundary properties:* Access only for instructor and registered students. *Powers of human components:* Program under complete control of instructor; powers of students limited to expressing approval or disapproval.

The sensitivity of the Psychology Department to the students' regard for the teaching it provided caused me to approach this, my first teaching, with more than my usual trepidation. I worked hard welding my Stanford and Lewinian background into what I am sure was a unique course of study. There were a few rough places in this setting, marked by some foot shuffling, but it ended with an acceptable round of applause. So I emerged with some confidence in my teaching ability and with a course outline that was a longtime asset.

Boring's Sack Lunch

Program: To combine an economical lunch with friendly conversation among colleagues. *Physical attributes:* Locus, Boring's office in Emerson Hall; table around which eight people could sit comfortably; sack lunches; in the background a desk and shelves filled with books. *Temporal characteristics:* 1:00 to 2:00 P.M. most weekdays. *Human components:* Boring and, usually, five or six staff members and visitors. *Boundary properties:* Access at Boring's invitation. *Powers of human components:* Boring's benign influence pervaded the setting.

I was flattered to be invited. I expected stimulating conversation of the kind I had heard took place at the high tables in the English colleges, but in this I was disappointed. Despite the high caliber and great achievements of a number of the attenders (B. F. Skinner, S. S. Stevens, Boring, occasionally Lashley and Beebe-Center), small shoptalk about equipment, library resources, particular research results, publishing problems, together with bantering but restrained gossip about current university, community, and national affairs prevailed. I emerged from this setting with some impressions of eminent and soon-to-be eminent people but nothing of professional value to me. It did strengthen my belief, originating at Stanford and strengthened at Iowa, that the effective men in the science were blue-collar, hard-hat workers, not gentlemen scholars. Here was Boring, well past middle age, the Mr. Psychology of the profession in America, eating his cold egg sandwich with the boys and discussing the nuts and bolts of research and writing, not lunching gracefully in the Harvard Faculty Club with his professional and administrative peers on the club's famous horsemeat steaks.

My time at Harvard was one of greatly expanded perspective, not of psychology as a field of study, but of the people, institutions, and cultural milieu of the science. Other settings that contributed to this expansion were conferences sponsored by the Macy Foundation, where I encountered the eastern wing of the child development movement and for the first time directly heard psychoanalysts expound their views.

Although I was no longer in the role of a student, I was still a probationer. As I understood the Harvard policy, it was: 3 years at most as an instructor and then up or out. As I saw no possibility of my moving up, I determined before the end of the year to seek another position. Behind this decision there were a number of considerations: uncertainty if I would be appointed for a second year and apprehension about finding a place in 2 or 3 years, when I would need one; the belief that 9 years as apprentice (6 years at Stanford, 2 at Iowa, 1 at Harvard) with the continual strain of being tested was enough; and the realization that I was veering sharply away from my goal of using psychology for the direct benefit of people. So when I heard that a position as assistant professor of educational psychology was open in the College of Education at the University of Illinois, I applied for it and was appointed. As it turned out, another year at Harvard was offered to me, and some surprise was expressed that I chose Illinois. But Louise and I went with few regrets; we were at last taking a hand in the direction of my professional career, our economic future did not come to a dead end in 1 or 2 years, and education was surely a promising place to apply what I had learned at Stanford and Iowa.

UNIVERSITY OF ILLINOIS, 1938–1942

We arrived in Urbana, Illinois, in July 1938 with our 2-month-old and 2-year-old children. We rented a house while looking for one to buy; we were ready to settle down.

STUDY AT HOME

Program: To get on at last with my own version of psychology. *Physical attributes:* We soon purchased an old house from a retired academic who had made himself a study to match, on a small scale, the library on Plimpton Street: paneled walls, a fireplace that worked, many shelves, stained glass windows, space for a large desk and work table. *Temporal characteristics:* Occurred at my discretion during the Illinois years. *Human components:* Myself, my students, Louise, and our children. *Powers of human components:* I was in overall charge, but in these years Louise began to participate in the research, a partnership that has continued, with some breaks when she has had outside jobs. *Boundary properties:* Penetrable to me, Louise, and children at any time; to students on invitation.

What I had prepared for the Harvard students of child psychology seemed good enough also for the Illinois students of educational psychology, so I turned early from preparations for my class to other undertakings. Two of these were rooted in Stone's laboratory, two in Lewin's offices, and one was a "do good" effort.

The question of whether differences in the attitudes and interests of premenarcheal and postmenarcheal girls have a basis in the social significance of their different physiques was left unanswered 5 years earlier, so I returned to it now and found evidence that, indeed, the adult associates of mature adolescent girls provide a different (more "mature") social environment for them than they do for immature girls. And I expanded my concern for the environmental significance of physique to physically disabled people and asked if they also live in a different environment from that of physically normal people by reason of their physiques. I began a long involvement with this question with two case studies. Although the roots of my interest in the environmental significance of physique were in Stone's laboratory, my interpretations and theories came from Lewin's office, and undoubtedly my expansion of this interest to physical disability was influenced by my personal experience with the problem.

The unfinished manuscript of the frustration research still occupied a prominent place on my desk, and I continued to wrest time from more immediately interesting new tasks to inch along toward its completion. And the conflict resolution study had become such an uncompleted task for me that I was impelled to replicate (and verify) the findings by an entirely different method.

My "do good" effort was carried out in collaboration with Herbert F. Wright, my fellow Fellow at Iowa, and Jacob S. Kounin, my new colleague at Illinois. This was a collection of reports of psychological research in the field of child development. It was intended to provide a "bookshelf" of primary research for students of child development and thereby promote scientific child study as a field for both practitioners and scientists. It is my impression that this was the first "reader," as they are now called, in child psychology, and perhaps in psychology as well (Barker, Kounin, & Wright, 1943).

My Study at Home was not only a place to get on with my version of psychology as a science; it became a place to teach my version, as well. In the early autumn of 1940 an acute phase of the bone infection occurred, and I was completely incapacitated for the term. Jack Kounin came to my rescue, taking over my classes, presumably for a short time. But as it turned out, I was out of commission for 4 months. Due to Jack's heroic efforts and the tolerance of the College and University, my pay continued. In the second semester, although still in a full body cast, I was able, again with the kind indulgence and special arrangements of the College, University, and students, to meet small classes in my Study at Home. Perched on a high tavern-type chair within a specially built surrounding pulpit, I was able to expound the word to a score of students at a time.

Again, as with Murray's clinic, my Study at Home saved me from possible disaster. This one nourished projects I brought to it from Stanford and Iowa, and in it new, long-continued undertakings originated.

EXTENSION CLASSES

Program: To teach educational psychology at the graduate level to primary and secondary-school teachers. *Physical attributes:* Located in classrooms of state teachers' colleges, which did not at that time offer graduate-level instruction. *Temporal characteristics:* Occurred on Saturday mornings for 2 hours during each semester. *Human components:* Instructor and 20 to 40 students from the schools of the area. *Boundary properties:* Only students satisfying registration requirements of the university were admitted. *Powers of human components:* Program controlled by instructor.

The Saturday trips from Urbana to outlying teachers' colleges, usually by automobile but in some cases by train, were enjoyable and satisfying. The mature, practicing teachers brought me into contact with real teaching problems in the towns where they taught; they educated me perhaps as much as I educated them. And the trips revealed to me something about the rural Midwest. I was intrigued with the small towns, and elsewhere I have related how the general problem that dominated the last 25 years of my professional life occurred to me as I was rushed through them by the train on the trip from Urbana in the center of Illinois to Carbondale in the south (Barker & Associates, 1978). In short, I had an overwhelming *negative* "Aha!" experience: Here I was, a native of the culture and an expert on child behavior (and especially on frustration) who knew no more about the everyday behaviors and environments of the children of the towns than laymen know. I was aware, too, that other child psychologists knew no more than I did, and furthermore, that we had no means of discovering more; no methods of determining the extent and conditions of frustration, joy, anger, success, conflict, problem solving, fear, and so forth among the towns' children. I thought how different the position of an agronomist would be. He would know or could determine the kinds, yields, and qualities of the crops we were passing, the properties of the soils in which they were growing, and the relations between soil conditions and output. This was the beginning of a growing conviction that a science that knows no more about the distribution in nature of the phenomena with which it is concerned than laymen do is a defective science, and it was the beginning of my impression that small towns of the kind I observed in Illinois and learned about from the teachers are favorable places to begin to remedy the defect. It was 7 years before the seed planted in the Extension Classes and on my trips across the plains of Illinois began to sprout.

It was not long after we went to Illinois to "settle down" that irritants began to appear. There were the disagreeable administrative impositions upon my teaching that finally became intolerable to me. And I was soon to discover that my flight from a marginal position vis-à-vis the upper uppers of the profession at Harvard had landed me squarely with the lower lowers. I attempted to establish collegial relations with psychologists in the psychology department but without success. Part of the difficulty was structural: I was separated from them spacially, temporally, and administratively; I was in a different building, their seminars and other gatherings often conflicted with my staff meetings and other duties, and administrative messages were on different communication networks. And in addition, I found that a psychologist in a college of education is distinctly lower class. This so impressed me and it was so important to me personally that I used my experience as evidence for an analysis of the values and dynamics involved. Finally, I became discouraged about my ability to combine scientific work with applications. I began to see that it required more than clear lectures to alter the practices of teachers. My own experience, namely that because of impositions from the encompassing system I could not practice in my own teaching at the university, the principles that my science showed me to be true should have made this immediately clear to me, but it took time. I struggled on with increasing dissatisfaction. Finally, in the spring of 1942, these multiple environmental stresses became so great that I wrote to Terman telling him of my disenchantment. To the surprise and delight of both Louise (who, surprisingly, did not thrive with a troubled mate) and me, Terman answered immediately with the offer of a place at Stanford for the duration of the war.

At Illinois I learned some important things about myself and about my profession; I closed out some unfinished tasks and initiated some new ones. I look back on the time there as a rough but beneficial passage.

STANFORD UNIVERSITY, 1942–1945

The Stanford appointment was as acting associate professor. I understood clearly that this was an emergency appointment to bolster a war-depleted staff. At the time its temporary nature did not trouble me or Louise; the advantages were many: I was free to teach as I pleased (the motto for Stanford of its first president, David Starr Jordan, "The winds of freedom are blowing," was fully realized in the classrooms of the Psychology Department): I was again a member of psychology's upper class; we were home among friends; Louise was welcomed back on a part-time teaching basis to her old school; my health was on the upgrade and promised to improve more in the California sunshine. We were in such good shape, in fact, that our third child was born in the spring of

1943. Furthermore, it turned out that I was able to make an important immediate application of my psychological knowledge.

But not all was rosy. The war was ever present on the West Coast, with blackouts, shortages, relatives and friends embarking for Asian combat, and casualties disembarking. The teaching load was heavy; in addition to the regular offerings, short cram courses were given for officers in training. I taught a number of subjects new to me, so I had to do much homework to keep ahead of the classes. Most of these 3½ years at Stanford were a steady grind. Only one setting stands out as of special significance for my career. It came about through a fortunate conjunction of (1) my desire to make a contribution to the war effort; (2) the national need for rehabilitation service for war casualties; (3) my interest in, my exploratory research upon, and my personal experience with, physical disability; and (4) resources that the Social Science Research Council (SSRC) made available. A crucial person in tying together these separate strands was my colleague Quinn McNemar, who was a member of the relevant SSRC committee; it was at his instigation that the council funded the preparation of a survey of what was known about the psychological aspects of the rehabilitation of the physically disabled (Barker, Wright, Meyerson, & Gonick, 1953). I set up a special study at home for this project.

OFFICE OF DISABILITY SURVEY

Program: Preparation of monograph *Adjustment to Physical Handicap and Illness. Physical attributes:* We were living in a house built by Walter Miles, my former professor and thesis adviser, which had a fine, spacious, isolated study; it became headquarters for the monograph project. *Temporal characteristics:* Occurred whenever I had time during the years 1943–1945. *Human components:* When the magnitude of the project became clear, I was fortunate in obtaining contributions from Beatrice A. Wright, Lee Meyerson, and Molly Gonick. *Boundary properties:* Ready access by the four participants. *Powers of human components:* Overall control was in my hands; others had complete autonomy for their own contributions.

In this setting I experienced some of the great satisfactions of my professional life, and they have continued to this day. In the first place, I felt competent; I believed I was as able any anyone to do the job at that time. Second, I saw this as my first opportunity to bring my skills to bear upon an urgent practical problem. As it turned out, the time was ripe for this; beginning with World War II, concern and services for the disabled have increased greatly, so any firm foundations laid in 1943 have had continuing consequences. And third, I believed at the time that I was able to contribute to this firm foundation by pointing out that some psychological problems of the disabled are not unique to them, that adolescents and ethnic minorities, for example, face the same problems; I was able to do this in terms of Lewin's concepts of marginal men and overlapping situations. I have not followed the course of rehabilitation psychology in recent years, so I have no firsthand knowledge of the permanence of this contribution, but I am told that the monograph is still in demand. Clearer evidence of the enduring consequences of the Disability Office is the fact that both Beatrice Wright and Lee Meyerson have become leaders of this field of psychological study.

In 1945 I wore the child psychology label, primarily, and there was not much demand for this branch of the science at Stanford. Members of the department had ambitions to develop a program of studies in child psychology, but money was scarce and progress slow; their principal efforts went to accommodating regular staff members returning from war service and to filling vacant, established slots. So in October 1945 I was told that there was no hope for me beyond the next spring semester. As of June 1946 I would be through at Stanford. The likelihood of this subsidence of the stream of my professional life had long been within my time perspective, but the reality was more vivid than the distant prospect. It gave a new urgency to the somewhat relaxed inquiries I had initiated before reality descended. I had communicated about possible jobs with a number of schools, including Clark University, and in the summer I had an interview with President Atwood about the vacant G. Stanley Hall Professorship in Child Psychology. I did not take this possibility seriously. So, when a definite offer came from Clark in November, Louise and I were almost overwhelmed by the drastic alteration in our prospects. But we were able to make the transfer; we arrived in Worcester, Massachusetts, for the second semester in January 1946.

Two firsts of some importance occurred during the 3½ years at Stanford. One was advising graduate students on their thesis research. In line with my interest in the disability problem and my work on the survey, three students undertook theses on attitudes toward the disabled. The other first was the establishment of the Disability Survey Office as a major behavior setting with a program after my own specifications; until this time, apart from minor side excursions, I had operated in behavior settings with programs arranged by others. At Stanford I was born as a psychologist, and on my return 15 years later I gained these two evidences that I had at last reached my majority.

Louise and I left Stanford older and with more experience of the stream of university life. We had drifted through the dangerous, white waters of Harvard, portaged to the slow Illinois channel with its sandbars and driftwood, portaged again to the steady, full flow at Stanford, on whose banks we were briefly stranded until an unexpected flash flood carried us to Clark. One more portage was to come.

CLARK UNIVERSITY, 1946–1947

Clark turned out to be a bayou for us. The top administrators changed 6 months after we arrived, the psychology department had been understaffed for some time and had an acting chairman, and I was uncertain of the direction of my next efforts, having completed the disability monograph. With so much in the process of change, all of us—the university, the department, and I—marked time. It was now that the seed planted in my mind on the plains of Illinois began to grow, and I seriously considered a project to discover and describe the living condition and behavior of the children of a small town. I took two actions. I explored the towns around Worcester, and I discussed the project with Kurt Lewin, who was then at the Massachusetts Institute of Technology and was living only 30 miles away. The exploration was discouraging. The small settlements of the region were not self-contained towns as in the Midwest; they were spacially dispersed and often specialized fragments of political units (towns) often straggling many miles along streams or across forested ridges. The children of these fragments did not have a common community environment as did the children of the towns I had seen in Illinois. But the discussions were encouraging, and in fact Lewin was enthusiastic. He, himself, was moving from laboratory experimental research to "action research" in communities and institutions to study the consequences for the inhabitants of induced changes in their structures and programs. So he was supportive of efforts to establish baselines in unaltered communities against which to assess the effects of changes. With his encouragement, I worked on an application for funds for a community study with the intention of doing the research at a distance from Worcester if necessary.

And now luck was with us. The United States Public Health Service was expanding its support of basic research, particularly on children. The advisory committees included persons familiar with my work whom I had met at Stanford, Iowa, Illinois, and the Macy Foundation and Topology Meetings. The project was approved, and the research was funded early in 1947. And then Dean Lawson of the University of Kansas turned up in Worcester. He was looking for candidates for the chairmanship of their psychology department. The department was at a low ebb, and the administration was ready to make a new beginning and provide the support required to bring psychology at Kansas to its former vigorous state.

Why should I be interested? I had just come to Clark, to an endowed professorship with some status and to a department that also was set to make new beginnings. One could interpret my career as exhibiting clear signs of instability; a solid and frank New Englander, on hearing from Louise of the towns in which we had lived, remarked, "I see your husband is something of a floater." Surely it was time to settle in and stay on course. But there was the research and the dispersed Massachusetts towns. I told Dean Lawson of the project and the kind of town it required. Did he know of such a town in the Lawrence area? "Yes," he said without any hesitation, "I know the place. I've spoken there several times. Its name is Oskaloosa." I made two trips to Lawrence that spring; on the second trip I asked my former fellowship colleague at Iowa, Herbert Wright, to come along and consider joining in the department and the research. We visited Oskaloosa. He came and he joined. So Louise and I made one more portage.

UNIVERSITY OF KANSAS, 1947–1972

We arrived in Lawrence in late August 1947 in a 115° heat wave. But, no matter, important things were underway. Fritz and Grace Heider were joining us, along with Herbert and Lorene Wright. There were houses to rent, a new department office to establish, instructors, teaching assistants to hire, and the university's rules and regulations to master.

I learned slowly why I had been chosen for this job over some other strong candidates. G. E. Coghill, a stellar name in biology in those days, had recently retired, and psychologists Raymond Wheeler, F. T. Perkins, and J. F. Brown had lately left the university. All of these men were well known for their "organismic" viewpoints. It was the wish of the two regular staff members who remained, Beulah Morrison and Anthony J. Smith, and of the administration, that this tradition be continued. Without making this explicit, Dean Lawson apparently saw that I would do this naturally and with enthusiasm. And in fact he had two immediate signs of the correctness of his insight when I recruited Herbert Wright and Fritz Heider within a couple of months. In the next 3 years we added Martin Scheerer, Alfred Baldwin, and Erik and Beatrice Wright. The new senior staff members were all from the center or the fringes of the Gestalt psychology movement.

Two behavior settings dominated my professional activities over the next 25 years; one of them was of my own creation, and I had considerable power over the other.

Office of Department Chairman

Program: To invigorate and expand the psychology department and to establish and administer settings subordinate to it according to University and Staff policies. *Physical attributes:* Suite of four rooms in Strong Hall with office furnishings and equipment. *Temporal characteristics:* My occupancy continued for 3 years; open for regular business weekdays 8:00 A.M. to 5:00 P.M. and for special business at any time. *Human components:* Myself, other staff members, students, secretaries. *Boundary properties:* Open access. *Power of human components:* The basic policies of the department were determined by external settings: those of the University administration and the setting Department Staff Meeting. Within the constraints imposed by these settings, the chairman had complete control of the Office.

In my 19 years of academic life the extent of my administrative experience was limited to registering and advising students at Illinois and Stanford and to voting on minor issues in the college staff meeting at Illinois. My former colleagues at Stanford expressed anxious surprise that I would or could become an administrator. Their surprise was not justified. They did not know the strength of my commitment to certain academic and educational principles and my eagerness to have more of a hand in promoting them than hitherto; and they did not know that administration was part of the package that included Oskaloosa, the crucial component. There were grounds for their anxiety, though not the ones they probably had in mind. They would know of my deficiencies in keeping appointments, answering correspondence, arranging schedules, making and keeping to budgets, gregariousness, and so forth. But they would underestimate, I think, the power of the behavior setting Office of Department Chairman to take me in hand in these respects. However, their anxiety (and mine, too) would have been justified had they known of the probable conflict between the duties of the Office of Department Chairman and those of the research setting Field Station in Oskaloosa. I lasted 3 years as chairman.

The usual conflict between administration and research was exacerbated in this case by a geographical factor: we found it impossible to do the research in Oskaloosa, 20 miles from Lawrence, without living there and having full-time headquarters there; and the urgencies that occurred in both places could not be scheduled. However, if I had found administration congenial and rewarding, I might have remained longer as chairman. But I did not. For one thing, I did not have easy relations with my superiors. Some sort of a personal status and power problem was involved. I saw myself as being too submissive to policy directives I opposed, and thereafter I felt guilty of betraying my principles. I did not stand up to authority in the way I thought I should. This was partly a matter of my divided commitment; I did not have the time to prepare for hassles with top administrators, but there was also inability to confront superior power. Another problem for me as chairman was the discovery that persons with whom I agreed and had harmonious relations were not always in agreement and harmony among themselves. My ambition was for a unified, amicable department, and with incredible naiveté I supposed that those with whom I was congenial would be congenial *inter se*. There were no great conflicts within the department, but not the unity I had hoped for. An added circumstance that interfered with maintaining a department with a common point of view on psychological matters was the rapid increase in the staff to serve the great increase in university enrollment after 1947. Inevitably those added were of a variety of psychological persuasions. In my 3 years in the chairman's slot, the Department was invigorated with staff members who received wide recognition as scientific scholars in the next two decades.

These were tremendously busy years for me, with increasing conflict between the demands of the chairmanship and the research, with increasing dissatisfaction with my relations with university administrators, and with some disappointment that my goal of a small, excellent, unified group of scholars was not more completely achieved. So, my occupancy of the chairman's position in the Office of the Department of Psychology brought me both satisfactions and regrets.

Classroom teaching was not clear sailing either. I had decamped when there was administrative interference with the way I wished to function as instructor at the University of Illinois. Now, it was discouraging to me to discover that there were other, more pervasive institutional obstacles to my teaching. The University of Kansas administration intruded very little in class operations, but a generally prevailing program of classroom instruction made it difficult for me to establish the kinds of programs I desired. This was my first experience with the fact that the settings of an institution may be so interdependent that deviant settings cannot function. My classes were arranged to foster students' skill in formulation of questions, finding and using the most relevant evidence, and writing reports on the basis of the evidence. Learning facts had no place in my classes; today's facts are obsolete tomorrow, and the current ones are always available if one knows where to find them and how to use them. My classes could operate best if the students had some unscheduled time: to think of interesting and answerable questions, to search for relevant evidence, and to analyze, organize, and present the findings. But who can think, search, analyze, and write when confronted with two quizzes a week in one class, 500 pages of reading in another, and 9 hours of laboratory attendance in another? As so-called standards went up and competitive grading became more severe, the students lost their freedom to act as inquirers, problem solvers, and expositors to the imposed demands of fact-, page-, and hour-oriented classes.

In addition to trouble with the teaching system within the University, I found that classroom settings and research settings do not mix—that the activities required by classroom teaching and by research are so conflicting as to be mutually injurious. I have observed this to be true for others, too. Both Terman and Lewin were excellent classroom teachers when they devoted themselves to it, but when they were deep in research, as they usually were, their teaching declined precipitately.

From the intrusions of the Illinois dean I escaped to Stanford; from the interference of the prevailing teaching system and the conflicts with research I escaped to Oskaloosa. Fortunately a Research Career Award from the National Institute of Health made this possible.

Field Station in Oskaloosa

Program: In the beginning, the program was to describe the living conditions and behavior of all the children of the town; later, all inhabitants were included. *Physical attributes:* Suite of offices in Oskaloosa, Kansas, with office furnishings and calculators; at intervals a satellite station was established in Leyburn, Yorkshire, England. *Temporal characteristics:* Operated during regular office hours, and often into the evening for particular staff members, from the fall of 1947 through the spring of 1972. *Human components:* Three to seven staff members, one to four graduate students, and occasional town residents. *Boundary properties:* Staff and graduate students selected and admitted by Station directors; they thereafter had free access; townspeople also had free access. *Powers of human components:* During the first 7 years, the Station was administered by the co-directors, Herbert F. Wright and me; we had power over the entire setting; when Herbert left the station, I was in charge. Next in power were professional scientists (fieldworkers, data analysts) who had complete control of their special operations; after them came the graduate students with power over their projects in consultation with their advisers, and finally the secretaries, who were masters of their own desks and secretarial facilities. Townspeople and other visitors had no power.

Here, at last, in the Midwest Psychological Field Station, the stream of my professional behavior entered a setting constructed to my own design: I initiated it, and its program was arranged cooperatively with Herbert Wright. Most other major settings I had inhabited had ongoing operations into which I was incorporated, with limited power to make alterations. I soon discovered, however, that in the Station I was not a free spirit but was captive of the setting I had established—a setting that embodied a past I could not escape and a future I could not control. Herbert and I had programmed the Midwest Field Station to describe the behavior and psychological habitat of the children of the town individually. With the setting underway (procedures developed and tested, staff trained, computer programs set up, citizens alerted and cooperative), it was not a simple matter when our insights and intentions changed to alter the program to one of describing extraindividual behavior within behavior settings. We had to struggle against our own creation. It makes one wonder how much of the stability of individual behavior has its source in the stability of the behavior settings people create and inhabit, a stability that is sustained by the fact that people establish new settings according to designs they carry with them from previous settings. The origins of some features we built into the Midwest Field Station are fairly clear: The aim to describe the living conditions and behavior of all of the children originated in the Extension Classes in Illinois; concern with the naturally occurring environment was brought from Stone's Animal Laboratory and the Iowa Nursery School Laboratory; disciplined, persisting concentration on a rather narrow program of activities, the policy that "dogged does it," came aboard in the Stanford settings; the dual importance of precise data and precise theories welded together characteristics of both the Stanford and the Iowa settings; the particular theories that undergirded the program of the Midwest research came from Lewin's Offices in Iowa; the importance attached to archives of atheoretical data originated in Stone's Animal Laboratory; the first data collecting system we installed, the narrative record, dated back to the Iowa Nursery School Laboratory; the importance given to community relations was first met in Miles's Later Maturity Facility. These problems, emphases, methods, and theories with which we endowed the Field Station were imported from earlier settings. We installed the past in the present. But the inheritances were assembled in new relationships, and new elements were added, including staff members, methods, ideas, and data; the Station developed a dynamic of its own with unforeseen consequences for its inhabitants. For me these were far-reaching. In this latest stretch of the stream of my professional behavior, I entered the Field Station as a psychologist aiming to study the naturally occurring behavior and environments of the people of the town as individuals. For a long time I clung to the view that this was the way to observe and explain their everyday activities. But the Field Station finally turned me around and showed me that more than people and the stimuli that impinge upon them individually are required, that an ecobehavioral science of extraindividual behavior and its nonbehavioral context is needed. The course of this change has been presented in a number of publications (Barker, 1960, 1963a,b, 1965, 1968; Barker & Associates, 1978; Barker & Gump, 1964; Barker & Schoggen, 1973; Barker & Wright, 1951, 1955).

OTHER PLACES, OTHER PEOPLE

I have had to omit many rewarding and pleasant reaches of my behavior stream and most of the people who shared parts of it with me and gave me tows and directions. Space is a factor here, but more important is absence of records of the early days. And there were important hidden settings (committees, administrative offices, and so forth), whose inhabitants I do not know, that gave me free time (Research Career Award: Fellowship, Center for Advanced Study in the Behavioral Sciences), research grants (U.S. Public Health Service, Society for the Aid of Crippled Children, Commonwealth Fund, Ford Foundation, Carnegie Foundation of New York, University of Kansas, Kansas University Endowment Association), honors (Kurt Lewin Award, Society for the Psychological Study of Social Issues; Research Contribution Award, American Psychological Association; G. Stanley Hall Award, Division on Developmental Psychology, American Psychological Association), and summer appointments (Columbia, Oregon, Colorado, California). I regret especially not being able to name the graduate students who studied with me at Stanford University, Clark University, and the University of Kansas, some of whom have become valued colleagues, and many of whom contributed greatly and still contribute to my intellectual development. My story would be too incomplete, however, without four prime influences on the odyssey. Louise Shedd Barker was an eager spectator, a frequent adviser, and an occasional stand-in in all the early settings. But when we discovered that the Station could not be operated from Lawrence, that it required us to live in Oskaloosa, Louise became an essential operative as chief fieldworker and our main line of communication with the community. She was well prepared. In her own professions she had experience as a field ecologist, first as biologist at the Stanford Marine Station and on the University campus, and then as high school "home visitor," searching out the homes of absent children and investigating the causes of their absence. Fritz Heider's ideas about media and things provided the link between people and behavior settings that prompted me to see the latter as more than convenient areas for sampling behavior but rather as entities (things) that impose patterns upon their components, including their human inhabitants (media). It was this insight that raised behavior settings for me from a technological convenience to the basic unit of an ecobehavioral science. Herbert F. Wright was co-equal developer of the Field Station's program during its first years, making unique contributions to the study of individual behavior; and Paul V. Gump was equally important in the latter years by bringing the Station's ideas and methods to bear on school and community operation.

CONCLUSION

I began this trip with the desire to benefit humanity. I have not, myself, been able to satisfy this desire, for I have found that, as with teaching, the time and skills required to make and disseminate applications have so conflicted with those required by the research as to make the former impossible for me. So the zeal and success of a small number of former staff members, students, and others to bring our methods and findings to earth in connection with hospitals, schools, architecture, town planning, child development, and even the movement "small is beautiful" have given me keen satisfaction. I began the journey, too, with reservations about my ability to make it in the scientific world. When I report that the self-doubt has not been dispelled, the response may well be: How greedy can he be? What does he want in brownie points? The answer: The stream of my professional life has skirted the areas of psychology that are currently richly cultivated and harvested, and in fact, it has finally landed me outside the turf of the psychology tribe. Being something of a maverick has its rewards from those (and there are many) who value what they hope will prove to be worthwhile innovations. The innovator hopes so, too, but in the meantime he is at a disadvantage vis-à-vis his mainstream associates, because he cannot keep up with them in the main channel. So, how can he be sure where he stands?

Acknowledgments

This offspring of my life has benefited greatly during its long period of gestation and labor from the skills and encouragement of Irwin Altman and Phil Schoggen. In addition, Irwin Altman had an important part in its conception, and Phil Schoggen was presiding pediatrician after its premature birth. To them I extend my most sincere thanks. However, as its sole natural parent, I must answer for its defects.

REFERENCES

Barker, R. G. (1960). Ecology and motivation. In M. R. Jones (Ed.), *Nebraska symposium on motivation, vol. 8* (pp. 1–49). Lincoln: University of Nebraska Press.

Barker, R. G. (1963a). On the nature of the environment. *Journal of Social Issues, 19,* 17–38.

Barker, R. G. (1963b). (Ed.). *The stream of behavior.* New York: Appleton-Century-Crofts.

Barker, R. G. (1965). Explorations in ecological psychology, *American Psychologist, 20,* 1–14.

Barker, R. G. (1968). *Ecological psychology: Concepts and methods for studying the environment of human behavior.* Stanford: Stanford University Press.

Barker, R. G., & Associates. (1978). *Habitats, environments and human behavior.* San Francisco: Jossey-Bass.

Barker, R. G., & Gump, P. V. (1964). *Big school, small school.* Stanford: Stanford University Press.

Barker, R. G., & Schoggen, P. (1973). *Qualities of community life.* San Francisco: Jossey-Bass.

Barker, R. G., & Wright, H. F. (1951). *One boy's day.* New York: Harper & Row.

Barker, R. G., & Wright, H. F. (1955). *Midwest and its children.* New York: Harper & Row.

Barker, R. G., Kounin, J. S., & Wright, H. F. (Eds.). (1943). *Child behavior and development.* New York: McGraw-Hill.

Barker, R. G., Wright, B., Myerson, L., & Gonick, M. R. (1953). *Adjustment to physical handicap and illness: A survey of the social psychology of physique and disability* (Bulletin 55, rev. ed.). New York: Social Science Research Council.

Lewin, K. (1935). *Dynamic theory of personality.* New York: McGraw-Hill.

Lewin, K. (1938). *The conceptual representation and measurement of psychological forces.* Durham, NC: Duke University Press.

Shaw, G. B. (1949). *Sixteen self-sketches.* New York: Dodd Mead.

4

Science and the Failure
of Architecture

AN INTELLECTUAL HISTORY

AMOS RAPOPORT

I WAS BORN ON MARCH 28, 1929, in Warsaw, Poland. After the outbreak of World War II, my parents—Joshua and Mala Rapoport—and I managed to get away and survive through a series of extraordinary events. In June 1941 we ended up in Shanghai, China (one of the few places where no visa was needed) where we were trapped by the outbreak of the Pacific war. I was lucky to attend an outstanding school—Shanghai Jewish School. Thus, when after the war we emigrated to Australia I was ready to begin my studies. I still think of myself as an Australian, although I have now lived in the United States, on and off, since 1963. Partly as a result of my travels I know a number of languages.

I graduated with a B.Arch from the University of Melbourne in 1955; obtained an M.Arch from Rice University in 1957 (which I attended on a Fulbright Fellowship, Houston Architects Fellowship, and a Graduate Assistantship/Fellowship), and a Postgraduate Diploma in Town and Regional Planning from the University of Melbourne in 1966. I am a registered architect in Victoria and New South Wales, Australia, a fellow of the Royal Australian Institute of Architects, and an associate of the Royal Institute of British Architects.

After some professional experience in the United States and Australia, and a year's study in France on a French Government Technical Cooperation Scholarship, I began my academic career as a lecturer at the University of Melbourne. I was then an assistant professor and assistant research architect at the University of California, Berkeley (1963–1967; lecturer at the Bartlett School of Architecture, University College, London (1967–1969); senior lecturer, in charge of Man–Environment Studies, University of Sydney (1969–1972); associate professor of architecture and anthropology, University of Wiscon-

AMOS RAPOPORT • School of Architecture and Urban Planning, University of Wisconsin–Milwaukee, Milwaukee, Wisconsin 53201.

sin–Milwaukee (1972–1974); professor of architecture and anthropology there during 1974–1979 and since 1979 I have been distinguished professor of architecture at the University of Wisconsin–Milwaukee.

I have always traveled extensively—it is both a hobby and central to my view of the academic profession. I have thus lectured extensively at universities and conferences in numerous cities and countries all over the world and have also been visiting professor or fellow in many countries.

I also regard writing as central to academic life and have been a prolific writer with over 200 papers, chapters, and articles, 4 authored books (one in press), several authored or co-authored monographs, and have edited or co-edited 5 books. My work has been translated into a number of languages, including several collections of shorter pieces in translation. I have also been editor-in-chief of one international journal, associate editor of another, and have served on many editorial boards.

I have served on the boards of a number of national and international organizations, including two periods on the EDRA Board (including the first). I have received a number of awards, including invitations to be a participant in several Delos symposia, a 3-year Research Professorship from the University of Wisconsin–Milwaukee, a Graham Foundation Fellowship, a Senior Sabbatical Fellowship from the National Endowment for the Arts, a Visiting Fellowship from Clare Hall, Cambridge, and a Career Award from the Environmental Design Research Association.

I have no hobbies outside reading, thinking, and writing, although I am addicted to jogging and thoroughly enjoy good food and wine.

My wife Dorothy and I were married in 1967. She has degrees in psychology and social work, and is very active in a range of volunteer activities. We have one son, Micah, who has recently started college and is now a sophomore at the University of Wisconsin–Madison, majoring in Chinese and Hebrew. This chapter is dedicated to him.

WHY INTELLECTUAL HISTORIES?

Intellectual histories differ from autobiography. Although both concern development over time, the former emphasize issues of some generality and are organized thematically rather than strictly chronologically. Their value is in clarifying the nature of fields, particularly new, interdisciplinary fields like Environment–Behavior Studies (EBS). Twenty years or so after we began, it seems useful to identify patterns. Knowing how things actually happened and happen is important for understanding any field.[1] It is useful to trace origins and map the routes whereby people reach particular positions within a domain.[2] Intellectual histories help explain why and how some people leave familiar, well-established fields for areas that may never become fields, how such people operate in the interstices among fields, and, in so doing, how they transform fields.

---

[1] It has recently become clear that a knowledge of the history of science is critical to complement philosophy of science in order to understand the domain.

[2] For example, the series of autobiographies of scientists sponsored by the Alfred P. Sloan Foundation, which includes Jacob (1988) and Kac (1985).

It has, for example, been enlightening to discover that molecular biology is partly the outcome of some physicists moving into biology, introducing new ways of thinking and thereby dramatically transforming the field. It may be useful to look at EBS in this way, particularly because it has been interdisciplinary from its inception and to try and understand how new ways of thinking may change mainstream design equally dramatically.

To me, EBS is defined in large part by its distinction from, and opposition to, mainstream architecture. What passes for debates in architecture (e.g., modernism vs. postmodernism) are not debates at all. The real alternatives are mainstream architecture in all its guises and EBS, seen as a science of Environment–Behavior Relations (EBR). The latter implies major changes in ways of defining the domain, of thinking and working, of approaching problems, the role of scholarship, research, and their application, the nature of theory, the nature of creativity in EBS vis-à-vis mainstream architecture, the rewards sought, and so on (Rapoport, 1983c). It then becomes essential to see how people in EBS work, particularly people from different disciplines: their starting points, the routes they follow and the positions they reach, of convergence and divergence. All these can help illuminate, and even define, the nature of that field.

Although I have spent my professional life largely in architecture, I did not really come from it; I just happened to get into it by chance. In fact, EBS allowed me to escape it intellectually by transforming it, redefining its domain, and approaching it very differently. It also enabled me to do what I most enjoy doing, and what I see as central to research and scholarship—seeking and finding connections among what seem to be disparate elements, things, events, or disciplines and above all *lateral* connections. This is what reveals patterns—and pattern recognition is central in science and research, particularly when allied to a cognitive style of generalization and abstraction and the seeking of explanation.

How I reached that point, and how that affected my work, is the result of my personal background and its interaction with chance and *Zeitgeist*.

PERSONAL BACKGROUND

At age 8 or 9 I decided to become a scientist—a theoretical astrophysicist, no less. Strange as it may seem, this is the key to my early involvement in EBS, my attitude to it and to architecture and my past, current and projected work, as well as the remarkable continuity in that work over the years.

It was mainly reading the astrophysicists Sir James Jeans and Sir Arthur Eddington that inspired that decision. I still remember the magical moment, the overwhelming feelings of awe at the ability of people, here on earth, to know what went on inside stars, how the universe began, how galaxies and stars were born, evolved, and died. Science, using concepts, mathematics, theory, and instruments allowed the human mind to see across distances of billions of light years and across billions of years to the beginnings of space and time, to the beginnings of everything. People could *know, understand,* and *explain* the apparently unknowable. These were, and are, to me the most wonderful things of which human beings are capable and my identification with science, which makes it possible, has grown stronger with the years. When I recently read that the molecular biologist Jacques Monod's last words as he lay dying, were "je voudrais savoir . . ." ("I want to know . . ."), it brought tears to my eyes. They captured the most profound and most human trait, which I find totally missing in architecture.

My decision lasted through the first week of my second year of a science degree in theoretical physics, when I decided that I would never make a good physicist. I also realized that although generalization and abstraction were my forte, they needed to be grounded in concrete *stuff*—physics seemed too separated from the rest of life. My later shift to EBS enabled me to link the patterns of science with the concreteness of the cultural landscape that was always there to perceive, to experience, to ponder, and to analyze. Thus although for a time, while in architecture, I apparently gave up science, it is the one constant in my history and, as will become clear later, since 1982, it has become central once again; I have come full circle. En route, however, my strong commitment to conceptual frameworks and theory, seeking interconnections and patterns, and a cognitive style of generalization and abstraction, which attracted me to science in the first place, continued. Thus my work can be seen as an ongoing attempt to know, to understand—and to try to explain—the ways in which people and environments interact. This requires understanding human characteristics, the nature of environments and their effects on people, and the mechanisms that link them (what I call the three basic questions of EBS). All my work over the years continues to try gradually to answer various aspects of these questions. It tries to do for our domain what other sciences do for theirs. It is a research program, intended to help create a scientific discipline of EBR.

Why, however, was I reading Jeans, Eddington, and the like at age 8? It was because I grew up in an environment of ideas and books, where the written word and the thoughts it expressed were the most important things in life, often to the detriment of other things, including income. Books were "sacred," reading them one of life's greatest pleasures, and writing them the highest calling. People were judged in terms of their commitment to the life of the mind. It was an environment one rarely encounters today; my parents and their milieu were members of an extraordinary generation of the East European Jewish intelligencia, often formally uneducated, poor, with no prospects and powerless, dedicated to ideas, learning, and books that were more important to them than comfort or money.

My mother was a schoolteacher who could recite poetry she loved for hours. My father was a writer—a literary critic, editor, and essayist. I hardly ever saw him do anything except read or write, oblivious to everyone and everything, doing just what he wanted; for this he sacrificed much. Although my domain is different, my attitudes and behavior are not. He was also my role model in his intellectual honesty, hatred of cant or hypocrisy, a refusal to compromise, and the need fearlessly to state the truth as one sees it, without fear or favor. I have adopted his confrontational approach, criticizing as strongly as necessary, pulling no punches and mincing no words. He paid dearly for this and had a difficult life materially, but he did what he wanted to, what he *had* to do—and enjoyed it passionately.

My father had little formal education. In part, he was taught at home; above all he was self-taught. His father, my grandfather, was also self-taught in secular subjects. He was not only a Talmudic scholar who published commentaries but, in a provincial city, in mid-nineteenth-century Eastern Europe, he knew eight languages and was a good enough amateur mathematician to correspond with many professionals around Europe. My father also knew a number of languages well enough to write in them and translate from them. He had an international reputation and lectured extensively; he edited newspapers and had published dozens of books and thousands of articles.

I thus knew that given interest and dedication, one can learn anything *by reading* and that is how I approach problems or other disciplines. It also shapes my view of academia; at universities one does not teach, students learn, and I much prefer the English term *"reading* a subject" to the American *"taking* a subject"—no one is *giving* anything. Academics may provide frameworks and the odd reference; mainly they serve as role models, provide guidance, answer questions, and provide creative criticism, they push students further than they think they can go and, most important, maintain high standards—students', peers', and their own. Above all, they create the literature that students (and others) read—*that* is the real teaching they do.

CHANCE AND PLACES

I have never systematically compared notes with others, but I think that the role of chance has been much greater than usual in my case. After I realized that physics was not for me, I drifted into architecture mainly because my best friend was in it and it seemed like fun. I have rarely initiated anything; graduate study, jobs, lecture tours, conferences, boards, visiting professorships; even books (authored and edited), papers, and chapters—including the very first—and often their topics have been invited. Even my early involvement in EBS was the result of chance. Of course, the mind needs to be prepared to grasp chance, but I believe with Ecclesiastes that

> the race is not to the swift, nor the battle to the strong, nor yet riches to men of understanding, nor yet favour to men of skill; but time and chance happeneth to all. (9:11)

Like most graduates in the early 1950s I found Australia isolated, provincial, and confining and wanted to travel. I also wanted to do graduate work in the United States, but deciding where to go and applying seemed too difficult. Chance intervened; our professor,[3] coming back from a trip, recommended

---

[3] Like in Britain, Australian university departments typically only had one professor who was also its permanent head.

Rice and helped me apply to just that one place. I was accepted, given two fellowships, made a TA and awarded a Fulbright. This gave me a chance to travel, by ship to San Francisco, stopping in New Zealand, Fiji, Hawaii, and Vancouver; then, before school started, by Greyhound bus for several months all over the United States. I mainly photographed recent work of architects but began to notice barns, slave cabins, industrial structures, small town main-streets, and the like. These were settings that I had never studied. They seemed to be ignored by academia and the profession (or implicitly strongly criticized, as in architecture vs. "mere building"). Although I still paid slight attention to them, there was a dawning realization that much of the built environment was of no concern to the field supposedly concerned with it; the ground was being prepared.

Rice proved the right place. I was one of only two graduate students in architecture and was able to work largely on my own, in the library, by reading and thinking—my natural way of working. A nonarchitecture minor was re-quired and, for some reason, I picked philosophy. It was a good choice, being a real academic subject taught by an inspiring professor. Not all of philosophy interested me, but I found metaphysics fascinating. This interest in ontology and epistemology has become central to my work since 1982, because these are central to any concern with explanatory, scientific theory that, in turn, is cen-tral to EBS as a discipline.

After more travel through the United States and Canada and a stimulating year working in New York, I convinced the Fulbright Foundation that, because travel was essential for architects, they should allow me to use the fare back to Melbourne for travel. I sailed down the St. Lawrence to Britain, then traveled through Europe and the Middle East before sailing through the Suez Canal to Australia, stopping in Aden, Colombo, Singapore, and so on.

However, it was Liverpool, of all places, where I landed, that proved seminal. Chance brought me to a bed and breakfast facing Sir Giles Gilbert Scott's unfinished Anglican cathedral. I rushed across to look at it. It was impressive, and the siting fascinating but, as I started back, there occurred what I still think of as a moment of enlightenment, a turning point in my intellectual development as important as reading Jeans and Eddington. The scales fell from my eyes: I suddenly *saw* the row of humble working-class terrace houses lining the street. They seemed more interesting than the cathe-dral, more important—even more beautiful. I also suddenly linked them with the barns and other structures I had begun to notice in the United States—I had realized that the domain with which we should be concerned is not only the cathedral but even more the streets and dwellings around, and the *rela-tionships* between the two. An important question seemed to be how such environments came to be through apparently independent decisions of many people over long periods of time, how those add up to highly distinctive, recognizable cultural landscapes. All this was clearly not instantaneous, but this question is still important in my most recent work and I have addressed it in as yet unpublished pieces.

I had "discovered" vernacular design. It was all around me yet, possibly because not the work of architects, I had never been told about it in 5 years of university. Although for some little time to come I still dutifully looked at, and often enjoyed, cathedrals, temples, mosques, castles, and palaces, the trip became a feast of vernacular design—buildings, settlements, markets, streets, alleys, and landscapes. I never photographed another architect's building and recently gave all my slides of such buildings taken before Liverpool to our library.

It was chance that the father of a classmate was the senior partner of a large firm in Melbourne; he hired me as a designer, a member of a small team planning Monash University. But I was dissatisfied and disappointed even working on such an unusually interesting project. Decisions seemed arbitrary and often based on senior designers' likes and dislikes. Although the most junior, I argued constantly, but my attempts to find a knowledge base were usually ignored. For example, to improve decisions about the scale and character of campus open spaces I created a "dictionary" of plans and sections of many green and built spaces, at least some of which we all knew. The intention, however inadequate, who to relate one's recalled sensory and affective experience to size, proportions, level of enclosure and the like of given spaces. That influenced few decisions, but I won a few skirmishes, and it was fun. It was, I now realize, an attempt to relate human reactions to objective attributes of settings.

When that relatively brief exercise was over, I somehow took over programming, identifying needs and requirements. The other designers seemed more than happy to let me do it—it was clearly not a glamorous task, yet critical because we were designing a campus before a single person had been appointed. It was also fun and allowed me to visit other universities and interview academics.

I have never forgotten two of the many lessons. First, in a flexibly designed chemistry building at Melbourne University, one wall had been moved 4" in over 20 years. Services however, which were *not* flexible, were being changed constantly. Flexibility, it seemed, was not self-evident nor a unitary concept. It seemed that terms and concepts that seemed self-evident needed analysis, clarification, and definition and that complex concepts needed dismantling. These two matters have been important in my work since then and are central at the moment, when we urgently need agreed-upon definitions of terms and concepts, explicit concern with taxonomy, and the like. The second, possibly more important discovery was that opinions about everything varied, often being contradictory. While programming hydraulics laboratories, for example, I interviewed several heads of departments; what Professor A regarded as ideal, Professor B denounced as intolerable or useless; even the most instrumental aspects of buildings were evaluated very differently. The professional (me!) had to decide, but there was little knowledge, and I had not been taught programming. I looked for commonalities, generalized, suggested flexible arrangements (shades of the chemistry building). But it all seemed most unsatisfactory—and I had not even talked to junior academics, technicians, or students. It was quite clear to me already then, in the late 1950s, that designing was essentially a problem-solving activity, but that to solve problems they first had to be discovered and identified and that to do that a *knowledge base* was essential; it was equally, or even more, essential in order to attempt to solve problems.

But the designers were not really interested. They included all the programmed equipment and facilities, but their hearts were not in it. Window proportions, mullion thickness, brick color, massing, and the like seemed much more important to them; so did single buildings rather than relations among them, the spaces on which I had worked so hard. Also, programming was coming to an end, and I would have to do what they did, and I knew that this was not how I wanted to spend my life.

By chance, during a bush hike, I heard that some French government fellowships were going begging. Here was an opportunity to travel and get away from "design" and architecture, and before long I was sailing to England (via the Panama Canal—6 weeks!) en route to Paris. Because I lived with a cousin, my generous stipend became available for a year of theater, concerts, and travel. Having found the proposed study of prefabricated housing systems dismal, I soon shifted to French vernacular settlements, although I did write two articles based on my study of French housing—one an evaluation of urban renewal, the other in which I first developed the notion of *perceived density* (in 1969), developed further in the late 1970s and early 1980s. Being able to borrow one of my cousin's cars and getting additional travel support from the agency allowed me to explore the country, its food and wine, and the variety of its vernacular design. That deepened my knowledge of, and admiration for, both. I also started the first of many travel notebooks that I have not yet really used. These include many sketches and *diagrams* that I realized were often much more useful than photographs because one had to think and analyze while drawing; photography could be almost mindless. I have believed since that diagramming is not just a way of communicating but a method of research, a way of thinking, conceptualizing, analyzing, and even synthesizing. I also began to realize that much needed to be recorded in words and even in numbers; the exclusively visual preoccupation of designers was a procrustes bed.

My cousin lent me money, and I took almost a year to get back to Australia, through Italy, Greece, Turkey, Israel, Iran, India ($3\frac{1}{2}$ months and 10,000 miles), Burma, Thailand, Cambodia, Singapore, Hong Kong, Japan, and the Philippines. This was helped by contacts I had made while in Paris when, because I could borrow a car and spoke French, I was often asked to take Asian fellows on my trips.

What a revelation. My education had ignored not only vernacular design and cultural landscapes but also numerous high-style traditions in architecture, urbanism, and landscape—Angkor Wat, Fahtepur Sikri, the gardens of Kashmir, the temples and castles of Japan, and so on and on. I had been *cheated!* Not only "design" was a problem in architecture, but the domain itself was pathetically distorted, and its history a parody. Rather than open my eyes to the built environment, architectural education had tried to close them. It had emphasized a tiny body of work that did not seem to be the most significant nor even, in my view, the most "beautiful," although the preoccupation with subjective aesthetic reactions already seemed unimportant and totally inadequate as a basis for analysis or design decisions.

Yet here I was, inexorably nearing Melbourne. After all I had discovered, a future in an office seemed a terrible fate. Although my shift from science to architecture had made all that travel possible in the first place, it now seemed like a terrible mistake. Even worse, private practice was impossible. My independent design work had made clear that architecture was a business—and my whole background made business and entrepreneurship unthinkable. It also made clear that social contacts were critical; one had to cultivate people—and that went against the grain; my style was uncompromising and confrontational.

In desperation I went to seek advice of my professor, and chance intervened again. He offered me a lectureship.[4] I was going to be an academic! In retrospect, academia, at least in its ideal form, seems my natural habitat, but I would never have dared aspire to it nor seek it; yet here it was being offered to me.

Thus, in 1962 I became an academic. Although I had to teach studio and a course on building construction (and proved very good at both), I was allowed to do a segment on vernacular in the history sequence. It was still very "architectural," emphasizing buildings, climate, materials, and construction; breaking free was difficult. But it was a beginning and, as far as I know, the first course taught on vernacular.

Then chance intervened again. A friend, who was already in the United States, felt that I should also be there. I am still not quite sure how he did it, but I was offered a position at Berkeley. I was excited but also worried; I was leaving a familiar place and giving up a tenured position for the unknown. But, almost before I knew it, I was on a ship once again, en route to Berkeley.

CHANCE—TIMES AND ZEITGEIST

Berkeley was the real turning point, the place where things began to crystallize, a process completed at the Bartlett in London.

I came to Berkeley at an interesting time but am reminded of the ancient Chinese curse: "May you live in interesting times." The period between January 1963 when I arrived and May 1967 when I left was difficult and frustrating in many ways, but I will neglect the negative attributes because they have no place in this narrative, important as they were, because the positive qualities proved more important. Combined with my personal characteristics, attitudes,

---

[4] In Australia that is equivalent to an assistant professorship, except that it then was tenured immediately.

and ways of working they led me into EBS almost before it existed. They provided both the stimulus and opportunities to begin my real work.

There were a few individuals in the College of Environment Design with new ideas, who were doing unusual things. Within weeks they introduced me to new things to read, among them, the historian of science Kuhn, the anthropologist Hall, the philosopher Langer and, above all, *Landscape* (about which more later). There were faculty seminars (e.g., by Chris Alexander and Horst Rittel) and heated debate at a rather high level. There was serious research in various areas. In a word, for a time there was more intellectual ferment than ever before, or possibly since, at any school of architecture except possibly the Bartlett. We had a faculty exchange program with them, and heard Llewellyn-Davies and others describe the rather radical developments there. One heard about architectural psychology at Utah and about geography at Clark. Richard L. Meier (an ex-physicist!) lectured about the origins of new disciplines and their institutional development, and Jack Calhoun talked about behavioral sinks. Many people and ideas intersected; the "invisible college" of the forming EBS was becoming visible.

At that time in that place the *Zeitgeist* led to both EBS and design methods as two responses to a number of perceived problems (Rapoport, 1970, pp. 11–12). Student dissatisfaction with purely subjective and individualistic evaluations of work played an important role. In rapidly changing conditions, designers, separated from clients and especially users, needed data that were not available. Research generally was flourishing, and theory became respectable because of its power, but the design fields were left out because they lacked a disciplinary base; yet one became necessary given the growing severity and complexity of problems. When new approaches based on research were used, as in the case of the Baltimore team headed by Skidmore, Owings, and Merrill, designers were able to change routes of urban highways by showing the presence of dense social networks defining neighborhoods and the presence of "seams," areas with few links, where freeways would do less damage. To me the impact of this event was overwhelming. The greater range of alternatives available to designers necessitated new ways of restricting the decision space. Design methods addressed the structuring of problems and information handling, whereas EBS addressed the nature of the information needed.

In a milieu like Berkeley, an emphasis in the emergent EBS on research, concepts, and rigorous methods was inevitable, so was the influence of the many exemplars all around the campus of new compound fields and multidisciplinary work. In our field, from the start, many disciplines were involved, each potentially capable of making contributions.

To me, that meant the university was more important than the college or department (and, in the longer run, that the larger, nonlocalized world of scholarship and ideas was the most important, so that one's allegiance was to it). Rather uncharacteristically, I interacted with many researchers and scholars from diverse disciplines. Some were my age and not yet widely known, others older and already famous. But, given my already extremely negative view of architecture, all had a similar effect on me, although I can only mention a few.

I discovered that what had taken a friend in electrical engineering years to master as a PhD student he could now teach in 10 minutes—a characteristic of science since documented in some detail. How wonderful, I thought, if architecture could be equally cumulative and progressive rather than always reinventing the wheel, the perfect exemplar of Sorokin's New Columbus Syndrome. And it could be, if it became a real discipline; this has been my goal ever since. A friend in mechanical engineering shifted from studying missiles to human blood flow. How wonderful, I was reminded, to have concepts, laws, and theories that could apply to both. In Calvin's new laboratory I observed attempts to replicate life from inert chemicals; knowledge had made it at least feasible. Allan Wilson was using biochemical analysis to study evolutionary linkages; this eventually revolutionized our view of these. Medawar lectured brilliantly about the difference between private science, as individuals do it, and public science, the record once admitted into the canon[5]—a distinction increasingly important in my current thinking about EBS and design (Rapoport 1983c, 1985, 1987). Koestler lectured, very badly, about creativity as the putting together of apparently unrelated fields, whereas McKinnon showed me that creativity could be studied scientifically—as it increasingly is.

From David Krech I heard about the effects of complexity on the brain; that work seemed to explain my intuitive arguments on pedestrian spaces in my M.Arch at Rice. A lecture on art by a clinical psychologist (Robert Kantor) also discussed complexity, and we collaborated on a paper about the importance of complexity for preference and hence as a component of environmental quality. We also proposed a joint course on environmental psychology and urban perception, which the department rejected.

Three individuals made a particular impact. Among the geographers whom I knew, Clarence Glacken and Paul Wheatley, who seemed inseparable, were the most scholarly people I had ever met. Glacken's monumental *Traces on the Rhodian Shore* was in press and arrived just as the course based on it (which I audited) ended; it was a history of ways in which people interacted with nature from antiquity to the eighteenth century. Wheatley was working on his monumental study of Chinese cities (*The Pivot of the Four Quarters*), on the dominance of religious and symbolic criteria for their layout and that of most traditional cities, although that appeared only in 1971. What most impressed me then was his book review, in *Pacific Viewpoint*, of Sjoberg's *The Preindustrial City*. That told one more than many books, and its 88 footnotes amounted to a literature review, using original sources in Sanskrit, Chinese, Japanese, and so forth. Clearly, I had never known real scholars before—and I certainly wasn't one.

And then there was J. B. (Brink) Jackson. In *Landscape*, which he founded and edited, EBS had been flourishing since 1951, although no one realized it, and it was not called that. In it, many apparently unrelated fields overlapped by studying the cultural landscape. That illustration of Koestler's argument I found most exciting, as I did Jackson's courses on the U.S. landscape, which I audited. But Jackson did more; he thought I had something to say and invited

[5] Francois Jacob (1988) calls these "night science" and "day science," respectively.

me to write for *Landscape*. As a child I wrote adventure novels, and I did pretty decent papers, and even articles, in school. But here I was, an academic at my second university, at age 34, and had never thought of writing. I clearly had writer's block. Jackson, in his quietly persistent way, unblocked it; I got my start in *Landscape*[6] as did so many others. My first-ever article, on Isphahan, Iran, linked several themes important in my work: the important role of vernacular and the relationships between it and high-style elements; the cultural specificity of the environment and how essential core elements often persist for millennia—hence the importance of history properly understood; the sensory, perceptual qualities in several modalities used to achieve such culture-specific goals, for example, to make the courtyards of mosques and medresses into models of Paradise. The second was a brief summary of a longer piece on shopping lanes that began to trace those general patterns that apply to pedestrian spaces on which I am still working. The third, an article on a Yagua dwelling I had visited in the Amazon jungle, illustrated some consequences of culture-specific design, for example, the identity of dwelling and settlement (and hence definitional problems), its relation to larger systems of settings, "unusual" privacy mechanisms, and changes in form related to culture change, again topics on which I am still working.

Berkeley's elective system enabled me to teach a course on vernacular. Significantly, the emphasis had shifted from the architectural aspects I had discussed in Melbourne to social, cultural, and conceptual (e.g., definitional) aspects, and there were guest lectures by geographers and anthropologists; the topics of student papers clearly show how things were changing in an almost preordained direction.[7]

There were other activities, people, and courses that played a role, but one chance event was particularly important in my explicit shift into EBS—a last minute assignment, in fall 1966, to teach a course on "social and cultural factors in architecture and urban design." I protested that I knew nothing about it, only to be told that neither did anyone else. I read as much as I could and then, with a very select group of students, we taught each other. It was exciting; each session generated new questions and uncovered relevant work in diverse fields. Some good papers resulted. There did seem to be something that could be studied, a field or domain that could be approached scientifically and could possibly become a new discipline.

It was feasible then, and for some time to come, to read everything because the literature was small, no matter how broad the approach. In fact, all of it could be known until the mid-1970s. Such mutual ignorance can sometimes be helpful in generating fertile new points of view—a point also made recently about molecular biology in its early days (Jacob, 1988, p. 227) and about an area of mathematics (Kac, 1985).

---

[6] My first article, "The Architecture of Isphahan" (*Landscape*, Winter 1964–1965), "A note on shopping lanes," (*Landscape*, Autumn 1966), "Yagua—An Amazon dwelling" (*Landscape*, Spring 1967).

[7] Topics included, in addition to specific *places*, attempts to define vernacular, personalization of mass housing, comparative and cross-cultural studies, culture change, and so on.

This mutual ignorance about EBR also applied to those disciplines that supposedly knew about human behavior. What they knew often proved inappropriate, but often they hadn't even thought of the questions. This made the gap between other disciplines and architecture less significant *in this new domain*. It was wide open and, both individually and as members of disciplines, all could contribute in their own way. This provided a wonderful opportunity to combine my interest in many disciplines and wide reading and my commitment to science and scholarship with my interest in the cultural landscape.

One more chance event proved critical. Not being very sociable, I rarely attend parties but, for some reason went to one. The host, Sim Van der Ryn, introduced to a geographer from Davis, Phil Wagner, who, he said, shared my interest in vernacular. By the end of the evening I had been commissioned to write a book for a series in cultural geography that he was editing. That turned out to be *House Form and Culture*. It almost wrote itself; I had all the material in course notes and files and hardly needed to consult a library. All that I had thought, seen, and taught came together because of this invitation, and its theses were simple. One could study the built environment as a system of settings and without considering appearance or making a single subjective aesthetic judgment; the main variables that influenced the shaping of environments were social and cultural, the traditional considerations of materials, technology, site, climate, and so on being secondary, modifying, or constraining; generalizations could be made if the topic was approached cross-culturally and comparatively; one needed to draw on a variety of disciplines, and the topic had more to do with geography and anthropology than with architecture—one could, in fact, define the domain of study without even thinking about architects and their designs; people, activities, schemata, relationships (e.g., the house settlement system) were all more important than buildings as artifacts. The importance of meaning, although discussed as early as 1967, was implicit but not adequately developed—an oversight corrected in a series of subsequent publications including the *Meaning of the Built Environment,* and even more recent developments (e.g., Rapoport, 1988). The final draft was done when the time came to leave Berkeley.

I never liked the social milieu of the town or department and would never get tenure; after all, I was commonly pointed to visitors as that weirdo ("nudge, nudge; wink, wink") who is interested in mud huts. Student unrest exploded in unfortunate ways and made Berkeley uninhabitable and the later 1960s such a terrible period, the effects of which are still eroding and corroding academic life and research, society, and politics.

Chance intervened again. Contacts with exchange faculty from the Bartlett led to a visiting appointment for 1 year (extended for one more) that proved almost as seminal as Berkeley.

Only when I came to London did I realize how oppressive Berkeley had become. I felt as though a heavy weight had been removed. The Bartlett was exciting and research emphasized; the small size of Britain made the whole country accessible. Shortly after arriving, while *House Form and Culture* was being typed, chance, in the form of a shared office resulted in my meeting the co-organizer of a forthcoming conference in Portsmouth, and I was added to what had been a final list of speakers. My paper, "Facts and Models," (Rapoport, 1969) an EBS critique of design methods, was a great success. It argued that one needed to understand culturally different ways of seeing things (what I would now call their emics) but that they *could* be undrstood, studied, and compared (through what I would now call the derived etics). It also suggested that by understanding EBR one could design in very different ways as long as conclusions were evaluated on the basis of knowledge, that is, EBS as a response to problems held more promise than design methods. As a result of that paper, I was inundated by invitations to lecture and write; moreover each activity generated further invitations, in Britain and elsewhere. Suddenly people wanted to hear what I had to say; the contrast to Berkeley was complete and extremely energizing. As a result I was very prolific. Even an incomplete listing would include an invited article on open-ended housing (in the *RIBA Journal*) as a way of allowing cultural and individual differences to be expressed, for personalization to increase congruence and satisfaction and also to achieve higher levels of complexity. One result was an invitation from Habraken to visit him at Eindhoven, another meeting others interested in this approach, including students. I wrote several programmatic pieces on the need for EBS, supplementing many lectures on the same topic. In co-editing an early issue of the *Architectural Association Quarterly* (AAQ), I invited people from a variety of disciplines to contribute.

I began a piece on Australian aborigines as a result of an invitation based on a question Paul Oliver asked me: how they define *place* (then, as now, a popular but unclear term) when they build so little. This was useful and important for several reasons: It showed how central social, cultural, and psychological variables, such as meaning, cognition, schemata, ritual, social relations, and so on were and how secondary the "hardware" was—environments are thought before they are built, and they may not be built at all. It also made me aware of a most important methodological principle—the value of beginning with *extreme* cases and, having understood the mechanisms, and so forth, moving to more subtle ones (*not*, note, simple to complex). I also did a comparative study of Pueblo and Navajo: Because the climate and site were comparable and the two groups in contact for centuries, differences in built form could very effectively be traced to specific cultural and social factors, further supporting the hypothesis of *House Form and Culture*. I also joined with a psychologist at the Bartlett, Ron Hawkes, in second paper on complexity in which a number of important changes were made, which I developed further later. I also wrote a more design-oriented piece on complexity in *AAQ*, and another emphasizing the point already made—the greater importance of urban *relationships* among elements, vis-à-vis the elements themselves, in a geography journal (*Area*).

Most important, it was all in my new capacity as an EBS type. While I was in London, an invitation arrived from Henry Sanoff, complete with funding to pay for the trip. It was to the first conference of the Environmental Design Research Association (EDRA 1). It had happened! We were a field; Meier's scenario about the origin and development of new fields was being reenacted before my eyes; what we now had to do was to make a *discipline* of it; that is still what needs to be done. At EDRA 1, my paper concerned two themes still important in my work—the notion of environmental quality and how it might be conceptualized and the importance of content-analyzing advertisements, novels, newspapers, travel literature, films, TV, and so on in order to understand environmental quality.

My new identity as an EBS type led to conflict with other team members when I headed the final year studio and was also in conflict with studio "culture." I resolved never to teach studio again, and I have not to this day.

But London was temporary, and chance intervened again. R. N. (Peter) Johnson, the head of architecture at Sydney, gave a seminar at the Bartlett. He was collecting data for a major project in his office—a federal courts building. I introduced him to EBS ways of approaching that problem; the result was a senior lectureship in Sydney, in charge of EBS within the first two-degree (3 + 2) program in Australia. EBS ran as an equal, compulsory sequence over the 3 years of the first degree. I gave an introductory course and organized a sequence of specially tailored courses in psychology, ethology, anthropology, and geography as ways to address design objectives, and political science to deal with constraints and implementation (cf. Rapoport, 1972). Time for this became available by reducing studio from four afternoons a week to two; and I did not teach any.

Johnson also arranged for me to write a weekly column in the national daily (*The Australian*). That was wonderful training in writing and also led to national exposure for the EBS point of view, trips, lectures, a successful campaign against an urban freeway. Service on an Institute of Architects awards jury meant that EBS criteria were at least considered. Among many invitations to write that I undertook while in Sydney was an edited book of commissioned papers (*Australia as Human Setting*). In it, people in a variety of disciplines were asked to consider the Australian cultural landscape. In my introductory chapter, I took the position that any change, by anyone, to the face of the earth was design—a position that informs much of my work; I again emphasized the role of social and cultural variables, continuing a campaign that seems to have borne fruit. At the moment, an emphasis on the role of cultural variables seems to be growing in EBS as shown by conferences, publications, and the like. My position also seems to be supported in many other fields, where the importance of culture is receiving increased emphasis.

While in Sydney, I was also invited to write what became *Human Aspects of Urban Form*. This took a long time to finish (partly because of my move to Milwaukee), but when it appeared, it had a number of important attributes. Among these: It was cross-cultural both regarding examples and the literature used; it adequately reviewed the literature up to the publication date (1,168 references by the publisher's count) and *synthesized* it, giving it a relatively simple order and, for the first time, using almost the full potential of diagrams; that synthesis is still, in my view, the closest thing to a theory in EBS, albeit not fully developed; all its concepts are still usable, and many have been greatly developed since. Moreover, its interpretations and predictions have not only stood the test of the 12 years since *publication* as I write this in mid-1989 but have been consistently supported by later work. In it I also greatly developed the process of dismantling concepts including "environment," "environmental quality," "culture," "privacy," and "environmental perception" that as used, I argued, was actually three major distinct things: preference and evaluation, cognition, and perception proper (which I, in turn, dismantled). It was highly condensed, having grown too large in the writing, so that paragraphs or even sentences can be expanded into a paper, several papers, or books. This is the case with most of my work; to give just one example, one paragraph in my chapter in *The Mutual Interaction of People and Their Built Environment* (1976) led to a report to the World Bank and became two papers on design in developing countries published in 1981 and 1983. When I turn to work on theory, part of the task will be to draw out many such implications and make them explicit.

In the meantime, while still in Sydney, *House Form and Culture* led to many invitations, including participation in Delos symposia. I realized again how little even the Delos luminaries knew about EBS. I was invited to join the board of the World Society for Ekistics—more trips to Athens and Paris; other trips to London and Geneva. I only mention these because I had not initiated any of that; what I think of as my "career by invitation" continued apace and has been even more important over that last 10 years.

Thus, by 1970–1971 my path was set. I worked on what I wanted to, mainly by invitation and, although formally in a department of architecture, my milieu was EBS and other disciplines. For example, I only taught EBS; ran a seminar organized jointly by the Institute of Architects and the department introducing EBS to the profession; I lectured on it to the institute and other schools; I gave talks to biologists, social workers, anthropologists, planners, and others. My publications included work on sacred space and the organization of space. I always continued to try and formulate some general principles of the field that had lateral connections to other bodies of knowledge and might turn it into a discipline. Other work related environmental quality to planning, new towns, and housing. I continued to explore the role of cultural variables in housing. That put a research project that Henry Sanoff and I had done at Berkeley into perspective. As a climatological study, it was first rate—and few have even duplicated it in the 25 years since. But it ignored cultural and life-style considerations, meanings, wants, and imagery that, in retrospect, were clear from surrounding evidence. Thus a self-help project for similar occupants (agricultural migrant workers) administered by Quakers sought a suburban image and accepted thermal conditions one would consider unacceptable. Using my work on complexity, I suggested in 1971—for the first time as far as I know—that the uniformity of conditions sought and achieved by environmental control systems may not be desirable and that more variability, including programmed variability, should be sought. There was much more—the amount of work was due partly to the fact that my teaching load consisted of one 50-minute lecture a week.

I liked Sydney, one of the most beautiful cities in the world, and trips were frequent enough to avoid isolation. Thus I intended to stay, particularly because I was given to understand that a chair was likely—a rare thing in Australia. (I was, in fact, offered one later.) But chance intervened again, in the form of a phone call inviting me to visit Milwaukee during our summer vacation; that led to an offer of a joint appointment in architecture and anthropology.

There were many disadvantages (one, a much higher teaching load), but two things swayed me. First I would be in the United States where EBS continued to develop. I missed EDRA 2, because nothing had been arranged for me but did attend EDRA 3 because Bill Mitchell organized funding; that conference was overwhelming. Although I work alone, proximity to people and ongoing work seemed useful—and so it proved. A chance meeting and discussion led to an invitation to organize a conference as part of the 9th International Congress of Ethnological and Anthropological Sciences. This I could do more easily in the United States and was the first thing I did after arriving in Milwaukee. The result was not only an edited book (*The Mutual Interaction of People and Their Built Environment*), it was also a realization of the value of, and need for, more small, invitational meetings. The 12 or so invited participants resulted in a meeting that we all still recollect with nostalgia. Unfortunately, although common in other fields, they are rejected in ours as "elitist" (a term of opprobrium that I regard as a major compliment). More important in my decision to move to Wisconsin was the joint appointment. Not only would I be in an academic department, but in a field in which I had never taken a single course. What a vindication of learning by reading! That I could not resist.

MY VIEW OF ARCHITECTURE

Many aspects of my architectural education were fun and personally satisfying but do not belong in this narrative. Others, more negative, were critical in allowing chance to play its role. If it takes a prepared mind to grasp chance, then the ultimate cause was my early commitment to science; the proximate was my dissatisfaction with architectural design. This began within weeks of starting architecture school and has become more extreme since, reinforced by further studies, travel, reading, working in architecture, and becoming an academic. My whole professional life is best seen as a rejection of architectural design as it is. The dissonance between what I do and being in a field—architecture—that, since student days, I felt did not belong in universities *as it was*, has been important in my work, which I have always defined in opposition to architecture.

What had become an unarticulated vague malaise crystallized in Berkeley; even the vaguest notion of EBS seemed self-evident.

But all this was later. At first I thought of changing fields again but couldn't because of financial reasons and because it meant losing another year, because, in the Australian system there were no credits to be transferred. But I also liked the domain, which was all around. One could study and analyze it while walking, driving, in buses, or looking down from airplanes. My discovery of vernacular environments and their inhabitants made this infinitely more interesting. It also meant that advertisements, novels, newspapers, TV, films and so on could also be used in research and teaching—and this has been an important and continuing theme in my work. It also made travel useful—one could get paid to travel! One's hobby could become one's work.

As long as science meant physics and the like, I could not see how built environments could be studied scientifically. But a new, broader view of science made it possible, at least in principle. EBS offered a perfect opportunity to "get out" of architecture by creating a science of EBR as a base for a science-based profession; it offered the possibility of introducing intellectual content, scholarship, rigor, research, empirical data, and theory. I could have both: I could study cultural landscapes in scientific and scholarly ways. That was irresistible because I immediately felt like a fish in water, although my negative view of architecture greatly influenced the way I saw EBS that, I repeat, I defined in opposition to the former.

But why my immediate rejection only of design in what was a strictly professional program? There were no electives; on entry, one knew what courses one would do and their order. With 1 year's office experience, most of it gained during the program, registration was automatic. During my second or third year I particularly enjoyed the only academic subject—art history (I regarded architectural history as at best semiprofessional). Although I have recently criticized it and architectural history based on it,[8] it did require an argument to be made and supported, however inadequately, by examples—a form of empirical evidence. In at least one paper, in which I compared Piero della Francesca and Mantegna, I managed to adumbrate several themes important in my later work: controlled comparison (by using their versions of a single subject (The Resurrection)), lateral connections, emphasis on cultural and conceptual issues rather than works of art, a broad conceptual framework (classicism vs. romanticism) much to the disadvantage of Mantegna's romanticism. This confirmed my dislike in high school of romantic literature (especially poetry) and a lifelong dislike of romantic music. Since then, I have an additional reason for the dislike. When first institutionalized as a movement, romanticism and the romantic spirit attacked rationality and science, a position now taken by its detestable twentieth-century equivalents.

I also accepted all other subjects; although mechanical services and surveying never thrilled me, they soon proved useful. Geology, structures, and construction, specifications, and professional practice I enjoyed and was very good at. In fact, I was regarded as a bit of an expert on the latter straight out of school. I had gotten very interested in it because the course materials soon became the standard book on the subject. This was an important lesson— university teaching should relate to one's research and interests.[9]

---

[8] In my as-yet unpublished book, *History and Precedent in Environmental Design* (to be published by Plenum Press in early 1990).
[9] Jacob (1988) makes the same point.

All those, and other, subjects made sense, seemed to have a knowledge base, a rationale, a logic and ways of deciding which of several alternatives was preferable—and why, which I regard as the essence of design.

But design as taught was different. From the very first day, it seemed vacuous, arbitrary, capricious, and based on nothing, yet surrounded by a mystique, meaningless verbiage, and arm waving. It also took far too much time, most of which was wasted.[10]

A very early first-year design project (following much rather meaningless "basic design"), a domestic kitchen, was the last straw. Our instructor, a very famous architect, marched in, pinned up some drawings, announced "this is the perfect kitchen; I designed it," and marched out. There was the problem in a nutshell. Not only ego getting in the way but a fundamental question: How could one "design" a kitchen without objectives by which the product could be evaluated; without users; without research (other than some inadequate ergonomics); without analyzing activities, including their latent aspects, and hence culture and meaning? Of course, I did not know those concepts then, just that something was wrong, that one cannot know whether a thing is well-designed, that is, does something well, unless one knows what it is supposed to do—and why. The most important part, *problem identification*, was missing; moreover, a solution to a problem may not be a setting at all.

My dissatisfaction was not due to the "uncertainty" of design versus the apparent "certainty" of science. I knew even then that science, although the most certain of all human endeavors, was not as certain as the undergraduate teaching of it. Moreover, that uncertainty was challenging; it promised many interesting problems and research; there was so much to be discovered—and finding out could be fun. At issue was the way uncertainty was dealt with.

Problems were never *discovered* or *identified*. This avoided difficult and real, hence challenging and interesting problems. Designers' problems were self-posed, hence trivial and easily "solved." One only needed to satisfy oneself. The basis for students' designs and the evaluation of studio critics and juries were personal preferences, without even knowing the reasons for them. Worse, there seemed no interest in finding out and reducing the area of uncertainty or ignorance through knowledge, unlike in other fields that did that constantly. The contrast between the beauty and excitement of the search for knowledge and understanding and the vacuous mindlessness of design were more than I could stand.

I responded initially by refusing to play the game. Because, however, I couldn't change my field again, for the first and last time I pretended to take seriously something I despised—design studio. It proved easy to do and I did well, even winning some design prizes. It also required very little time, and it was then that I developed the habit of never working evenings or weekends.

---

[10] Note that in 1949, during the heroic period of the modern movement in Australia, design was at least semirational and user requirements sometimes present in word if not in deed. Things are much worse now.

My projects were usually finished days or even weeks early—there was so little to it!

But I still fought it. I failed in attempts to change design education by helping to organize students in Australia and New Zealand. I succeeded by sneaking in my own agenda whenever possible. Thus when it became possible just in time for me to do a written research part (in *addition* to design) of the B.Arch thesis, all my efforts went into that. The redesign of the main Melbourne railway station became an excuse to study pedestrian movement by using some Swedish and U.S. mathematical models that treated it like fluid flows. The design was an afterthought as far as I was concerned.

But these problems with design continued into practice. Although offices had many competent people doing useful and important things, designers were the elite and seemed to do the same trivial things we did in school with no more knowledge. As described earlier, clients and users did not seem to know much either, and as a designer my professional responsibility was to know what they did not. The critical issue was *knowledge*, not so much about how to do things, although designers lacked knowledge even about that, but about identifying problems and about *what* to do, and *why*.

Design work I had done—in offices, on my own, and as a consultant— also lacked valid criteria. All I could say about my own designs was that *I* liked them, *I* thought them good, *I* thought they solved the problems as *I* defined them. That was no basis for design. If I rejected these criteria for others, in schools and the professions, I could not use them in my own work. Nor could I criticize others' work—all it meant was that I did not like it. Yet, as I now put it, a good design for a particular situation may be one the designer himself hates. Clearly there was a need for knowledge about what to do and why, about how to justify objectives and discover whether the choices made had achieved them.

The intervening years have only increased my dissatisfaction with a profession that lacks any real basis for design decisions or judgments, other than "I like it" or "I don't like it." Who cares? That is relevant only regarding one's own settings and provides no basis for anything else. I make this point to students during my lecture on complexity in our introductory EBS course, by reading the first two sentences of Venturi's *Complexity and Contradiction in Architecture:* "I like complexity and contradiction in architecture. I do not like . . ." (p. 22) and suggesting that this is totally irrelevant. The approach, I argue, is to discover whether complexity is liked or important, for whom, where and when, and why; how it can be defined and operationalized and requisite levels established; how it differs from contradiction or ambiguity; how one can achieve it and know whether one has. Answering these questions and many others like them that are important and interest me has been my objective in EBS and central to my work.

MY VIEW OF ENVIRONMENT–BEHAVIOR STUDIES (EBS)

For me, the purpose of EBS has never been to help design with information, design guides, programming, or Post Occupancy Evaluations (POEs) but to replace it with a science-based profession. Hence making research "relevant" to designers, or understandable to them, was unnecessary; it was *designers* that needed changing, to see research as essential. The way things are, even if understood, research is not used (Rapoport, 1986b). In any case mainstream design will not, or cannot, change, and EBS needs to work directly with users and clients, and design should become applied EBS. But that did not concern me much either because I was never interested in *changing* the world (much as I object to much of it) but in *understanding* it. Of course, history shows that ultimately only understanding permits effective change, in desired and predictable ways. Valid practice is impossible without empirical research and theory development; only explanatory theory is powerful enough to be applied reliably.

Design, thus redefined, would be concerned with problem identification and decisions about what to do and why. Design is the process of choosing among alternative courses of action to achieve certain predicted effects based on explicit objectives. This I have called the *choice model of design*. It applies to *all* design—vernacular or high style, traditional or contemporary. What varies is who makes the choices and why, that is, the choice criteria used, their order, the temporal scale involved, the ideal schema that choice is trying to approach, and so on. As in most of my work a single, relatively simple model can be applied extremely broadly, possibly universally, as long as the correct specifics (discovered through research) are introduced and used. To be valid, objectives must be based on the best available knowledge; how to achieve goals, what means are available to achieve objectives, and how one can judge whether these have been reached also require theory and knowledge of mechanisms and are amenable to research. *Design can then be seen as hypotheses,* the results of which can be tested rigorously and publicly. In this way, a cumulative body of public science *in design* could develop. Seen thus, design and research are quite similar and can follow very similar models.[11] This means that applied research

---

[11] This became very clear from a project I had students do over a number of years in my EBS introductory course in Sydney and Milwaukee. They were exemplars of research and design at the same time. What was meant to be a simple model of research clearly was also a model of design as it should be. Students were to pick a setting and observe and otherwise study ongoing behavior in it. On the basis of the research literature, that is, *knowledge*, they were to hypothesize about the mechanisms linking the setting and behavior. On the basis of this they were to suggest change(s) to the setting that would result in some changes in behavior (understood broadly) of the occupants. They were then to make these changes and see whether the predictions were borne out. This is obviously a highly simplified description of research. One observes the world and identifies certain patterns, questions about which constitute problems. Inferences are then made from prior knowledge, theory, and intuition about mechanisms that might explain these patterns and hypotheses derived that can be tested. In my view, this is also what design is all about. It is usually the result of an attempt to solve a perceived problem in the physical environment. A proposed solution is then a hypothesis (or rather a set of hypotheses) of the form: Given an analysis of the problematic situation, and given knowledge of theory, mechanisms, etc., so and so should be done to achieve such and such objectives, for the following reasons. One then needs to check whether this set of hypotheses is correct, both before and after implementation. Such rigorous and *public* testing would lead to a cumulative body of knowledge *in design* (e.g., Rapoport, 1983c).

is important, wherever it occurs. It also means that EBS must go it alone, totally independent of mainstream design, not only as a discipline but also as an applied field; for both, explanatory theory is central.

Thus I hold strong and fairly concrete views on design and how changes in it can improve the performance and credibility of designers. But application is not my major concern; moreover a science can only be applied once it exists. Because what distinguishes EBS from mainstream architecture is that it is scientific, I have always seen EBS primarily as a new discipline concerned with the study, understanding, and explanation of a particular domain—EBR. Because science is the best (if not only) way so far found of achieving that, EBS is then like other sciences in *their* particular domains.

Like many new disciplines, EBS is the result of an overlap of many fields. It began by interacting with a few social sciences but, as the study of man increasingly involves evolutionary science, ethology, sociobiology, neuroscience, cognitive science, and so on, so does EBS. Its links are not with specific disciplines but with all domains that contribute to its objective—the scientific study of human interaction with the cultural landscape and material culture. In this way I have been able to introduce ever new disciplines into my work, while retaining an unchanging objective. The specific linkages have changed and grown with changes in knowledge.

That study requires using the full spectrum of evidence for pattern recognition, generalization, theory development, and testing. In that, it is truly humanistic in the sense that it considers the full range of human environments and relies on a wide variety of work in many disciplines, places, and times, not neglecting popular media, advertising, and so on. Science itself is, of course, the most human of enterprises; it and humanism are not opposites—they are one. This approach is also rigorous and opposed to "holism"; one must dismantle, study the components, their linkages and interconnections, identify causal mechanisms, and reassemble using many techniques, including simulation, to show understanding. One can use data already available to constrain theorizing and also learn from the successes and failure of other fields.

Given this broad orientation, a number of more or less conscious decisions followed. I would do pure, basic, scholarly research without any concern for application. Both empirical research and theory construction and the requisite analysis of philosophical bases were missing in architecture. Theory, however, seemed central because it, not data, is the most important product of science. Also, emphasis on real, that is, explanatory, theory would show up what passes for "theory" in architecture.

I would, therefore, do no empirical work because too much of it can even be counterproductive because the sheer mass of material becomes overwhelming. Also, as Eddington pointed out, facts mean little until confirmed by theory. I would use empirical studies by others, which are often "lost" and not used and become useless without a framework of theory. Instead, I would synthesize, generalize, search for patterns, define the domain, develop and clarify concepts. I would try to synthesize and to seek interconnections—particularly lateral ones. I would search for patterns and, through them, for generalizations, abstraction, conceptualization, and so on as a way of getting to *explanation*—the things that attracted me to science in the first place. This goal has influenced the way I conceptualize the field; all the concepts, frameworks, and theoretical formulations were always meant to be fundamental enough to be useful for developing explanatory theory. This, I feel, has now advanced sufficiently for me to begin actively to work on it. This was also congenial to my original interest in *theoretical* science, which is clearly differentiated from its experimental counterparts.

There are institutions concerned with application and applied research; basic scholarly work can only occur in universities (cf. Rapoport, 1979). Thus I would pursue ideas and data wherever they led. I would move into whatever disciplines I needed and into new areas at will; I would overlap fields. My approach would be eclectic and based on extensive *reading* in my rather idiosyncratic way. I would combine the concepts and ways of thinking of many scientific disciplines in unusual ways, in a search for patterns and connections, particularly *lateral* connections.

Extensive reading helps to identify those disciplines that have addressed given problems and to discover what has been done. Before doing anything, one must know the maximum possible about what has been done; before moving into new areas, one needs at least a good idea of current thought in it. This fitted my characteristic since childhood of being a voracious reader, and I also reacted against the lack of this in architecture; unfortunately this is now emerging in EBS. "New" insights or findings are announced that have been in the literature for years. There are arguments against literature reviews; worse, these are often *pro forma* and not really used. Worse still, work in many disciplines is ignored that becomes clearly relevant if approached at a sufficiently *conceptual* level; hence the wheel is often reinvented.

Only at a university could one work in this way and avoid the constraints of applicability and funded research. The latter particularly makes this ideal impossible, even in applied research, leads to compromises, distorts the line of development because of sudden shifts of emphasis due to shifting fashions reflected in the availability of funds; research follows money. Important theoretical research is unlikely to be funded because it is open ended and results highly uncertain. Long-range research also suffers because it may take years even to get started. Some reading on history and theory that I expected to take a few months took 7 years and continues. One result has been to link a host of new disciplines to EBS; that also would have been impossible with funded research because overlapping fields in this way violate the administrative milieu of funding agencies.[12]

Even worse, like studio and committees, funded research wastes time, in writing proposals, administering assistants, and accounting for funds to bureaucracies—time to do important things. It also turns academics into entrepreneurs, expected to help support universities, departments, and students; this I regard as destructive to research and academia.

[12] This does not apply to *Fellowships;* in fact, this work was partly supported by those.

My decision to do basic, scholarly research and theory development had the advantage of being inexpensive. It was the ultimate small science, and I could work on my own; all I needed was a library, paper and pen and, possibly, access to a copy machine. I could be completely independent—and I see the university as a collection of independent scholars whose main commitment is to the world of ideas and scholarship and to their work.

CONTINUITY IN MY WORK

My commitment to science, to understanding and explanation, the rejection of architectural design, and an emphasis on a scholarly approach based on very extensive readings in many disciplines have provided the overall continuity to my work as a whole that, when I look over the rather large amount done, is quite striking and remarkable.

There has also been continuity in parts of my work, although I can only give a few examples of the many possible. Pedestrian movement, first studied in my B.Arch thesis (1954) was developed further, with some reference to vernacular design in my M.Arch thesis; then in several papers on complexity, in *Human Aspects of Urban Form,* several recent chapters, and it is part of the as yet unpublished book on history. This line of work has emphasized the relation between *perceptual* attributes of the environment and walking and has shown how principles can be derived from an analysis of the many vernacular examples found in almost all cultures over thousands of years. Particularly because walking *as an activity* has not changed. Also, the role of culture is weaker, being mainly with regard to the willingness or readiness to walk. I first considered learning from vernacular (as opposed to an interest in it for its own sake) in my M.Arch. thesis (1957), continued in some design work done in the early 1960s, discussed it at EDRA 1, and then developed it in a series of papers and chapters through 1988, including its relevance to design for developing countries; it is one of two major themes in the book mentioned in footnote 8. The concept of the house settlement system was introduced in my first published piece on Isphahan in *Landscape* (1964–1965); was developed in *House Form and Culture* and *Human Aspects of Urban Form,* then in a series of chapters and papers showing its great usefulness; its theoretical development is the subject of an as yet unpublished paper, and it has proved very useful in teaching.

An important aspect of that continuity has been the need for the broadest and most varied body of evidence necessary for pattern recognition, valid generalization, and theory development. This required a redefinition of the domain through a systematic sequence of steps that may appear like a series of distinct topics. It is significant that these also identify the characteristics that distinguish that domain from mainstream architecture. First, I introduced preliterate, vernacular, and popular environments and spontaneous settlements. That immediately involved the full range of cultures—and hence the need for comparative, cross cultural work and tracing patterns at higher levels of abstraction. I then included the whole environment, defined as the cultural landscape and conceptualized as a system of settings and including all of material culture. This led to the great importance of semifixed elements. Most recently I included the full span of history, even extending into evolutionary aspects. In this final expansion, explored in some papers (e.g., Rapoport, 1986a) and particularly in my *History and Precedent in Environmental Design*, the point is made that defining the domain in this way is not only essential but has major theoretical implications. One is that the study of the history of that domain becomes part of EBS, and hence scientific, rather than part of art history (for one thing, design is no longer an art but a science-based profession). The second is that any patterns and generalizations that are needed for theory development must include evidence from this broad domain, including historical data.

This also has had methodological implications, such as the use of multiple methods, the need for cross-cultural and comparative work, and the use of archaeological, pictorial, and written materials that I have emphasized in papers, chapters, and books since EDRA 1. It has also led to shifts in the *specifics* of what I have read, although not the need to begin with what is known, so as not to lose it and to be cumulative. At Berkeley I began with anthropology, geography, and psychology. Then, over 10 years or so, I combined those with the burgeoning EBS literature. Starting in 1982, I concentrated on the "new" history and archaeology, philosophy of history and historiography, historical geography, history of medicine, and the various "historical" sciences, such as geology, biological evolution, paleontology, cosmology, and so on. These helped support the position that the study of the past can be scientific and that in turn, that study is essential for EBS: History and EBS need each other. In preparation for a book on theory that I hope to start during 1990/1991, I have concentrated on a variety of sciences, their theories, findings, and controversies in them; philosophy of science; the history, sociology, and psychology of science, and so on.

As emphases have changed, so have the subjects read; but always the goal has been to read extensively in all relevant disciplines, to find out as much as I could about a given topic. Within some limits, time is of no concern because I am not funded by grants.

Because of the continuity that I see in my work, I regard it as a *research program*, based on the desire to achieve that cumulativeness that first impressed me in Berkeley. Each piece of work is part of a larger pattern, a "brick" in an edifice under construction; each has been built on previous ones and, in turn, forms a basis for others. These linkages seem so clear to me, that this work should be read as one; this is why I cite my own work so much.

Connections are made not only within each piece of work, and among them, but between them and ever new fields and disciplines. Through all this, theory has been developing, resulting in a highly elaborated theoretical framework, with many even more elaborated parts. This framework encompasses the whole field and seems to accommodate ever new work from very many different fields, which often confirm predictions made earlier. In fact, I have been struck repeatedly by how the "predictions" I have made or are implicit in my position have been supported by published work, dissertations, and on-going work by students and others or by work in other fields. Moreover, the very large amount of material in many new (to EBS) disciplines that I have read and continue to read fits into, and seems to support, my emergent framework. This is why my earliest pieces make even more sense now, within this larger pattern.

That research program has had two major parts or bodies of work. Some have seen these as antithetical, particularly as, since 1983, my theoretical work has emphasized science more. But that is not the case. The first, my work on vernacular and the like, involved the redefinition of the domain of the cultural landscape and material culture over its full cross-cultural and temporal range. The second has been concerned with its scientific study in order to develop theory in EBS. Thus I have moved from an interest in vernacular as such, to learning from it through EBS concepts and theory (i.e., as precedent), to using it as an entry point into EBS. I linked EBS concepts to culture-built form relations and applied that synthesis to developing countries, which more clearly show general patterns, given their much more extreme situations. Most recently I have linked all of those with history and the latter with EBS theory.[13]

RECENT WORK

My work over the last 10 years can be divided into two periods—before and after my 1982–1983 sabbatical.

During that whole period I have increasingly worked by invitation and even the *topics* have mostly been given me—some of which I had never thought about. That means that the role of chance has become even more important; it also illustrates an important aspect of my research program. Invited topics offer a particularly good opportunity to test my approach, conceptual framework, and emerging theory. These are tested effectively to the extent that I am able to tackle topics about which I had never even thought, and I do that relatively quickly and easily. This has worked for many topics, among them nomads, the elderly, children, the concept of place, housing, regionalism, tradition, dry stone architecture, interior design, spontaneous settlements, and design for developing countries. Students have also been able to test these frameworks, using an even larger variety of topics, numerous locales, periods, and so on. In no case have these conceptual frameworks had to be "stretched" or modified to any significant extent. In each case, reading was topic-specific and confined to aspects of the substantive content, suggesting that the conceptual framework is, indeed, broadly applicable, rather simple and capable of having many specifics "plugged" into it. This, in turn, suggests to me that there is, in fact, an emergent and implicit theory there. To discuss it, however, I have felt it essential to tackle the nature of theory as already mentioned and to be briefly discussed later.

[13] For example, Rapoport, 1980, 1982, 1983a,b, 1986a,b, in press; also *History and Precedent in Environmental Design*.

The 1982–1983 sabbatical was a watershed. I have continued the previously mentioned process of using invitations to reexamine terms and definitions, consider taxonomy as a neglected but most important topic, refine concepts and frameworks, redefine terms and concepts, and dismantle complex ones. This I have now done, among others, for "culture," "environment," "region," "tradition," "environmental quality," "privacy," and "life-style," and also shown how, once redefined and dismantled, various linkages can be established, given knowledge of mechanisms. I have also tried to relate these activities to the use of diagrams, which as already discussed, I see not just as a means of communicating ideas, but as a way of thinking, analyzing, and synthesizing. I also began a longer range, more fundamental reexamination of concepts, frameworks, and so on, and the philosophical bases of the field. Both activities are thus mutually reinforcing and share a concern with an emerging theory, with its *what* and *why*—what it might be and what it should do.

The importance of explanatory theory in EBR has been a constant theme, but major emphasis began after I had completed defining the domain by analyzing the role of history. I had intended history and theory to be a single project; it should complete the domain definition and also outline a theory of it. But this history alone took 5 years, and I am still preparing to start writing on theory in 1990.

Since 1982 I have read systematically in a wide range of fields better to understand the nature of science, scientific theory, and their philosophical bases. This does *not* involve philosophy in general but only the philosophy of science as modified by many other relevant fields because my concern is *scientific* theory. The object is to help clarify the essential characteristics of science and research, theory, explanation, empirical confirmation, and so on. Also, the role of philosophy is to clarify issues—concepts, definitions, theories, and test logic and consistency. Philosophy is good at that and at asking questions; it is not very good at giving answers—in any case, *that is the role of research*. This systematic reading has changed what had been a firmly held, but only partly formed, view into concrete and, in my view, unassailable fact that science, properly understood, was the only model to follow.

This work suggests that many of the things I have talked, thought, and written about and the multitude of new things discovered are coming together into real frameworks. My courses also are increasingly about frameworks, with readings confined to specific topics rather than reviews of the literature in general; I also use newspapers, novels, and advertisements more than EBS papers. In fact, I do not read that much EBS now.

This is partly because of the state of the literature. My dissatisfaction with architecture now also affects EBS. Not only has it been on a plateau for a decade or so, but it has become preoccupied with design applications rather than aiming to become a science of EBR. Not only does it continue to be too empirical, lacking conceptual clarification and theory development, but it also seems, like architecture and the social sciences, to be affected by a strongly antiscientific, that is, antirational attitude.

I cut architecture readings to almost nothing a long time ago, although I still read the publications of the two architectural institutes to which I belong; belonging makes my critique more meaningful. (This is also why I maintain my registration as an architect in two Australian states.) During 1982–1983, as part of my reading program on theory, I tried to look at "architectural theory" but soon stopped. There was no theory; in fact there was nothing. Clearly, any theory development in EBS will need totally to ignore all that and begin elsewhere. It is not a matter of rejecting the bases of mainstream architecture—it simply has no bases; the emperor has no clothes.

All this is a natural development of my early commitment to science. Unlike others who shifted from science to architecture and rejected science, I rejected architecture and went into EBS to make it a science. The relentless attacks since the 1960s on science and rationality have had a devastating effect on the social sciences and EBS. Many in them have been infected by doubt about objectivity and have lost confidence in rationality. This is revealed by certain key words, especially attacks on "positivism" or "positivistic science" (used as an incantation) or on "reductionism," or demands for "holism." Another dead giveaway are certain standard quotations, usually Kuhn and Feyerabend. There is little apparent knowledge of the fields I have mentioned or even of what the terms mean and major analytical distinctions within and among them.

My own reaction to these assaults has been the exact opposite. I have ignored neo-Marxism, existentialism, phenomenology, the "counterculture" (better—anticulture), consciousness raising, and "new age" movements of all sorts, mysticism, various forms of spirituality, holism, hermeneutics, deconstructionism, and other varied assaults on rationality. I have increasingly seen science as the only bit of sanity left in a world gone mad. At present, it is the only human enterprise that has succeeded brilliantly; attacks on it probably represent resentment against this very success. Science and, with very few exceptions, its practitioners have ignored most of that noise and stood firm as a bastion of rationality, objectivity, and truth. As a result, they have revealed ever more wonders about the world, making it intelligible and explaining it. Above all, science exemplifies the wonderful ability of humans to do all that— what first inspired me in reading Jeans and Eddington.

In terms of *knowing, understanding, and explaining,* and that is what I take EBS to be, science is the only approach that has worked and works ever better—at least thus far. It is also the only self-correcting and progressive activity and, in spite of attempts to deny it, there is rapid (and ever accelerating) progress and cumulativeness in all fields of science.[14]

Only in science is rational criticism of theory and findings possible; in fact criticism is central. This turns private science into reliable knowledge. That distinction seems ever more important, specially in terms of the role of intuition and architects' preoccupation with creativity. It is clear that individual

---

[14] Hence the title of this chapter, as a reaction to Perez-Gomez's *Architecture and the Crisis [sic!!] of Modern Science.*

scientists are quirky, intuitive, and affected by chance. Although infinitely better prepared than architects, and starting at the state of the art in cumulative disciplines, the major difference is, first, that they themselves test their products rigorously before those see the light of day. This is because, second, the field subjects those products to even more rigorous testing. The results are only accepted or admitted into the canon if they pass this rigorous winnowing process, attempts at refutation, testing, questioning, and so on, which are the role of public science. Only fit ideas and findings survive the natural selection of scientific evolution, and even lapses are eventually corrected. There is an urgent need for an equivalent in design (cf. Rapoport, 1983c).

Science is not, of course, perfect because it is a human activity, but, among all human activities, it is *the only one* that still gives me some hope for humanity. The less said about social or political attitudes the better. Most social sciences are increasingly becoming what the Australian philosopher David Stove recently called "festering intellectual slums." In my view, this is because they are preoccupied with "social" (in an ideological way) and have rejected science, possibly because it would reveal their biases and hidden agendas.[15] The so-called humanities are worse, and art simply irrelevant to the study of the cultural landscape and material culture, and even to their design.

Moreover, much of what currently passes for art is, at best, a bad joke. I agree with Judson (1980) that science is the art of the twentieth century. That is where beauty is found, the beauty of the discovery of patterns; of the elegant and simple mechanisms behind the most complex phenomena; of gradually revealing reality; above all, the beauty of the human mind capable of knowing, understanding, and explaining not only the furthest reaches of the universe, but itself. All this is sublime and breathtaking, a beauty far greater than any other. The study of EBR can be like that.[16] All this also makes the claims that our domain is too complicated to understand sound like a bad joke and, in turn, explains why so much architectural, social science, and humanities writing is incomprehensible. There is a clear tendency deliberately to obfuscate, to make relatively simple things seem so complex that they cannot be understood. I believe with most scientists that fundamentally, and once understood, things are relatively simple—so is any theory, the task of which (among many others) is to simplify further.

In this view of science, in being eclectic and broad, in emphasizing synthesis and theory rather than empirical work, in pursuing questions because

---

[15] This is well described in two passages that I have used as epigraphs in my *History and Precedent in Environmental Design;* (1) "For many antiscientists objectivity is not so much impossible as reprehensible," John Passmore, *Science and its Critics,* New Brunswick, NJ, Rutgers University Press, 1978, p. 91. (2) "With its deconstructionists in literary criticism, its ordinary language and other philosophers, and its novelists, our age may one day come to be known in intellectual history for its role in the advancements of techniques to prove that reality does not exist." Joseph Epstein, "The sunshine girls," *Commentary,* Vol. 77 No. 6, June 1984, p. 67.

[16] What all this means specifically, and the establishing of an explicit link between science and EBS will have to await future work.

they are interesting and seem important rather than because they can be applied or funded, I am out of step with many. That also is an aspect of continuity in my work. I stubbornly stick to what I feel needs to be done, and fashion plays no part in it. Frequently real advances are made by those who work at unfashionable subjects. Particularly in developing theory, a long-range goal and program are essential, and one cannot allow oneself to be distracted by changes in fashion. Of course, I cannot tell what invitations I will get, if any, but other than that I expect to be developing theory from now on.

CONCLUSION

So I am back where this history began, ever more involved with science, although I feel that I have now adequately defined the domain of EBS—both its subject matter and some of the important questions in it. My current reading in many sciences and the philosophy, history, psychology, and sociology of science (*not*, please note, the "sociology of *knowledge*"), although still extremely broad, is now highly directed. It is a reading program, focused on concepts, topics, and theories, not fields; in any case, new fields come up constantly. This program has involved reading over 1,000 books on these topics since 1982, and I continue at the rate of two or three a week. It is *that* kind of immersion that I believe to be essential before a topic can be tackled. It is intended to allow me to discuss theory and develop a theoretical, or metatheoretical base, that will avoid problems I see with the work so far on this topic in EBS, caused by ignoring the relevant literature. I intend to show that only by filling these gaps can one even begin to outline the nature of an explanatory theory of EBR, let alone begin to develop a theory. For me, everything else is, at the moment, secondary, even trivial; it will follow "automatically" once such theory is even partly developed.

Thus I will continue to cultivate my own garden, doing what I do, pursuing ideas wherever they lead, and, above all, enjoying myself because, essentially, scientists and scholars work for fun and for their own satisfaction. And it has all been great fun. Thinking about it for this chapter has made that clear and has been a wonderful experience; in fact too much so—this essay is a précis of what has become a book!

When I read Jeans and Eddington and fantasized about being a scientist, I did not know what that meant and never really believed I would be one. When I became the first member of my family to attend university I never dared dream that I would be one of the elite who *are* the university. When I seemed trapped in architectural offices doomed, it seemed, to engage in vacuous and trivial pursuits, I never thought that there would be a way out. When I became an academic, I seemed doomed to teach design, graphics, construction just like every one—but haven't for 20 years.

I have been able to do what I have always wanted to do and to combine science and scholarship with a wonderful and fascinating domain that is all around us—the cultural landscape and material culture—and to do it my own way. Extensive travel has been part of my work, and work has been my hobby.

Even getting angry at the architectural milieu within which I have had to work has sometimes been fun; I often enjoy being angry, although it has sometimes been almost too much. But, all in all, few people have been as lucky.

Above all, I have had the privilege of playing a part, from the beginning, in creating a new field of study and in contributing to its development. Now, starting where I began at age 8 or 9, I will concentrate on trying to turn it into a discipline, by exploring its theoretical bases and trying to outline an explanatory theory of EBR. Only time will tell if I will succeed—but it should continue to be great fun.

REFERENCES

Jacob, F. (1988). *The statue within*. New York: Basic Books.

Judson, H. F. (1980). *The search for solutions*. New York: Holt, Rinehart & Winston.

Kac, M. (1985). *Enigmas of chance*. New York: Harper & Row.

Rapoport, A. (1969). Facts and models. In G. Broadbent and A. Ward (Eds.), *Design methods in architecture* (pp. 136–144). London: Lund Humphries.

Rapoport, A. (1970). Man-environment studies—A review. In A. Rapoport and B. Davis (Eds.), *Man-environment studies seminar* (pp. 11–22). School of Architecture, University of Sydney and NSW Chapter, Royal Australian Institute of Architects.

Rapoport, A. (1972). The undergraduate man-environment course at Sydney. In W. F. E. Preiser (Ed.), *Environmental design perspectives (MES Focus I)* (pp. 42–48). Blacksburg, VA: College of Architecture, Virginia Polytechnic Institute and State University.

Rapoport, A. (1979). Pure research in architecture and urban planning. *Wisconsin Architect* (September), 15.

Rapoport, A. (1980). Vernacular architecture and the cultural determinants of form. In A. D. King (Ed.), *Buildings and society: Essays on the social development of the built environment* (pp. 283–305). London: Routledge & Kegan Paul.

Rapoport, A. (1982). An approach to vernacular design. In J. M. Fitch (Ed.), *Shelter: Models of native ingenuity* (pp. 43–48). New York: Katonah Gallery.

Rapoport, A. (1983a). Environmental quality, metropolitan areas, and traditional settlements. *Habitat International, 7*, 37–63.

Rapoport, A. (1983b). Development, culture change and supportive design. *Habitat International, 7*, 249–268.

Rapoport, A. (1983c). Debating architectural alternatives, *RIBA Transactions 3, 2*, 105–109.

Rapoport, A. (1985). On diversity, and designing for diversity. In B. Judd, J. Dean & D. Brown (Eds.), *Housing issues I: Design for diversification* (pp. 5–8 and 30–36). Canberra: Royal Australian Institute of Architects.

Rapoport, A. (1986a). Settlements and energy: Historical precedents. In W. H. Ittelson, M. Asai, & M. Ker (Eds.), *Cross-cultural research in environment and behavior* (pp. 219–237). Tucson: University of Arizona Press.

Rapoport, A. (1986b). Culture and built form: A reconsideration. In D. G. Saile (Ed.), *Architecture in cultural change: Essays in built form and culture research* (pp. 157–175). Lawrence: University of Kansas.

Rapoport, A. (1987). Statement for the ACSA 75th anniversary (Jubilee) issue. *Journal of Architectural Education, 40*, 65–66.

Rapoport, A. (1988). Levels of meaning in the built environment. In F. Poyatos (Ed.), *Cross-cultural perspectives in nonverbal communication* (pp. 317–336). Toronto: C. J. Hogrefe.

Rapoport, A. (in press). Defining vernacular design. In M. Turan (Ed.), *On vernacular architecture: A collection of essays*. Aldershot, England: Gower.

5

From the Pragmatic to the Spiritual

AN INTELLECTUAL AUTOBIOGRAPHY

CLARE COOPER MARCUS

I WAS BORN IN 1934 IN ENGLAND and raised in the north London suburb of Finchley, except for the period of World War II, when I was evacuated to the country. I was educated in public and private schools, and in 1952 entered the University of London, where I majored in historical geography. I completed a master's degree in cultural and urban geography at the University of Nebraska in 1958 under the direction of James E. Vance, Jr., and Leslie Hewes. After teaching cartography and working as an urban planner in Britain for 3 years, I returned to the United States as an immigrant in 1961. A second master's degree in city and regional planning at the University of California, Berkeley, in 1965 under Melvin Webber turned my attention to the built environment and to the need for postoccupancy evaluation research in housing. After working for several years as a research associate in the Institute of Urban and Regional Development at Berkeley, I started to teach in the Department of Landscape Architecture in 1969. My entire teaching career has been at the University of California, Berkeley, where I am now a professor with a joint appointment in the Departments of Architecture and Landscape Architecture.

I have served on the board of directors of the Environmental Design Research Association and on many juries for design awards and competitions. I have received a number of awards, including an award for exemplary design research from the National Endowment for the Arts; the Career Award of the Environmental Design Research Association; and a Guggenheim Fellowship.

I love my work, my family, and my home, and in my spare time I enjoy canoeing, hiking, gardening, watercolor painting, and photography. I dedicate this chapter to my teenage children—Jason and Lucy.

CLARE COOPER MARCUS • Department of Architecture and Department of Landscape Architecture, University of California at Berkeley, Berkeley, California 94720.

INTRODUCTION

I cannot remember a time when I was not interested in the physical environment. A World War II childhood necessitated evacuation from the London blitz to the relatively calm countryside of Buckinghamshire. Ironically, wartime restrictions minimized such parent-perceived dangers as excessive traffic or the presence of strangers. My explorations covered a wide rural territory; the normal need to be aware of the environment was intensified by the blackout, and by the removal of all official signs indicating direction or location—a measure taken to confuse the enemy if invasion occurred. I am sure that a keen visual sense was born at that time.

As I reached the middle years of childhood, my curiosity about the cultural landscape increased. Why were the fields different shapes? Why were the cottages in our village built of stone, whereas only 10 miles away, they were built of flint? Armed with a precious and influential book—*The Observers' Book of Architecture*—a friend and I bicycled around the countryside examining churches for clues of Saxon or early English traits in their design. A decade later, when I went to University College, London, as an undergraduate, I chose to major in cultural and historical geography.

My understanding of the landscape deepened immeasurably, tramping through the hills and byways of England on undergraduate field trips. What I choose to focus on now may have changed from soil types and field boundaries to the personalization of porches and public behavior in city plazas, but the rigorous training—not only to look but also to see and to question—is one for which I am immensely grateful. During later study for a master's degree in geography at the University of Nebraska, my training was further enhanced by a seminal teacher—James E. Vance, Jr.—who, guiding us through the byways of Lincoln and Omaha, caused me to shift my questioning curiosity from the rural to the urban landscape.

My consciousness about how cities *might* be began to be aroused. A year of academic teaching in geography at the University of Sheffield convinced me that theories about how the contemporary landscape came to be were not enough to satisfy my wish to influence the future. Geographers—at least then (late 1950s)—were not interested in what might be, in predicting or guiding the future. My childhood curiosities had been satisfied; I wanted a more active role in shaping the environment.

IMMIGRATION TO THE UNITED STATES AND EARLY HOUSING RESEARCH

Urban planning seemed to be a possible outlet for my interests in cities and in working for change. For 2 years I worked as a planning researcher for the Ministry of Housing and for London County Council, but my yearning for academia and for the United States could not be quelled. I returned to do a second master's degree in city and regional planning at Berkeley. Fortuitously, my immigration to the West Coast coincided with the start of the social ferment of the 1960s. Antiwar rallies and civil rights marches roused Berkeley to near boiling point. City planning students called a strike and refused to go to classes until we were taught what we perceived as more relevant material. The elitism of professional architecture seemed repugnant to many of us. When one of our professors made disparaging remarks about the "ticky-tacky boxes" of suburban Daly City and their inhabitants, we quickly conducted a door-to-door survey. People were delighted with their homes; their views on urban aesthetics were totally at odds with what we were being taught.

This period at Berkeley radically changed my world view. Two outspoken women iconoclasts provided role models. Catherine Bauer Wurster's seminar on federal housing policies, suburban sprawl, and public housing design called into question much of what had gone before, and design professionals listened. Bauer's formal training was in English, not in the social sciences or design; she called a spade a spade and knew how to speak and write in persuasive ways. So too did Jane Jacobs, the New York journalist whose *Death and Life of Great American Cities* we consumed with relish. Here was a muckraker par excellence who looked at the changing city, and with a no-nonsense prose devoid of jargon or rhetoric, questioned what she saw.

A focus for my concerns began to emerge: I wanted to look at designed settings and find out how the user viewed and felt about them. In particular, I wanted to investigate residents' reactions to subsidized housing. But I found myself poorly prepared for what I wanted to do. Though I could interpret topographic maps, read aerial photos, and do land-use surveys, my knowledge of social research was minimal. I sought out academic advisors who could counsel me and started pursuing questions about resident needs in housing that would motivate my work for many years to come. An especially supportive mentor at this time was Melvin Webber, a professor of city planning. Under his guidance, I began to find inspiration in studies that had tangentially considered the links between the designed environment and human behavior (White, 1946; Young & Wilmott, 1957); studies that considered mental health and the environment (Taylor & Chave, 1964, Wilner, 1962); studies that specifically looked at the influence of physical settings on neighboring (Festinger, Schacter, & Back, 1950; Gans, 1961; Kuper, 1953; Madge, 1964); and those few studies, at the time, where residents were questioned about many aspects of their reactions to housing and neighborhood design (for example, Lamanna, 1964; Wilmott, 1964). Interestingly, virtually all the articles at this time that were drawing attention to the misfits between design and human needs were appearing in the pages of the *Journal of the American Institutes of Planners* (for example, Fried & Gleicher, 1961; Lamanna, 1964; Rainwater, 1966; Rossow, 1961; Seeley, 1959). This was the period when redevelopment and urban poverty were receiving close government and academic scrutiny. In city planning seminars, we read seminal authors who were questioning the standard perceptions of slums (Schorr, 1963; Seeley, 1959), challenging the goals of urban renewal (Gans, 1962), and reporting on the severe psychological stress of forced relocation (Back, 1962; Fried, 1963).

The notion of questioning housing designers about their motives and then questioning residents about the result seemed such an obvious approach that I was surprised to find few precedents in the literature. In its simplest terms, it was market research; in later terminology, it became known as postconstruction and later, postoccupancy evaluation (POE). My first large-scale POE case study was at Easter Hill Village, a public housing project in Richmond, California, dating from the 1950s. It comprises 300 two-story row houses, and its population at the time of my study (1963–1965) was mixed white, black, and Chicano. I chose to study this project because it had won several design awards and was perceived as successful by the architectural and housing professions; because its designers (Vernon de Mars, Donald Hardison, Lawrence Helprin) were know to have a "social" bias and were available locally for me to interview; and because it was accessible by public transport (I did not learn to drive or own a car until my midthirties).

The detailed results of this case study are too many to report here and appeared later as a monograph and eventually as a book (Cooper, 1965, 1975). Suffice it to say, the designers correctly predicted certain social needs and correctly translated them into physical form—for example, the need for fenced backyards for enclosing children or animals, for gardening, sitting outside, and the like. They sometimes correctly predicted a need, but the translation into form was not meaningful to the residents—for example, the need to have a house facade that looked individual—but many of the physical means employed to express this via design were not "seen" by the residents. Finally, the designers sometimes predicted a need that was not important to the residents, but the physical solution fortuitously provided for a resident need that had not been predicted—for example, a maze of footpaths for adult visiting were barely used for that purpose, but did provide highly valued routeways for children's play.

In retrospect, the methods I used at Easter Hill Village were somewhat simplistic: I interviewed only the architects and the landscape architect and thought I had obtained a full view of the design process. In a later postoccupancy study (St. Francis Square, San Francisco) my coauthor (Phyllis Hackett) and I started our study the same way but were quickly urged by one of the architects (Robert Marquis) to interview the client, housing consultant, building contractor, and so forth to obtain a more accurate overview of the complexities of the design process. A portion of that case study research that we thought would take a few weeks engaged us for 6 months and resulted in a working paper of some length and complexity (Cooper & Hackett, 1968). We learned a good lesson: Within reason allow yourself to be side-tracked; the result may be more fruitful than the direction you had set out upon.

I had chosen to focus on a housing co-op—St. Francis Square—for my second case study because it was famous locally as a highly successful social experiment. The board of directors of the pension fund of the International Longshore Workers Union used seed money from the federal government to sponsor this 300-unit, low-rise apartment project in a newly cleared redevelopment area of San Francisco known as the Western Addition. The co-op is administered by a board of directors elected from among the residents, and with the support of the adjacent black community, it has maintained an informal quota system to ensure an ethnic balance of residents—one-third black, one-third Asian, and one-third white. In the late 1960s, when our study began, it was already a favorite place for local redevelopment officials to show to visitors as a successful project. It seemed important to look at a setting that was apparently well liked and appreciated by its residents and to investigate what part design had to do with that success.

At Easter Hill Village, I had naively thought that personal interviews with residents would tell me all I needed to know about their reactions to design. By this time I had become a little more sophisticated in terms of social research. Texts had begun to appear that focused on methods of qualitative and observational research (e.g., Webb et al., 1966). On annual visits to England (still perceived then—as now—as "home"), I combed the shelves of Her Majesty's Stationery Office for the latest case studies emerging from the Sociological Research Section of the Ministry of Housing (Ministry of Housing, 1969a, 1969b, 1970); from the Building Research Station (Hole, 1966); and from the Architectural Research Unit at the University of Edinburgh (Architecture Research Unit, 1966, 1969; Gilmour et al., 1970). In these studies, interview surveys were being combined with systematic observation techniques. Soon I had an opportunity to experiment with the latter during an unexpected year's sojourn in Sweden. I spent countless days exploring the newly built Stockholm suburbs of Vällingby and Fårsta and experimenting with my own methods of unobtrusively recording activities in playgrounds, courtyards, and shopping malls. I was hooked! I found this unobtrusive observation of human behavior in public places to be totally absorbing. Although geographical fieldwork had trained me to observe the physical environment with a questioning eye and although interviewing at Easter Hill Village had thrown me into verbal communication with people about the environment, behavioral observation allowed an unobtrusive overview of human action in, toward, and with the environment while it was happening.

Thus, in this second major postoccupancy study of St. Francis Square, data collection comprised a combination of resident interviews with a random sample of residents; systematic behavior mapping of outdoor activities; recording of behavior traces; and documenting of resident changes to the environment over time. This multifaceted approach—though now standard practice—felt pioneering at the time (1969–1971). A few years later (1973–1974), my husband (landscape architect Stephen Marcus), our infant son Jason, and I moved into St. Francis Square to live in a sublet apartment for a year. While there our daughter Lucy was born, and I continued my studies of St. Francis Square as a participant observer, resident, and mother. This experience was very important in my intellectual development. Though I had read *The Urban Villagers* (1962) and *The Levittowners* (1967) by Herbert Gans, I had not appreciated how much richer were insights gained from participant observation data than from the quantitative data I had previously collected. Issues emerged that I had not dreamed of asking questions about; earlier findings that had seemed puzzling, now—with personal experience—seemed eminently "right." Our behavior mapping recordings, for example, had ceased at 8:00 P.M. because I assumed children would be inside by that time; casual observations from our third-floor balcony indicated a heavier use of the play area at 10 P.M. by teenagers than at 3:00 P.M. by children! Until I noticed myself picking up litter in "our" courtyard yet ignoring it on the public street side of our building, I did not fully comprehend the instinctual caring attitude toward shared territory that is truly communal and the relative ignoring of that seen as public. Until I documented in a journal the slowly expanding cognitive map of "our neighborhood," I had not fully appreciated the effect of time on the appropriation of space. I'm sure I did not fully appreciate residents' fear of crime in adjacent neighborhoods before I myself was held at knife point for money on a pedestrian overpass. Until this happened, I had unconsciously dismissed residents' fears as being part of their reality but not mine. Overall, the participant–observer experience was so meaningful in enhancing a deeper interpretation of data already collected, I determined never again to do a housing case study unless I could live in the setting and experience it at first hand.

Although lack of funds and family circumstances prevented me from turning the data from St. Francis Square into a book, publication of the most interesting results in the *American Institute of Architects' Journal* (with enthusiastic follow-up commentary by one of the architects) exposed my work to the profession with whom I most wanted to communicate. But I soon understood that more was needed than an occasional article in *Landscape Architecture* or the *AIA Journal*. The last chapter in my study of Easter Hill Village (which appeared as a book in 1975b) was a set of design guidelines based on those results from my work that seemed to be corroborated in other similar studies. Although the pragmatic, applied nature of this chapter pleased me, I suspected that few professional designers would ever see it because the book appeared to be—and was—a case study of one particular project.

I started work (unfunded) on drawing together the results of dozens of POE studies that by then were starting to proliferate, and turning them into design guidelines. In the late 1960s and 1970s, studies of resident views on housing and POE case studies of specific housing schemes began to appear with greater frequency, though it often took some sleuthing to locate them. A few appeared as published books (e.g., Boudon, 1972; Jephcott & Robinson, 1971) or articles in professional or academic journals (e.g., Hinshaw & Allot, 1972; Miller & Cook, 1967; Rapoport, 1968). But among the most detailed, influential, and inspiring were those that appeared as monographs published by centers for housing research, such as that at Harvard University (Zeisel & Griffin, 1975); at the University of Edinburgh (Byrom, 1972); at Cornell University (Becker, 1974); at the University of Illinois, Urbana-Champaign (Francescato, Weideman, Anderson, & Chenoveth, 1980; Saile *et al.*, 1972; Weideman & Anderson, 1979); at the University of Michigan (Lansing *et al.*, 1970); at the University of Winnipeg (O'Brien, 1972); and by quasi-governmental bodies concerned with housing markets (Norcross, 1971); or the welfare of residents (Maizels, 1961; Stewart, 1970). Traveling to give lectures at this time in schools of architecture and landscape architecture in the United States and Canada, I began to discover pioneering work appearing in unpublished senior and master's theses such as those by Ellen Bussard, Bettye Rose Connell, and Steven Tulin at Cornell (Bussard, 1974; Connell, 1975; Tulin, 1978); by Carmel Gatt at the University of British Columbia (Gatt, 1978); by John MacCleod at the University of Manitoba (MacCleod, 1977); by Julia Robinson at the University of Minnesota (Robinson, 1980); and by Mary Griffin at Brown University (Griffin, 1973). This was work I began to call "research in hiding;" but for personal contacts at conferences or on lecturing visits, I doubt that I would have discovered such studies until much later. Finally, in this search for usually nonpublished case studies, chance encounters lead to the discovery of useful in-house POE reports by architectural firms in the U.S. (Parish & Parish, 1972); in Canada (The Eikos Group, 1980); and in Britain (Ellis, 1976; Shankland Cox and Associates, 1969). Interestingly, most of this early case study work on resident reactions to housing was being done by architects or in academic departments of architecture or landscape architecture. Very little was being conducted by psychologists or sociologists. This is ironic considering the fact that now psychologists tend to be in the majority in organizations such as EDRA, and members bewail the fact that few designers attend the annual meetings. It seems to have been forgotten that it was largely professional planners and designers who started the groundswell that launched our field.

A felicitous meeting with a like-minded Canadian planner–researcher, Wendy Sarkissian, while I was on sabbatical leave in Australia in 1973, initiated a rewarding co-authorship of what later became the book, *Housing as if People Mattered: Site Design Guidelines for Medium-Density Family Housing* (1986a). We drew inspiration from current and earlier work of my architectural colleagues at Berkeley—Christopher Alexander, Sara Ishikawa, Murray Silverstein, *et al*'s *A Pattern Language* (1977); Van der Ryn and Silverstein's *The Dorms at Berkeley* (1967); Roslyn Lindheim, Helen Glaser, and Christie Coffin's *Changing Hospital Environments for Children* (1972); and Fred Osmon's *Patterns for Designing Children's Centers* (1971). They, too, as architect researchers, had struggled with the issue of making research results usable at the drawing board. Should we add "Possible Design Responses" as suggestions for how to fulfill our guidelines as Zeisel, Welch, and Demos had done in *Low-Rise Housing for the Older People: Behavioral Criteria for Design* (1977), or would designers "take offense" at being told too much? Should we word guidelines as behavioral or attitudinal statements, or as performance standards? Should we illustrate our guidelines with line drawings of ideal solutions or photographs of real situations? Although this book broke no theoretical ground, it certainly stretched our minds in terms of how to communicate research to a largely non-research-oriented audience. Our firm belief was that to communicate with another profession, one must go more than halfway to meet them. The fact that this book received positive reviews in many major American design magazines suggests that we did achieve our goal.

TEACHING: THE EARLY YEARS

In 1969, Michael Laurie—a former teacher from whom I had learned much about landscape design—encouraged me to start teaching; he felt that what I had reported in my studies of Easter Hill Village and St. Francis Square represented a missing component of design education. Nervously, I offered my first elective course in 1969; I had no conscious plan to "become a teacher." That first year, 9 people enrolled, then 17, and by the third year, the faculty proposed that this course (Landscape Architecture 140—Social and Psychological Factors in Open Space Design) become a required course for all undergraduate and graduate students in landscape architecture. The enthusiasm of those late 1960s/early 1970s students was infectious and heartening to a new teacher. A group of the first students in this course, including Mark Francis (now a professor at the University of California at Davis), resurrected a student-run magazine, Landmark, and published a handsome issue comprising excerpts from many papers written by students in LA 140. Many students saw the significance of a "user" approach to design before most of the faculty.

The same year I started teaching, I attended my first Environmental Design Research Association conference (EDRA 2, Pittsburgh). It was an enormously morale-boosting experience; I found I was not alone, delving into this emerging field-without-a-name. On contemplating teaching, I had approached the then chair of the Department of Landscape Architecture at Berkeley—an eminent designer. "Well . . . ," he said, without enthusiasm, "I hope one day we'll be able to afford such a luxury." "One day," I responded with uncharacteristic confidence, "I hope this field will be considered a necessity and not a luxury." I am happy to see, not so many years later, that courses in this field are seen as a necessity in most reputable schools of design and that the annual conference of EDRA continues to be, for most of us, a primary source of inspiration and encouragement.

My first course (LA 140) has remained the basic core of my teaching. It is one of three survey courses in this field offered at Berkeley; the other two are Environmental Psychology taught by Kenneth Craik, and Social and Cultural Aspects of Architecture, taught by Russ Ellis, Galen Cranz, and myself. Student enrollment in any or all of these courses ranges from sophomores to PhD students, requiring considerable flexibility on the part of the faculty.

My philosophy in LA 140 is to teach basic theories, concepts, methods, and research results in environment and behavior studies and to do so in a way that will appeal to design students. This means relating everything I talk about to real-life examples, illustrated with blackboard diagrams and slides. With regard to the latter, I make it a point of taking my camera almost everywhere to catch "chance" events that may one day be useful in a lecture; I also make specific photography trips—to British and Scandinavian new towns, to downtown plazas, to housing projects, and so on—whenever I am traveling. Though I am still searching for the "ideal cataloging method," my personal collection of many thousand slides is invaluable to me and is half the reason why design students in LA 140 seem to get excited about this subject matter. The other salient reason for their enthusiasm is that I insist on a considerable amount of fieldwork, which they seem to enjoy. Students observe the use of San Francisco plazas and compare the results with William Whyte's Manhattan research in *The Social Life of Small Urban Spaces* (1980); they conduct a POE of a neighborhood park of their choice using behavior mapping, behavior trace observation, and informal interviews and conclude this research exercise with a redesign of the park based on user needs. The fact that I require students to redesign helps them see the connections between research and practice.

In developing a style of teaching, I soon found that design students seem to learn most easily from observation assignments in the real world. Although lectures or reading about personal space or territorial behavior are necessary to introduce pertinent concepts, it is the observation and experiencing of such behavior that confirms and roots these ideas in students' minds. Because students are taught, in design studios—implicitly or explicitly—to draw upon personal experience when approaching design problems, it is reasonable to suggest that the most effective mode of awakening their consciousness of people–environment concepts is to do so via observing themselves and others in real environments.

For almost two decades now, students in Landscape Architecture 140 have been conducting postoccupancy evaluation studies in the parks, playgrounds, plazas, and streets of the Bay Area. Much of their work has been of a high professional standard. Inspired by their insights, I compiled a second major volume of design guidelines, together with a PhD student, Carolyn Francis. This book, entitled *People Places: Design Guidelines for Urban Open Space* (Van Nostrand Reinhold, 1990), covers such topics as neighborhood parks, mini-parks, downtown plazas, day-care outdoor space, hospital outdoor space, elderly housing outdoor space, and campus outdoor space. Several chapters are written by current and former students whose theses have focused on a specific open space topic. This book, like *Housing as if People Mattered* (1986d), is structured for use at the drawing board and is highly illustrated.

While preparing these two books for publication, I have had many debates with colleagues, co-authors, and prospective users of design guidelines about how this material might be worded, organized, illustrated, supported. Some of the results of this thinking were pulled together in a working paper entitled "Design Guidelines: A Bridge between Research and Decision-Making" (Cooper Marcus, 1986b). I feel there is much more to do on this topic—the communication of research. We need to do "postpublication evaluations" of our books and monographs: Who is using them? Which formats seem most acceptable? How might we improve the construction of this "bridge"? Although such applied work may not seem very appealing or prestigious to our colleagues in social science departments, I believe it is essential if we are to do more than talk to each other or preach to the already converted.

CONSULTING

An important component of my intellectual growth has been involvement in consulting with designers. This work—assessing existing environments that need rehabilitation, preparing design programs for newly constructed settings—forces one to evaluate, summarize, and communicate research findings to colleagues who have little time for footnotes but a pressing need for practical guidance. I have found this work to be challenging, exciting, and immensely rewarding. The rewards come from a sense of teamwork and camaraderie that I have rarely experienced in academia and from seeing the results in a tangible, socially responsive environment. I also feel I have been forced to learn a lot, often at the fast pace demanded by a design office. In an early consulting job, in which I was hired by a firm of civil engineers to develop a design program for a large, water-oriented regional park (Lake Cunningham, Santa Clara County, California), I found almost nothing to draw upon in the research literature. Rapid-fire observations of use of comparable parks in the Bay Area was all that I could do in the time available. When hired by a San Francisco architectural firm (Marquis and Associates) to be a consultant on the conversion of a defunct high-rise housing project into elderly housing, I was relieved to find Sandra Howell's (1980) eminently readable book, *Designing for Aging*. Using this, and other research-based material (Zeisel, Epp, & Demos, 1977), I was able to keep one step ahead of the design team, provide them with information in the form of charts and diagrams pinned to the walls of our brainstorming room, and critique their preliminary designs from a user perspective. At one prophetic meeting, I had Howell's book with me. "What's that?", one of the architects inquired. "Oh this . . . This is the "Bible" I'm consulting! If you read this, you wouldn't have to spend money hiring me," I responded, half in jest. They pushed the book back at me. "Oh no," they laughed, "we'd rather you read the book and tell us what it says . . ." When the job was successfully completed, I asked architect Bob Marquis why they had hired me; his response is significant for those of us in the applied side of environment and behavior studies. "Because we want you to read the literature and translate it for us. Because we think the client will be more persuaded by you than by us on user issues. Because we don't trust our own judgment in form/function tradeoffs. Because we think you can write and talk better than us. And because if you're in at the beginning, you won't be able to criticize our work in the magazines!"

In fact, I had done just this some years before. An article in the *AIA Journal*, criticizing some aspects of this firm's rehabilitation of a project at Hunters Point, San Francisco, had annoyed Marquis (Cooper Marcus, 1978a). But when some of my tentative predictions turned out to be correct, he reassessed his position on environment and behavior thinking. If this experience is anything to go by, perhaps we should more openly and frequently criticize design "solutions" in those very magazines read by designers and their peers. We need to take a few more risks—be willing to speak out when we see something questionable being built or proposed. To make a difference, it is not sufficient for us to talk to each other at EDRA or IAPS or IAAP or to publish theories and research that are only read by our academic peers.

Not all my consulting work has resulted in satisfying outcomes. Marquis and Associates and I were rehired by the San Francisco Housing Authority to create some alternative redesigns for the Hayes Valley project, a 1950s, low-rise apartment scheme in San Francisco, racked by problems of vandalism and drug dealing. Fieldwork had to be carried out surreptitiously because we were viewed as possible police informers by the drug dealers. Resident interviews were well-nigh impossible because people feared reprisals for talking with us. We developed and costed out a series of alternative redesign plans based on defensible space principles. So far, none has been implemented. If and when one is, we know that the drug-dealing problem would not be "solved," but merely be shifted to another place. As four spaced-out heroin addicts stumbled out of a boarded-up apartment on our initial site visit, we began to appreciate the comments of the project manager who told us, "Forget about architecture—get these people jobs and training, and they might not want to do drugs . . . it relieves the hopelessness for a few hours . . . " There is no easy answer for those of us who will be hired to render housing projects more secure: Do we move the problem down the block, or do we refuse the job as an inadequate band-aid solution to a complex societal problem? For my part, I will accept the job, because, like most problems, this one needs to be approached via multiple channels. If we believe (as I do) that our responsibility is primarily to those made most vulnerable by environment–behavior problems, then improving security in housing projects for the coming generation of children should be a high priority. One single-parent mother at Hayes Valley who was willing to talk with us had lost a 14-year-old daughter caught in the crossfire of a police raid; she no longer lets her other children go out to play. Waiting for the federal government and the police to solve the drug problem is no answer for those children.

Interestingly, I find that being a woman is something of an advantage in this kind of consulting: Because many low-income families are single-parent and female-headed, it is somewhat easier for a woman than for a man to gain access for interviewing. My sense is, too, that many male architects find it easier to "accept" critiques of their work from women consultants because women are "supposed to know about all that social stuff." As a woman, I am heartened by the fact there were many women pioneers in our field who saw the significance of "user needs" long before there were peers or organizations to support them. I think of Margaret Willis, a lone sociologist speaking for people's needs in the architecture department of London County Council (Willis, 1963a,b,c); Vere Hole, at the Building Research Station in Britain, a lone voice calling for consideration of children's needs in housing (Hole, 1966); feisty New York journalist, Jane Jacobs, who pointed out many of the ills of the modern city that were later confirmed by empirical research (Jacobs, 1961); Joan Maizels, a social worker in London, Pearl Jephcott and Hilary Robinson in Glasgow, and Anne Stevenson, Elaine Martin, and Judith O'Neil in Melbourne, Australia—all of whom published studies challenging the wisdom of housing families with small children in high-rise buildings, long before architects and politicians listened (Jephcott & Robinson, 1971; Maizels, 1971; Stevenson, Martin, & O'Neill, 1967). And looking to the early student theses that paved the way for what we now call postoccupancy evaluation research, a remarkable number were by women (Bussard, 1974; Connell, 1975; Gatt, 1978; Griffin, 1973; O'Brien, 1972).

Teaching and consulting will continue to be important components of my work. Both of these activities force us to keep abreast of, summarize, and communicate environment and behavior research to people outside the field. Sometimes, admittedly, the goal of educating design students and influencing the practice of design is a disheartening undertaking. Architects are trained to see the world largely through a sensory mode and strive to create settings that evoke particular feelings. Environment and behavior researchers perceive environments primarily via a functional mode and strive to understand how settings work. Though a minority of socially conscious designers does appreciate and use the burgeoning literature of design guidelines, the majority does not. Sandra Howell was right, many years ago, when she urged us to aim our applied findings at the fee-paying clients of buildings, rather than at the designers (Howell, 1974). Increasingly, I find it is clients who hire me as a consultant (or instruct the designer to do so); those who pay for, manage, and maintain designed settings have much more incentive to create satisfied users than do the architects who do their work and must often move on rapidly to another job.

In one sense, this is an exciting time to be in the applied side of environment and behavior studies. The fruits of our labors over two decades are emerging in print. Research-based guidelines on elderly housing, play areas, special hospital settings, group homes, disabled-accessible environments, and the like are appearing in book form; no longer can designers or clients complain that research is too hard to find, or read, or comprehend. On the other hand, ironically, this is an especially difficult time to interest design professionals in socially responsive design; fashion has swung away from the form–function dialogue of the modern movement, to postmodern concerns for facade design, decoration, aesthetic theory, and designer in jokes. Although the future may look good for programming consultants hired by building clients, it is a disheartening time for many of us who teach in schools of design. Form is "in"; function—let's hope only temporarily—is "out."

BENEATH THE SURFACE: THE ENVIRONMENT AS METAPHOR

Parallel with my concern for pragmatic, applied work, another part of my mind (it seems) has been hungry to explore beneath the surface of obvious functions and meanings. This urge was undoubtedly nurtured by another movement that had its beginnings in California in the 1960s—the so-called human potential movement. It seemed that residents of the most affluent state in the nation were avid to find some direction and meaning in their lives beyond career, money, and material possessions. Although initially concerned with understanding intrapsychic conflicts, most members of the much maligned "me generation" later expanded their concerns to social issues and new intellectual directions. Having been raised in a culture that discouraged the overt expression of strong emotions, I was initially drawn to workshops and lectures for purely personal reasons. Work with Fritz Perls and his colleagues at the Esalen Institute in Big Sur immeasurably expanded my consciousness of self and of others. A fortuitous meeting with a maverick Berkeley psychologist led to numerous guided experiences with hallucinogenic drugs (LSD, mescaline, peyote, etc.). My awareness of other states of consciousness was vastly expanded. I began to be interested in the phenomenon of altered states of a less extreme nature being triggered by introspective experiences in the natural world (wilderness, ocean, viewpoint, forest, running water). Though I have never formally pursued this interest, I keep journals of my experiences in, and feelings about, various natural settings. So far, these have seemed too personal to expose to more than a few friends, but eventually I expect to write about these issues more fully. In a recent experimental seminar, "Experiencing a Sense of Place" (1989), design students and I explored together the emotional and symbolic experience of viewpoints, oases, retreat spaces, and so on. This work will eventually emerge in co-authored writing; for me, the balance of an intellectual and experiential approach is essential in studying a topic such as "sense of place".

In the early 1970s, the tension between personal growth and academic concerns became more and more uncomfortable. The turning point, for me, was discovering the writing and philosophy of Carl Jung. His concepts, which seemed to fuse the experiential and the intellectual, the personal and the collective, were enormously appealing. To my dismay, I found the University of California offered no courses on Jung; I turned for my education to the Carl Jung Institute in San Francisco, workshops at various growth centers, and the shelves of Berkeley's alternative bookstores. Once again, I seemed to be plunging into an area for which I was poorly trained in a formal academic sense; this time—not because I had majored in the "wrong" subject—but because academia seemed resistant to the social and philosophical debates swirling around it. Although many social science departments at the University of California remained unyielding in their clinging to traditional concepts and methodologies, the University's Extension Division (a semiautonomous body) offered courses on Jung and other seemingly frontier topics. It was here in a course taught by a remarkable woman analyst in her 80s that I learned about Jung's life and work (Jung, 1967) and was encouraged to write a paper, "The House as a Symbol of Self," which was later reprinted in two environment and behavior readers (Cooper Marcus, 1974b, 1976). This article brought me more unsolicited letters from strangers than anything else I have ever written. The general thesis of this paper—that we express who we are not only via our appearance and clothes but via the houses in which we live—seemed rather obvious and universal in American culture. I found theoretical support from Jungian notions of symbols and archetypes, and anecdotal support from the writings of novelists, poets, playwrights, and autobiographers. Although this particular essay has been criticized by some peers as "armchair" research and not concerning itself sufficiently with sociopolitical realities (Duncan, 1982), it has had an apparent triggering effect on the thinking of others—for example, Kim Dovey's master's of architecture thesis in Australia, entitled *The Dwelling Experience* (Dovey, 1978) and to some extent his later work (Dovey, 1985); Katherine Anthony's

PhD dissertation, *International House: A Home away from Home* (Anthony, 1981), and her later work on the meaning of home to families experiencing divorce (Anthony, 1989); and Tadishi Toyama's PhD dissertation in Sweden, *Identity and Milieu* (Toyama, 1988). I am inspired by their and others' insights and see all of our studies as an emerging body of work pushing at the boundaries between consciousness and the environment.

MERGING ACADEMIC AND PERSONAL CONCERNS

I suspect it may be easier for men than for women to separate personal and family concerns from those of work and career. With the birth of two children as I continued my academic work and secured tenure at Berkeley, such a separation became impossible to maintain. Gradually, I began to see some benefits from the fusing of these two important components of my life. My long-term interest in children's environments was now expanded by observations of my own children in playground and day-care settings. My empathy for the lives of single parents was immeasurably deepened by my own entry into their ranks. Now that my own children are teenagers, I experience firsthand some of the joys and tribulations of urban life for this maligned and under-studied age group.

But most of all, it is my own experiences with self and house that have fueled and inspired my continued work on the environment as metaphor. A divorce put my own house temporarily in jeopardy and aroused such profound emotions that I was motivated to expand "The House as Symbol of Self" into something more than a maverick think piece. While in a women's group, I reencountered the Gestalt therapy technique of role playing. Listening to a woman "speak" to the Arizona desert that she had just left and profoundly missed, I had one of those prophetic "Aha!" experiences. If she could "dialogue" with an inanimate phenomenon such as the desert, could I get people to do the same with their houses? I found that I could. Once again expanding into an area that was not my own, I entered a training group led by a Gestalt therapist and learned enough about role playing to use it with some facility as a research tool.

With more than 40 dialogues between people and their dwellings completed, my understanding of this deeply emotional relationship has expanded immeasurably. I see the dwelling as a significant component of the Jungian process of individuation. It is a screen onto which we project, often unconsciously, facets of the psyche; the dialogues I conduct allow people to recognize and acknowledge that projection (Cooper Marcus, 1986c). My work in this area has developed so that my interviews comprise both research and therapy. I feel comfortable with this, because it reflects my ongoing concern to bridge the gap between theoretical and applied work.

One of the advantages of doing work on the frontier of a field is that one has freedom to develop new methods and conceptual frameworks. A distinct disadvantage is that one's work appears to fall between disciplinary cracks and funding boundaries. I am embarrassed to see the years expanding between my initial think piece and a book-length manuscript (to be completed in 1990). The fact that "fringe" work must be accomplished unfunded in one's "spare" time is a burden to be borne if one chooses an unconventional path.

My work on the house as a symbol of self began with my own involvement with and feelings for home. But there is more to the fusing of home and work, personal and professional concerns, than the easing of logistics or cognitive tensions. It seems to me that if one can take a personal issue and expand it into a study that has universal meaning, that work becomes imbued with creative passion. I never did believe in the possibility of total objectivity in social research. The older I get, the more I find I must work on topics that represent a merger of personal and academic interests, for only then do I feel whole in what I do.

TEACHING: NEW DIRECTIONS

With the encouragement of Roslyn Lindheim—an architecture professor who was challenging the traditional ways of doing architecture and who had obtained a large grant from NIMH to foster a social and cultural factors emphasis in the architecture department at Berkeley—I began teaching in that department. I offer seminars on social aspects of housing design; on design and social responsibility (co-taught with architectural historian Stephen Tobriner); on public life and a sense of place; and on environments for the life cycle (originally co-taught with the late Roslyn Lindheim and with psychiatrist–planner, Len Duhl). I co-teach graduate design studios in the landscape architecture department with Michael Laurie, and occasionally co-teach in architectural studios with Ray Lifchez, Sara Ishikawa, Sam Davis, Mui Ho, and Sandy Hirshen. I have found a subtle but discernibly more open acceptance of the social approach to design in landscape architecture than in architecture. I attribute this to a less fashion-oriented, "star designer" emphasis in landscape architecture and a long tradition of recognizing that aesthetic goals must be balanced with other requirements in landscape design (for example, ecological needs, microclimate, plant growth requirements). Thus, although I have held a joint appointment between architecture and landscape architecture for many years, I still find myself slightly more at home in the latter department.

But in one important respect the architecture department is, for me, a place of intellectual growth; here is based a PhD program that attracts outstanding students in the field of environment and behavior (or as we call it, "social factors in design"). Together with faculty colleagues Russell Ellis and Galen Cranz (sociologists who teach in the architecture department) and a core of 6 to 10 doctoral candidates, I form part of the social factors emphasis in that department. These are the students who stretch our minds and keep us on our toes. Many are foreign students who conduct their dissertation research in their home countries: Recently graduated students include Gunawan Tjahjono who did his dissertation on symbolism in traditional Javanese architecture and returned to his faculty position in Indonesia; Gerald Magutu, who wrote a dissertation on squatter settlements in Kenya and returned to teach in architecture at the University of Nairobi; and Amita Sinha who did her dissertation research on women and children's use of the environment in a traditional and a modern housing development in an Indian town and is currently teaching at the University of Illinois, Urbana. As in any academic department, it is the PhD students who are perhaps the greatest stimulus to intellectual growth. My years as an adviser to Kim Dovey, for example, were ones that expanded my consciousness in many areas. Although he is now back in Australia on the faculty at the University of Melbourne, Dovey and I are currently working on a co-authored paper on experiments in Dutch cooperative housing (Dovey & Cooper Marcus, 1990). Closer to home, I have co-authored with current PhD candidate Carolyn Francis (Cooper Marcus, Francis, & Meunier, 1987a; Cooper Marcus & Francis, 1990) and expect to do more of this in the future.

A very significant influence on my teaching was a workshop in which I was a participant with 27 students from the College of Environmental Design in 1977. This was a "taking part" workshop led by Lawrence Halprin with Sue Young Li Ikeda of Roundhouse, San Francisco. For 9 days we lived and workshopped together at Sea Ranch (Northern California Coast) and then in San Francisco. Lawrence Halprin, internationally known landscape designer, had led such workshops for many years, both with students and with communities engaged in participatory planning and design. In the introduction to a report on this workshop, Halprin wrote of his philosophy as a teacher:

> My own interests have increasingly focused on the interaction between people and their environment—not one without the other, but what happens to each in response to the interaction between the two. . . . Instead of telling students what I think and know and trying to impart knowledge *to* them, I felt it would be a more meaningful learning experience if we could explore together the essential qualities of the human/environment interaction. . . . The workshop leader is not called upon to transmit information. Instead he/she establishes the nature and location of interactions, helps students penetrate their own experience, and then helps valuact (evaluate) that experience. . . . A willingness to communicate one's own experiences to the group become essential . . . it requires not only being open to the experience itself but being able to externalize the experience . . . you are asked to have the trust necessary to reveal your feelings and experiences to others. . . . In sum, these interactions produce a whole new dynamic which results in a group as well as individual set of experiences—a phenomenon which I call "collective creativity." (Halprin, 1979, pp. 7–8)

In this workshop, we took part in a sensory walk and recorded our experiences in haikulike statements; we chose places in the landscape for life and for death and communicated them via drawings; we explored the relationship between the body and land forms; we broke into male and female groups and communicated via a dramatic performance how we experienced a particular environment; we created personal spaces on a beach, and then—without words—planned and created a community space. The experience of these 9 days still resonates with me as I bring modified forms of these exercises into studio and seminar teaching.

My teaching goals early on in my career consisted almost exclusively of introducing design students to environment and behavior research. It was the era of user needs; I wanted my students to be more attuned to socially responsive environments. As I became more aware of how my own background and experiences had influenced the direction of my work, I realized that my approach to consciousness raising among design students left out one very important person—the student him/herself. Starting first with a favorite childhood place exercise that Robin Moore and I introduced into a studio dealing with play design, I expanded this into experiences about other remembered environments and finally into a paper, "Environmental Autobiography," which I now require in almost every class. The interest that this paper arouses (among students admittedly not enamored of writing!) and the often profound insights into the influence of past environments on current values convince me that this is an essential exercise. Just as therapists need to go through psychoanalysis to understand their own emotional biases, so too, I believe, must design students understand their values and where these have come from in order not to impose biased solutions onto their clients.

It is intriguing to note that this exercise evolved simultaneously at several places before we knew of each other's work: it was introduced by Robin Moore and myself in landscape architecture at Berkeley (Cooper Marcus, 1978b, 1979); by Kenneth Helphand, Department of Landscape Architecture, University of Oregon (Helphand, 1977, 1978); by Florence Ladd at the Graduate School of Design at Harvard (Ladd, 1977); and by Randy Hester, Department of Landscape Architecture, University of North Carolina (Hester, 1979). No doubt it proves to be a particularly appropriate exercise for landscape students because the favorite childhood places recalled are frequently outdoor environments and the insights gained have immediate potential application in outdoor design for children.

After some years of assigning this paper in a large survey course, students began to ask for more, though what "more" was neither they nor I was sure. I developed a seminar, Personal Values and Design, in which the whole class revolved around the environmental autobiography. Breaking with tradition, we never met on campus. With a limit of 10 graduate students, we met one evening per week in students' homes for the 10-week quarter. Each class began with the student presenting his or her home as a "mirror of self"—in many cases we saw a different aspect of that person than was revealed on campus. A different guided fantasy exercise each week helped students (and me) reveal layer upon layer of their values as they related to environmental design. These were recorded in individual journals. Close to the end of the class, students swapped journals and "constructed" ideal dwellings for each other on a San Francisco beach. Some students reported that this was one of the most revealing classes they had taken; a few changed their career directions as a result. Ironically, I felt I had to keep the true nature of this seminar half obscured from my colleagues, who I feared would judge it as too "'60s, touchy-feely." However, word got around among the students, and the course never wanted for participants, despite its somewhat ambiguous catalog description.

In teaching, as in research, I have sometimes felt the need to push the boundaries of what is considered "appropriate." I don't believe academia has a corner on learning; indeed it does well at accumulating and disseminating knowledge and theory but poorly at nurturing wisdom. Just as the medical profession is beginning to look guardedly at alternative healing practices (acupuncture, herbal cures, visualization, stress-reducing techniques, and so on), so, I believe, must we be open to a range of approaches for harmonizing people and environments. Empirical research on people–environment relations is only one answer. In a recent seminar on sense of place, not only did we spend half of each meeting in an environment, recording sensations and feelings that we later analyzed in class, we also brought to the class experts and practitioners in Eastern and Western methods of environmental sensing (feng-shui, geomancy, dowsing). The fact that these methods have never been fully explained in a scientific sense is of no consequence to me; the fact that they are age-old methods for the propitious siting of buildings is all the more reason to consider them. We need always to bear in mind that the scientific method is useful for discovering only those truths that can be revealed by the scientific method; that leaves out a lot of other phenomena—some of which are surely of concern to us in the environment and behavior field.

INTROSPECTION AS INSPIRATION

Academic training in social research encourages us to be objective, to be rational, to quantify—in short, to exercise our left brain functions. "Feminine" intuition, introspection, and convergent thinking are acceptable if you are a poet or novelist but barely so in environment and behavior research. In teaching students whose primary mode is intuitive and visual, however, I have found it necessary to create assignments that allow them to exercise these talents, as well as those that are more objective. For example, before conducting a detailed POE of a neighborhood park, I ask design students first to write about how they experience the park via the senses of sight, smell, and sound; and second, I ask them to "become" the park and to write what it feels about itself. Remarkably, many—in this short paragraph—correctly grasp the essence of the park's assets or problems. Later these issues are confirmed by more objective data collection and analysis. I am not suggesting that in my own work, or in my teaching, I have given up on rational/objective approaches but rather that I now strive to blend the rational with the intuitive/subjective in order to shape a more holistic approach.

I believe that right brain intuitive thinking needs support and exercise, the more so for those of us in academia. My own retraining in these modes of thought took place while residing for a year in the alternative community of Findhorn in Scotland. I had gone there for two reasons: because I was personally attracted to its philosophy of nondogmatic spiritual seeking and because I was intrigued by its remarkable success as a community. I had no desire to spend my sabbatical at an academic institution, absorbing more of the same. After brief visits to attend workshops at Findhorn, I knew that I could only come to know the richness of this remarkable community by living and working within it, not as an academic trying to study it from some pretended objective viewpoint. This is the first lesson I learned there—the value of surrender: To understand the community and what it exemplifies, one must fully experience and immerse oneself into the daily flow of life, surrendering all preconceptions. To surrender does not mean ignoring the responsibilities of work and daily life but to be totally open and receptive to whatever is happening.

Though not the path for everyone, for myself, the encouragement of open awareness and intuitive insight seemed a necessary balance to the heady rationality of academia. To "go within" and listen to the innate wisdom of one's own inner teacher may have little place in the university; all the more reason to seek guidance elsewhere. In his perceptive study *The New Gnosis* (1984), Robert Avens defines gnostic knowledge as "the knowledge of the soul," or as Jungian James Hillman puts it, "a seeing through . . . a moving from the surface of visibilities to the less visible" (Hillman, 1975, pp. 140–141). Thus gnostic knowledge, meditative insight, and some aspects of phenomenological enquiry might be thought of as aids to seeing things as they really are. Avens writes:

> Heidegger's concept of phenomenology implies a radical reversal of our habitual subjectivistic and scientific way of thinking: it is not we who "objectively" decide what things are; things themselves speak and how themselves if they are let be in their own manner of being. (Avens, 1984, p. 29)

Or as Vycinas eloquently described his interpretation of the phenomenological attitude—"a respectful stand in face of reality which allows this reality to appear on its own way. We do not dictate reality, reality dictates us" (Vycinas, 1969, p. 29).

My lack of formal training in philosophy or psychology prevents me from adding anything useful to the academic debate on the nature and meaning of phenomenology. I am fascinated, however, with how those debates seem to be part of an overriding contemporary concern at many levels of humanity with the notion of "bridging the gap." The middle and later decades of this century seem to be characterized as never before by movements seeking balance between seemingly opposite points of view: the struggle for a balance between communism and democracy in eastern Europe, China, and the U.S.S.R.; environmental movements seeking a more healthy balance between economic growth and ecological renewal; animal rights and other forms of activism aimed at replacing an exclusively human-centered viewpoint with one that is life centered. In many Western, industrialized societies, the last few decades have seen the emergence of civil rights movements seeking a balance between majority and minority viewpoints and feminist movements seeking to redress imbalances inherent in patriarchal societies. In our own academic circles, we have witnessed debates concerning the differences between phenomenological psychology and empirical psychology (Kockelmans, 1971), between humanist and positivist geography (Christensen, 1982), and between phenomenological and empirical approaches in environment and behavior research (Seamon, 1987). Finally, few who have attended the annual meetings of EDRA could have avoided the "bridging the gap" debate between design and social science, between practice and theory, between application and research.

The parallels between the quantitative/qualitative debate in the social sciences and the reductionist/holistic debate in the natural sciences are revealing. In the past decade, numbers of books accessible to the layperson have explored holistic science and the analogies between emerging thought patterns in physics and traditional Eastern mystical beliefs. Among these are Fritjof Capra, *The Tao of Physics* (1975a), Gary Zukar, *The Dancing Wu Li Masters: An Overview of the New Physics* (1979), and Paul Davies's *God and the New Physics* (1983). Faced with phenomena that could not be "explained" in normal scientific terms, many physicists turned to modes of awareness that are remarkably similar to parts of Buddhist holistic philosophy. David Bohm, in his pivotal work, *Wholeness and the Implicate Order*, described the new approach thus:

> A centrally relevant change in descriptive order required in the quantum theory is thus the dropping of the notion of analysis of the world into relatively autonomous parts, separately existent but in interaction. Rather, the primary emphasis is now on "undivided wholeness," in which the observing instrument is not separated from what is observed. (Bohm, 1980, p. 134)

Living in the Findhorn Community—where there is every encouragement to experience "undivided wholeness"—gave me the support I was unconsciously seeking to develop new modes of relating to the world. Science and the modes of thinking that it gives rise to have trapped us in a partial mode of seeing. What is happening at Findhorn, where people seek to live and be in a more balanced way is but a reflection of what is happening in a more global sense as we challenge the scientism of the last few centuries and explore a new way of relating to the world that has been termed *the new paradigm*.

THE NEW PARADIGM

Findhorn, although the best known of today's alternative communities, is certainly not alone in its embracing and promotion of new ways of living and relating to the world. It is only one of hundreds of such communities, worldwide (McLaughlin & Davidson, 1986); only a small but visible component of a significant paradigm shift that many have written about (Capra, 1982; Davies, 1983; Keys, 1982; Russell, 1982; Smith, 1984; Thompson, 1982).

The so-called "old paradigm" had its beginnings in the scientific and industrial revolutions and gradually replaced the predominantly ecclesiastical model of the Middle Ages. To know the world, its proponents argued, we don't have to accept what the church tells us. We must stand apart and observe the world objectively. We must set aside self, emotion, and feeling and discover the true nature of the world via vigorous observation, documentation, and quantification. Parallel with the rise of this mode of thought, people began to see the world around them as raw material for manufacturing and processing. The physical environment was put at a convenient cognitive and affective distance so that we could more easily observe, evaluate, and exploit it. As a consequence, much of humanity lost its understanding of our profound affective connections to the natural environment. The old view of the world as Mother Earth, an intimate part of who we are, had to be replaced.

But—many observers have argued—the tide is beginning to turn again. The environmental movement, feminism, and the resurgence of interest in ancient spiritual practices (shamanism, Taoism, Sufism) are indications that our intimate holistic links with Nature are beginning to be rediscovered. In a paper published in *Landscape*, I suggest that the current revival of interest in Britain in dowsing, ley-lines, and sacred sites and the current interest in the United States in Chinese geomacy (*feng shui*) are perhaps glimmers of a return to traditional views of interconnectedness with the environment that were swept under the rug by the scientific revolution because they could not be "proved" (Cooper Marcus, 1987). Western medical practice, with its emphasis on the treatment of symptoms with drugs, is being challenged by the holistic health movement and its concern for treating the whole person. The significance of the natural environment itself as a healing medium is being rediscovered (Ulrich, 1984, 1986). Business is looking to new modes of decision making and corporate structure. Within environment and behavior research, changes are beginning to appear comparable to those already cited but so far with little public discussion.

All of these trends, and many more, are part of a subtle but profound shift of consciousness, the end result of which—many argue—is to effect a more balanced, holistic world view. Without it we may be doomed as a species. This is not a political movement in the usual sense of that term; it has no leader or dogma. It is rather a gradual, undirected, unfolding of a new ethos, a new set of assumptions on which to base our views of the world and everything in it. Findhorn is but a microcosm of this larger movement. But it is an important one because by visiting and living in this community (it hosts about 4,000 guests annually) one can experience first hand how this new world view feels, how it is to live it. In that respect, the community can be looked upon as a social experiment, a colony of the future where new ways of relating to each other, to community, and to the physical environment around us can be "tried on for size."

Findhorn and Berkeley continue to be the two critical poles of my life. They represent not so much opposites as complements of each other. At each, I try to bring to the setting a little of what the other has to offer. Occasionally, I bring experiences of meditation and guided fantasy into my seminars and studios at Berkeley. Before I left Findhorn, I found myself conducting resident workshops and a survey on future housing needs; the community had just purchased land and needed to make plans for the future. With a little reluctance, I attempted to merge the intuitive awareness mode of Findhorn with the more rational mode of Berkeley. Nominated as a Findhorn Fellow, I continue to visit the community and offer advice, when appropriate, on housing and planning issues. I now feel comfortable in this balanced approach both at Findhorn and at Berkeley. A paper on Findhorn at EDRA (Cooper Marcus, 1985) and an invitation to contribute a chapter on the community to a book edited by David Seamon have enabled me to express in an academically acceptable medium the insights I have experienced while immersing myself in this extraordinary community (Cooper Marcus, 1990). I doubt that I will ever again write about a setting without immersing myself within it as a participant observer. My year's residence at St. Francis Square began to teach me that. My stay at Findhorn confirmed it: Only via the combination of objective knowledge and intuitive awareness-as-participant can people–environment interactions on a community scale be comprehended in all their complexity and richness.

FUTURE WORK

The house and housing have been abiding interests in my work. A discovery that I shared with two students—a fascination for visiting model homes in new suburban subdivisions—led to a jointly authored article in 1987, "Mixed Messages in Suburbia: Reading the Suburban Model Home" (Cooper Marcus, Francis, & Meunier, 1987). My continuing interest in this area will, I hope, lead to further jointly authored work on this topic.

In the near future, I expect to explore more fully the links between housing and a sense of community. A Guggenheim Fellowship will enable me to spend the 1989–1990 academic year developing case studies of a range of settings known for their sense of community. I will live briefly as a participant–observer in several housing co-ops in Denmark and The Netherlands; a "family hotel" in Sweden; a communal suburban neighborhood in Illinois; an alternative community in rural California; an energy-saving subdivision in Davis, California. I am deliberately focusing on highly successful projects. My observations in these settings, together with work already completed at Findhorn and St. Francis Square, will contribute to an analysis of what appear to be the design and organizational communalities among all these places. By the intimate observation of settings known for their sense of community, I hope to draw some conclusions of use to designers and planners in the future.

This study will hopefully expand into work of perhaps even greater import: recommendations for the redesign of the American suburb. In the near future, the enormous suburban expansions of the 1950s will come under scrutiny as areas of renewal and densification. Debate in the U.S. architectural world has recently focused on a new form of suburban development in Seaside, Florida, a small "new town" drawing its inspiration from Main Street and small-town America. Though built primarily for the wealthy (and currently largely a second-home community), Seaside breaks new ground in terms of building codes and zoning. Earlier, in Davis, California, Village Homes broke new ground as a solar energy and ecologically oriented suburban subdivision. Current suburban experiments in southern California are turning to recycling, sustainable landscapes, and energy-conserving design. The publication of an attractive book, Co-Housing: A Contemporary Approach to Housing Ourselves (McCamant & Durrett, 1988), has introduced American audiences to the many successful experiments in shared living in Denmark. Small groups in Berkeley, San Francisco, and Seattle have formed to create similar communities in their cities. It is clearly a time for experimentation and debate: Seaside is not for everyone, nor is Village Homes. The future will hopefully expand choices in suburban living so that different life-styles and family-types can find the most suitable settings for themselves. This is an important time for us as environment and behavior researchers to turn our attention to suburbia and not to be afraid to make recommendations, to write for the popular press, and to spark intelligent debate on how Americans might want to live in the twenty-first century.

The more I investigate environment–behavior interactions, the more I am convinced of the need to delve more deeply into the emotional and health components of people's experience. Among the most exciting work I have encountered in recent years is that by geographer, Robert Ulrich (currently at Texas A & M). His research indicating that postsurgery patients with a view of exterior greenery recover more quickly than those with a view to buildings, seems to me to be an important breakthrough (Ulrich, 1984, 1986; Ulrich & Simons, 1986). A recent unpublished study of my own asking more than 100 undergraduate and graduate students where they might go in the public domain if they were upset or depressed confirmed a marked preference for natural settings (beach, park, trail, and viewpoint). As our cities (and probably, too, our older suburbs) become more densely built up, the visual, symbolic, air quality, and stress-reducing aspects of accessible natural areas will become more and more important. It will be incumbent upon our field to supply proof of the value of these spaces, for budget-strapped cities and profit-conscious corporations, developers, and hospital boards are unlikely to be convinced by aesthetics alone. With an aging population (some of us among them!), the provisions of elderly housing, nursing homes, and geriatric hospital settings with sensitive access (visual and functional) to green spaces may be a small but vital component of reducing stress, promoting health, and enhancing the quality of life in later years. For adolescents and young adults, a wilderness, hiking, or mountaineering trip may be a pivotal experience in enhancing feelings of self-esteem. For those in the crucial middle years of childhood, near-home access to explorable natural settings may have untold repercussions in enhancing capacities for imagination and creativity. One critical area of environment and behavior studies to which I hope to contribute is, then, the significance of natural settings for the health and emotional well-being of human beings.

Another allied area that I will continue to pursue will be the affective component of person/home relations. The many dialogues I have conducted between people and their present (or past) homes convince me of the profound, barely understood salience of dwelling/person interactions. Bachelard's justly famous book, *The Poetics of Space* (1964), and psychiatrist Harold Searles' lesser known volume, *The Non-Human Environment in Normal Development and Schizophrenia* (1960), awakened our consciousness to levels of person/environment connections beyond the everyday. However, the number of studies confirming or expanding their insights has been minimal. Are we as leary of dealing with emotion in our professional work as we are sometimes in our personal lives? Is the investigation of "satisfaction" with an environment sufficient, or does it suggest—in part—a suspicion of feelings more deeply expressed? We need to devise new methods for tapping and understanding the often profound connections between people and their homes, gardens, neighborhoods, and "special places." If people are willing to lay down in front of bulldozers to save beloved trees or risk their lives to relcaim their neighborhood from drug dealers or to prevent further exploitation of tropical rainforests by cattle barons, there are clearly emotions at play as deep as those expressed for other human beings. It seems unlikely that any field but our own will ever feel motivated to investigate these feelings. At a global scale, our understanding of such connections may be critical to our very survival as a species.

Beyond the emotional connection of person and place, there is—for some people in some places—a connection even more difficult to describe or prove. This might be termed a spiritual or psychic connection. Certainly the Druids felt it (or created it?) at Stonehenge; many Japanese sense it at Mount Fuji; many traditional peoples experience and revere it at sacred places and holy mountains. My own work and writing on this theme has focused on the island of Iona, off the west coast of Scotland. I have been drawn back to its shores many times. In using myself—my feelings and perceptions—as a "receptor," I am trying to understand why so many people sense this particular island as "magic." Although I am not quite ready to go public with this work, I sense that one day, the time and my writing will be right.

A recent California conference on "sacred space" (Davis, California, 1988) brought together a remarkable collection of academics, artists, writers, outdoor educators and Native Americans. For them, there is no doubt of the sacred dimension of people–environment relations. This is a dimension and subfield of our profession we need to recognize. Whether scientific proof will ever be forthcoming is problematic. Documentation may be more significant at this stage, and this task may have profound political and cultural significance as the sacred places of different subgroups begin to be recognized and legally protected. A sacred place may be every bit as important to a culture as home is to the individual.

And what of that environment sacred to us all—planet Earth? News of the Gaia hypothesis (Lovelock, 1979), proposing that the planet itself is a self-regulating organism, seems barely to have touched academia, let alone the field of environment and behavior studies. An inspiring 1988 conference on the topic in San Francisco was addressed by theologians, psychologists, feminists, and philosophers, and met in a Unitarian church. Whether the Gaia hypothesis can ever be proven seems less important than acknowledging its power as a myth to guide us. Global warming, oceanic pollution, acid rain, nuclear accidents—these and other phenomena are warning us that unless we recognize and curb our assaults on Gaia, we may not survive. Surely this symbol is one worthy of our attention as researchers in the field of environment and behavior. Are we able and willing to deal with the environment at all scales from the house lot to the planet? Are we able and willing to address human concerns from the most pragmatic to the emotional to the spiritual? These—it seems to me—are the critical questions for our immediate future.

REFERENCES

Alexander, C., Ishikawa, S., Silverstein, M. *et al.* (1977). *A pattern language.* New York: Oxford University Press.

Anthony, K. (1981). *International House: Home away from home?* Unpublished doctoral dissertation, Department of Architecture, University of California.

Anthony, K. (1989). *Breaking up is hard to do: The meaning of home to parents and children of divorce.* Paper presented at the International Housing Symposium, Gavle, Sweden.

Architecture Research Unit. (1966). *Courtyard and houses, Inchview, Prestonpans.* Edinburgh: University of Edinburgh.

Architecture Research Unit. (1969). *Traffic separated layouts in Stevenage New Town.* Edinburgh: University of Edinburgh.

Avens, R. (1984). *The new gnosis.* Dallas: Spring Publications, Inc.

Bachelard, G. (1964). *The poetics of space.* New York: Orion Press.

Back, K. W. (1962). *Slums, projects and people: Some psychological problems of relocation in Puerto Rico.* Durham, NC: Duke University Press.

Becker, F. D. (1974). *Design for living: The resident's view of multifamily housing.* Ithaca, NY: Center for Urban Development and Research, Cornell University.

Bohm, D. (1980). *Wholeness and the implicate order.* London: Routledge & Kegan Paul.

Boudon, P. (1972). *Lived-in architecture: Le Corbusier's Pessac revisited.* Cambridge: MIT Press.

Bussard, E. (1974). *Children's spatial behavior in and around a moderate density housing development: An exploratory study of patterns and influences.* Unpublished master's thesis, Department of Design Analysis, Cornell University.

Byrom, J. B. (1972). *Shared open space in Scottish private enterprise housing.* Edinburgh: Architecture Research Unit, University of Edinburgh.

Capra, F. (1975). *The tao of physics.* Berkeley: Shambhala.

Capra, F. (1982). *The turning point: Science, society and the rising culture.* New York: Simon & Schuster.

Christensen, K. (1982). Geography as a human science: A philosophic critique off the positivist-humanist split. In P. Gould & G. Ollson (Eds.), *Search for common ground.* London: Pion Press.

Committee on Housing Research and Development (1972). *Families in public housing: An evaluation of three residential environments in Rockford, Illinois.* (Research Report). Urbana-Champaign: University of Illinois.

Connell, B. R. (1975). *Behavioral science research for design decision-making: The processes of programming and evaluation and an evaluative case study of multi-family housing.* Unpublished master's thesis, College of Human Ecology, Design and Environmental Analysis, Cornell University.

Cooper, C. C. (1965). *Some social implications of house and site plan design at Easter Hill Village: A case study.* Center for Planning and Development Research. Berkeley: University of California.

Cooper, C. C. (1970a). Adventure playgrounds. *Landscape Architecture, 18–29,* 88–91.

Cooper, C. C. (1970b). To Zima Junction and beyond: A journey across Russia on the Trans-Siberian Express. *Landscape.*

Cooper, C. C. (1971a). Landmark '71. *Annual Student Journal of Landscape Design Club,* Department of Landscape Architecture. Berkeley: University of California.

Cooper, C. C. (1971b). St. Francis Square: Attitudes of its residents. *AIA Journal,* 22–27.

Cooper, C. C. (1971c). *The house as symbol of self.* (Working paper #120.) Institute of Urban and Regional Development. Berkeley: University of California.

Cooper, C. C. (1972). Resident dissatisfaction in multi-family housing. In W. M. Smitth (Ed.), *Behavior, design and policy aspects of human habitats* (pp. 119–145). Green Bay: University of Wisconsin.

Cooper, C. C. (1974a). Children in residential areas: Guidelines for designers. *Landscape Architecture, 65,* 372–377, 415–419.

Cooper, C. C. (1974b). The house as symbol of self. In J. Lang (Ed.), *Design for human behavior* (pp. 130–146). Stroudsburg, PA: Dowden, Hutchinson & Ross.

Cooper, C. C. (1975a). Children's play behavior in low-rise, inner city housing development. In D. Carson (Ed.) (*EDRA 6*) (pp. 197–211). Washington, DC: Environmental Design Research Association.

Cooper C. C. (1975b). *Easter Hill Village: Some social implications of design.* New York: The Free Press.

Cooper, C. C. (1976). The house as symbol of the self. In H. M. Proshansky, W. H. Ittleson, & L. G. Rivlin (Eds.), *Environmental psychology: People and their physical settings* (pp. 435–448, 2nd ed.). New York: Holt, Rinehart & Winston.

Cooper, C. C., & Hackett, P. (1968). Analysis of the design process at two modern income housing developments. (Working paper #80.) Center for Planning and Development Research. Berkeley: University of California.

Davies, P. (1983). *God and the new physics.* New York: Simon & Schuster, Inc.

Department of the Environment (U.K.). (1971). *New housing in a cleared area: A study of St. Mary's oldham.* (Design Bulletin 22). London: Her Majesty's Stationery Office.

Department of the Environment (U.K.) (1972). *The estate outside the dwelling: Reactions of residents to aspects of housing layout.* (Design Bulletin 25). London: Her Majesty's Stationery Office.

Department of the Environment (U.K.) (1973). *Children at play.* London: Her Majesty's Stationery Office.

Dovey, K. (1978). The dwelling experience: *Towards a phenomenology of architecture.* Unpublished master of architecture thesis, University of Melbourne, Australia.

Dovey, K. (1985). Home and homelessness. In I. Altman and C. Werner (Eds.), *Home environments: Human behavior and environment* (pp. 33–64). New York: Plenum Press.

Dovey, K., & Cooper Marcus, C. (1990). Designing for community, (unpublished, forthcoming).

Duncan, J. (1982). *Housing and identity: Cross-cultural perspectives.* New York: Holmes & Meier, Inc.

The Eikos Group (Planning and Environmental Design Group Ltd., Vancouver). (1980). *Children's perceptions of a play environment: A study of three low cost housing developments in Vancouver.* (Research Project 4 for International Year of the Child). Ottawa: Canada Mortgage and Housing Corporation.

Ellis, P. (1977). *A social psychological study of the outside spaces in the Chalvedon housing area.* London: Ahrends, Burton and Kuralek, Architects.

Festinger, L., Schacter, S., & Back, K. (1950). *Social pressures in informal groups: A study of human factors in housing.* New York: Harper & Row.

Francescato, G., Weidemann, S., Anderson, J. R., & Chenoweth, R. (1980). *Residents' satisfaction in HUD-assisted housing: Design and management factors*. Washington, DC: U.S. Government Printing Office.

Fried, M. (1963). Grieving for a lost home. In L. Duhl (Ed.), *The urban condition* (pp. 151–171). New York: Basic Books.

Fried, M., & Gleicher, P. (1961). Some sources of residential satisfaction in an urban slum. *Journal of the American Institute of Planners, 27,* 305–315.

Gans, H. (1961). Planning and social life: Friendship and neighbor relations in suburban communities. *Journal of the American Institute of Planners, 27,* 134–140.

Gans, H. (1962). *The urban villagers*. Glencoe, IL: Free Press.

Gans, H. (1967). *The Levittowners*. New York: Pantheon.

Gatt, C. (1978). *Privacy in private outdoor spaces in multi-family housing projects*. Unpublished master's thesis, Department of Architecture, University of British Columbia.

Gilmour, A., Byrom, C., Campbell, S., Helgason, I., & Liddell, H. (1970). *Low-rise high density housing study*. Edinburgh: Architecture Research unit, University of Edinburgh.

Griffin, M. E. (1973). *Mount Hope courts: A social physical evaluation*. Unpublished American civilization senior honors thesis, Brown University.

Halprin, L. (1979). *A report on taking part at College of Environmental Design*. Berkeley: Center for Environmental Design Research, University of California.

Helphand, K. (1977). *Environmental autobiography: An anthology* (mimeo, unpublished).

Helphand, K. (1978). Environmental autobiography. *Childhood City Newsletter, 14,* 8–11.

Hester, R. (1979). A womb with a view. *Landscape Architecture, 69,* 475–481.

Hillman, J. (1975). *Re-Visioning Psychology*. New York: Harper & Row.

Hinshaw, M., & Allot, K. (1972). Environmental preferences of future housing consumers. *Journal of the American Institute of Planners, 38,* 102–107.

Hole, V. (1966). *Children's play on housing estates* (National Building Studies research paper no. 39). London: Her Majesty's Stationery Office.

Howell, S. (1974). Needed: Performance specifications for using behavioral science. *Industrialization Forum, 5,* 25–29.

Howell, S. (1980). *Designing for aging: Pattern of use*. Cambridge: MIT Press.

Jacobs, J. (1961). *Death and life of great American cities*. New York: Random House.

Jephcott, P., & Robinson, H. (1971). *Homes in high flats: Some of the human problems involved in multi-storey housing*. Edinburgh: Oliver and Boyd.

Jung, C. (1967). *Memories, dreams, and reflections*. London: Fontana.

Keys, D. (1982). *Earth at Omega: Passage to planetization*. Boston: The Branden Press, Inc.

Kockelmans, J. J. (1971). Phenomenological psychology in the United States: A critical analysis of the actual situation. *Journal of Phenomenological Psychology, 1,* 139–172.

Kuper, L. (1953). Blueprints for living together. In L. Kuper (Ed.), *Living in towns* (pp. 7–202). London: Cresset Press.

Ladd, F. C. (1977). Residential history: You can go home again, *Landscape, 21,* 15–20.

Lamanna, R. A. (1964). Value consensus among urban residents. *Journal of the American Institute of Planners, 30,* 317–323.

Lansing, J., Marans, R. W., & Zehner, R. B. (1970). *Planned residential environments*. Ann Arbor: Institute for Social Research, University of Michigan.

Lindheim, R., Glaser, H., & Coffin, C. (1972). *Changing hospital environments for children*. Cambridge: Harvard University Press.

Lovelock, J. (1979). *Gaia: A new look at life on earth*. London: Oxford University Press.

MacLeod, J. (1977). *Open space and walk-up apartments: A case study of user needs and landscape design*. Unpublished practicum for master's degree. Department of Landscape Architecture, University of Manitoba, Winnepeg. Mimeo.

Madge, J. (1964, December). *Privacy and social interaction*. Paper delivered to the Bartlett Society, Mimeo.

Maizel, J. (1961). Two to five in high flats. London: The Housing Center.

Marcus, C. Cooper (1977). User needs research in housing. In S. Davis (Ed.), *The form of housing* (pp. 139–170). New York: Van Nostrand Reinhold.

Marcus, C. Cooper (1978a). Evaluation: Rehabilitated housing at Hunter's Point. *American Institute of Architects' Journal, 67,* 48–55.

Marcus, C. Cooper (1978b). Remembrances of landscape past. *Landscape, 22,* 34–43.

Marcus, C. Cooper (1978c). Evaluation: A tale of two spaces. *American Institute of Architects' Journal, 67,* 34–39.

Marcus, C. Cooper (1979). *Environmental autobiography.* (Working paper #301). Institute of Urban and Regional Development. Berkeley: University of California.

Marcus, C. Cooper (1985). Environment and community: A case study of Findhorn, an alternative community in Scotland. In S. Klein, R. Werner, & S. Lehman (eds.), *Environmental Change/Social Change: Proceedings of 16th Annual Conference of EDRA* (pp. 144–154). New York: EDRA.

Marcus, C. Cooper (1986a). Design as if people mattered. In S. Van Der Ryn & P. Calthorpe (Eds.), *Sustainable design* (pp. 121–129). San Francisco: Sierra Club Books.

Marcus, C. Cooper (1986b). Design guidelines: A bridge between research and decision-making. In W. H. Ittleson, M. Asai, and M. Ker (Eds.), *Cross cultural research in environment and behavior: Proceedings of the 2nd U.S.-Japan seminar* (pp. 56–83). Tucson: University of Arizona (Reissued as a paper by Center for Environmental Design, Berkeley: University of California, 1986).

Marcus, C. Cooper (1986c). House-as-haven, house-as-trap: Explorations in the experience of dwelling. *Proceedings of annual conference of Associated Collegiate School of Architecture.*

Marcus, C. Cooper (1987). Alternative landscapes: Ley lines, Feng-Shui, and the Gaia Hypothesis. *Landscape, 29,* 1–10.

Marcus, C. Cooper (1988). Pink palace to Rosa Parks Towers: High rise rehabilitation using environment and behavior research. *Looking back to the future: Proceedings of the 10th Biennial Conference of the International Association for the study of People and their Physical Surroundings (IAPS)* (pp. 411–420). Delft: Delft University Press.

Marcus, C. Cooper (1990a). Designing for a commitment to place: Lessons from the alternative community Findhorn. In D. Seamon (Ed.), *Dwelling, seeing and building: Toward a phenomenological ecology.*

Marcus, C. Cooper (1990b). The garden as a symbol of planet earth. In R. Hester and M. Francis (Eds.), *The meaning of the garden.* Cambridge: MIT Press.

Marcus, C. Cooper & Francis, C. (Eds.). (1990). *People places: Design guidelines for urban open space.* New York: Van Nostrand Reinhold.

Marcus, C. Cooper, & Hogue, L. (1977). Design guidelines for high-rise family housing. In D. J. Conway (Ed.), *Human response to tall buildings* (pp. 240–277). Stroudsburg, PA: Downden, Hutchison and Ross, Inc.

Marcus, C. Cooper, & Moore, R. (1976). Children and their environment—A review of research. *Journal of Architectural Education, 29,* 22–25.

Marcus, C. Cooper, & Sarkissian, W. (1986d). *Housing as if people mattered: Site design guidelines for low rise medium-density family housing.* Berkeley: University of California Press.

Marcus, C. Cooper, & Wischemann, T. (1987b). Open spaces for living and learning. *Landscape Architecture, 77,* 52–61.

Marcus, C. Cooper, Francis, C., & Meunier, C. (1987a). Mixed messages in suburbia: Reading the suburban model home. *Places, 4,* 24–37.

Miller, A., & Cook, J. (1967). Radburn estates revisited: Report of a user study. *Architect's Journal, I.*

Ministry of Housing and Local Government (U.K.). (1969a). *The family at home: A study of households in Sheffield.* London: Her Majesty's Stationery Offfice.

Ministry of Housing and Local Government (U.K.) (1969b). *Family houses at West Ham: An account of the project with an appraisal.* London: Her Majesty's Stationery Office.

Ministry of Housing and Local Government (U.K.). (1970). *Families living at high density: A study of estates in Leeds, Liverpool and London.* London: Her Majesty's Stationery Office.

McCamant, K., & Durrett, C. (1988). *Co-housing: A contemporary approach to housing ourselves.* Berkeley: Habitat Press.

McLaughlin, C., & Davidson, G. (1986). *Builders of the dawn: Community lifestyles in a changing world.* Shutesbury, MA: Sirius Publishing.

Norcross, C. (1973). *Townhouses and condominiums; Residents' likes and dislikes.* (Institute Special Report). Washington, DC: Urban Land Institute.

O'Brien, N. J. (1971). *A comparative behavioral study of row housing developments.* Institute of Urban Studies, University of Winnipeg, Winnipeg, Canada.

Osmon, F. L. (1972). *Patterns for designing children's centers.* New York: Educational Facilities Laboratories.

Parish, S., & Parish, D. (1972). *A study of four Bridgeport housing developments.* Bridgeport, CT: Zane Yost and Associates.

Rainwater, L. (1966). Fear and the house-as-haven in the lower class. *Journal of the American Institute of Planners, 32,* 23–31.

Rapoport, A. (1968). The personal element in housing: An argument for open-ended design. *Royal Institute of British Architects' Journal, 75,* 300–307.

Robinson, J. W. (1980). *Images of housing in Minneapolis: A limited study of urban residents' attitudes and values.* Unpublished master's thesis, Department of Architecture, University of Minnesota.

Rosow, I. (1961). The social effects of the physical environment. *Journal of The American Institute of Planners, 27,* 127–133.

Saile, D. G. et al. (1972). *Families in public housing: An evaluation of three residential environments in Rockford, Illinois.* Champaign: Housing Research and Development Program, University of Illinois.

Russell, P. (1982). *The awakening earth: The global brain.* London: Routledge & Kegan Paul.

Seamon, D. (1987). Phenomenology and environment-behavior research. In G. T. Moore and E. H. Zube (Eds.), *Advances in environment, behavior, and design* (pp. 3–27). New York: Plenum Press.

Seeley, J. R. (1959). The slum: Its nature, uses and users. *Journal of the American Institute of Planners, 25,* 7–14.

Searles, H. (1960). *The non-human environment in normal development and schizophrenia.* New York: International Universities Press.

Schorr, A. (1963). *Slums and social insecurity.* Washington, DC: U.S. Department of Health, Education and Welfare. Social Security Administration.

Shankland Cox and Associates. (1969). *Private housing in London: People and environment in three Wates housing schemes.* London: Author.

Smith, H. (1984). *Beyond the post-modern mind.* Wheaton, IL: Theosophical Publishing House.

Stevenson, A., Martin, E., & O'Neil, J. (1967). *High living: A study of family life in flats.* Melbourne: Melbourne University Press.

Stewart, W. F. R. (1970). *Children in flats: A family study.* London: National Society for the Prevention of Cruelty to Children.

Taylor, S., & Chave, S. (1964). *Mental health and environment.* London: Longmans.

Thompson, W. I. (1973). *Passages about earth.* New York: Harper & Row.

Thompson, W. I. (1982). *From nation to emanation: Planetary culture and world goverance.* Findhorn, Scotland: Findhorn Publications.

Toyama, T. (1988). *Identity and milieu.* Stockholm: Department of Building Function Analysis, Royal Institute of Technology.

Tulin, S. J. (1978). *Residents' use of common areas in condominium developments.* Unpublished master's thesis, Department of Environmental Analysis, Cornell University.

Ulrich, R. (1984). Views through a window may influence recovery from surgery. *Science, 224,* 420–421.

Ulrich, R. (1986). Human responses to vegetation and landscapes. *Landscape and Urban Planning, 13,* 29–44.

Ulrich, R., & Simons, R. P. (1986). Recovery from stress during exposure to everyday outdoor environments. In J. Wineman, R. Barnes, & C. Zimring (Eds.), *The cost of not knowing: Proceedings of the 17th Annual Conference of EDRA* (pp. 115–122). Washington, DC: EDRA.

Van der Ryn, S., & Silverstein, M. (1967). *The dorms at Berkeley.* Berkeley: University of California, Center for Planning and Development Research.

Vischer, J., & Marcus, C. Cooper (1982). Design awards: Who cares? In P. Bart, A. Chen, & G. Francescato (Eds.), Knowledge for design: Proceedings of the 13th international conference of the Environmental Design Research Association (pp. 210–223). College Park, MD: EDRA.

Vischer, J., & Marcus, C. Cooper (1986). Evaluating evaluation: Analysis of a housing design awards program. *Places: A quarterly journal of environmental design, 3,* 66–85.

Vycinas, V. (1969). *Earth and gods: An introduction to the philosophy of Martin Heidegger.* The Hague: Martinus Nijhoff.

Wallace, A. C. F. (1952). *Housing and social structure.* Philadelphia: Philadelphia Housing Authority.

Webb, E. J., Campbell, D. T., Schwartz, R. D., & Sechrest, L. (1966). *Unabtrusive measures: Nonreactive research in the social sciences.* Chicago: Rand McNally.

Weidemann, S., & Anderson, J. (1979). *Resident heterogeneity in multi-family housing: A source of conflict in space.* Urbana-Champaign: Housing Research and Development Program, University of Illinois.

White, L. E. (1946). *Tenement town.* London: Jason Press.

White, R. W. (1957). *A study of the relationship between mental health and the residential environment.* Unpublished master of city planning thesis, Massachusetts Institute of Technology, Cambridge, MA.

Whyte, W. (1980). *The social life of small urban places.* Washington, DC: The Conservative Foundation.

Willis, M. (1963a). Designing for privacy: (1) What is privacy? *The Architects' Journal, 137,* 1137–1141.

Willis, M. (1963b). Designing for privacy: (2) Overlooking. *The Architects' Journal, 137,* 1181–1187.

Willis, M. (1963c). Designing for privacy: (3) Personal relationships. *The Architects' Journal, 12,* 1231–1236.

Willmott, P. (1964). Housing in Cumbernauld—Some residents' opinions. *Journal of the Town Planning Institute, 50,* 195–200.

Wilner, D. M., Walkley, R. P., Pinkerton, T. C., & Tayback, M. (1962). *The housing environment and family life: A longitudinal study of the effects of housing on morbidity and mental health.* Baltimore: Johns Hopkins Press.

Yancey, W. (1971). Architecture, interaction and social control: The case of a large-scale public housing project. *Environment and Behaviour, 3,* 3–21.

Young, M., & Willmott, P. (1957). *Family and kinship in East London.* London: Routledge & Kegan Paul.

Zeisel, J., & Griffin, M. E. (1975). *Charlesview housing: A diagnostic evaluation.* Cambridge: Architecture Research Office, Harvard University.

Zeisel, J., Epp, G., & Demos, S. (1977). *Low rise housing for older people: Behavioral criteria for design.* U.S. Department of Housing and Urban Development. Washington, DC: U.S. Government Printing Office.

Zuckar, G. (1979). *The dancing Wu Li Masters: An overview of the new physics.* New York: Bantam New Age Books.

6

Environmental and Personality Psychology

TWO COLLECTIVE NARRATIVES AND FOUR INDIVIDUAL STORY LINES

KENNETH H. CRAIK

I WAS BORN IN PAWTUCKET, RHODE ISLAND, on April 10, 1936. My parents, Margaret Conlon and Robert Craik, were first-generation Americans. My maternal grandparents had come from counties Cavan and Monaghan in Ireland; my paternal grandmother was born in Rosemarket, Wales, whereas my paternal grandfather, Henry Craik, was born in Tweedmouth, in the border district linking England with Scotland. My wife, Janice, also born in Pawtucket, and I were married in Providence in 1957; she earned her BA degree in English at the University of California at Berkeley in 1962. Two of our children, Jennifer and Kenneth, have received their undergraduate degrees from the University of California at Berkeley, while Amy is now beginning her studies at Reed College.

I was educated in the public school system in Pawtucket. I majored in psychology at Brown University, receiving my BA degree, magna cum laude, with honors in psychology, in 1958. I was privileged to participate in an experimental program, "the identification and criticism of ideas," which entailed small seminar courses with senior faculty and the use of original sources for much of the first and second undergraduate years. While at Brown, I was a Francis Wayland Scholar, a James Manning Scholar, and was elected to Phi Beta Kappa in my junior year.

In 1956–1957, I was a psychiatric aide at the Rhode Island Hospital for Mental Diseases, as it was then called, and in 1957–1958, a social worker for the Division of Public Assistance in Providence. Both positions made me more sensitive to issues of social ecology than did my undergraduate and graduate training in psychology. I had, just barely, managed to resist the temptation of an interdisciplinary major in American civilization. Following my graduation from Brown, Jan and I spent the summer bicycling across the United States, from New England to Nebraska, experiencing some of the diversity of our culture and its environments.

KENNETH H. CRAIK • Institute of Personality Assessment and Research, University of California at Berkeley, Berkeley, California 94720.

We were heading for Berkeley, where I then earned a PhD in psychology in 1964. There I gained research training in personality and social psychology and professional training in clinical psychology, with internships at the VA Neuropsychiatric Hospital, in Menlo Park, and the VA Mental Hygiene Clinic, in San Francisco. As a graduate student, I had become associated with the Institute of Personality Assessment and Research (IPAR), led by its founding director, Donald W. MacKinnon. By the time I was awarded my PhD, Nevitt Sanford, who had been IPAR's founding associate director, had left to establish a research center at Stanford University. I was fortunate to be appointed to the vacant joint position in IPAR and the Department of Psychology, continuing my association with both units to this day.

I enjoyed admirable support at Berkeley when my research interests turned toward the new field of environmental psychology and was encouraged to take part in its development. I have served as founding president of the Division of Environmental Psychology of the International Association of Applied Psychology, president of the Division of Population and Environmental Psychology of the American Psychological Association, and was founding co-editor of the *Journal of Environmental Psychology*. At the University of California at Berkeley, I have served as director of IPAR and as chair of the faculty of the College of Letters and Science. During 1970–1971, I was senior postdoctoral fellow in environmental psychology in the joint geography–psychology program at Clark University, which afforded an exceptional opportunity to broaden my background in geography and natural resources management. More recently, a sabbatical leave award from the James McKeen Cattell Fund has allowed me to spend a year in London attempting to organize my interests in environmental, personality, and social psychology and in history and to formulate contextual approaches to the study of persons.

INTRODUCTION

Intellectual histories of individuals hold the promise of conveying something about collective history, in the instance of this volume, about the field of environment and behavior, its community of practitioners, and its history. The recounting of individual and collective histories exemplifies the narratory character of human existence, which is receiving increasing acknowledgment by philosophers of history (Carr, 1986; White, 1984) and psychologists (Sarbin, 1986). Persons tend to give accounts of actions and other events in storied form, and narratory activity is held to be a constituent feature of human action and experience (Carr, 1986; Mink, 1978; Passmore, 1987; Sarbin, 1986).

Of course in pure narrative, there is a storyteller in a retrospective position who knows the entire plot (beginning, middle, and end). However, Carr (1986) argues that our experiences of our own actions possess a quasi-retrospective character that corresponds to the future perfect tense; thus although they unfold in time (and often in unanticipated ways), our intended actions at the outset are envisioned by us from the retrospective of their having already been completed. Thus we seek in daily life to create our own plots (Mancuso & Sarbin, 1983) and self-narratives (Gergen & Gergen, 1983), "constantly striving with more or less success to occupy the story-teller's position with respect to our own lives" (Carr, 1986, p. 127).

At the level of individual life histories, the extent to which the narrative constitutes a single, overarching coherent story remains an open question

(McAdams, 1988; Runyan, 1982). In pure narrative, the plot not only provides a principle of organization but also a basis for exclusion of the extraneous; in life, everything is left in. Carroll (1988) has taken a skeptical stance on the claim that entire life stories have a single narrative structure but joins Carr in noting that

> individual events and actions are storied; and these stories, in turn, compose storied or configured chains, even though these chains are interrupted and crisscrossed by other storied events. Out of the multiplicities of our doings, we separate out story-lines, each constituted by intentions, retentions, protensions, recollections, and projections. (Carroll, 1988, p. 302)

For this essay, I have selected four story lines from my intellectual history. Two serve to illustrate the influence of personality psychology upon environmental psychology; two illustrate the subsequent influence of environmental psychology upon personality psychology.

In preparing this account, I have come to realize that to convey these four story lines succinctly, I must draw upon a fifth story line concerning my role as a framer of collective narratives. Carr (1986) has argued that just as the first person singular question, "Who am I?", can be answered in terms of self-narratives, so also the first person plural question of social entities, "Who are we?", can be and typically is addressed in terms of collective narratives, both with regard to the contemporary structure of group action and with reference to group identity.

> A community in this sense exists by virtue of a story which is articulated and accepted, which typically concerns the group's origins and its destiny, and which interprets what is happening now in the light of these two temporal poles. (Carr, 1986, p. 128)

In 1977, I offered a collective narrative on the development of environmental psychology (Craik, 1977). This collective narrative provides the context for my first set of individual story lines regarding the extension of the personality research paradigm into environmental psychology. In 1986, I presented another collective narrative in the form of an historical perspective upon the development of personality research methods (Craik, 1986a). This collective narrative offers a framework for my second set of individual story lines, illustrating the subsequent influence of environmental psychology upon my current approach to personality psychology. The collective narratives were offered by me as a member of these two scientific communities, seeking to render our present and future endeavors more comprehensible in light of our pasts but not as a professional historian—a distinction of some importance (Carroll, 1988; Lowenthal, 1985). The exercises were also manifestations of my long-standing intellectual interest in the psychology of time (Craik, 1964; Craik & Sarbin, 1963) and my disposition to be historically minded (Craik, 1988a,b).

COLLECTIVE NARRATIVE I: THE INVASION OF THE PARADIGMS IN THE DEVELOPMENT OF ENVIRONMENTAL PSYCHOLOGY

By the mid-1970s, I had been observing the emergence of environmental psychology as a distinct field of scientific inquiry for a decade. My interest in my own research program was equalled by my fascination with the development of the new field as a whole and with its prospects (Craik, 1966, 1970, 1973a).

My vantage point for considering the nature and fate of environmental psychology was the Institute of Personality Assessment and Research (IPAR) at the University of California in Berkeley, where I had served a research apprenticeship while also receiving training in clinical and social psychology within the Department of Psychology. The institute's founding director, Donald W. MacKinnon (Craik, Gough, Hall, & Helson, 1989) and associate director, R. Nevitt Sanford (1980), had been at Harvard University in the 1930s together, when Gordon W. Allport had published his classic textbook in personality psychology (Allport, 1937), and they had worked with Henry A. Murray on the influential *Explorations in Personality* (Murray, 1938). Thus a sense of continuity with the historical origins of personality psychology as a distinct field of inquiry in the United States was very much present in the intellectual environment of the institute. I soon discerned how the mid-1960s were to environmental psychology what the mid-1930s had been to personality psychology. I considered myself privileged to be a participant–observer in the creation of a new field.

The institute's research program was responsible for my serendipitous acquaintance with environmental psychology. By 1964, IPAR had completed an intensive assessment study of creative architects (Hall & MacKinnon, 1969; MacKinnon, 1978). The project had yielded important new knowledge concerning the personality characteristics that differentiate more and less creative architects, but little was known about how these dispositions bore upon the everyday pressures and conduct of architects. I had completed my PhD dissertation in January, 1964, and was awaiting appointment in July to a joint position in the department and at IPAR left open when Nevitt Sanford was called to Stanford University to establish a new research center. In the meantime, I was happy to take on a project, conceived by MacKinnon, to conduct an informal field study of the principal architect of a San Francisco Bay Area firm who had served in the sample of creative architects assessed at IPAR.

Thanks to the openness of the architect, Charles Warren Callister, and his associates, this task expanded into an exploration of the functioning of the architectural firm (Craik, 1968a, 1969b). It soon became evident that the architects in this moderate-sized firm were intrigued by having a research psychologist on the premises, and I was introduced to the questions architects asked and those they failed to ask (Gutman, 1965–1966) at that time. The firm had earned its reputation for outstanding design on the basis of small projects such as residences, schools, and churches. But when I arrived, it had underway the planning and design of an entire retirement village for several thousand persons and was competing for the master planning of a valley in southern California envisioned as the future residence of tens of thousands.

Instead of interacting closely with families during the design of their new residence, the architects were now dealing with intermediary clients on large-scale projects whose residents could only be identified subsequent to design and construction. This new administrative and social distance from their ultimate user–clients provoked many inquiries to me from the psychologically minded members of the firm. Moreover, during the frequent quiet periods in my observations of drafting room activities, I had an opportunity to note and ponder these issues, as well as other unquestioned psychological assumptions that appeared to guide planning and design decisions. Although the psychological research literature had not yet dealt with these matters, it was clear that available concepts and methods were at hand to address many of them (Craik, 1966).

Thus it was that my personal discovery of environmental psychology occurred *in situ* rather than through reading and discourse with other psychologists. However, a young architect at the firm, Daniel Solomon, now a prominent practitioner and professor, had introduced me to a friend from Stanford University named David Stea (1987), who was even then a step or two ahead of me and had offered his first course in environmental psychology in 1964. Initially through him, I became linked to the emerging network of pioneers in the environment and behavior area. My primary teaching in the department was in personality psychology, but I soon established a graduate seminar in environmental psychology and then established our undergraduate course in that field.

Although debate had centered at that time upon the proper name for the new field, *environmental psychology* was obviously the correct term at Berkeley, where the Departments of Architecture, City and Regional Planning, and Landscape Architecture had recently grouped themselves into the new College of Environmental Design. The generic concept *environmental* was the topic of much discourse and controversy but to a largely liberating and exciting effect. Thus Berkeley immediately provided supportive colleagues, such as Robert Twiss and Burt Litton (Twiss & Litton, 1966), and informed graduate students, such as Brian Little in my first and Clare Cooper Marcus in my second seminar on environmental psychology.

What I had managed to learn about the new field was summarized in an essay (Craik, 1970) that attempted to gather together the disparate remnants available at the time and to display them with as much assurance as possible, as if they constituted the coherent fabric of a distinctive discipline. Soon the *Annual Review of Psychology* was ready to acknowledge environmental psychology with a review chapter (Craik, 1973a), but by the mid-1970s the field showed a number of puzzling attributes.

During my first decade of observing it, environmental psychology had become a vigorous and bewilderingly diverse research area. Unlike the case of some other urgent societal problems that seemed unable to generate productive research programs, examination of the psychological facets of person–environment relations had quickly taken hold scientifically. But at the same time, research meetings and conferences revealed serious misgivings about the state of our new field. Environmental professionals complained about the esoteric nature of research reports and their sometimes seeming lack of relevance. Researchers published stocktaking pieces regretting the lack of a common conceptual framework (Altman, 1973; Wapner, Kaplan, & Cohen, 1973; Wohlwill, 1973). Others expressed disappointment in the carryover of research as usual and the failure to generate fresh approaches distinctively fitting to the person–environment context (Sommer, 1973).

I had been far from alone in speculating about how Kuhn's (1962) concept of paradigm and his formulation of the development of science might apply to contemporary psychology. In his analysis, the unit that produces scientific knowledge is a group of practitioners bound together by common apprenticeship and education, aware of each other's work, displaying consensus on technical judgments, and committed to the refinement, articulation, and extension of a shared paradigm. Not merely a theory, the paradigm is generated by exemplary achievements whose elaboration sets an agenda of worthwhile puzzles entailing precision of measurement, testing of predictions, conceptual clarification, and applications to new contexts (Kuhn, 1962). In their development, scientific fields move from a preparadigmatic stage to the typically prevailing state of paradigmatic or normal science, and then sometimes on to a revolutionary state of paradigm crisis or succession.

While on a family retreat in the autumn of 1975 to an old cabin on the edge of Echo Summit overlooking the Lake Tahoe Basin, I had a chance to read the proceedings of a London conference on Kuhn's work. In them, Margaret Masterman (1970) had contributed the argument that particularly in the social sciences, a multiple paradigmatic stage must be recognized, during which several strands of normal science are spun concurrently. For me, her perspective immediately clarified the nature of mainstream scientific psychology, within which a number of research traditions could be identified. More important, I could interpret the current intellectual–scientific structure of environmental psychology at that time as an array of autonomous and distinctive strands of normal science undertaking that had separately invaded the realm of person–environment relations and found engaging puzzles within that context.

This analysis of the developmental–historical pattern of environmental psychology accounted for several features that characterized the field in the mid-1970s. The invasion of mature research traditions was an asset in facilitating its early and noteworthy scientific productivity, by providing an effective readiness to identify researchable puzzles and the conceptual and methodological equipment for addressing them. At the same time, the multiple paradigm structure severely challenged researchers to communicate not only with other disciplines and professions but also across several distinctive research guilds. Finally, the ready extension of established research paradigms carried the threat of cognitive and strategic rigidity and a possible thwarting of efforts to view person–environment relations in new and more appropriate ways.

I presented this formulation at the International Congress of Psychology in Paris in 1976, illustrating it with six paradigms: ecological psychology, environmental perception, environmental assessment, personality and the environment, environmental cognition, and functional adaptation (Craik, 1977). The paradigms drew upon other fields as well as psychology (e.g., geography, landscape architecture), whereas ecological psychology was perhaps more accurately viewed as an early settler rather than a recent invader. Daniel Stokols (1978) adapted this framework for the second environmental psychology chapter in the *Annual Review of Psychology*, and I have employed it in organizing my undergraduate course.

The multiple invasion of paradigms was compelling to me autobiographically because my major research programs during this decade represented the extension of the personality assessment paradigm in two ways: the observational assessment of environments and the assessment of persons' environmental dispositions.

INDIVIDUAL STORY LINE: OBSERVATIONAL ASSESSMENT OF ENVIRONMENTS

My initial research interest was drawn to the question of how we can systematically study the ways in which persons comprehend their everyday physical environments and how we can use their descriptions and evaluations in the systematic assessment of places (Craik, 1966, 1968b, 1971, 1972a, 1973b). In doing so, I sought to extend to environmental psychology what I had learned at IPAR about the observational assessment of persons.

The institute had been established in 1949 with the purpose of studying highly effective persons through the assessment center method. In IPAR's personality assessment program, a group of 10 to 12 participants are brought together to interact with a staff of 10 to 12 assessors and each other at a center for 1 to several days. Various specific assessment procedures can be employed, including life history interviews, projective techniques, personality scales and inventories, and situational tests (such as the Leaderless Group Discussion, Role Improvisations, and the game of Charades) (MacKinnon, 1978). In addition, the assessment program constitutes an overarching social occasion, with informal interaction between participants and staff members at meals and social hours.

Earlier assessment programs (e.g., Murray, 1938; OSS Assessment Staff, 1948) had made use of the impressions formed by staff members of each participant in subsequent staff discussions, termed *diagnostic councils*. The IPAR research team had at the outset committed itself to making more systematic use of the independent judgments of each staff member, which would then be combined quantitatively. For example, new procedures were developed at IPAR to facilitate the comprehensive debriefing of staff members concerning their individual impressions of each participant, including Gough's *Adjective Check List* (Gough & Heilbrun, 1965) and Block's (1978) *California Q-Set*. Block (1961) had also advanced a compelling case for use of the aggregated judgments independently made by staff members, whose composite reliability can rival the reliability of personality scales.

For the undergraduate course I taught in personality assessment, I had developed a conceptual model to organize the issues raised by the observational assessment of persons, identifying the major facets of the problem. That is, to understand any observer-based description or evaluation of a person one must consider who made the assertion (observer characteristics), by what means the assessed person was presented to the observers (media of presentation), by what method the observers' impressions had been recorded (response format), and by what criteria the impressions might be appraised for validity or accuracy.

I soon recognized that this conceptual framework applied equally well in analyzing observers' impressions of places and that it could organize and guide an interesting research program in environmental psychology (Craik, 1968b). I subsequently published the schemes for both persons and places (Craik, 1971, Tables 2 and 3) in order to highlight the analogous relationships. In both cases, the distinction between trait attribution and trait designation is clarifying. If an observer asserts that "Person X is dominant" or "Place Y is cozy," then researchers can treat the assertion as a trait attribution and examine the influences and processes that led the observer to make it. This avenue of research leads to the study of person perception and environmental perception. However, if a panel of observers displays adequate composite reliability regarding the same statements, then they can be treated as trait designations and considered for research purposes as denoting properties of the person or place assessed. This use of consensual designations contributes an important approach to personality assessment (Wiggins, 1973) and environmental assessment (Craik & Feimer, 1987).

My Berkeley colleagues in landscape architecture, Twiss and Litton (1966), had recognized that landscape arises from the interplay between material reality (landform and land use) and the human observer. In collaboration, we began exploring response formats to facilitate the recording of observers' experiences and impressions of landscape, an interest I still hold (Craik, 1986b). The *Landscape Adjective Check List*, a 240-item procedure, for example, draws upon the rich descriptive terminology of ordinary language (Craik, 1971, 1972a, 1975).

The next step in the research agenda flowing from this conceptual model called for examination of the influence of observer characteristics and media of presentation upon the impressions observers form of everyday environments (Craik, 1968b). Once again, my good fortune in collaborators held true. I had met Donald Appleyard in 1966 when I gave a talk in the research seminar series, Psychology and the Form of the Environment, which Stephen Carr had organized at MIT. Shortly thereafter, Appleyard came to Berkeley to take a joint appointment in the Departments of City and Regional Planning and Landscape Architecture. He brought with him his interest in dynamic environmental simulation through the use of tiny lens probes moving through scale models of environments and quickly assembled preliminary laboratory equipment to explore this medium of presentation. Our mutual interests in environmental perception generated a research program, supported by the National Science Foundation, that combined the framework of observational assessment with the aim of appraising alternative media of presentation, including simulations to be produced by a new and more advanced Berkeley Environmental Simulation Laboratory (BESL) (Appleyard & Craik, 1978; Bosselmann & Craik, 1987).

The research program was ambitious in scope and complexity. A study site in Marin County as selected, and a 9-mile standard auto tour through it was identified. At the BESL, a scale model of the site was constructed, a new gantry and camera carriage was engineered, new lens probes designed, and stop-frame computer-guided film methods introduced. A battery of observational assessment formats was developed, including the *Environmental Adjective Check List* and the *Regional Q-Sort Deck*, and instruments were selected for assessing observer characteristics. Simulated film and videotaped tours through the scale model were made, to be compared with real-world tours. Samples from the general public and environmental professionals were recruited (total $N = 1,148$) who were then randomly assigned to one of the media of presentation. They came to our research field station in Marin County in groups of about 25 for day-long assessment sessions. Our experience with this project was taxing and exhilarating, as model makers, lens designers, engineers, filmmakers, computer technicians, environmental researchers, and research psychologists worked together on it. Our filmmaker, John Dykstra (1977) later won an Academy Award for special effects when he continued his innovative use of computer-guided simulations from scale models in the film "Star Wars."

The research had two major aims. The first was to gauge the psychological effectiveness of the dynamic simulations; the second was to estimate the influence of observer characteristics and media of presentation upon environmental perception and cognition (Appleyard, 1977; Craik, 1983; McKechnie, 1977). Descriptive and evaluative responses showed extremely high similarity between the auto tour and the filmed simulation; cognitive spatial measures somewhat less so. Observer characteristics, assessed by an array of personality, attitude, and background variables, were revealed to exert far more influence upon environmental impressions than did media of presentation (Bosselmann & Craik, 1987; Bryant, 1984; Craik, 1983; Feimer, 1979, 1984).

The death of Donald Appleyard at the age of 54 in a highway accident in Athens in 1982 was a stunning loss for us at Berkeley personally and for our field (Anthony, 1983; Craik, 1983). Fortunately, our colleague Peter Bosselmann has continued the operation and program of the BESL, realizing much of what we initially envisioned for it in research and applied use, and more besides (Bosselmann, 1983; Bosselmann & Craik, 1987).

The research program on the Marin County site dealt with factors that influence observers' impressions and judgments of environments. When adequate composite reliability is demonstrated for them, the same kinds of measures can focus upon the environments represented, affording observer-based assessments of places. A major application of observational assessments of environments is found in research and planning regarding natural and urban landscapes (Craik, 1973b; Daniel & Vining, 1983; Zube, Sell, & Taylor, 1982). The typical data sets in these studies are large and complex, entailing samples of observers, samples of landscapes, varied media of presentation, and multi-item and often multiform response formats. Our research program at Berkeley has sought to clarify the psychometric principles and forms of pertinent data analysis for these assessment studies (Craik & Feimer, 1979, 1987; Feimer, Smardon, & Craik, 1981; Smardon, Feimer, Craik, & Sheppard, 1983).

A second role for observational assessment of environments occurs in the devising and understanding of indices for environmental quality. In 1974, I had served on a panel of the National Academy of Sciences–National Academy of Engineering (1975) on planning for environmental indices of the kind called for by the 1970 U.S. National Environmental Policy Act (NEPA). Most of the participants were drawn from the environmental sciences and public health. As we went around the table giving our recommendations, my turn came last, and when it did, I attempted to make the obviously neglected case for observer-based indices of environmental quality, pointing out that for each physically based index (e.g., for water quality, air quality), complementary experiential indices could be devised, whereas for some if not all cases, they were indeed definitive (e.g., scenic quality, noise pollution). After failing initially to make much headway, I slipped into referring to perceived environmental quality indices (PEQIs), and suddenly facial expressions of understanding and even open-mindedness shined around the table.

I was scheduled to spend the following year on sabbatical leave at the Institute for Man and Environment (IME) at the University of Massachusetts at Amherst. IME was directed by Ervin H. Zube, whom I had met among a remarkable gathering of geographers and environmental psychologists at Clark University during a year of residence in 1970–1971. An account of that exciting period is given in a recent special issue of the *Journal of Environmental Psychology* (Canter & Craik, 1987). The notion of environmental quality indices was very much on Zube's mind, and indeed he had established a center within IME that reviewed the adequacy of all environmental impact statements required by the State of Massachusetts' equivalent of NEPA. Zube was not only experienced in observational assessment research (Zube, 1974) but alert to the policy issues that would be relevant to PEQIs.

We quickly organized a series of research workshops at IME exploring the role of PEQIs for the domains of ambient (air, water, sound), institutional (residential, work), and natural (scenic, recreational) environments (Craik & Zube, 1976). Later we formulated research for coastal zone PEQIs (Zube & Craik, 1978) for which unfortunately we have been unable to secure funding, whereas the Carps have extended the concept to the assessment of neighborhood quality (Carp & Carp, 1982). Most recently, Karl M. Dake and I, with colleagues in architecture, have been applying the PEQI conceptual framework to the assessment of thermal annoyance and comfort in office environments (Craik, 1987b; Craik & Dake, 1988).

INDIVIDUAL STORY LINE: ASSESSING ENVIRONMENTAL DISPOSITIONS

My initial research program in environmental psychology had adapted techniques for the observational assessment of persons to guide research on the experience and assessment of places. My second focus was a more straightforward extension of the personality research paradigm to the task of assessing persons with regard to their orientations toward the everyday physical environment.

By the mid-1960s, personality scales and inventories constituted a mature and relatively well-understood method of personality research. The technique had been deployed for assessing interindividual differences among persons across an array of traditional domains of personality variables, including interpersonal traits (e.g., dominance), intrapsychic dynamics (e.g., self-acceptance), personal values, cognitive capacities and styles, vocational interests, social attitudes, and psychopathological propensities. Indeed, the California Psychological Inventory (CPI), one of the most effective and widely used multiscale personality inventories, had been constructed at IPAR by Harrison G. Gough (1957).

Assessing how persons vary in the ways they tend to experience and act toward the everyday physical environment had been neglected by this research tradition, however. I noted how the development of a Pastoralism Scale, for example, might capture individual differences with regard to the major theme of American cultural and intellectual history, that is, the idyllic vision of the rural environment (Craik, 1966). Two of our Berkeley graduate students, Brian Little and Nancy Marshall, were already undertaking the development of procedures to assess thing versus person orientation (Little, 1976a,b) and orientations toward privacy (Marshall, 1970, 1972).

In the meantime, I had advocated the construction of a multiscale environmental trait inventory but at the same time pointed out the formidable challenge of generating an appropriate new item pool for which few precursors were available (Craik, 1970). In 1968, Theodore R. Sarbin (Allen & Scheibe, 1982), my colleague in social psychology who had chaired my PhD dissertation committee in 1964, one day introduced me to a new graduate student in psychology he had recruited from Wesleyan University. George E. McKechnie was keen to gain experience in constructing personality scales and had an interest in aesthetics and the environment. The problem of assessing environmental dispositions had found its master, and McKechnie set about with skill and industry to develop the Environmental Response Inventory (ERI) (McKechnie, 1972, 1977a, 1978). McKechnie also played a major role with Appleyard and myself in formulating the early research program at the BESL (McKechnie, 1977b); its first research project was officially entitled "Environmental Dispositions and the Simulation of Environments."

The final version of the ERI (McKechnie, 1974) is an excellent state-of-the-art 184-item inventory that assesses eight environmental dispositions and a test-taking index: pastoralism, urbanism, environmental adaptation, stimulus seeking, environmental trust, antiquarianism, need privacy, mechanical orientation, and communality.

In mapping out the possibilities of extending the technique of personality scales to environmental psychology, I had also noted the promise of taking the reflexive position (Little, 1972) and treating every person as an amateur environmental scientist and policymaker (Craik, 1966, 1970). Taking an implication from that stance, I have more recently undertaken the development of environmental attitude and belief scales when conducting research with David M. Buss and Karl M. Dake on perceptions of technologies and preferences regarding their societal management.

We began with the personological assumption that individuals do not respond to specific technologies (such as refrigerators, nuclear power plants, genetic engineering, movie special effects) in a psychological vacuum but rather as part of a broader sociotechnological environment, which encompasses not only technological processes and their artifacts but also the societal decision-making structure for their development, deployment, and management (Buss, Craik, & Dake, 1987; Craik, 1985b). We also worked from the observation that over the past three decades, changes in industrial societies have presented citizens with a host of issues worldwide in scope around which individual attitudes may form: resources, population, environment, technology, economic development, energy, and risk. We have assumed that persons take a stance toward this evolving issues complex in more or less organized and coherent fashion guided by wide-ranging contemporary worldviews (Buss & Craik, 1983b).

Scales assessing two contemporary world views have now been shown to relate systematically to perceptions of specific technologies and to preferences regarding how decisions about the societal management of technologies should be reached and who should be involved in the process (Buss, Craik, & Dake, 1986).

In a splendid chapter for the *Handbook of Environmental Psychology*, Little (1987) has reviewed the invasion of the personality paradigm into environmental psychology. He captures the spirit and importance of this research tradition and offers a broad and insightful conceptual analysis to guide future research on the study of personality and the environment.

COLLECTIVE NARRATIVE II: HISTORICAL FATES OF PERSONALITY RESEARCH METHODS

My current research is directed to the development of contextual approaches to personality. They take two forms: the use of field studies from an act frequency approach and the use of naturalistic observational assessment in the reputational analysis of personality.

These endeavors can be placed within and are partly guided by an historical perspective upon research methods in personality (Craik, 1986a). By identifying five historical eras in personality psychology and seven major forms of research method, one can trace the fate of each method. The five historical periods include (1) the preidentity era prior to the appearance of the first major textbooks in personality psychology by Allport (1937) and Stagner (1937); (2) the World War II era through to 1945; (3) the post-World War II era, which was dominated by the personality scale and inventory method, through 1973; (4) the contemporary era, which has seen a reexamination of the personality and prediction model; and (5) within this period, the current situation since 1980, which has seen a revival of personality psychology. Within this framework, four research methods have shown continued development: laboratory methods, observer judgments, projective techniques, and personality scales and inventories. Two methods have seen interrupted development: field studies and biographical/archival methods. One method has suffered arrested development: reputational analysis by use of naturalistic observational assessment.

This historical perspective conveys a collective narrative about the field of personality psychology. Once upon a time, at the scientific emergence of the field, at least seven more or less distinct methods were available for personality research. Over the past half century, the development of some methods was arrested or interrupted, whereas that of others continued steadily. During the post-World War II era, personality and prediction studies using scales and inventories predominated in mainstream research. Toward the end of the 1960s, this method had matured in its scientific accomplishments. The subsequent period of stocktaking and challenge saw the revival of pre-World War II conceptual issues and a reconsideration of alternative methods, especially those whose development had been arrested or interrupted.

It is noteworthy that the methods that have been relatively neglected over the past 50 years in personality research are contextual in nature. Field studies examine the person's conduct within the everyday context of naturally occurring circumstances and settings. Reputational analysis investigates the kinds of impressions of the individual that prevail throughout the person's everyday social ecology. Life history analysis places the person within an historical context, not only that of the individual's life narrative but also within the societal narrative that constitutes history in the broader sense. My efforts have been primarily dedicated to the further development of the first two methods, although I remain fascinated by the relation of life history to societal history as well (Craik, 1988a,b).

Individual Story Line. Field Studies in Personality: The Act Frequency Approach

In retrospect, from the vantage point of the late 1980s and my version of the collective narrative concerning personality research methods, it is not surprising that a major extension of personality psychology into environmental psychology took the form of the ERI and other scales assessing environmental dispositions. But in 1975, when I prepared an account of this research program (Craik, 1976), merely describing the development and use of new scales and inventories would not suffice. Partly instigated by Mischel's (1968) critique of mainstream research, a major reconsideration of approaches to personality was underway.

Person-by-situation analysis was receiving attention, but in ways that, as Ozer (1986) has demonstrated, were excessively narrow conceptually. I was more impressed by the need to give closer conceptual scrutiny to the basic notion of disposition, which lay at the heart of the personality paradigm. During my undergraduate days at Brown University, my first inclination to-

ward a major field of study, before I shifted to psychology, had been philosophy, influenced by one of my professors, John Ladd (1963). The British ordinary language or analytic school of philosophy had had some presence at
Brown at the time, in that Austin Duncan-Jones, advisory editor of *Analysis*,
had been in residence, and guest lectures had been given by G. E. M. Anscombe and others from that tradition. When I was a graduate student at
Berkeley, Sarbin had urged us to read or reread Gilbert Ryle's (1949) *The Concept
of Mind*, which provided a close and influential analysis of the concept of
disposition. As I later developed and taught my undergraduate course in personality assessment in the 1960s, I had added treatment of Stuart Hampshire's
(1953) alternative formulation of disposition to my lectures on that topic.

By the mid-1970s, the work of these two British philosophers struck me as
critically pertinent to the reexamination of the personality paradigm (1976).
Ryle (1949) treats dispositions as hypothetical propositions. Thus the assertion
that "Mary is dominant" is akin to the assertion, "The glass is brittle": Each
takes the form: it is likely or a good bet, if certain circumstances occur (a, b, c),
then the entity will respond in certain ways (x, y, z). In contrast, Hampshire
(1953) considers dispositional assertions to be summarizing statements, taking
the form: "So far, the term *dominant* is the right word to summarize the general
trend of Mary's conduct" and are akin to other dispositional claims, such as
"The New England weather is changeable."

These formulations of Ryle and Hampshire both point to the direct relevance of dispositional concepts for the field study of persons' everyday conduct in naturally occurring circumstances. I had concluded:

> Indeed, the person-centered observational strategies pioneered at the Midwest
> Psychological Field Station (Barker, 1963) hold considerable promise for the cur-
> rent phase of personality investigation, although what is needed is not *One Boy's
> Day* (Barker & Wright, 1951) but, for example, *One Dominant Boy's Day*. The
> failure of personologists to have studied unobtrusively the stream of behavior of
> persons assessed or reputed to be, e.g., highly dominant, constitutes a remark-
> able oversight. (Craik, 1976, p. 69)

Upon my return from sabbatical leave at the University of Massachusetts, I
was delighted to find a talented new graduate student at Berkeley who shared
my fascination with the manifestations of dispositions in everyday conduct. In
the fall of 1976, David Buss and I decided to explore Hampshire's (1953) cate-
gorical summary formulation of disposition. We selected it because it did not
impose the heavy requirement of knowledge about conditional contingencies
posed by Ryle's (1949) analysis and because it struck us as being closer to
ordinary usage.

What the summary approach did demand was a systematic specification of
what kinds of acts "count" as instances of a given disposition. By treating
specific dispositions as cognitive categories of acts, we were able to mobilize
our Berkeley colleague Eleanor Rosch's (1978) analysis of human categorization
for our purposes. Rosch argued that object categories do not entail dichoto-
mous or either-or membership decisions. Rather, instances of a category vary
in their prototypicality, ranging from core or exemplary instances to peripheral

or borderline members. To explore the cognitive structure of the disposition of dominance, for example, we required a set of potentially relevant act descriptions that could be judged for their prototypicality for that category of acts.

By the spring of 1977, we had combined an act nomination procedure used earlier by Jaccard (1974) with an adaptation of Rosch's instructions for prototypicality judgments (Rosch & Mervis, 1975) to begin our act-based exploration of dominance (Buss & Craik, 1980) and other dispositional constructs drawn from Wiggins's (1978) circumplex model of interpersonal behavior (Buss, 1981; Buss & Craik, 1981, 1984). Subsequently, we have contributed a general theoretical formulation of the act frequency approach to personality (Buss & Craik, 1983c,d, 1986), discussed its implications for personality description and taxonomy (Buss & Craik, 1985), illustrated the role of act trend indices as criteria for the appraisal and conceptual analysis of personality scales (Buss & Craik, 1983a, 1984, 1989), and extended its application to the analysis of personality disorders (Buss & Craik, 1987a, 1987b). In addition, Buss (1985) has shown how the concept of environmental act trends can facilitate assessment of interpersonal environments and the analysis of person–environment correspondence.

Our research program to date has focused upon act-based conceptual analyses of dispositional constructs and on summary act trend indices assessed by retrospective act reports from target persons and their close acquaintances. The next challenge for the research program is finally to attempt the dispositional analysis of everyday conduct through comprehensive on-line monitoring (Buss & Craik, 1983d, 1989). In my judgment, our best models for this endeavor remain the behavior specimen records of the daily conduct of children made by Barker and Wright's research team (Barker & Wright, 1951, 1955; Barker, Schoggen, & Barker, 1955). These projects demonstrated that a reasonably continuous and inclusive description of a persons' daily conduct can be generated by means of a sequence of verbally depicted behavior episodes made by members of a monitoring team (even if each record may require a 422-page document) (Barker & Wright, 1951).

The act frequency approach can be seen as continuing the person-centered phase of the Barker and Wright research program, but from an explicitly personality perspective. Conceptual and technical developments point to some procedural alterations, however. First, contributions from social cognition (Collett, 1980; Newtson, Engquist, & Bois, 1977), social psychology (Rommetveit, 1980), and philosophy (Anscombe, 1979; Davidson, 1980; Feinberg, 1965) suggest that possible alternative descriptions of the same act event should be incorporated into the record of a person's daily conduct. Second, findings from research within the act frequency approach (Angleitner & Demtroder, 1988; Borkenau, 1986; Buss & Craik, 1986) indicate that the same act description can be judged highly prototypical of more than one dispositional category. Thus in computing act trend indices, multiple dispositional categorization of acts must be considered (Buss & Craik, 1989). Finally, hand-held battery-powered video cameras offer a potentially important supplementation to verbally depicted records of conduct.

Once the comprehensive recording of the daily conduct of a person is accomplished, then dispositional analysis of the individual's acts can proceed by category sortings and prototypicality judgments. A beginning along these lines was made by the Barker and Wright team in their analysis of "action modes" (Barker & Wright, 1955; Barker *et al.*, 1955) but not within a personality framework.

I am happy to note that David Buss and I are not working in isolation in moving toward field studies of personality. Also within the dispositional approach, Wright and Mischel (1987, 1988) are now exploring the hypothetical conditional formulation of Ryle (1949). Another approach is to examine a person's personal goals (Pervin, 1983), strivings (Emmons, 1986), projects (Little, 1983, 1987), and life tasks (Cantor, Norem, Niedenthal, Langston, & Brower, 1987). With regard to methodological options, a number of researchers are gathering self-monitored reports of daily experience and action in everyday settings (Csikszentmihalyi & Figurski, 1982; Hormuth, 1986; Pawlik, 1985). My own expectation is that field studies will show that, in general, self-monitored reports of daily conduct lend themselves to analysis by goal and project concepts whereas reports of daily conduct made by monitoring teams of the Barker and Wright kind are particularly fitting to dispositional constructs.

Initially, I had not been favorably impressed by Mischel's (1968) challenge to the personality paradigm (Craik, 1969a), interpreting it as failing to recognize the implications of important evidence for the temporal stability of personality measures and as seeming to discount the value of reliable composite observer judgments of personality. I am in better agreement with his subsequent views on these issues (Mischel & Peake, 1982; Wright & Mischel, 1987). But on one important point in his 1968 volume, I had failed to appreciate Mischel's concern about how personality constructs and research typically did not manage to "mirror" behavior. I now see more clearly how act-based data offer an essential complement to the traditional forms of personality data (i.e., self-report data, laboratory data, observer-based data, and life outcome data) (Block, 1977; Buss & Craik, 1983c, Cattell, 1979). Act-based data offer a route to better understanding of how personality constructs and research can more closely mirror conduct within the context of the naturally occurring settings of daily life.

INDIVIDUAL STORY LINE: NATURALISTIC OBSERVATIONAL ASSESSMENT AND THE REPUTATIONAL ANALYSIS OF PERSONALITY

Field studies in personality seek to understand persons on the basis of trends in their everyday conduct. A second contextual source of information about individuals resides in the impressions formed by members of the community of observers within the person's everyday social ecology.

My initial interest in this topic was provoked by Paul G. Petersen's (1965) PhD dissertation examining individual differences among IPAR assessment participants with regard to the judgments made about them by the assessment staff. Petersen was not primarily concerned about the substance of the observational assessment, that is, whether the person was seen as affiliative, hostile, and so forth. Instead, he was interested in gauging the number of dispositional assertions the assessment staff was ready to make about the person and the degree of consensus it displayed in making them. For example, on the 300-item *Adjective Check List*, each assessment staff member described each participant by checking those adjectives (ranging from absent minded to zany) that appeared to be characteristic of the person. For a sample of 100 Air Force officers assessed at IPAR, Petersen found that the total number of adjectives checked by 10 observers (which could range from 0 to 3,000) showed a range from 289 to 704. Thus, at the end of the assessment program, some participants emerged as over twice as *socially visible*, in Petersen's term, as others. Second, eight staff members had described each participant using an early version of the *California Q-Set*, with an average composite reliability for the total sample of +.83. However, when Petersen examined the composite reliabilities for each participant, he found that they ranged from +.34 to +.96. Thus the degree of consensus regarding the impression of an individual's personality held by a team of observers turns out to be an interesting individual difference variable in its own right. Furthermore, an index of composite reliability for the *Adjective Check List* descriptions made by the assessment staff (i.e., average number of checks per adjective checked) correlated +.73 with the *California Q-Set* index of reliability, showing cross-method convergence for this personality metavariable.

In my undergraduate course in personality assessment, I have always given detailed attention to Petersen's fascinating report. In addition, I speculated about the implications of social visibility and degree of observer consensus for an individual's everyday social life, beyond the assessment center. To have members of a person's social ecology ready to assert a good deal about the individual and to concur in it (whether favorable or unfavorable) must have different social consequences for the person than to have fellow citizens willing to say little and tending to disagree even about that. Furthermore, although it may be technically sound to focus upon ensuring adequate composite reliability in the observational assessment of persons, it is also important to look beyond it to areas of difference as well as consensus among impressions observers form of a person.

These considerations suggest strongly to me that the professional observational assessments gathered at IPAR and similar centers from staff members be supplemented by naturalistic observational assessments gathered from stratified representative samples drawn from the individual's everyday community of observers (Craik, 1985a, 1986a). Use of social network analysis (Fischer, 1977) and identifying observers from the person's daily or monthly behavior setting inventory (Barker, 1968) would assist in constructing a comprehensive specification of an individual's distinctive audience.

Conceptually, this approach revives a reputational or "social stimulus value" analysis of personality (May, 1932) and addresses important issues concerning how persons exist and have social meaning within their everyday life settings. Implications of the size and extent of a person's community of observers have not been adequately studied, although the related phenomena of celebrity and fame warrant scientific attention (Braudy, 1986; Schickel, 1985). Petersen's query about whether consensus or dissensus prevails in the impressions held about a person can be extended into everyday settings. Some persons may generate unified views of themselves; others may socially exist in the form of multiple public personalities, depending upon behavior setting or subaudience, whereas truly enigmatic individuals may leave in their wake a trail of disagreement among observers as they move through settings, audiences, and life (Craik, 1985a). Finally, the degree of accuracy persons display regarding the nature and structure, as well as substance, of their public personalities or reputation deserves investigation within a social ecological framework.

In his influential textbook, Allport (1937) dismissed the reputational conception of personality (May, 1932) as dealing with mere rumor or gossip. In subsequent use of peer ratings and observer judgments, systemic and broad sampling of observers has not been employed in personality research. Instead, consensus has been assured by requiring and working until, adequate composite reliability is secured (e.g., Block, 1971; Cattell, 1945). Comprehensive specification and sampling of the individual's community of observers, adaptation of observational assessment techniques in gathering stratified representative impressions of the person, and examination of the structure of variation as well as consensus in the person's public personality constitute an ambitious research agenda.

However, the problem of reputation also requires attention to how information about a person's everyday conduct affects the impressions formed by immediate observers of it and how it then flows to and is assimilated by secondary and tertiary audiences. The channels through which reputational information flows (Goode, 1978; Rommetveit, 1980) and the efforts of the person to manage this process and its outcome (Emler, 1984; Hogan, 1982) must also be considered. Thus the reputational analysis of personality depends in part upon progress in understanding the social dynamics of reputation (Bailey, 1971; Bromley, 1986), the traditions and psychosocial foundations of defamation law, through which persons seek to protect their reputation (Helmholz, 1985; Post, 1986) and even as Allport noted, the social psychology of gossip and rumor (Rosnow & Fine, 1979).

CONCLUSIONS

INFLUENCES UPON INDIVIDUAL STORY LINES

My intellectual history has been pervasively influenced by the assessment research tradition embodied in the program of the Institute of Personality Assessment and Research (IPAR) (MacKinnon, 1978). My introduction to environmental psychology was made possible by two outstanding facilitators of the creative process in others, Donald W. MacKinnon at IPAR and Charles Warren Callister at the then firm of Callister and Payne. The intellectual impact of the work and example of my graduate school mentors, MacKinnon and Theodore R. Sarbin, is even more evident in these pages than I had anticipated. My good fortune in research collaborators has been continuous and obvious.

Perhaps less apparent in this narrative are the benefits accruing from graduate and undergraduate teaching. In addition to those graduate students with whom I have become a collaborator and colleague, I have also gained from ongoing interaction with other talented young scholars attracted to the PhD programs in environmental design and psychology at Berkeley. Involvement in individual reading tutorials, seminars, and, yes, even the oral examinations conducted by the qualifying examination committees affords a continuing forum for discourse about developments in environmental and personality psychology.

Finally, I have discovered in preparing this narrative that the undergraduate courses I have taught over the years have played an important part in the individual story lines recounted here. Organizing the material on observational assessment of persons for my personality assessment course in the mid-1960s provided the conceptual framework for my later research on the observational assessment of environments. Furthermore, when my general activities in environmental psychology over two decades led me to be increasingly committed to exploring more contextual approaches to personality, I was able to draw upon my treatment of dispositions in the personality assessment course and my treatment of the early person-centered phase of ecological psychology (Barker, 1968) in my environmental psychology course in formulating the act frequency approach with David Buss. And I have subsequently been able to draw upon my treatment of Petersen's (1965) PhD dissertation in the personality assessment course in advancing the notion of reputational analysis of personality via naturalistic observational assessment. The important point to emphasize is that these topics were not central to my research program at the time I introduced them into my undergraduate lectures, but some years later, they became critical ingredients of new research directions.

INDIVIDUAL STORY LINES AND COLLECTIVE NARRATIVES

The emerging field of environmental psychology as I found it in the mid-1960s was certainly engaging in its own right. However, in retrospect, my attraction to it was also a function of the character of that era of the 1960s in the collective narrative of personality psychology. The good ship *personality* at that time appeared to have sailed into the doldrums. The impressive accomplishments and products of the personality and prediction model must of course continue to be recognized and to exert sustained influence upon the field (Hogan & Nicolson, 1988; Wiggins, 1973). However, by the late 1960s, its primary method of personality scales and inventories had been well examined. Nevertheless, the issue of response sets regarding personality scales was consuming an excessive expenditure of scientific effort (Block, 1965; Edwards, 1957; Rorer, 1965), while failing to yield understandings of the method that were not already available in the field, and certainly failing to advance our understanding of personality. Fortunately, the past decade has seen a return to examining basic conceptual issues, a commitment to a broader array of research methods, and a general resurgence of scientific vitality (Craik, 1986a).

What has been the collective narrative of environmental psychology over the past decade? In the mid-1970s, I had envisioned several possible outcomes of the invasion of multiple research paradigms into the person–environment domain (Craik, 1977). One possibility was simply the continued coexistence and extension of the paradigms within environmental psychology. Certainly, much unfinished business remains in 1989 for each research tradition. A more attractive possibility was the gradual merging of the paradigms, with the person–environment domain providing the synergizing context for a more coherent and integrative scientific psychology (Craik, 1977; Stokols, 1978). Some merging has occurred, but to document it would entail another story altogether. A third possibility was the eventual collapse of every paradigm back into mainstream psychology and the disappearance of environmental psychology as a distinct field. The monumental *Handbook of Environmental Psychology* (Stokols & Altman, 1987) testifies to the invalidity of that forecast. If nothing else, the continued involvement of other disciplines and the relatively more applied research programs would assure our field's separate identity.

Although I have enjoyed a privileged vantage point as co-editor of the *Journal of Environmental Psychology* (Canter & Craik, 1981), I have found it difficult to generate a coherent collective narrative for our field's activities beyond the mid-1970s. The tale now requires more than an account of the invasion of the paradigms, although that perspective continues to offer an essential intellectual map. Research guilds have formed around major pertinent societal issues, such as housing, landscape assessment, crime and the environment, and society at large can be counted upon to turn attention to new topics, such as risk analysis (Canter, Craik, & Brown, 1985). The fate of the paradigm invasion has revealed an outcome I had not anticipated, namely the strong impact from environmental psychology back upon mainstream psychology (Canter, Craik, & Griffiths, 1984). Two of my own story lines fall into that narrative type. Finally, the rapid international expansion of environmental psychology represents a promising potential source of change and diversity for our field (Canter, Craik, & Griffiths, 1983; Craik, 1987a). Whatever the appropriate collective narrative for this most recent period, it will entail a continuing story of scientific vitality for environmental psychology.

I feel even less ready to forecast the future. Many years ago, I speculated about the nature of environmental psychology beyond the year 2000 (Craik, 1966). What I thought at the time to be an ambitious scenario now pales beside what has already been accomplished, and we have a decade more to go.

CONTEXT IN ENVIRONMENTAL AND PERSONALITY PSYCHOLOGY

I have offered two individual story lines that illustrate specific contextual approaches to personality. I view them as emergents from my joint interest in environmental and personality psychology. The linking concept is that of *context*. Contextual strategies are receiving increasing attention in environmental, personality, and social psychology (Rosenberg & Gara, 1983; Sarbin & McKechnie, 1986; Stokols, 1987).

Initially, environmental psychology had close reference to study of the everyday *physical* environment. Yet analysis of the physical environment necessarily entails reference to sets of scientific and professional constructs (Craik, 1972b) and cultural concepts (Lowenthal & Prince, 1976). Thus contextual strategies might reasonably refer more generally to study of human conduct within the everyday environment.

A number of theoretical meanings of "contextual" can now be identified (Altman & Rogoff, 1987; Little, 1987; Sarbin, 1977; Stokols, 1987). My own preference at this time is to avoid commitment to grand theoretical structures and instead to refer to a contextual orientation to research that emphasizes study of a person's conduct within its everyday circumstances. The spirit of this orientation is still best expressed by Barker's (1968) evocation of a naturalistic style of inquiry, although I view the notion of behavior setting as simply one of many conceptual resources now available to us.

A focus upon the contextual study of persons as they move through their daily rounds of conduct and settings is, in my judgment, exactly what is required for progress in personality psychology—the specificity of everydayness. Furthermore, we will never achieve an adequate contextual theory for environmental psychology until we have a contextual formulation of the person.

Acknowledgments

Organization of this chapter derives from my current collaboration with David Lowenthal on the comparative study of accounts of the individual and collective past, undertaken during my tenure as honorary research fellow at University College London. Portions of the chapter were presented in talks at the British Psychological Society's 1988 meetings in London and in the Environmental Psychology Program at the University of Surrey, in conjunction with my appointment as honorary visiting professor at the University of Surrey. Preparation of the chapter was supported by a 1988–1989 sabbatical award from the James McKeen Cattell Fund.

REFERENCES

Allen, V. L., & Scheibe, K. E. (1982). *The social context of conduct: Psychological writings of Theodore R. Sarbin.* New York: Praeger.

Allport, G. W. (1937). *Personality: A psychological interpretation.* New York: Holt.

Altman, I. (1973). Some perspectives on the study of man-environment relations. *Representative research in social psychology, 4,* 109–126.

Altman, I., & Rogoff, B. (1987). World views in psychology: Trait, interactional, organismic, and transactional perspectives. In D. Stokols & I. Altman (Eds.), *Handbook of environmental psychology* (pp. 7–40). New York: Wiley.

Angleitner, A., & Demtroder, A. I. (1988). Acts and dispositions: A reconsideration of the act frequency approach. *European Journal of Personality, 2,* 121–142.

Anscombe, G. E. M. (1979). "Under a description." *Nous, 13,* 219–233.

Anthony, K. H. (1983). Major themes in the work of Donald Appleyard. *Environment and Behavior, 15,* 411–418.

Appleyard, D. (1977). Understanding professional media: Issues, theory and a research agenda. In I. Altman & J. F. Wohlwill (Eds.), *Human behavior and the environment* (Vol. 2, pp. 43–88). New York: Plenum.

Appleyard, D., & Craik, K. H. (1978). The Berkeley Environmental Simulation Laboratory and its research programme. *International Review of Applied Psychology, 27,* 53–55.

Bailey, F. G. (Ed.). (1971). *Gifts and poison: The politics of reputation.* Oxford: Basil Blackwell.

Barker, R. G. (Ed.). (1963). *The stream of behavior.* New York: Appleton-Century-Crofts.

Barker, R. G. (1968). *Ecological psychology: Concepts and methods for studying the environment of human behavior.* Stanford: Stanford University Press.

Barker, R. G., & Wright, H. F. (1951). *One boy's day: A specimen record of behavior.* New York: Harper & Row.

Barker, R. G., & Wright, H. F. (1955). *Midwest and its children.* Evanston, IL: Row, Peterson.

Barker, R. G., Schoggen, M., & Barker, L. S. (1955). Hemerography of Mary Ennis. In A. Burton (Ed.), *Case histories in clinical and abnormal psychology, Volume II: Clinical studies of personality* (pp. 768–808). New York: Harper & Brothers.

Block, J. (1965). *The challenge of response sets: Unconfounding meaning, acquiescence and social desirability in the MMPI.* New York: Appleton-Century-Crofts.

Block, J. (1971). *Lives through time.* Berkeley: Bancroft.

Block, J. (1977). Advancing the psychology of personality: Paradigmatic shift or improving the quality of research? In D. Magnusson & N. S. Endler (Eds.), *Personality at the crossroads: Current issues in interactional psychology* (pp. 37–63). Hillsdale, NJ: Erlbaum.

Block, J. (1978). *The Q-sort method in personality assessment and psychiatric research.* Palo Alto, CA: Consulting Psychologists Press. (Original 1961.)

Borkenau, P. (1986). Toward an understanding of trait interrelations: Acts as instances for several traits. *Journal of Personality and Social Psychology, 51,* 372–381.

Bosselmann, P. (1983). Visual impact assessment at Berkeley. *Urban Design International, 7,* 34–37.

Bosselmann, P., & Craik, K. H. (1987). Perceptual simulations of environments. In R. Bechtel, R. Marans, & W. Michelson (Eds.), *Methods in environmental and behavioral research* (pp. 162–189). New York: Van Nostrand Reinhold.

Braudy, L. (1986). *The frenzy of renown: Fame and its history.* New York: Oxford University Press.

Bromley, D. B. (1986). *Case study methods in psychology and related disciplines.* New York: Wiley.

Bryant, K. J. (1984). *Geographical spatial orientation ability and the representation of real-world and simulated environments.* Unpublished doctoral dissertation, University of California at Berkeley.

Buss, D. M. (1981). *The act frequency analysis of interpersonal dispositions.* Unpublished doctoral dissertation, University of California at Berkeley.

Buss, D. M. (1985). The act frequency approach to the interpersonal environment. *Perspectives in Personality, 1,* 173–200.

Buss, D. M., & Craik, K. H. (1980). The frequency concept of dominance: Dominance and prototypically dominant acts. *Journal of Personality, 48,* 379–392.

Buss, D. M., & Craik, K. H. (1981). The act frequency analysis of personal dispositions: Aloofness, gregariousness, dominance and submissiveness. *Journal of Personality, 49,* 175–192.

Buss, D. M., & Craik, K. H. (1983a). Act prediction and the conceptual analysis of personality scales: Indices of act density, bipolarity and extensity. *Journal of Personality and Social Psychology, 45,* 1081–1095.

Buss, D. M., & Craik, K. H. (1983b). Contemporary worldviews: Personal and policy implications. *Journal of Applied Social Psychology, 13,* 259–280.

Buss, D. M., & Craik, K. H. (1983c). The act frequency approach to personality. *Psychological Review, 90,* 105–125.

Buss, D. M., & Craik, K. H. (1983d). The dispositional analysis of everyday conduct. *Journal of Personality, 51,* 393–412.

Buss, D. M., & Craik, K. H. (1984). Acts, dispositions, and personality. In B. A. Maher & W. B. Maher (Eds.), *Progress in experimental personality research: Normal processes, Volume XIII* (pp. 241–301). New York: Academic Press.

Buss, D. M., & Craik, K. H. (1985). Why *not* measure that trait? Alternative criteria for identifying important dispositions. *Journal of Personality and Social Psychology, 48,* 934–946.

Buss, D. M., & Craik, K. H. (1986). The act frequency approach and the construction of personality. In A. Angleitner, A. Furnham, & G. Van Heck (Eds.), *Personality psychology in Europe, Volume 2* (pp. 141–156). Berwyn, PA: Swets North America.

Buss, D. M., & Craik, K. H. (1987a). Act criteria for the diagnosis of personality disorders. *Journal of Personality Disorders, 1,* 73–81.

Buss, D. M., & Craik, K. H. (1987b). Acts, dispositions, and clinical assessment: The psychopathology of everyday conduct. *Clinical Psychology Review, 6,* 141–156.

Buss, D. M., & Craik, K. H. (1989). On the cross-cultural examination of acts and dispositions. *European Journal of Personality, 3,* 19–30.

Buss, D. M., Craik, K. H., & Drake, K. M. (1986). Contemporary worldviews and perception of the technological system. In J. Menkes & V. T. Covello (Eds.), *Contemporary issues in risk analysis: The social and behavioral sciences* (pp. 93–130). New York: Plenum Press.

Canter, D., & Craik, K. H. (1981). Environmental psychology. *Journal of Environmental Psychology, 1,* 1–12.

Canter, D., & Craik, K. H. (1987). Environmental psychology at Clark University: Circa 1970–1972. *Journal of Environmental Psychology, 7,* 281–288.

Canter, D., Craik, K. H., & Brown, J. (1985). Psychological aspects of environmental risk. *Journal of Environmental Psychology, 5,* 1–4.

Canter, D., Craik, K. H., & Griffiths, I. (1983). Editorial. *Journal of Environmental Psychology, 3,* 1–3.

Canter, D., Craik, K. H., & Griffiths, I. (1984). Environmental bridge-building. *Journal of Environmental Psychology, 4,* 1–5.

Cantor, N., Norem, J., Niedenthal, P., Langston, C., & Brower, A. (1987). Life tasks, self-concept ideals, and cognitive strategies in a life transition. *Journal of Personality and Social Psychology, 53,* 1178–1191.

Carp, F. M., & Carp, A. (1982). Perceived environmental quality of neighborhoods: Development of assessment scales and their relation to age and gender. *Journal of Environmental Psychology, 2,* 295–312.

Carr, D. (1986). Narrative and the real world: An argument for continuity. *History and Theory, 25,* 117–131.

Carroll, N. (1988). Review essay: *Time, narrative and history,* by David Carr. *History and Theory, 27,* 297–306.

Cattell, R. B. (1945). The description of personality. Principles and findings in factor analysis. *American Journal of Psychology, 58,* 69–90.

Cattell, R. B. (1979). *Personality and learning theory, Volume I: The structure of personality in its environment.* New York: Springer.

Collett, P. (1980). Segmenting the behaviour stream. In M. Brenner (Ed.), *The structure of action* (pp. 150–167). New York: St. Martin's Press.

Craik, K. H. (1964). *Social and asocial patterns of temporal behavior.* Unpublished doctoral dissertation, University of California at Berkeley.

Craik, K. H. (1966). The prospects for an environmental psychology. *IPAR Research Bulletin, 1,* 1–18.

Craik, K. H. (1968a). *A sociopsychological study of an architectural firm.* Berkeley: Unpublished report, Institute of Personality Assessment and Research, University of California.

Craik, K. H. (1968b). The comprehension of the everyday physical environment. *Journal of the American Institute of Planners, 34,* 29–37.

Craik, K. H. (1969a). Personality unvanquished: Review of *Personality and assessment* by W. Mischel. *Contemporary Psychology, 14,* 147–148.

Craik, K. H. (1969b). The architectural student in architectural society. *Journal of the American Institute of Architects, 51,* 84–89.

Craik, K. H. (1970). Environmental psychology. In K. H. Craik, B. Kleinmuntz, R. L. Rosnow, B. Rosenthal, J. A. Cheyne, & R. H. Walters, *New directions in psychology 4* (pp. 1–122). New York: Holt, Rinehart & Winston.

Craik, K. H. (1971). The assessment of places. In P. McReynolds (Ed.), *Advances in psychological assessment, Volume Two* (pp. 40–62). Palo Alto, CA: Science and Behavior Books.

Craik, K. H. (1972a). Appraising the objectivity of landscape dimensions. In J. V. Krutilla (Ed.), *Natural environments: Studies in theoretical and applied analysis* (pp. 292–346). Baltimore: Johns Hopkins University Press.

Craik, K. H. (1972b). An ecological perspective on environmental decision-making. *Human Ecology, 1,* 69–80.

Craik, K. H. (1973a). Environmental psychology. *Annual Review of Psychology, 24,* 402–422.

Craik, K. H. (1973b). Psychological factors in landscape appraisal. *Environment and Behavior, 4,* 255–266.

Craik, K. H. (1975). Individual variations in landscape description. In E. H. Zube, R. O. Brush, J. Fabos (Eds.), *Landscape assessment: Values, perceptions and resources* (pp. 130–150). Stroudsburg, PA: Dowden, Hutchinson & Ross.

Craik, K. H. (1976). The personality research paradigm in environmental psychology. In S. Wapner, S. Cohen, & B. Kaplan (Eds.), *Experiencing environments* (pp. 55–80). New York: Plenum Press.

Craik, K. H. (1977). Multiple scientific paradigms in environmental psychology. *International Journal of Psychology, 12,* 147–157.

Craik, K. H. (1982). Obituary: Donald Appleyard, 1928–1982. *Journal of Environmental Psychology, 2,* 169–170.

Craik, K. H. (1983). The psychology of the large-scale environment. In N. R. Feimer & E. S. Geller (Eds.), *Environmental psychology: Directions and perspectives* (pp. 67–105). New York: Praeger.

Craik, K. H. (1985a). Multiple perceived personalities: A neglected consistency issue. In E. E. Roskam (Ed.), *Measurement and personality assessment* (pp. 333–338). New York: Elsevier Science.

Craik, K. H. (1985b). Psychological perspectives on technology as societal option, source of hazard, and generator of environmental impacts. In V. T. Covello, J. L. Mumpower, P. J. M. Stallen, & V. R. R. Uppuluri (Eds.), *Environmental impact assessment, technology assessment and risk analysis* (pp. 211–226). New York: Springer-Verlag.

Craik, K. H. (1986a). Personality research methods: An historical perspective. *Journal of Personality, 54,* 18–51.

Craik, K. H. (1986b). Psychological reflections on landscape. In D. Lowenthal & E. C. Penning-Roswell (Eds.), *Meaning and values in landscape* (pp. 48–64). London: Allen & Unwin.

Craik, K. H. (1987a). Aspects internationaux de la psychologie de l'environnement. *Psychologie Francaise, 32,* 17–21.

Craik, K. H. (1987b). Environmental perception and environmental annoyance: Issues of measurement and interpretation. In H. S. Koelega (Ed.), *Annoyance in the environment: Characterization and measurement* (pp. 45–50). New York: Elsevier Science.

Craik, K. H. (1988a). Assessing the personalities of historical figures. In W. M. Runyan (Ed.), *Psychology and historical interpretation* (pp. 196–218). Oxford: Oxford University Press.

Craik, K. H. (1988b). *Personality and sense of history.* (Unpublished paper presented at the meetings of the Second World Congress on Heritage Presentation and Interpretation, University of Warwick, Coventry, England, August 30–September 4, 1988).

Craik, K. H., & Drake, K. M. (1988). *Psychology assessment of thermal comfort: Findings from a field study of office environments.* Berkeley: Unpublished report, Institute of Personality Assessment and Research, University of California at Berkeley.

Craik, K. H., & Feimer, N. R. (1979). Setting technical standards for visual assessment procedures. In G. Elsner & R. C. Smardon (Eds.), *Our national landscape* (pp. 93–100). Berkeley: U.S. Forest Service.

Craik, K. H., & Feimer, N. R. (1987). Environmental assessment. In D. Stokols & I. Altman (Eds.), *Handbook of environmental psychology* (pp. 891–917). New York: Wiley.

Craik, K. H., Gough, H. G., Hall, W. B., & Helson, R. (1989). Donald W. MacKinnon (1903–1987). *American Psychologist, 44,* 731–732.

Craik, K. H., & Sarbin, T. R. (1963). Effect of covert alterations in clock rate upon time estimations and personal tempo. *Perceptual and Motor Skills, 16,* 597–610.

Craik, K. H., & Zube, E. H. (1976). (Eds.), *Perceiving environmental quality: Research and application.* New York: Plenum Press.

Csikszentmihalyi, M., & Figurski, T. J. (1982). Self-awareness and aversive experience in everyday life. *Journal of Personality, 50,* 1–28.

Daniel, T. C., & Vining, J. (1983). Methodological issues in the assessment of landscape quality. In I. Altman & J. F. Wohlwill (Eds.), *Human behavior and the environment, Volume 6* (pp. 39–84). New York: Plenum Press.

Davidson, D. (1980). *Essays on actions and events.* Oxford: Oxford University Press.

Dykstra, J. (1977). Miniature and mechanical special effects for "Star Wars." *American Cinematographer, 58,* 702–705, 732, 742, 750–757.

Edwards, A. L. (1957). *The social desirability variable in personality assessment.* New York: Dryden.

Emler, N. (1984). Differential involvement in delinquency: Toward an interpretation in terms of reputation management. In B. A. Maher & W. B. Maher (Eds.), *Progress in experimental personality research: Normal processes, Volume XIII* (pp. 173–239). New York: Academic Press.

Emmons, R. A. (1986). Personal strivings: An approach to personality and subjective well-being. *Journal of Personality and Social Psychology, 51,* 1058–1068.

Feimer, N. R. (1979). *Personality and environmental perception: Alternative predictive systems and implications for evaluative judgments.* Unpublished doctoral dissertation, University of California at Berkeley.

Feimer, N. R. (1984). Environmental perception: The effects of media, evaluative context and observer sample. *Journal of Environmental Psychology, 4,* 61–80.

Feimer, N. R., Smardon, R. C., & Craik, K. H. (1981). Evaluating the effectiveness of observer-based visual resource and impact assessment methods. *Landscape Research, 6,* 12–16.

Feinberg, J. (1965). Action and responsibility. In M. Black (Ed.), *Philosophy in America.* London: George Allen & Unwin.

Fischer, C. S. (1977). *Networks and places: Social relations in an urban setting.* New York: Free Press.

Gergen, K. J., & Gergen, M. M. (1983). Narratives of the self. In T. R. Sarbin & K. E. Scheibe (Eds.), *Studies in social identity* (pp. 254–273). New York: Praeger.

Gough, H. G. (1957). *Manual for the California Psychological Inventory.* Palo Alto: Consulting Psychologists Press. (Revised, 1987).

Gough, H. G., & Heilbrun, A. B., Jr. (1965). *The Adjective Check List manual*. Palo Alto, CA: Consulting Psychologists Press. (Revised, 1980).

Goode, W. J. (1978). *The celebration of heroes: Prestige as a social control system*. Berkeley: University of California Press.

Gutman, R. (1965–1966). The questions architects ask. *Transactions of the Bartlett Society, 4*, 49–82.

Hall, W. B., & MacKinnon, D. W. (1969). Personality inventory correlates of creativity among architects. *Journal of Applied Psychology, 53*, 322–326.

Hampshire, S. (1953). Dispositions. *Analysis, 14*, 5–11.

Helmholz, R. H. (Ed.). (1985). *Select cases of defamation to 1600*. London: Seldon Society.

Hogan, R. (1982). A socioanalytic theory of personality. *Nebraska Symposium on Motivation, 30*, 55–89.

Hogan, R., & Nicolson, R. A. (1988). The meaning of personality test scores. *American Psychologist, 43*, 621–626.

Hormuth, S. E. (1986). The sampling of experiences *in situ*. *Journal of Personality, 54*, 262–293.

Jaccard, J. J. (1974). Predicting social behavior from personality traits. *Journal of Research in Personality, 7*, 358–367.

Kuhn, T. S. (1962). *The structure of scientific revolutions*. Chicago: University of Chicago Press.

Ladd, J. (1963). The issue of relativism. *Monist, 47*, 585–609.

Little, B. R. (1972). Psychological man as scientist, humanist and specialist. *Journal of Experimental Research in Personality, 6*, 95–118.

Little, B. R. (1976a). *Personal systems and specialization*. Unpublished doctoral dissertation, University of California at Berkeley.

Little, B. R. (1976b). Specialization and the varieties of environmental experience: Empirical studies within the personality paradigm. In S. Wapner, S. Cohen, & B. Kaplan (Eds.), *Experiencing environments* (pp. 81–116). New York: Plenum Press.

Little, B. R. (1983). Personal projects: A rationale and method for investigation. *Environment and Behavior, 15*, 273–309.

Little, B. R. (1987). Personality and the environment. In D. Stokols & I. Altman (Eds.), *Handbook of environmental psychology* (pp. 206–244). New York: Wiley.

Lowenthal, D. (1985). *The past is a foreign country*. Cambridge: Cambridge University Press.

Lowenthal, D., & Prince, H. (1976). Transcendental experience. In S. Wapner, S. Cohen, & B. Kaplan (Eds.), *Experiencing environments* (pp. 117–131). New York: Plenum Press.

MacKinnon, D. W. (1978). *In search of human effectiveness: Identifying and developing creativity*. Buffalo: Creative Education Foundation.

Mancuso, J. C., & Sarbin, T. R. (1983). The self narrative in enactment of roles. In T. R. Sarbin & K. E. Scheibe (Eds.), *Studies in social identity* (pp. 233–253). New York: Praeger.

Marshall, N. (1969). *Orientation towards privacy*. Unpublished doctoral dissertation, University of California at Berkeley.

Marshall, N. (1972). Privacy and the environment. *Human Ecology, 1*, 93–110.

Masterman, M. (1970). The nature of paradigm. In I. Lakatos & A. Musgrave (Eds.), *Criticism and the growth of knowledge* (pp. 59–89). Cambridge: University of Cambridge Press.

May, M. A. (1932). The foundations of personality. In P. S. Achilles (Ed.), *Psychology at work* (pp. 81–101). New York: McGraw-Hill.

McAdams, D. P. (1988). Biography, narrative, and lives: An introduction. *Journal of Personality, 56*, 1–18.

McKechnie, G. E. (1972). *A study of environmental lifestyles*. Unpublished doctoral dissertation, University of California at Berkeley.

McKechnie, G. E. (1974). *Manual for the Environmental Response Inventory*. Palo Alto: Consulting Psychologists Press.

McKechnie, G. E. (1977a). The Environmental Response Inventory in application. *Environment and Behavior, 9*, 255–276.

McKechnie, G. E. (1977b). Simulation techniques in environmental psychology. In D. Sokols (Ed.), *Perspectives on environmental and behavior: Theory, research and application* (pp. 169–190). New York: Plenum Press.

McKechnie, G. E. (1978). Environmental dispositions: Concepts and measures. In P. McReynolds (Ed.), *Advances in psychological assessment, Volume 4* (pp. 141–177). San Francisco: Jossey-Bass.

Mink, L. O. (1978). Narrative form as a cognitive instrument. In R. H. Canary & J. Kozicki (Eds.), *The writing of history: Literary form and historical understanding* (pp. 129–150). Madison: University of Wisconsin Press.

Mischel, W. (1968). *Personality and assessment.* New York: Wiley.

Mischel, W., & Peake, P. K. (1982). Beyond déjà vù in the search for cross-situational consistency. *Psychological Review, 89*, 730–755.

Murray, H. A. (1938). *Explorations in personality.* New York: Oxford University Press.

National Academy of Sciences–National Academy of Engineering (1975). *Planning for environmental indices.* Washington, DC: National Research Council.

Newtson, P., Engquist, G. A., & Bois, J. (1977). The objective basis of behavior units. *Journal of Personality and Social Psychology, 35*, 847–862.

Office of Strategic Services (OSS) Assessment Staff (1948). *Assessment of men.* New York: Rinehart.

Ozer, D. J. (1986). *Consistency in personality: A methodological framework.* New York: Springer-Verlag. (Revision of a doctoral dissertation, University of California, Berkeley, 1982).

Passmore, J. (1987). Narratives and events. *History and Theory, Beiheft, 26*, 68–74.

Pawlik, K. (1985). Cross-situational consistency of behavior: Models, theories, and in-field tests of the consistency issue. In E. E. Roskam (Ed.), *Measurement and personality assessment* (pp. 307–314). New York: Elsevier Science.

Pervin, L. A. (1983). The stasis and flow of behavior: Toward a theory of goals. *Nebraska Symposium on Motivation, 30*, 1–53.

Petersen, P. G. (1965). *Reliability of judgments of personality as a function of subjects and traits being judged.* Unpublished doctoral dissertation, University of California at Berkeley.

Post, R. C. (1986). The social foundations of defamation law: Reputation and the Constitution. *California Law Review, 74*, 691–742.

Rommetveit, R. (1980). On "meanings" of acts and what is meant and made known by what is said in a pluralistic social world. In M. Brenner (Ed.), *The structure of action* (pp. 108–149). New York: St. Martin's Press.

Rorer, L. G. (1965). The great response style myth. *Psychological Bulletin, 63*, 129–156.

Rosch, E. (1978). Principles of categorization. In E. Rosch & B. B. Loyd (Eds.), *Cognition and categorization* (pp. 27–48). Hillsdale, NJ: Erlbaum.

Rosch, E., & Mervis, C. B. (1975). Family resemblances: Studies in the internal structure of categories. *Cognitive Psychology, 7*, 573–605.

Rosenberg, S., & Gara, M. A. (1983). Contemporary perspectives and future directions of personality and social psychology. *Journal of Personality and Social Psychology, 45*, 56–73.

Rosnow, R. L., & Fine, G. A. (1979). *Rumor and gossip: The social psychology of hearsay.* New York: Elsevier.

Runyan, W. M. (1982). *Life histories and psychobiography.* New York: Oxford University Press.

Ryle, G. (1949). *The concept of mind.* New York: Barnes and Noble.

Sanford, R. N. (1980). *Learning after college.* Orinda, CA: Montaigne.

Sarbin, T. R. (1977). Contextualism: A world view of modern psychology. *Nebraska Symposium on Motivation, 24*, 1–41.

Sarbin, T. R. (Ed.). (1986). *Narrative psychology: The storied nature of human contact.* New York: Praeger.

Sarbin, T. R., & McKechnie, G. E. (1986). Prospects for a contextualist theory of personality. In R. Rosnow & M. Georgeoudi (Eds.), *Contextualism and understanding* (pp. 187–207). New York: Praeger.

Schickel, R. (1985). *Common fame: The culture of celebrity*. London: Pavilion Books.

Smardon, R. C., Feimer, N. R., Craik, K. H., & Sheppard, S. R. J. (1983). Assessing the reliability, validity and generalizability of observer-based visual impact assessment methods for the western United States. In R. D. Rowe & L. G. Chestnut (Eds.), *Managing air quality and scenic quality resources at national parks and wilderness areas* (pp. 84–102). Boulder, CO: Westview Press.

Sommer, R. (1973). Evaluation, yes; research, maybe. *Representative Research in Social Psychology, 4*, 127–134.

Stagner, R. (1937). *Psychology of personality*. New York: McGraw-Hill.

Stokols, D. (1978). Environmental psychology. *Annual Review of Psychology, 29*, 253–295.

Stokols, D. (1987). Conceptual strategies of environmental psychology. In D. Stokols & I. Altman (Eds.), *Handbook of environmental psychology* (pp. 41–70). New York: McGraw-Hill.

Stokols, D., & Altman, I. (Eds.). (1987). *Handbook of environmental psychology*. 2 volumes. New York: Wiley.

Twiss, R. H., & Litton, R. B., Jr. (1966). Resource use in the regional landscape. *Natural Resources Journal, 6*, 76–81.

Wapner, S., Kaplan, B., & Cohen, S. B. (1973). An organismic-developmental perspective for understanding transactions of men in environments. *Environment and Behavior, 5*, 255–290.

White, H. (1984). The question of narrative in contemporary historical theory. *History and Theory, 23*, 1–33.

Wiggins, J. S. (1973). *Personality and prediction: Principles of personality assessment*. Reading, MA: Addison-Wesley.

Wiggins, J. S. (1978). A psychological taxonomy of trait descriptive terms: I. The interpersonal domain. *Journal of Personality and Social Psychology, 37*, 395–412.

Wohlwill, J. F. (1973). The environment is not in the head! In W. F. E. Preiser (Ed.), *Environmental design research, Volume II* (pp. 166–181). Stroudsburg, PA: Dowden, Hutchinson, & Ross.

Wright, J. C., & Mischel, W. (1987). A conditional approach to dispositional constructs: The local predictability in social behavior. *Journal of Personality and Social Psychology, 53*, 1159–1177.

Wright, J. C., & Mischel, W. (1988). Conditional hedges and the intuitive psychology of traits. *Journal of Personality and Social Psychology, 55*, 454–469.

Zube, E. H. (1974). Cross-disciplinary and inter-mode agreement on the description and evaluation of landscape resources. *Environment and Behavior, 6*, 69–89.

Zube, E. H., & Craik, K. H. (1978). Indices of perceived coastal quality. *Coastal Zone 78, Volume II* (pp. 1008–1018). New York: American Society of Civil Engineers.

Zube, E. H., Sell, J. L., & Taylor, J. G. (1982). Landscape perception: Research, application and theory. *Landscape Planning, 9*, 1–33.

7

Paths toward Environmental Consciousness

LEANNE G. RIVLIN

MUCH OF MY LIFE HAS BEEN SPENT in the Borough of Brooklyn in New York. A graduate of its public schools and Brooklyn College, I went to Teachers College, Columbia University, for a PhD in developmental psychology that I received in 1957. While a graduate student I taught in the psychology department at Brooklyn College. After completing my degree, I was a research consultant on a 2-year study of creativity at Hunter College High School. With the termination of this project, I began my association with Bill Ittelson and Hal Proshansky in their environmental research that was based first at Brooklyn College, then at the Graduate School of the City University of New York in Manhattan.

Although anchored in New York, I have had many opportunities for travel in the United States and abroad. A number of summers in North Africa where my husband, Ben Rivlin, was engaged in research, have deepened my appreciation of the cultural imprint on people's lives and introduced me to the impressive architecture of the region. Although I see myself as a New Yorker, I have felt quite at home in Paris, Rabat, and the lovely Berber village of Azrou in the Middle Atlas Mountains of Morocco. A teaching career suits my interests—my love of reading, writing, and travel. I am grateful to Hal Proshansky for encouraging my move into academia and to my husband and my son, Marc, for their support and tolerance of my absorption with this life.

SOME CAUTIONS ABOUT PERSONAL ACCOUNTS[1]

Some years ago while reviewing publications in our environmental psychology library, we came across a Council of Planning Librarians' history and bibliogra-

[1] For the caring and sensitive reading of an earlier draft of this chapter, I wish to express my appreciation to Louise Chawla, Sheila Lehman, Ben Rivlin, and Nora Rubinstein.

LEANNE G. RIVLIN • Environmental Psychology Program, The Graduate School and University Center of the City University of New York, 33 West 42nd Street, New York, New York 10036.

phy on the development of our program and the contributions of individual members of the faculty. It was written by students from a distinguished school in another country, people who knew our work from written sources. The biographies were amusing accounts, obviously shaped by our vitae and publications, with a rational approach to our careers as environmental psychologists. It was as though each of us—William Ittelson, Harold Proshansky, Maxine Wolfe, Gary Winkel, and I—were preordained to enter this field based on a series of calculated steps related to our professional interests and training that seemed especially significant to our future work. But, of course, much of the speculation was fiction. What the writers could not know was the serendipitous nature of our development into environmental psychologists, the values and concerns that shaped the decisions each of us had made in choosing the directions we took.

I thought about this account of our program when faced with the task of writing this chapter. How easy it is to round off the rough edges of contradiction in a person's life, fill in the gaps, ignore the side roads, false starts, and chance events that characterize most people's development. Even with a personal memory of the events, it may be easier for the writer and clearer for the reader to smooth out the details and strive toward a logical story rather than an accurate one. But this kind of deception would, in effect, defeat the point of this history. It would, to a great degree, change the intention of our mandate to discuss the evolution of our ideas in environmental psychology. For it was the rough shaping of our interests that led me, and others, to this special area because we came to this field from many directions. Although I have no doubt that my story will include some fiction, at least I carry with me the memory of the Council of Planning Librarians' amusing history and the points it could not make.

MY NEW YORK IDENTITY

The City of New York has been a major force in shaping my interests, my professional work, and my style of life. Although I have lived elsewhere for short periods of time and have traveled in other countries, including time spent in North Africa, New York has formed my life world, for better or worse, becoming part of my place identity (Proshansky, Fabian, & Kaminoff, 1983). The city has influenced me on two levels. The larger sphere is a general sense of being part of a large, culturally rich city with a great deal of stimulation available a subway or bus ride away. On a deeper level, a powerful, closer influence has emerged from neighborhood life, being part of a smaller, more intimate geography in three Brooklyn communities, all of them close to Prospect Park. This magnificent Olmsted creation has probably been the single most powerful environmental influence from my childhood up to today. It was my Depression-era "Playland," a place to ride my tricycle and run freely; later, my access to nature and beauty and my son's playground as well. This park and my neighborhoods have produced two themes that helped to define directions for me. The neighborhoods in which I have lived and worked, gone to school, shopped, and found recreation have been enriched with diverse populations—Italians, Irish, blacks, Orthodox Jews, secular Jews, Puerto Ricans—always with variety, although more in some areas than others. Each one showed me how a single geography could support different cultures, although not necessarily without conflict. These experiences have shaped my food and housing preferences, my interests and attitudes. Whenever I am away from this diversity for any length of time, I find that I miss it sorely.

But neighborhood life has shaped my world in other ways. The ability to look out of my apartment window and see faces I know in the street, children playing, people of different ages, is satisfying and comfortable. Am I too much affected by Jane Jacobs in this view? Perhaps, but how can one ignore the support of neighbors in creating residential satisfaction? And what does it mean to have no neighbors, or frightening ones, or people rejecting your presence? These kinds of questions have intruded on my professional life for many years.

My first neighborhood study and research on diversity came out of undergraduate course assignments at Brooklyn College. The diversity study was undertaken in a philosophy class where we were required to deal with a question, any kind of question, that could be examined from different perspectives. I chose the problem of racial relations in South Africa, where the grandfather I never knew had spent many years. I interviewed blacks, Indians, and Afrikaners who were native to that country and considered their views in light of the racial problems in the United States. It was my first empirical study in which interviews formed a major source of information, and the instructor's requirement that we dig into the meaning of the questions and responses was advice that was to influence my work in many ways.

The neighborhood research became a term paper for a class on the sociology of communities where we had to do an analysis of a sector of New York. My study examined a few blocks in the Williamsburg section of Brooklyn, an area that was largely Hasidic in its population. I selected this neighborhood because it provided an opportunity to look at a group of Orthodox Jews that was unfamiliar to me, a chance to learn about a sect that had a distinctive way of living. It was an early environmental experience in which both the nature of the housing and commercial development had to be related to the ideology and life-style of the residents. This was a task I was to repeat in my later professional life in research on Lubavitcher Hasidim in Crown Heights (Rivlin, 1982), my open space research (1986), and my current work on homeless communities (Rivlin & Imbimbo, 1989). In fact, the need to look at geographic areas and define their form and functions became central to my work. But the course assignments also sharpened my view of New York's neighborhoods and the different populations that lived in the city. My enthusiasm for the heterogeneity of New York and my sense of myself as a New Yorker have shaped my research interests, my way of thinking, and my community work in many ways.

THE CHANGING PATHS

Neither philosophy nor sociology was my major area of study as an undergraduate. After considerable shopping around across broad territories, I realized that I could not settle on a single specialty and instead took a double major in English and psychology. To the end, the decision as to which path to take was a difficult one, but I finally settled on developmental psychology that was the closest thing my advisor could suggest when I expressed an interest in the psychology of "ordinary people."

My training came at a period when developmental psychology was heavily involved in tests and measurement, and I did considerable work in that area. When I came to do my dissertation, I designed a field study of creativity in teenagers in which I assessed their attitudes toward themselves and their social preferences and also interviewed them in a follow-up study (Rivlin, 1959). In reflecting on my graduate training, I can see how the requirements to observe children closely demonstrated the value of this method in understanding the messages conveyed by behavior and the significance of looking at real-world events rather than simulated ones. In retrospect, this was another important methodological lesson that very likely influenced the change in my interests and my current work. It was to be reinforced in my first step toward environmental research.

In the late 1950s, Bill Ittelson, who was then chair of the psychology department at Brooklyn College where I was teaching some courses, asked whether I would be interested in joining his research project on psychiatric ward design. At the time, I could see no connection to my research on creativity and little in my training (other than experience in teaching abnormal psychology) that would attract me, apart from the opportunity to work with Bill. I declined the offer and went on to conduct a 2-year study at Hunter College High School that was closer to my interests. As this work was coming to a close, a chance meeting between my husband, Ben Rivlin, and Hal Proshansky brought the Ward Design Study into my life again. The invitation to join the project (in which both Bill and Hal were then involved) was initiated with receipt of a document on the history of psychiatric care, which had been prepared as a first step to empirical research (Ittelson, Proshansky, & Rosenblatt, 1960). It was a comprehensive overview of attitudes toward people with behavior perceived as "disordered" and an analysis of the relationship of these views to the ways people were treated, including any physical settings that might be provided. This use of history to understand social issues was different from the kind of history I had read before. It also contrasted with the analysis of psychiatric care available in psychology texts. I believe that this report influenced my decision to join the project, although this may be hindsight. I do know that my colleagues' description of the research—the opportunity to look at the ways psychiatric wards function before we came up with a research plan—did intrigue me, although I had no sense of how all this would make use of my developmental background.

The years ahead provided considerable experience in observing psychiatric hospitals. Although the issue of psychiatric care had an inherent interest of its own, what was most compelling was the opportunity to look at all components of a setting and all the people there playing out their roles in a relatively closed system, one that could be observed over time without creating a major disruption in what was happening. It became clear that obtaining an understanding of the functions of a system could not be forced into a conventional working day. It was essential to go to the hospitals in the evening and at night to develop a sense of the life on the wards and that life did not end at 5 P.M. We discovered the activities of the dark hours, the restlessness of many patients despite their medications (or perhaps because of them), and the pressures on night staff and their loneliness because staffing was very limited after midnight. Our team of researchers experienced the night life of the city as we traveled to and from our research sites, the vitality of the streets after midnight and in the early morning hours.

We spent many hours on the psychiatric wards speaking to patients, nurses, aids, psychiatrists, and housekeeping staff, getting familiar with hospital life and bureaucracy. Some of our contacts were informal ones, but we also interviewed the patients and personnel and undertook formal observations, over time. Even as we were working in the hospitals, we recognized the significant role of the physical place and the neglect given to this domain in the past. But we also realized that we were looking at a people/place relationship that extended beyond the specific psychiatric context of our research to cover broader principles of behavior. When we reviewed the results of our observations, which Bill Ittelson called "behavioral mapping" to call attention to its geographical context, and when we listened to the concerns of patients and staff that emerged from interviews, it became clear that there were significant behavioral domains that were salient issues, if not basic needs, for people. Although our data were based on psychiatric ward experiences, these domains resounded with human experience, whatever the context. It was recognition of this fact that led to further work and a search in the literature for like-minded colleagues. What had begun as a single piece of research developed into what ultimately became part of the interdisciplinary specialization of environmental psychology.

It was not difficult, at the time, to find others working in the area. The environmental consciousness and self-questioning of the 1960s had led to critiques of the status quo and reflections on a broad range of alternatives. The environment was the object of increasing criticism from many professions. We found Robert Sommer in the publications he was producing (Sommer, 1969; Sommer & Ross, 1958), Irwin Altman (Altman & Haythorn, 1965, 1967), Humphry Osmond (1957), Kiyo Izumi (1965), Kevin Lynch (1960), Robert Gutman (1966), Robert Kates (1968), Roger Barker and his associates (Barker, 1963, 1968; Barker & Gump, 1964), David Canter (1961), Paul Sivadon (1965), and others. Coming from different disciplines with interests covering many aspects of environment–behavior study, these colleagues were articulating an agenda for environmental research that was central to the emergence of the field.

It was the work of this disparate group of people and the need we felt to begin to define the domains of an environmental psychology that led us to put together a book of readings in the late 1960s (Proshansky, Ittelson, & Rivlin,

1970a). Included were some of our own papers that were based on the ward design studies. Two of them outlined core concepts that had emerged from our research, some of which were appearing in the publications of the environment and behavior professionals. The consideration of how the physical environment influences behavior generated assumptions that, in my view, largely hold up over time and place (Proshansky, Ittelson, & Rivlin, 1970b). The ability to extract these principles from data on psychiatric wards underscored the general relevance of our work to a larger framework.

One direction that emerged from this thinking as well as from the work of others in the area (Goffman, 1961; Osmond, 1957; Sommer, 1969; Sommer & Ross, 1958) was the gradual development of ideas on institutional form. I found great inspiration in Goffman's work, but it was extensive subsequent research with Maxine Wolfe on a children's psychiatric hospital (Rivlin & Wolfe, 1972, 1985), on schools and day-care settings with Marilyn Rothenberg (Rivlin & Rothenberg, 1976), and facilities for developmentally disabled persons with Marian Golan, Vincent Bogert, and Robyn Cirillo (Rivlin, Bogert, & Cirillo, 1981) that provided day-by-day evidence of institutional qualities. These indicators emerged from our intensive observations of the same settings, over time, covering complete days (and nights in the case of hospitals), over years. We were able to document the institutional impacts on the daily routines in the sites, their physical arrangements, and the degrees of freedom available to the occupants to use and personalize the settings in an individual manner. The opportunity to consider a range of settings from the total institution of psychiatric hospitals to the partial ones of schools and day-care centers reiterated the continuity of environmental influences and the fact that institutional qualities are not exclusive to places labeled as institutions (Rivlin, 1976).

Another early paper included in our book defined some central environmental concepts by outlining a perspective on freedom of choice that considered privacy, territoriality, crowding, and change (Proshansky, Ittelson, & Rivlin, 1970c). Drawing heavily on the hospital studies, we were able to examine the individual's need for freedom, privacy, and control over both the immediate domain surrounding the person and in the larger urban, suburban, and rural contexts, as well. The constructs provided key issues around which to understand the relationship between person and environment, directing attention to the total life world rather than a limited sphere, recognizing that each domain transacts with others. This perspective acknowledged that people's needs for privacy and the values about it extended over the entire life of the individual from the home, to the school, to settings for work and recreation, a formulation vital to my later concerns with homeless children and adults.

The view that emerged from the early work required a research ideology that differed greatly from the one in which I had been trained. Rather than focus on single variables, it forced me to consider all aspects impinging on the dimensions under study. Privacy and crowding became key concepts in my work and the issue of change a central consideration.

The early environmental research was instructive in charting a course that influenced my future work in many ways.

- It verified the value of studying questions in the field rather than looking at laboratory simulations of complex phenomena.
- It emphasized the necessity of looking at people in settings over time, rather than at brief episodes in their lives. Settings had a rhythm, a series of time frames in which changes occurred, and it was crucial to identify these time frames in trying to understand change.
- It convinced me that no one discipline held the answers to complex questions, that professional boundaries must be crossed in environmental research. This obligates environmental researchers to read both widely and intensively on an area that is new and to recognize that their questions have been posed, and sometimes answered, by people with other disciplinary identities.
- It underlined the requirement to examine problems in an historical context, not for specific answers from the past but for an understanding of the ways that different forces—social, political, and economic—impinged upon conditions in the past as they may also in the present. A journey into the past makes it easier to see these forces operating than is possible in restricting the study to the present. The patterns from the past are more visible, providing directions as to what to investigate in the contemporary realm and clues for detecting connections.
- It revealed the richness of a multiple methods approach to questions, examining data from a number of techniques rather than a single data set. It demonstrated the importance of talking to all the people in a setting, not just the powerful or conspicuous people, to look closely at what was happening, to check for archival information, and to put all of this evidence together in analyzing the questions under study and in writing the final report.
- It demonstrated the value of collaborative work in which each member of the study team is an active participant in designing and conducting the research. This does not imply a consensus model of research but rather the discussion of everyone's ideas and consideration of alternatives in an open manner. This approach has turned out to be, in my view, the best way to conduct quality research and the most effective way to train people in research skills. It also has the advantage of realism in the light of time pressures, unexpected events, and personal involvements characteristic of field research.

BEYOND THE INSTITUTIONS

After a number of years of institutional research, Maxine Wolfe and I began a book that would enable us to reflect on our work—both studies on which we had collaborated and work that we each had undertaken individually. The focus was on institutional environments for children, which we wanted to place in an historical context while reflecting on our own findings in contemporary times. Because the research had been completed, we felt that it would be a relatively simple matter to examine the past and summarize the findings.

The task of addressing history turned out to be far from simple and was extremely time consuming but essential to the story we were telling. It was necessary to search out original source materials and read extensively in historical texts in order to unravel the origins of children's psychiatric hospitals, schools, and day-care facilities, the subjects of our writing. But the information we uncovered was vital to our consideration of contemporary institutions and provided an understanding of the ways the philosophy of a time influences its physical forms and programs. For the second time I recognized the inseparability of the social, political, and economic contexts of a physical form and its contemporary functions. By looking both at the development of the concept of childhood and the creation of settings prescribed for children, we were able to understand why psychiatric hospitals for children exist, the implicit and explicit functions of schools and day care, and the gaps between the ostensible philosophies of therapy, education, and child care and actual practices (Rivlin & Wolfe, 1985).

In the case of psychiatric facilities for children, the emergence of a complex, bureaucratic, and largely ineffective system for the treatment of children perceived to be "disordered" occurred over a number of years, stimulated, in large measure, by the various reforms offered by well-intentioned citizens, social reformers, and professionals. Prior to the 1800s, the orphan asylum constituted the primary child-caring institutions in the United States with almshouses accommodating impoverished children and their families. By the early nineteenth century, children who were orphaned, poor, or whose parents were judged incompetent had a variety of public and private institutions available for their care and education. Children convicted of petty crimes or vagrancy and those considered to be "willfully disobedient" (Rothman, 1971, p. 209) could be turned over to the authorities and placed in the Houses of Refuge, reformatories for disobedient children and youth. This was a period of reform that had confidence in the value of isolating inmates from the corrupting influences of family and the community and optimism about the malleability of the young. By providing a strict routine that emphasized the value of hard work, obedience to authority, and punishment for "misbehaviors" that included physical abuse, the authorities felt that they were creating therapeutic, educational settings for learning proper values and skills that would enable inmates to fit into society. The professionals often described their programs in family terms, although neither the physical setting nor the institutional routine bore any resemblance to a home. This is a mythology that has persisted in the creation of various kinds of institutions where homelike conditions have been uniformly absent, although the settings might be identified as "Children's Homes."

The historical view pointed to important guidelines for contemporary research. The gaps between rhetoric and reality, between ideology and practice might be easier to see through hindsight but were no less powerful in the institutions and their programs that we were studying. The writing also required that we examine the developmental literature, and I was able to return to the specialty in which I had been trained. The analysis reified the essential nature of an historic perspective to research and has influenced my later work on homelessness and on public spaces in significant ways.

THE PUBLIC ARENA

My interest in public space began when Mark Francis and Stephen Carr were teaching in our program in 1981. We decided that we wanted to work together and developed a study of public spaces on which we would collaborate. The goal was to undertake a critique of contemporary public spaces and to offer a perspective on their design and management. Andrew Stone, then a student in our program, joined our effort, and over the years we have been preparing a manuscript on the development and use of public space.

With the end point of this project now in view, I can look back and recognize the qualities that make it an excellent example of collaborative work. Although it has been difficult to sustain the momentum with Mark Francis in Davis, California, Steve Carr in Cambridge, Massachusetts, and Andy and me in New York, the richness of the material we have gathered—case studies of public spaces, historical analyses of public life, examples of effective and ineffective design and management—has nurtured our own analyses and moved us along. For myself, the work has uncovered the public arena in ways that I had not perceived before, raising issues about the public/private components of people's lives and the role that they play in different societies. It has made me more conscious of the worlds I move through because unlike the special settings of institutions, public spaces are everywhere.

In looking at public life, I realized that a good deal of it took place in settings that were not designed for the purposes they were serving. The steps of buildings, streetcorners, areas in front of shops, all were filled with people-watchers, performers, peddlers, and persons engaged in conversation. They were important additions to the conventional settings and in many cases, far more successful. Ahuva Windsor and I found that when people were asked about "found" spaces, they were able to describe a variety of different sites they used. Our observations of a number of found places confirmed an array of activities there and regular use by many of those who were present (Rivlin, 1986; Rivlin & Windsor, 1986).

Both the designed and found public spaces were serving many of the functions of a home, an office, a playground, and a balcony on life. For homeless users, these settings were living rooms, places to pass time, rest, eat, talk to others, or sleep. In the years ahead, I learned much about the role of public spaces in the lives of homeless persons.

DEALING WITH HOMELESSNESS

Homelessness first came to my attention in dramatic form in 1978 when students in a class in methods in environmental psychology began to study

Grand Central Terminal in New York (Rivlin, Francis, & Paxson, 1979). Even then, we discovered that the waiting room was a gathering place for homeless persons, although they were not welcomed by the space managers. The following year, the methods class was assigned the Port Authority Bus Terminal as a study site, and again we found large numbers of homeless persons were regular users of seating areas and bathrooms. These were my initial, direct contacts with homelessness and my first recognition that New York had large numbers of unhoused citizens. My early interests in nomadic groups were revived by what I saw, and I began to read, collect newspaper clippings, and raise questions about this serious social problem.

No research in which I have been involved has encompassed my interests and raised my sense of outrage as much as this work on homelessness. Although the studies of institutions uncovered many injustices and were stressful, none reached the level of this present work. The examination of homelessness has tapped a broad array of my concerns—about New York, the history of homelessness in this country, housing policies, deinstitutionalization, diversity, and the nature of public and private behaviors. In the years that followed my original recognition of the scale of homelessness in New York, the problem escalated onto the front pages of newspapers, and it became clear that this was a national crisis. Homeless people were everywhere in the public spaces I was studying—parks, plazas, and in found spaces such as the steps of monumental buildings and transitional areas where peddlers sold their wares—in doorways, in libraries, in front of the building in mid-Manhattan where my university is housed. Not only did homelessness raise questions that resounded with my own interests, I came to see it as a quintessential contemporary environmental issue, one that addressed the central concerns of environment and behavior researchers and practitioners.

My approach to the study of homelessness required recognition that I could not stand apart from the problem and examine it from a distance. Too many years of research in environmental areas had disabused me of any desire to look at questions from a laboratory view, to pretend at scientific objectivity. I was convinced of the value of examining problems in their context, of keeping a close view of issues and the settings in which they were embedded. However, this did not mean that unreflected personal experiences should parade as data. What was needed was a way of getting a detailed view of people's experiences and providing an analysis of results that exposed both my own perspective on the problems and my methods in addressing them. A systematic approach was required, and I was able to draw on my past history for lessons on how to proceed.

As a start, much as I had to spend time looking at psychiatric wards, earlier in my work, I had to be immersed in the reality of homelessness, at least to the degree possible for a person with a home. I began by volunteering in a small, privately sponsored shelter that also might have relieved some of my guilt about studying a disastrous situation without contributing some effort to alleviate the suffering.[2] Although I never saw the purpose of my time as a volunteer as direct data gathering, it did confront me with the day-by-day experiences of homelessness as I listened to the stories of the 10 men who came to our shelter. What became clear were the different aspects of homelessness that had to be considered. The first one concerned the meaning of home to people and the significance of the loss of a home setting.

As I began to work with homeless families, the question of the impacts of homelessness on each family member, especially on the development of children, was in the forefront. Interestingly, despite the increasing numbers of professionals involved in homelessness, few have addressed the developmental–environmental questions on the impacts of losing a home or of living in a series of temporary facilities. Attention has been placed on the symptoms identified in homeless persons rather than on the significance of home or the long-range consequences of being homeless.

Drawing on work on environmental biographies (Cooper Marcus, 1978a,b; Hester, 1978; Horwitz & Klein, 1978); home (Horwitz & Tognoli, 1982); place identity (Proshansky, Fabian, & Kaminoff, 1983); and place attachment (Shumaker & Taylor, 1983; Stokols & Shumaker, 1981), it is possible to articulate the serious emotional, physical, and intellectual threats to children and adults who live in emergency shelters, welfare hotels, transitional residences, and other forms of precarious housing. I am convinced that if environmental researchers do not attend to this issue, it will not receive the attention it requires from other professionals who are directing themselves to different concerns.

The second aspect of my present work has been to describe the diversity of homeless persons, to counteract the tendency evident in the press to exaggerate the incidence of mental disorders among homeless populations. Of those homeless persons showing behavioral problems, many are deinstitutionalized psychiatric patients thrown onto their own resources with little preparation for independent life and placed in precarious circumstances that intensify rather than ameliorate their problems. Although it has been estimated that about 30% of the homeless persons seen in shelters and in the streets have some form of behavioral difficulties, the fastest growing group among the homeless is families with children. I have tried to understand something of the lives of a broad range of homeless persons including homeless families, single men and women, and homeless groups. With the help of colleagues, I have been documenting the experiences of two self-help homeless communities, groups of homeless persons who live together cooperatively, often on empty lots or in abandoned buildings, managing through the efforts of participants. Many of these people grew up in the area and feel strong attachments to the neighborhoods in which they are living. The struggles of these homeless persons provide a lesson in dealing with municipal bureaucracies and urban survival strategies in

---

[2] The shelter where I have been a volunteer for the past 6 years is part of the Partnership for the Homeless interfaith system of shelters located in churches, synagogues, and meeting houses.

the face of threats of eviction, severe weather, and limited resources, other than personal ones (Rivlin & Imbimbo, 1989).

Most recently I have been talking to homeless families moving through the conventional New York City system for rehousing, in order to consider the long-term experience of being homeless. We are including each person's environmental history, place attachments, and finally are looking at the effects of relocation, over time. From this longitudinal perspective on the ecology of homelessness, the entire experience can be evaluated with a view toward understanding the significance of home and neighborhood within a grounded critique of homeless policies.

It also has been important to understand the history of homelessness in the United States, again to identify some of the factors that contribute to the loss of home. Through a study of newspapers, archival materials, and other primary and secondary sources, I have been examining periods when homelessness has been prevalent, looking for explanations for the problem and the policies for dealing with it. These all were times of severe economic difficulty, with financial panics and depressions, including the second half of the nineteenth century and the Great Depression of the 1930s. One project in this area has involved a review of the *New York Times* from 1865 through 1900, examining articles dealing with homeless children and adults, particularly the views expressed toward them and the measures taken. Lynne Manzo and I have documented the language used to describe the homeless persons, the prejudices reflected in the attitudes toward them, and the morality, both Puritanical and Victorian that led to the measures taken (Rivlin & Manzo, 1988). In looking at these articles on homeless children in New York, we have found the ideology of poverty reflected onto the young, the prejudices toward immigrants, and the old distinctions, seen throughout earlier history and in contemporary times, between "deserving" and "undeserving" poor. The nineteenth-century newspapers also reflected a different concept of childhood, with an expectation that poor children, even those as young as 6 or 7, should work for their food and shelter whether on the streets or in the lodging houses provided for homeless youth. In the next years I plan to examine this history in greater detail with attention to the nature of housing policies and the availability of low-cost housing during different periods of widespread homelessness.

THE NEW YORK CONTEXT

The City of New York has been a partner in my research, much as the many collaborators with whom I have been fortunate to work, over the years. It is a context for my studies but also a stimulus to the research directions I have pursued as well as the style of the research.

It is not unusual to hear colleagues from other locations qualify the results of New York-based research suggesting that findings cannot be generalized beyond this area. "New York is unique" or "New York is different" are frequent comments. Although I will not deny the special qualities of my native city and the place where I work, I would conclude that the individuality of New York, which is a product of the diversity of its components, the heterogeneity of its populations and the variety of its problems, makes it a superb setting for research. New York is the quintessential context for studies of a broad-ranging sort. At our doorsteps are more questions than a lifetime could contain, more problems needing attention than any single person could address, and enough environmental work for generations of professionals. Although it is essential to acknowledge that it is a huge and diverse city, it is equally important to recognize that New York is characteristic of the culture of the United States into which it is embedded. Every place is unique, a fact that we often find easy to forget. It is the researcher's obligation to identify the individual qualities of the research setting, its context, and the participants as well as the qualities shared with other sites and people.

WITH A VIEW TOWARD THE FUTURE

In preparing this chapter, I rummaged through some cartons in the back of my closet containing old files from my undergraduate and graduate studies and came upon notes from my first psychology course taken in 1950. We had used Norman Munn's textbook (1946) covering the standard topics of the time—on response systems, growth and development, conditioned responses, learning, remembering and forgetting, thinking, physiological drives, social motives, emotions, attending, perceiving, and then each of the senses (vision, hearing, other senses), statistics, intelligence, aptitudes, and personality—each topic encapsulated in its separate chapter. In glancing through the class notes and notes on the textbook I was struck by their neatness, the certainty of the various theories displayed, the "science" displayed with diagrams and outlines. It was psychology as I once knew it, but it was far from my present concerns and the way I do psychology today. Although I continue to be interested in many of the topics from the past—human development, learning, social motivation, emotions, and perception—they have become enmeshed in larger environmental issues in which I am immersed. In another file I found a lengthy report prepared for a course in experimental psychology, "A Study of Verbal Learning and the Dynamics of Retroactive Inhibition," summarizing a laboratory study undertaken with an unnamed partner. But most surprising was a paper completed as a graduate student to fulfill requirements in a memorable course on the Rorschach given at the New School for Social Research by Ernest Schachtel. This class, in fact, was a journey through the ways people constructed their perceptions of the world. The paper, "A Critical Study of the Dd Response," impressed me, for I have long forgotten the details of this diagnostic instrument. It contained a critical assessment of the Dd or small detail response to the Rorschach blots. However, my final sentence was rather unexpected in light of my training at the time. After evaluating different professional interpretations of the Dd response I concluded:

This is not to suggest that all these dynamics lie behind each case of excess Dd, but in the light of the class lectures, and the literature in the area, it is clear that the meaning of details in the test might be better understood when we examine some of the other needs and forces in the life space of the individual.

It is unreasonable to believe that this reflected a philosophic ember that ignited when the opportunity to pursue environmental research was offered to me. That interpretation would be completely fictional. However, looking at the comment from a distance, I was delighted that it was there, for it reassured me that this path is one that resounds well and long with my thinking, in whatever area that thinking was applied. The training offered by my past research and by my students' work over the years has underlined the value of thinking contextually, considering all responses as the end points of multiple factors, recognizing the diverse past histories of people who have individual cultural backgrounds, physical makeups, personalities, and different views of the world. Thus, attention to the life space of any individual, as Lewin (1936) has expressed it, identifies the interaction of internal and environmental forces as influences on behavior, although Lewin did not delineate contributions of the physical world. This contextualization of research questions, I would hope, will continue to characterize environmental research in the future.

One of the characteristics of much research, including environmental studies, has been the neglect of contextual information (including historical detail) that is necessary to interpret findings with accuracy and rigor. Further development of environmental methodologies that respect these requirements is a task that must be addressed. Although we can learn much from other disciplines, for example, from history and anthropology, the specific demands of environmental research require particular attention to the social, cultural, political, and economic realities that transcend individual specializations and single points in time. The kinds of problems that we are addressing are complex, multidisciplinary, and require both a broad and deep approach to study.

As we move toward the end of the twentieth century, we need to take on the challenges presented by the many environmental issues that confront us— the housing and homelessness crises, critiques of our educational system, threats from environmental risks, and dangers from pollution and contaminants—but we must do so with confidence in our methods and movement beyond the conclusions of individual studies into theory development. With strong theory grounded in empirical evidence we can offer the most effective arguments for policy change. We can encourage the empowerment of people on their own behalf with confidence that solid, professional research (hopefully, research in which they have participated) underlies the voices that are heard and the theories that the voices illustrate.

To some degree, I have a luxury at this stage of my work, a freedom to explore what interests me without concern for promotion committees, peer review, and the like. But this also is a time to reflect on what has disappeared, over the years, interests that have not received sufficient nourishment to persist. It amazes me that I can pass a day without sketching and not feel deprived or that my writing has been directed exclusively toward professional papers and conference presentations rather than to other sources. I am reminded of my early research on the artistic and scientific efforts of youth and the evidence of the decreasing range of their interests, as time progressed. I look for models in people who have retained a breadth in their work, people who have defied the trends toward narrow specialization.

My own future work will continue to address homelessness, at least until people are no longer threatened by the loss of their homes. I am developing some research that will consider the situations in other countries and am searching for international contacts, colleagues interested in pursuing these questions. I have no doubt that new areas will attract me as well. The inherent interest of our work and the stimulation it offers are qualities I deeply appreciate. There are too many intriguing questions: the different lives of people from similar backgrounds (I would like to look closely at different branches of my family tree now living in England, France, Israel, Brazil, and Uruguay); the learning process associated with understanding complex geographies (I would like to study the ways children learn to get around intricately laid-out cities such as Fes in Morocco); the basic questions surrounding the meaning of home, a question that has plagued me in the past and will continue to do so, probably forever (I would like to return to work on nomads that I began years ago and, fueled by my recent work with people having ephemeral grasps on home, generate a perspective on the significance of homes over the course of life; I would like to understand the ongoing work of creating a home and threats to that process). Although there no doubt is much that I cannot or will not accomplish, I am confident that others also will be intrigued with these questions and take them on in the years ahead.

REFERENCES

Altman, I., & Haythorn, W. W. (1965). Interpersonal exchange in isolation. *Sociometry, 28,* 411–426.

Altman, I., & Haythorn, W. W. (1967). The ecology of isolated groups. *Behavioral Science, 12,* 169–182.

Barker, R. G. (1963). *The stream of behavior.* New York: Appleton, Century.

Barker, R. G. (1968). *Ecological psychology: Concepts and methods for studying the environment of behaviors.* Stanford, CA: Stanford University Press.

Barker, R. G., & Gump, P. V. (1964). *Big school, small school.* Stanford, CA: Stanford University Press.

Canter, D. (1961). Attitudes and perception in architecture. *Architectural Association Quarterly, 1,* 24–31.

Carr, S., Francis, M., Rivlin, L. G., & Stone, A. (under review). *Making Public Space.*

Cooper Marcus, C. (1978a). Remembrance of landscapes past. *Landscape, 22*(3), 34–43.

Cooper Marcus, C. (1978b, December). Environmental autobiography. *Childhood City Newsletter,* 3–5.

Goffman, E. (1961). *Asylums.* Chicago: Aldine.

Gutman, R. (1966). Site planning and social behavior. *Journal of Social Issues, 22,* 103–105.

Hester, R. (1978, December). Favorite spaces. *Childhood City Newsletter,* 15–17.

Horwitz, J., & Klein, S. (1978, December). An exercise in the use of environmental autobiography for programming and design of a day care center. *Childhood City Newsletter,* 18–19.

Horwitz, J., & Tognoli, J. (1982). Role of home in adult development: Women and men living alone describe their residential histories. *Family Relations, 31*, 335–341.

Ittelson, W. H., Proshansky, H. M., & Rosenblatt, D. (1960). *Some factors influencing the design and function of psychiatric facilities.* New York: Brooklyn College.

Izumi, K. (1965). Psychosocial phenomena and building design. *Building Research, 2*, 9–11.

Kates, R. W. (1968). *Natural hazards in human ecological perspective: Hypotheses and models.* Natural Hazard Research Working Paper No. 14. Toronto: Department of Geography, University of Toronto.

Lewin, K. (1936). *Principles of topological psychology.* New York: McGraw-Hill.

Munn, N. (1946). *Psychology.* Boston: Houghton Mifflin.

Osmond, H. (1957). Function as the basis of psychiatric ward design. *Mental Hospitals (Architectural Supplement), 8*, 23–29.

Proshansky, H. M., Fabian, A. K., & Kaminoff, R. (1983). Place identity: Physical world socialization of the self. *Journal of Environmental Psychology, 3*, 57–83.

Proshansky, H. M., Ittelson, W. H., & Rivlin, L. G. (Eds.). (1970a). *Environmental psychology: Man and his physical setting.* New York: Holt, Rinehart & Winston.

Proshansky, H. M., Ittelson, W. H., & Rivlin, L. G. (1970b). The influence of the physical environment on behavior: Some basic assumptions. In H. M. Proshansky, W. H. Ittelson, & L. G. Rivlin (Eds.), *Environmental psychology: Man and his physical setting* (pp. 27–30). New York: Holt, Rinehart & Winston.

Proshansky, H. M., Ittelson, W. H., & Rivlin, L. G. (1970c). Freedom of choice and behavior in a physical setting. In H. M. Proshansky, W. H. Ittelson, & L. G. Rivlin (Eds.), *Environmental psychology: Man and his physical setting* (pp. 173–183). New York: Holt, Rinehart & Winston.

Rivlin, L. G. (1959). Creativity and the self-attitudes and sociability of high school students. *Journal of Educational Psychology, 1*, 147–152.

Rivlin, L. G. (1976). *Some issues concerning institutional places.* Paper prepared for the 3rd International Architectural Psychology Conference. Strasbourg, France.

Rivlin, L. G. (1982). Group membership and place meanings in an urban neighborhood. *Journal of Social Issues, 38*(3), 75–93.

Rivlin, L. G. (1986). *A study of "found" public spaces.* New York: City University of New York, Center for Human Environments.

Rivlin, L. G., Bogert, V., & Cirillo, R. (1981). Uncoupling institutional indicators. In A. E. Osterberg, C. P. Tiernan, & R. A. Findlay (Eds.), *Design research interactions: Proceedings of the twelfth international conference of the Environmental Design Research Association.* Ames, Iowa.

Rivlin, L. G., & Imbimbo, J. (1989). Self-help efforts in a squatter community: Implications for addressing contemporary homelessness. *American Journal of Community Psychology, 17*(6).

Rivlin, L. G., & Manzo, L. C. (1988). Homeless children in New York City: A view from the 19th century. *Children's Environments Quarterly, 5*(1), 26–33.

Rivlin, L. G., & Rothenberg, M. (1976). The use of space in open classrooms. In H. M. Proshansky, W. H. Ittelson, & L. G. Rivlin (Eds.), *Environmental psychology: People and their physical settings* (pp. 479–489). New York: Holt, Rinehart & Winston.

Rivlin, L. G., & Windsor, A. (1986, July). *Found space and users' needs.* Paper presented at the 21st International Congress of Applied Psychology, Jerusalem, Israel.

Rivlin, L. G., & Wolfe, M. (1972). The early history of a psychiatric hospital for children: Expectations and reality. *Environment and Behavior, 4*, 33–72.

Rivlin, L. G., & Wolfe, M. (1985). *Institutional settings in children's lives.* New York: Wiley.

Rivlin, L. G., Francis, M., & Paxson, L. (Eds.). (1979). *Grand Central Terminal: A human perspective.* New York: City University of New York, Center for Human Environments.

Shumaker, S. A., & Taylor, R. B. (1983). Toward a clarification of people-place relationships: A model of attachment to place. In N. R. Feimer & E. S. Geller (Eds.), *Environmental psychology: Directions and perspectives* (pp. 219–251). New York: Praeger.

Sivadon, P. (1965). Space as experienced: Therapeutic implications. *L'Evolution Psychiatrique, 3,* 477–498.

Sommer, R. (1969). *Personal space: The behavioral basis of design.* Englewood Cliffs, NJ: Prentice-Hall.

Sommer, R., & Ross, H. (1958). Social interaction on a geriatrics ward. *International Journal of Social Psychiatry, 4,* 128–133.

Stokols, D., & Shumaker, S. A. (1981). People in places: A transactional view of settings. In J. H. Harvey (Ed.), *Cognition, social behavior, and the environment* (pp. 441–488). Hillsdale, NJ: Lawrence Erlbaum Associates.

8

Thinking . . . As Much Fun as Sex, Drugs, and Rock 'n Roll

MICHAEL BRILL

My father was a gifted artist, calligrapher, and a high-school teacher of art and photography. My mother kept our household, ran it frugally, warmly, and well, and she sang, listened to music, and read. They were both born in New York City of parents of mixed ancestry: German, Rumanian, Russian, English, and Portuguese, I believe. My younger sister is a gifted photographer, graphic designer, calligrapher, and a teacher of photography. We both were born in Brooklyn, New York, I in 1936 and went to public school and high school there, both located a block from our small fourth-story apartment. It was a small world and much about the arts. That seems to continue, for I have four sons, now 28, 26, 23, and 17—an actor, an artist–illustrator, a designer of jewelry, and a cartoonist.

After a year's study of chemical engineering at Rensselaer Polytechnic University, I transferred to the School of Architecture at Brooklyn's Pratt Institute, receiving its bachelor of architecture degree in 1953. Right after school, I spent 2 years as a designer for Eero Saarinen in Michigan, then returned to New York City to teach and practice architecture, and passed my architect's licensing examination in 1957. I designed a wide variety of buildings as senior designer in several firms. Simultaneously I taught a design studio at Pratt for 7 years and had a small private practice creating fantasy shopping environments. Several of my works were published. In Washington, DC, from 1967 to 1969, I was a senior systems research architect at the U.S. National Bureau of Standards, exploring ways to make buildings and the design process more responsive to the needs of its end users.

In 1969, I helped John Eberhard establish the new and innovative school of architecture at the State University of New York at Buffalo and was the first chairman of its graduate program. In parallel, we founded the research unit of this school, called

MICHAEL BRILL • The Buffalo Organization for Social and Technological Innovation, 1479 Hertel Avenue, Buffalo, New York 14216, and School of Architecture, State University of New York at Buffalo, Buffalo, New York 14214.

BOSTI, the Buffalo Organization for Social and Technological Innovation, Inc. In 1973, I became BOSTI's president. As of this writing, I am a professor of design at the university and president of BOSTI.

I serve and have served on many boards and councils, often as a chair, trustee, or governor, some quite actively and some not. The more active ones have been Environmental Design Research Association; New York Foundation for the Arts; New York Council on the Humanities; New York State Council for the Arts; National Endowment for the Arts/Design Arts Program; International Design Education Foundation; and the David Gordon Pick-up Company, a postmodern dance/theatre company.

I am a frequent speaker at conferences and to professional groups, a guest design critic and speaker at university schools of architecture and landscape architecture, serve as a juror for national or statewide architectural design competitions, as an evaluator of proposals for several agencies, and consult to corporations, nonprofit groups, and government agencies.

Some awards have been made to me: a Senior Sabbatical Grant from the National Endowment for the Arts; an Individual's Grant from the Ford Foundation and the New York State Council for the Arts; a Career Award from EDRA; five awards for applied design/research from *Progressive Architecture* magazine; two from *Industrial Design* magazine; and an Outstanding Alumni Achievement award from Pratt. I have been made a national Honorary Member of the American Society of Interior Designers, and I am a systemwide Faculty Exchange Scholar of the State University of New York.

I am proudest of three things:

- Maintaining a full-time, multiperson practice in design/research for over 20 years, whose clients' payment of over $8 million in fees demonstrates the viability of such an enterprise and suggests that design/research can be a "mainstream" activity in our society's making and using of places
- My continued curiosity about a wide variety of things that finds sustenance in a willingness to change intellectual directions
- Continued joyous co-learning and real kinship in an active, dependable, and growing network of friends/colleagues.

INTRODUCTION

My recollection of first really using my mind was when it was set reeling by two particular book experiences, books looked at before I could even read, and afterwards, read again and again. The first was my art-teacher father's set of three large-format books with tipped-in and perfect color plates of all the great postimpressionist paintings, with text about the painters' lives and the paintings; the text was read only much later and quite perfunctorily. These books are now mine and looked at still. The second was a child's set of the *Wonderland of Science*, recognized now as simplistic, but fascinating then, and long since gone. I read these alternately and frequently and have felt there was some kind of imprint from this art/science oscillation. I did not mix art and science in my head then. They were separate interests and worlds, for they were in separate books.

My father was a painter and a calligrapher, a gifted teacher of art and an amateur in science. He pursued and earned a degree in geology at age 40 for fun. He encouraged both interests in me. He took great pleasure in teaching me what he knew, about all sorts of things, and he was patient and encouraging. I still hope to become the teacher he was. We often looked at paintings together in books and museums, and he talked about them. Painting's magic captured my imagination and still does, far more than any art form. Conversely, the determinism, order, elegance, and majesty of science appealed to me. Perversely, I chose neither art nor science to study, not ever.

Both the magic of art and the probe, recognition, and release of rigorous thought are enormous pleasure for me and always have been. I am primarily a designer, an architect by trade, and a designer of places. In my search to make better places, I have grown very curious and thoughtful about why we engage in acts of place making; about how they affect people and how people affect them; about the meanings embodied in the places; and about the origins and mechanisms of our responses to these places. For over 20 years now, my work's emphasis has been in thinking about place making far more than in actually making places. And in retrospect, my intellectual struggle has been to try to preserve the poetry while understanding the pragmatics of design.

A QUIRKY MIND THAT SPATIALIZES ALMOST EVERYTHING

Since childhood, I have always designed and made drawings and objects with the purpose of representing something in order to understand it. I made representational drawings to capture something's structure; little models that were interpretations of things around me or in my imagination; primitive geometries constructed to help me visualize complicated forms; and later, grown-up and for a living, diagrams made to provoke thought and make sense of complex systems. Although each was for use, I remember that making those physicalities had a metapurpose for me—to explore and understand something—my way of learning and knowing. I have never been curious about how "real" things worked, like a bicycle or a printing press, but quite interested in how nonphysical systems worked, how they evolved, elaborated, and behave.

I have always best related to and understood most phenomena, physical and ephemeral, by giving them a *spatial pattern,* searching for the one I though implicit. My mind seems always to form, give shape to, and graphically configure situations as a way of knowing them. I have always "seen" diagrammatically, and this is the way I know most things and know them best. This was, from the beginning, not an artist's need to make, not a form of creative expression, but my chosen way of being curious, of exploring and learning. The physical form of something, or, more important, the form I give it to know it, has always been the most satisfactory point of entry for me, in almost every situation, even when the situation is one without any real physical form, such as an economic system or a societal relationship. For me, the patterning of information is a major source of information in any situation. This preferred way of knowing, innate, a quirk, simply the way it happens, has improved through years of its exercise. Lately in my readings about mythic thought and its origins, I have noted how culturally widespread spatialization was as an ancient way of knowing. Sharing in this transcultural, transepochal mode pleases me and provokes my curiosity about different ways of knowing.

Like all modes of knowing, this one has its drawbacks. I now understand my early beliefs in fairly simple causation paths in research, for to see-as-form (to receive impressions of phenomena in spatial terms) or to give form (to express phenomena in spatial terms) is an act of concretization and of resolution. The very nature of spatialization suggests that each phenomenon has "a" form, place, and clear relationship to others. And although many phenomena are characterized by their dynamic and changing nature, "seeing" them spatially requires at each moment that they have either, or both, a unique form and unique location. Spatialization's weaknesses, and mine, are not being well-suited to sustaining ambiguity for very long; a tendency toward an over-emphasis on simple causality; and by emphasizing space, there is a corresponding deemphasizing of time as an element in knowing.

After years of thinking in this way, I came to recognize these tendencies when they started to surface, and then I tried to be less intellectually dependent on causative explanations, more conscious of time, rhythms, and pace in a situation and tried to embrace ambiguity more. Refusing to give up my spatial patterning, my solution was to try to project these nonspatial phenomena onto spatialized thought, but I seem to have spatialized these as well and now "see" ambiguity as form, and time's rhythm and pace as form, so I have found a strategy that uses spatialization in an odd way, using it to deal with its own limitations. However it happened, I now can sustain far more ambiguity for much longer, am much more conscious of rhythm and pace as necessary to knowing, and am far, far less wedded to simple, causal explanations. But it remains an effort to do this.

PAYING ATTENTION TO PATTERNS AND PEOPLE

I have always paid great attention to everything. My mates and children have, correctly, often found it a fault, as in "Mike, let something go by . . . you're so damned *alert*." Paying attention and then the intellectual curiosity about that which has been seen has always been an obsession. I've always felt there wasn't enough life to satisfy all the curiosity I had. Finding out something, figuring out something, seeing connections among seemingly disparate phenomena, the "aha" of really seeing, has always been big fun, a form of great pleasure—right up there with sex, drugs, and rock and roll.

I've always had an inductive thought process, building patterns from particulars. While paying careful attention to particulars, I'm also placing them in some larger pattern, wondering how they relate, go together, or sort themselves out. Rather than a grasp, this thinking is more a playful embrace. This pattern making focuses on the characteristic properties of something (what it is like) rather than on its definitive particulars (what it is). I then use those properties as a way to see the similarities or differences among things, using the properties to classify them in an attempt to know them. And I play with alternative classificatory concepts until finding one that pleased, the pleasure being in learning something both from that particular classificatory perspective and from the sequence of perspectives used. A continuing game.

I have always resisted specialization, sensing it to be narrowing. As well, I've simply been unable to do it. As I learn about something, its connections to other things expand my curiosity outward to other things, rather than inward. I never wanted to (or could) know everything about anything but wanted to know something about everything.

I never thought of myself as an intellectual because I thought intellectuals were supposed to really know a lot about something. I've read relatively little compared to many others I know and painfully few of the great books. I had a poor education, first some engineering, then an architect's education. Both professions read little and are not often challenged to think deeply. Neither profession's education is sufficient, I think, for a reasonable intellectual life.

Although I can't entirely blame an architectural education for its deemphasis on scholarly modes of thinking, I feel somewhat cheated by being denied the goad of assigned books and their classroom discussion. I've often felt somewhat ignorant and been appalled at how long it still takes me to fully comprehend a paragraph or page of a deep, dense, rich thinker, like Cassirer or Foucault.

Much of my learning comes from talking with others, finding out about the frameworks and assumptions they use to think about what they know rather than finding out *what* they know. I have friends in a variety of different worlds, and we meet and talk often and intensely of these worlds. In this informal network, I send, and they send me work of theirs and of others, work always prized because it has been prescreened by someone whose perspective I know and admire. This is slow and spotty as a learning process but well suited to someone gregarious and very attentive to other people's conversation.

NOT MUCH AND NOT VERY HIGHER EDUCATION

After high school, I made a "career choice" of engineering that was determined by a proficiency in mathematics (now totally lost) and for crisp drawing (retained); by not caring very much what I did ("teenager drift"); and by President Eisenhower's public statements that America had suffered a technological humiliation in outer space from Russia's preemptive launching of the orbiting rocket *Sputnik*. He asked that America quickly produce a generation of engineers. I gallantly responded to that call but had no idea which branch of engineering would be interesting or useful and so randomly chose chemical engineering.

Attending Rensselaer Polytechnic Institute in 1954–1955, I was an average student of chemical engineering. It was intriguing, but engineering students were not, and by the end of 1 year I decided I didn't want to spend a professional life with people uninterested in art. (Facing a lifetime of humiliation around differential and integral calculus was not so attractive either.) The dorm room next door housed a student of architecture, and his work looked like fun, and his colleagues had wide-ranging interests. I wanted that, and so quit engineering, and moved back to Brooklyn to study architecture at Pratt Institute. I loved it immediately. The ordering of space to enhance life, the yoking of poetry to pragmatics seemed perfect for me, and the thinking through and making of a system of esthetics appropriate to each designed place was a source of delight.

Good teachers have influenced me greatly, in high school, college, and now, something I try to remember every time I think I've "had enough of teaching." From 1955, through my architectural degree in 1959, I had three truly special teacher–architects at Pratt, each with a special view of architecture, and taken together, they presented architecture as a rich set of possibilities. Bill Bregler's architecture was a rigorous system of thinking manifested in form; Stan Salzman's was a sensitive vehicle for feeling; and Harold Edelman's architecture was, unabashedly, art.

Because I had no basis from which to choose among these, and they graciously didn't force choice or allegiance, I didn't select from among them but was permitted to see architecture as all of them, acting simultaneously, a rich system for making places. From them I learned about architecture and about one of its supports, basic design. Basic design suggested that design of all things (as various as posters, chairs, spoons, locomotives, buildings, floor patterns, rooms, clothing, and cities) rested on a learnable language of basic design elements and on systems for their manipulations. I was especially fond of the idea of a common substrate underlying all design, but permitting each product to be unique, and this concept has colored all my thinking about design. Believing this freed me to approach the design of anything with some confidence (even hubris) and helped me think of myself as a "generic" designer, albeit most frequently a designer of places.

A FINISHING SCHOOL AND EARLY TEACHING

After receiving my architectural degree, my first major employment was with a widely acknowledged master architect, Eero Saarinen, in Michigan, from 1959 to 1961. He spoke openly of hiring an officefull of only the best design students, about 100 of them. It felt like a "finishing school." About his architecture, Eero said that he was "doing research," and he was exploring an esthetics, for each of his buildings looked totally different from all his others, in contrast to most other architects of the period. Although his research was primarily about esthetics, I liked the idea that architecture could be research, a way of finding something out.

At the Saarinen office, I met a group of young, bright, devoted designers and learned much from them and was excited to be involved in "big-time" architecture-with-a-master so swiftly, even though my input was modest. There is a rigid caste system in famous architects' offices, and all of my effort was in support of the Masters' design concepts, me thinking about the design of small parts of his large buildings. (I spent a good deal of time obsessively designing and detailing the world's handsomest toilets, whose beauty may be seen to this day in the John Deere Headquarters in Moline, Illinois.) In this role of support designer, I learned much about the actual detailing of buildings, something poorly or not taught at all in schools. I began then to understand how parts and wholes of buildings are each other, something that only reappears 30 years later as I begin to understand how parts stand for wholes in mythical thought, through reading Ernst Cassirer, Joseph Campbell, and Mircea Eliade. And only recently do I hear of a teacher of architecture who presents students with a detail of a building and asks that they conceive of and reconstruct the building from the detail, much like Woody Allen's hilarious movie skit of cloning a live person from a dead one using their salvaged-during-life nose.

After 2 years of Saarinen's finishing school, I felt "finished" enough to accept an offer to teach and practice back in New York City. Returning to the university at which I'd studied, I was a very young architect teaching even younger architects. I taught an architectural design studio at Pratt Institute, from 1961 to 1966, and simultaneously worked as a senior designer in several firms, designing hospitals, theatres, religious buildings, high-end housing, and for fun on my own, several fantasy shopping environments in Greenwich Village.

From the first day, teaching was wonderful for me, a perfect fit. I had no design ideology (other than *not* to have one) but was interested in helping students to form, explore, and present theirs, even for one project. I did this through a kind of homemade Socratic discourse. This involved looking very carefully at their work, and through a series of directed questions, teasing out from them and in their words what seemed "present" in their work. I slipped naturally into this mode of discourse, for my teachers had done it, and in using it, I tried to help my students make their implicit and ill-shaped assumptions into explicit ideas. I encouraged them to become self-conscious about how they did this, as a way of developing a process of self-examination in design. Because each student's response to the problem given to the group was different, it was largely through teaching that I became better at exploring a single problem, invoking multiple perspectives, and recognizing how many alternate views there can be that satisfy or address the problem.

EMPHASIZING ESTHETICS IN DESIGN

The received wisdom about architectural esthetics prevalent in the 1950s was that design decisions were based largely on criteria of an idealized esthetics. Architecture was judged this way by most architects, by many who taught it, and in the journals. Emphasized was expression of an underlying visual and structural order and harmony in architecture, rather than, for example, the disorder of the life that architecture housed.

I knew that in order to express this ideal esthetics, that serving the building's various purposes had to be somewhat repressed, or certainly left unexpressed in the building's form. Function was often treated as a servant to some higher order of concerns about esthetic perfection.

My own architectural interests were also primarily esthetic, but my esthetics had a functionalist base, an esthetics derived from the purposes to be housed in places. But I confess that I was far less interested in actually *serving* those purposes than in *using* those purposes to seek an esthetic I liked.

I too had an idealized esthetic: I idealized forms derived from use, but it was still an ideology of esthetics, rather than an ideology of use. This surely related to my lifelong delight in things clearly marked in ways I see as particularly human and are thus sweetly and painfully imperfect; that embody a humanist's rather than a geometer's poetry; that show the mark of the human hand. (As an example, calligraphy has always given me great pleasure.) All the architecture and art I like best are odd, peculiar, marked by their maker or their making, baroquely asymmetrical, each one having something expressive that is idiosyncratically human.

So in each architectural project, I sought human, programmatic, and organizational differences and needs as primary material for my esthetic manipulation. I taught design and did design, largely within this paradigm, for some 10 years. I don't know exactly when this began to feel inadequate or inappropriate, but it did begin. In 1966, 3 years of my work on a single building was completed with the opening of a really beautiful and fine building I'd designed. It was a large theater complex on a campus in central Massachusetts, and it was lauded as handsome, site sensitive, an excellent theatre to go to and to work in. For me, somehow it felt like not enough product for the large amount of time spent; it felt, and I felt, somewhat socially irrelevant. I began to feel that designing buildings with so little real information about those who used it wasn't a good thing. I also started to feel that the much-coveted commissions to design places for social elites extended social inequities.

Transition from a Paradigm of Esthetics to One of Users

My ideas about architecture's "true purpose" started to change profoundly in a 5-year period in the mid-1960s. There was a mosaic of simultaneous events, meeting new people and interacting with interesting institutions that, all together, started to reshape my intellectual emphases in the following ways:

- In my exploration of peoples' purposes and functions as fodder for my funky, let-it-all-hang-out, functionalist esthetic, somehow, peoples' needs within places actually became more important to me. I felt an increasing desire to truly serve purpose and less desire to find a richer esthetic.

- That desire to serve was reinforced by the increasing social conscious-ness of the mid-1960s, a subcultural shift in consciousness I shared, even though it was one I only partially embraced—I was, after all, just over 30. There was an emerging notion that our buildings were some-how alien, not connected to the rightness of things. For me, there was a faint dawn of ecological consciousness, of the interconnectedness of things. I felt a need to serve better those then poorly served by our buildings.
- In teaching some students at Pratt who were poor designers of form but very thoughtful about making architecture more relevant to its users, we developed some ways to increase the knowledge base about people in design projects by finding out what people actually did or wanted to do in places and how they felt about them. We had no skills or back-ground for this, and these methods now seem very primitive. I dis-covered later on and with some amusement that my students and I had independently developed "folk versions" of methods in common use by systems analysts to explore problems with many variables.
- This work with students at Pratt captured the attention of some people at the Institute for Applied Technology at the U.S. National Bureau of Standards, who were themselves exploring ways to make the design process more information-rich and more humane and seeking ways to make the entire "facilities realization process" more rational and more responsive to this enhanced information base. I was asked to join this group, and did, moving from New York's Greenwich Village to Wash-ington's Dupont Circle, from teaching and a private practice in architec-ture, to thinking about it within a public sector group.
- The institute was led by the extraordinary and passionate John Eber-hard, a major influence on many of us because he understood how to embed ideas in institutional fabrics, how to commit organizations to action based on an idea. There I met a group of remarkable people in government service, in private practice, and in academic settings who shared a vision: they were interested in user-responsive design, in doing research about it, and in trying to embed what they learned in those institutions responsible for making places. Among people who influenced me then were John Eberhard at NBS; Don Schon of NBS and then of OSTI in Boston; Coryl LaRue Jones, Clyde Dorsett, and Matt Dumont at the National Institutes of Mental Health; Ezra Ehrenkrantz and Christopher Arnold of building-systems fame; Horst Rittel, Clare Cooper, Roz Lindheim, Christopher Alexander, and Sim Van DerRyn at Berkeley; Dick Krauss and Mike Pittas at Arrowstreet, and many others with whom and from whom I learned.
- After 2 years, I left NBS with John Eberhard who had been asked to establish a new school of architecture in Buffalo, a school that was to be based on, promulgate, and be a proselytizer for this emerging para-digm. I was to design and chair the graduate program. It was a thrilling chance to design and make an educational institution to serve a set of

ideas and a chance to hire and work with good and like-minded people in a context with no institutional history and thus no politics and no acrimony.

- Simultaneous with the founding of the school, we founded BOSTI, an acronym for the Buffalo Organization for Social and Technological Innovation, Inc. This was a not-for-profit research and educational organization and was intended to act as the clinical component of this innovative school and as the primary mechanisms by which the school would play a role in the development of a new paradigm. All faculty and all students worked through BOSTI and simultaneously were part of the university, and the two seemed quite congruent. BOSTI was, however, administratively separate from the school so it could be nimble and entrepreneurial, unconstrained by university bureaucracy; so it could engage in work with a wide variety of user and consumer groups, some not seen by the university as "legitimate"; and so it could pay much larger stipends to its students than the university would. BOSTI/school sought and attracted older, more experienced students, most already working in a wide variety of disciplines, whose multiple perspectives we valued highly. BOSTI was consciously founded as a place dedicated to developing and promulgating a paradigm about design that affirmed the needs of the inhabitants of place as the primary determinants of design. We knew that we had more ideas than we had knowledge, and BOSTI's roles were to develop this knowledge through research in action, to develop a cadre of people skilled at, and dedicated to it, and to demonstrate the benefits available from its use. Quite overtly, our teaching was a vehicle for rapid collaborative learning in a new field and would be used, somehow, to define the field. (Later on, as the field emerged, BOSTI would shift roles, becoming more practice oriented, rather than teaching oriented.)
- My earliest BOSTI colleagues, Terry Collison, Ibrahim Jammal, and George Borowsky, planners from the University of Pennsylvania, had wild yet rigorously analytical minds and introduced me to their own homemade brand of general systems theory and the idea that you could analyze anything systematically and can keep on doing it from slightly different perspectives and that you would learn a lot from the exercise.
- In 1969 I attended the first meeting (and almost all subsequent ones) of "the-thing-that-became-EDRA" (the Environmental Design Research Association) and occasionally participated in organizations exploring how to better understand design, such as the Design Methods Group. These emerging groups were, and are, a vast resource for me and a source of much validation.

At that time, what started to knit these events together was the emergence for me of a cohesive pattern of thought about what architecture might be. As I write it, I understand that it can be read as polemic, and by now, a polemic that is well known. Its base was arrived at intellectually, but its "rightness," for me, has made me somewhat passionate about it. I don't know how to easily disentangle the intellectual content from my belief in it. Anyhow, I thought the following then, and still do.

Much in architecture promotes and sustains a vision that is architect-oriented, where the enterprise is viewed more from the perspective of its creators than of its consumers. This tends to set the enterprise at some distance from its culture. Designed places should be more about the people who use them and less about those who design them. Because, as Bob Bechtel has said, it is behavior and not space that is enclosed by architecture, architecture should be largely about the people who *use* it and less about those who *design* it. Thus, architecture should be more a *biography of its users* and less an *autobiography of its designers*.

If architecture is to be more about its inhabitants, then the design process must really learn about the inhabitants, who they are, what they do, what they want, how they feel, and what has meaning for them. Thus architecture should be a learning process, research, inquiry, a seeking. And those in the design process must learn *how to learn* about those they serve, for their untrained intuitions about these matters are seldom good enough and sometimes wrong.

Viewed from the perspective of the inhabitants, the process of place making and place using extends over a very considerable period of time, much longer than the time it takes simply to design it. But normal practice strongly emphasizes design and tends to deemphasize most other aspects. It is not surprising that this is so. The education of designers, their publications, honors, and awards focus emphatically on design. Few other aspects receive much attention.

Yet the inhabitants need much more in order to have places that meet their needs over time. There is then often a grave mismatch between what clients need and what we provide them with, both in the process and the products, the made-places. Clients and inhabitants, lacking alternatives or even visions of alternatives, "make do." They do manage to house themselves and provide places for their operations and people and get their work done in the places they've got but probably at a substantial hidden cost. Without any model of an alternative way of doing things, individuals and the society will continue to bear these costs, some of them unnecessary, and it is also highly likely that the most vulnerable groups will bear a disproportionate burden.

The thought then was to develop an alternative model of practice, which had at its base a different idea about what "good design" is about, who it is for, what the appropriate determinants of design are, how better information might be used in the process, and about how much of inhabitants' lives design could reasonably and beneficially touch.

Very little of my education or practice as an architect, nor my teaching, had prepared me for trying to understand, in any systematic way, the relationships between purposes, people, and places. In the 1960s, this began to feel like a critical necessity.

This whole next phase, emphasizing psychosocial needs of users in design, saw my intellect largely yoked to problem solving in service of a vision about how we might design places in ways more responsive to people's needs.

For me, it was not primarily done in a meditative or scholarly mode, nor did I permit my natural intellectual curiosity to veer far from the problems I'd set. Fortunately, the problems were grand and complex enough to sustain my great interest. Another form of discipline for me was to engage in all this within the framework of a *business,* one that strove to produce ideas useful enough to organizations so that they'd financially support their development. I have had great fun patterning and exploring large scale sociotechnical problems with many interlocking subcomponents and found always that explorations in one increased my understanding in others and presented new problems. A giant puzzle and one quite worth the attention and energy.

EMPHASIZING PSYCHOSOCIAL NEEDS OF USERS IN DESIGN

In this period, from the late 1960s to now, and largely one of working within the framework of BOSTI, I came to think of architecture more as a *functional and psychosocial instrumentality* than an esthetic one. I thought of myself as a designer, taking a sabbatical, to develop a better way to design and then intended to come back and design places that were a better fit for peoples' activities, behaviors, and aspirations. My conception of architecture was not a new one but seemed to hold more promise at the time because it seemed that a number of then-current ideas, if linked simultaneously, would have more power.

I thought that if we had more and better information available to the design process about the functional and psychosocial needs of the users; if we had a design process that could and would use this new and better information and be more open to users as participants in the design-decision process; if we produced designs that permitted users some freedom to change their environments over time; if we had a facilities delivery system more socially equitable and more responsive to the needs of all groups, then we might be able to have places that better fit, supported, and satisfied the people for whom they were intended. (I have pursued all these ideas for some 20 years now.)

Rather than receiving an existing paradigm, I found myself making one among a group of pioneers. I call it design/research. I felt I had a cause, something to profess. It was a heady experience. (One possible pitfall with committing youthful energy to the making of a new paradigm is that you may think you need, as I did, a contrasting error-ridden paradigm to emphatically reject. I chose as the enemy high-style, socially insensitive architecture, and I started to diminish, even denigrate, the previous importance of esthetics to me. In retrospect, I would not do that again. I would try to find a way to integrate the content of paradigms as my interests shifted.) This all broadened my interests with dizzying swiftness, and I became, once again, in many things, a passionate novice, ignorant of much that I wanted to know.

FINDING SOME USEFUL INTELLECTUAL TOOLS

To diminish the terror of ignorance and to be able to approach problems without preconceived models for their solutions, I searched for some intellectual tools that had power to help organize the search for the knowledge I thought we needed to do the tasks we set ourselves. Although I eventually learned a fair amount about useful tools from the social sciences, of primary utility for me were general systems theory and the performance concept, both attractive to me because they could be "seen" as spatial patterns.

General Systems Theory

Thomas Kuhn's work was useful for understanding this emerging paradigm as a metaframework. A basic strategy in the new paradigm we seemed to be guiding was that rather than intervening in each unique building, it might be better to intervene in the overall systems that produced environments, like the banking and building industry, and to do this we needed to understand these somewhat alien systems.

The attraction of general systems theory (as proposed by Von Bertallanffy and practiced by Churchman and Ackoff and early lauded by Alexander) was that it suggested complex sociotechnical systems could be understood if focused on. Colleagues and I engaged in systems analyses of large-scale complex systems, often with the aid of flow charts 15 feet long, sometimes analyzing the interactions among several hundred events or tasks organized within two dozen major variables in a time sequence, done before computers were widely available. Here my quirk of facile spatialization was fully used.

With this tool I thought I could look at any set of phenomena, be able to conceive of them as a system, analyze its behavior, test changes, and predict outcomes. This seemed like real intellectual leverage. I could identify the system's elements and participants, describe the sequence and pattern of their relationships and the multiple pathways in which power, information, and resources moved, and identify how changes in one part of the system supposedly caused changes in others. I could understand this all in terms of how it actually worked, not as it appeared or was formally constituted. I began to see how the appearance of a system or its administrative structure often masked its actual performance and true structure and that this masking was often the root cause of problems. After gaining comfort with general systems theory, I thought this way almost as a matter of course, and it was very useful in gaining useful perspective on many problems and development of possible "solution spaces" for them.

This attraction to general systems theory eventually waned because it was clearly not very useful in probing and understanding situations that had a large psychosocial component, one very human and messy and containing politicized, pluralist demographics. And some of the systems I was interested in had that character, such as the way we designed, produced, and distributed housing. Horst Rittel, Berkeley's brilliant systems analyst, successfully challenged my perhaps excessive belief in general systems theory and argued it wittily and well, saying that general systems theory was somewhat like handling children—it dealt best with what he called "well-behaved" problems, in goal-seeking situations, like getting a monkey in a rocket to the moon but not very well with "wicked" problems like that of sustaining a rich public life downtown. After this extended passionate fling with general systems theory, I have come, more happily, to understand, accept, and appreciate complexity, ambiguity, a lot more mess and "wickedness" in situations, and be able to work within a permanent dialectic among dynamic phenomena held in sensitive tension. But it was often useful and always good exercise and a method I still use when appropriate.

The Performance Concept

Although general systems theory was completely borrowed from its inventors, I helped develop, test, and use the performance concept in the late sixties. When a discipline matures, it has a standard repertoire of standard solutions to what it sees as standard problems. The performance concept suggests that it is highly probable that problems are being seen as, or worse, shaped to be standard when they are not and that this operates to preclude innovation and change within a discipline and in each instance or project within the discipline and that the very existence of a mature discipline assures that it will be seen as the only source of solutions even when some problems presented to it may be solved in other venues, which precludes innovation across disciplines.

Let me offer some examples at different levels: When someone goes to an architect, that act alone specifies a solution, not a problem. If you go to an architect, you will get a building as a solution, whatever the problem is. (And if you go to a lawyer or a doctor, you will get their standard solutions, overlooking other "solution spaces" to the problem.) The U.S. Post Office came to us, requesting a design for a swiftly erectable mail-sorting building, many of which were needed in Chicago to handle an overload. A performance concept analysis suggested that mail might be sent to other, less-burdened cities that had slack capacity in their building inventory—a solution of rerouting, rather than building. But what architect would suggest such a solution? Or search for it? A discipline looks "inside" for solutions, not "outside."

As well, specifying an auditorium, or a 10-inch brick wall, is naming-a-solution rather than describing a problem in a way that might permit several solutions. Selecting normative things, like auditoriums and brick walls, have the same effect—by naming solutions before articulating problems we often rob our intervention processes of thoughtfulness.

The goal of the performance concept is to reemphasize thinking about purpose, by articulating desired ends rather than prescribing means, and doing it without regard to a discipline's normal or preferred solutions. (It is not easy to do.) In architecture the concept has these social purposes: It suggests multidisciplinary approaches; forces assessment of peoples' needs; spurs innovation; harnesses some creativity and capability normally unavailable to the processes of place making; and provides places (or other solutions) whose performance more satisfies needs.

But once it is decided that a building is a reasonable solution to the problem, the performance concept then describes crisply what kind and level of performance the building (and each of its spaces and elements) must provide to its users, and over time. With this concept, one can think of buildings as being more "alive," as participants in situations that have purposes, as performers. The concept is also intended as a way to harness the formidable intelligence that resides in two groups who have the least input into design—manufacturers and builders (major resources in the process of building) and the users and occupants of buildings (major sources of information about best use).

Seldom asked about their needs or listened to, prospective building occupants have little or no say in how it shall perform. Architects or the client's building committee often act as a surrogate for the users and make critical planning and design decisions. Because the process often takes 3 years and much changes in an organization's life in that time, we frequently make buildings that don't quite fit on opening day.

The performance concept offers as twin solutions a careful assessment of the performance that users need from buildings and an opportunity to build flexibility into buildings so that performance can change as needs change. This requires that users be involved in design and flexible buildings and building subsystems be produced. To achieve this flexibility requires that manufacturers be asked early enough in the building process to make intellectual contributions and that they be given sufficient and clear information about desired performance to enable them to play a more creative role.

We used general systems theory to analyze the building industry and to develop more reasonable flows of information and more appropriate roles and relationships for the various actors. Using the performance concept, we developed ways to assess users' needs and ways to help manufacturers and builders be more involved and more responsible for the in-use performance of buildings. We developed performance-based methods of designing and specifying buildings and their spaces and how they might be better managed over time. We were involved in the performance-based design of building systems, a very sophisticated form of prefabrication, kits-of-parts that were developed with end-user performance as their primary determinants, and preengineered to permit a wide range of high-performing configurations, with a great deal of user-friendly flexibility so that inhabitants had a building that could change to accommodate changing needs.

DESIGN/RESEARCH AS A BUSINESS

As I became more active in paradigm building, I chose to emphasize research-in-action as my primary mode of engagement, more than the search for knowledge through scholarship. It was not really much of a choice for I was an architect, with little training and experience in scholarship. Change was my goal, and knowledge its necessary servant.

At its inception, BOSTI was intertwined with the newly founded school of architecture in Buffalo. (In fact, it was entirely congruent with the graduate program. One of them was a "paper" program, but we never decided which.) After its first 5 years, I took on BOSTI's presidency, and to resolve some of the tension I saw between the pace and needs of quality education and the pace and needs of sponsored research in an academic enterprise, I moved BOSTI outside the school. BOSTI maintained an educational goal, acting as a clinical experience for students and supported them financially, but it was now to emphasize a more professional attitude toward sponsored research and be more dependent on senior analysts than graduate students for actual knowledge production. I made BOSTI a free-standing organization with no institutional support, one that would have to survive in the marketplace. It would continue to be run as a not-for-profit educational and research corporation but now be totally self-supporting. I felt that action-oriented research was valuable, would be directly useful to organizations, and wished to prove that.

So, in contrast to those engaged in scholarly and research activities in academic life, the framework for much of my intellectual life and work has been *as a business*. This has been both a burden and an opportunity and has shaped my intellectual history. For the past 15 years, BOSTI has supported from 5 to 15 people, requiring me to be entrepreneurial and to secure about $425,000 each year, about 85% from research and consulting contracts and some 15% from grants. (A major spur to entrepreneurship has been for me to think of BOSTI as a mouth needing to be fed $35,000 each month, or worse, over $1,000 a day.)

As well as being a viable business, I insisted BOSTI be a vehicle for collegiality and a good life, for doing good work aimed at very high standards, to provide a satisfying worklife for all, a place to have some fun with great flexibility and few rules, to enable beneficial cross-disciplinary interaction and mutual learning, and have an appropriate scale and character.

My intellectual growth and change in this two-decade period has certainly been colored by this BOSTI framework, dependent on client satisfaction and support, and where most projects' results were to have direct use applications. Such work generally results in a broad and shallow, rather than a narrow and deep spectrum of engagement, and I've had the opportunity to explore only a few areas for a long time and in great depth. I loved these few and always seek them. Some of BOSTI's work was very much like research, with knowledge a primary goal, whereas most of it was directly applicable consulting with beneficial intervention as the goal.

Although I have, of course, become somewhat expert in some areas since BOSTI's 1969 origin, I think I have been fortunate to never truly specialize and to maintain a general practice doing design/research. This was based on several factors: personal preference for variety; the broad and systemic nature of most of the problems we approached; and on the simple necessities of running a business whose product, design/research, was not then or now one that brings long lines of customers.

Early on, we took on any work we could get, boldly assuming that our way of thinking and my quirk of pattern seeking and making could approach any problem that linked the use of place with people. I remember feeling that just as my training as a generalist designer had equipped me to design anything, I now felt that general systems theory, the performance concept, pattern recognition, great enthusiasm, and being a "quick study" would serve me well as a generalist in this new world.

Thirty years ago, few people and fewer building clients understood what predesign programming was or what a diagnostic evaluation of a building interior was or was for or even that there was information from the social and behavioral sciences that could be useful in design. Given the client's obvious difficulty in really knowing how we might help them, we priced our work cheaply, so we'd get it. To those who became our clients, we seemed to promise a lot for their investment, and then we worked hours far beyond the project's budget so we could actually deliver a product that met their, and our, expectations. We wanted design/research to have a "good reputation." Of course, we did not then, or now always succeed, for a hallmark of systematic "finding out" is the risk that clients don't always like what they get, nor does what they get always make sense, nor are the recommendations for action always feasible.

After a period of some success, we wanted to take more control over selecting the kinds of problems we'd explore. So we spent a lot of time talking about and predicting where and what kinds of problems might arise 5 years out and dabbled in futurism and trends analysis as a framework within which to understand emergent possibilities. As a kind of premarketing reconnaissance, we investigated various urban systems, such as housing, transportation, social services, communications, and education, trying to identify current or near-term future problems within them that we might explore and whose exploration some institution might support. We formally identified many targets where we thought the use of a design/research sensibility and methods might prove useful, and then we were proactive, did some preliminary work on the problem to frame it thoughtfully, developed some evidence that it really was a problem, and then made contact with those institutions we thought would have a stake in dealing with problems we'd identified.

During this 20-year phase, I learned a great deal about a very wide range of place types, place users, and place behaviors. In order to do this work reasonably well, we had to search for methods and where none seemed appropriate, to occasionally invent them. In order for any of this to actually make a difference, we sought also to change the way organizations saw the role of the physical environment in achieving their goals. As self-appointed change agents, we often engaged in education. This was a form of marketing as well, for convincing leaders of organizations of the importance of the physical environment to their success is the equivalent of developing a market. And, we tried to understand how institutions behaved in order to embed our results in their framework so they would continue successfully when we were gone.

In this phase, some 20 years of BOSTI experience, my target audiences were largely those involved in commissioning, designing, managing, and using places, and less so my colleagues in the academic community. I learned how to embed academic research in an applied practice whose primary clients were organizations needing help in making their places work better and often as part of their competitive strategy. Our work was reasonably welcomed in the design worlds, for even though they have little tradition of research, there is desire to know more to design better. And manufacturers supported research when they saw some advantage or benefit from it, often but not necessarily an economic one. Some wanted to be seen as leaders in their field, taking a statesmanlike position, supporting "important work."

Where we were asked to study and improve a client's facilities, we found they would be less comfortable acting on results that were presented as extensively "qualified" the way good academic research would demand and be more comfortable with results presented in ways that had commonsense validity. Although our research was done using academic standards, it was seldom presented like that. In this way, we could more easily "bridge" the worlds of research and applications. And I'm sure I have sometimes overstated the case to clients, in the sense that I've deemphasized the "qualifications and limits to generalizability" in those situations where I've used research as the suggested basis for an intervention.

I've managed several hundred research and consulting projects for BOSTI, each of which originated because of some problem or opportunity related to the physical environment. Let me present three examples of work, selected because they are works pursued over a considerable period of time and in depth; display the range of my version of design/research; and show the insistent patterning in my work.

These three are

- *PAK: The Planning Aid Kit*, a method for community-based planning of mental health services.
- *Using human factors analyses in exploring accidents* involving *elements of buildings*, such as windows and stairs, and *consumer products*, like chain saws.
- *Using office design to increase productivity*, explorations of the facets of the office environment which affect individual, workgroup, and organizational effectiveness.

Example 1: PAK/The Planning Aid Kit

PAK, an acronym for the Planning Aid Kit, is a structured process for use by a group especially formed to identify and prioritize the mental health problems needing attention in a particular community, to plan mental health programs and facilities that would help solve those problems, and to identify and secure necessary resources. The planning is done according to a prepared set of agendas; in structured group meetings of service providers, service users, and community representatives; and led by a skilled discussion leader. PAK welcomes a wide variety of participants and highly disparate and politicized agendas. It is a group-process mechanism for the surfacing and resolution of conflict about allocation of limited resources in service of a goal.

In the late 1960s, mental health concepts changed drastically, toward it as part of a community ecology and suggesting that community stress and normative treatment modalities were sometimes part of the problem and a more caring and supportive community part of the solution. Within this new framework, I was part of a group in government that helped the National Institutes of Mental Health (NIMH) to think about a new facilities alternative to mental hospitals. After some reflection and analysis, we felt there could not be a generic facility solution for use everywhere but there might be a way to develop programs and facilities tailored for each unique community, in a process that examined each community, its mental health problems, and its priorities. Community-based planning seemed to be a more important problem for us to address than developing a generic facility, and we did.

The intellectual content for me consisted largely of my studying and learning about process-related issues, such as small-group processes, creative problem solving, and the various forms of equitableness in group decision making in resource-constrained situations. And I studied what was happening at the federal, state, and local levels in the mental health field; the history of madness and changing social attitudes towards it; and the historic bases for legislation relating to it.

With the architect Dick Krauss at NBS, I had developed a very primitive version of such a process for NIMH in 1968. It was one that heavily emphasized mental health facilities and drew heavily on our strengths as architects. A substantial grant now came from NIMH to develop two versions of a new PAK. These new versions were to be, essentially, a program planning process and would emphasize facilities only insofar as groups chose to. I worked with sociologists and psychologists for over a year, and I learned much about group process, the qualities and training of discussion leaders, about the selection of participants, the formation of task-oriented groups, and ways to have these groups be efficient and effective while being equitable. The actual product was a structured series of self-training workbooks, slides, and videotapes that form a system for planning.

The process was used some 10 times in New York, some 20 times in Massachusetts, and actually delivered high task productivity, the creative resolution of genuine conflict, and reasonable program plans. Interestingly, the results seldom included major attention to mental health facilties—it was used mostly as a needs assessment and service program planning tool in situations where broad community participation was desired or mandated.

Example 2: Using Human Factors Analyses in Exploring Accidents

Around 1970, I became interested in the enormous number of accidents people had in interaction with buildings. This was of special interest because of how salient seemed the interactions between behavior and environment and how highly imageable and patternable these interactions are. I suspected that there were hazards accidentally designed-in to many of our environments; that these played a major role in accidents; and that if we looked carefully, we would find strong patterns in these accidents, suggesting that the phenomena were neither accidents nor randomly occurring. If all this were true, it meant that you could understand how and why accidents happened and possibly design places that reduced them.

Over a 10-year period, we successfully sought support for a dozen projects from a wide variety of sources. As a first task, we found out whether the problem of accidents caused by peoples' interactions with designed settings was of sufficient magnitude to engage society's concern. To do this, we searched various sources for and found information about the magnitude of place-implicating accidents.

In a detailed epidemiological analysis of some 50 years of the accident literature, we selected accidents occurring in the home and/or with elements built into the home and sorted them into discrete types within a taxonomy especially designed to support further etiological and ergonomic analysis. Following this, we developed some 30 detailed accident "scenarios," using human factors analyses, and developed performance-based requirements for safer stairs, doors, windows, kitchens, and bathrooms. Of great interest was our economic analysis of the enormous annual dollar costs to the nation of having these accidents.

We developed a model data base for a single product, windows, and then in an exhaustive analysis developed: a dozen human-factors-based accident scenarios; patterns of forces in glass breakage; a current-standards analysis; performance-based specifications and designs for safer windows and glazing; and benefit–cost analyses.

For all home accidents, we prepared safety manuals for homeowners, architects, and builders; designed public education programs; recommended new ways of data collection and training for people who investigated accidents in the field; and prepared a desk-reference document for architects and builders to use in design of safer dwellings.

We then realized we had developed a method of analysis useful in understanding how all accidents happened. We had made a generic metascenario for accident analyses, and using this, could build a specific scenario for any accident. We had applied it to our primary interest, the dwelling, and felt it could also be applied to *consumer products* involved in accidents. We used it successfully in several projects examining products as varied as chain saws, electrical extension cords, skateboards, CB antennas, Christmas tree lights, space heaters, swimming pools, hair dryers, snowmobiles, and playground equipment. As a little triumph of pattern recognition, we developed a method whereby a maximum of six mutually exclusive human-factors-based hazard patterns for each product would account for at least 95% of all the accidents for that product.

We found the information collected by accident investigators in the field not so well suited to human factors analysis and scenario building, and so we proposed and developed a manual of guidelines for how to collect such information, and we gave a series of 4-day information-rich training courses to accident investigators, teaching them a human factors perspective in their work. We later modified these courses to train corporate product designers and manufacturing engineers to enhance the safety of their product designs.

Finally, analysis turned from consumer products to *user groups*, particularly the elderly, a group vulnerable to certain accident types, and materials were developed for groups serving the elderly that would sensitize them to their special safety problems.

Example 3: Using Office Design to Increase Productivity

Understanding how the design of offices affects group and individual productivity and the quality of working life is my longest lived research interest and best known work. Starting in 1969, we used the performance concept in the design and procurement of many federal office buildings. This work linked human performance directly to that of the environment and started my interests in office work, workers and workplaces, at the same moment a revolution in office design was happening, the controversial introduction of open offices and systems furniture, designed to support newer theories of at-work interactions.

Clients, designers, and manufacturers engaged in heated but information-poor discussions about the office and, wanting to enrich that discussion, I did an analysis of the literature and began a series of user-based evaluations of offices for organizations. Around 1975, I conceive of both a "grand" research project and an entrepreneurial scheme in which BOSTI would offer to do detailed diagnostic evaluations of their offices' performance for many organizations, giving each a report but also using each as part of a larger data base, whose analyses would be of interest to major manufacturers and to national research institutions. Each and all would receive a product of value, and all the analyses, looked at together would provide a far more comprehensive understanding of the office than we had.

This program continues now and has had multiple sponsors and sources of data, including many *Fortune 500* companies, federal and state governments, nonprofit organizations, and research-support agencies. This research program examined some 8,000 office workers in about 80 offices nationwide and developed data about which aspects of the office environment related most to productivity and quality of worklife for a variety of job types. The research design involved both cross-sectional and before-and-after measures of job performance, job satisfaction, ease of communication, and environmental satisfaction of office workers at multiple sites, all linked to evaluations and physical measurements of some 20 facets of the physical environment. The results, methods, and experience gained have acted as a "core" for BOSTI's consulting to organizations and for pro-bono work, where we have developed and distributed design guidelines for the offices of small businesses and for nonprofit organizations.

The results suggested the work environment was a tool that could be purposefully manipulated to enhance organizational effectiveness, and the project received extensive national press, journal, and lecture-circuit attention because the findings showed there were substantial effects related to the environment, and moreover, our economic analysis showed that the dollar value of these effects was quite enough to warrant organizational expenditures for more user-oriented planning and design. The economic analysis yielded extraordinary leverage in our dealings with organizations.

As the core of all our office research and consulting, this program has provided a vehicle for me to explore many ways to use research-gained information of value to organizations. Over the past ten years, I have designed and been able to deliver a series of consulting services which include these, taken verbatim from BOSTI's brochure:

- *Diagnostic evaluations of workplaces* in which we measure the effects of current workplaces on individual productivity, workgroup performance, psychosocial phenomena, quality of worklife, and comfort. Our risk assessments measure or predict both the positive and the negative impact on environmental "misfits" for all workers.
- *Development of predesign programs and design guidelines and standards* in which we develop detailed recommendations for planning and design. Use of our recommendations can provide productive and satisfying workplaces with attention to required functions, psychosocial support for work, and concerns for enhancing organizational culture.
- *Human factors analyses* in which we analyze workers, work processes, equipment, furniture, and the environment as a system with interlocking performances. We compare what is needed to perform the tasks against human capabilities in order to develop design requirements to assure optimum performance.
- *Assisting in the selection of an appropriate design team and design collaboration* in which we work with architects in ways that respect their creativity while ensuring that the critical objective of organizational effectiveness is fully realized in planning and design.
- *Teaching best use of environment:* Around move-in time, we prepare and deliver seminars and take-away materials so that people can become wiser users of complex high-performance environments, and better neighbors to each other in their workspaces. We have developed award-winning videotapes and manuals, like a *User's Guide to the Open Office*.
- *Postoccupancy evaluations (POEs):* After some 8 months of use, we measure the effects of recent environmental changes on employees' productivity and job satisfaction and make recommendations for further fine-tuning of the physical environment. As well, the results of POEs are used to modify your planning, design, and workspace standards.
- *Economic analyses* in which we provide benefit–cost and return-on-investment analyses and estimate the dollar value of the costs or benefits of selected physical changes.
- *Support for facility managers:* Through the development of facilities management concepts and strategies and the development and documentation of facility policies and procedures, we help facility managers evalu-

ate problems, set priorities, make wise trade-offs, and reposition facilities in the life of the organization.

From the mid-1970s to mid-1980s much of the research and consulting work BOSTI had been doing was about office work, workers, and the workplace. Much of this work was framed within a patched-together but workable alternative to the conventional model of architectural practice, and the work was often satisfying focused on the user's biography. But I began to sense that the user's biography we focused on was shallow compared to what it could be, although it certainly felt deeper than the one conventional design practice plumbed. The work simply did not account for a major portion of what I had begun to sense the wonder of places could be. With very few exceptions (and none mine), offices were simply not places where the full richness of place design could be strongly expressed, and my work felt somehow constrained, incomplete, and a touch dull.

Workspace is not an appropriate venue for exploring the richness or meaning of place. I think nobody was ever awed, stunned, or centered by the design of office space, and there *are* places that awe or stun, ones filled with "charge," that nurture revery and dreams, that center the soul, and that link us to others in especially human ways. I now wanted to find out *why* or *how* these places had such effects. This desire led to a third major phase in which how I think and what I think about has changed. For me, there seems to be a pattern; of finding a set of ideas important and useful for a time and then finding them insufficient in some substantial way. I begin to sense that *any* strongly held intellectual emphasis is both a source of focused strength and, simultaneously, the origin of insufficiency, except of course, for the zealot and ideologue. Years ago, when I sensed the hollowness in design-as-functionalist-esthetics (no doubt coincident with getting really good at it), I slowly replaced it with design-as-psychosocial-support. After years of work, I felt again this hollowness. But wiser now, I saw no need for rejection of the old as a new emphasis was revealed. Now I see embracement and integration as a way to think and am less ideological about ideas. I recognize myself more as an open system, continually curious, and eminently reprogrammable, but now with the capacity and desire for integrating rather than erasing the old program.

A Field of Intellectual Changes

This shift came about, again, within a field of other intellectual changes. I can describe them but cannot easily sequence them or give more weight to one than others. This field of changes includes the following:

Engagement with the Arts. In the phase when I reconceived of architecture as a psychosocial support system, I still taught, not design, but what I thought the design process most lacked, emphatic and affectionate attention to supporting peoples' needs. I taught courses in predesign programming and how behavior and space are related. I limited my contact with design and with its poetry. Reading the architectural journals, I was still occasionally stunned by a wonderful building, but thought most I saw were overblown or trivial, precious social resources wasted.

But I stayed fully engaged with other arts and thought a great deal about painting, dance, the movies, emergent art forms, landscapes, especially those termed "sublime," the places marked by megaliths, cave paintings (sadly, only from the books), calligraphy from many cultures, and music from non-Western cultures. A lifelong food scholar and lover of many cuisines, I continued to be amazed at the remarkable artistry the world's cuisines embodied.

These experiences were powerful to me, often of wonder and species pride, and I felt connections across these arts, and myself being connected to something both old and always. I knew that many of these works had excited such feelings for many people in many places and were thus experiences that might be cross-cultural and across time, that perhaps I was experiencing a response that might be species wide.

Architecture in the 1970s and 1980s seemed so trivialized, with proponents of various styles proselytizing all others as to their "true way" and each with such vigor (modernists, postmodernists, neoclassicists, metabolists, deconstructionists, etc.). As in Mao's "hundred flowers," I welcomed these ideas but rejected all their claims to rightness, for each was a style, would experience style's capricious trajectory, and eventually be retired.

But some made-places I saw had a quality that placed them outside of style and called the very idea of style into question. These seemed, somehow, to be "true" or "right" without any accompanying media-feeding polemic. From readings and discussion with others, my feelings seemed widely shared and may always have been, and I was very interested in that phenomenon—the wide and deep sharing of powerful feelings about certain places. I suspected that there might be characteristics common across all such places.

Traveling and Public Life and Public Space. I'm a "city person" and have always been comfortable in cities anywhere, even in ones where I spoke none of the language. Starting in the late 1970s and continuing through the 1980s, I business-traveled a great deal in the United States and Canada, largely related to design/research projects for BOSTI, and I spent some pleasure time in Rome, Hong Kong, Paris, Istanbul, Warsaw, and London. In large cities and small, I always sought out their public places and public life and noted the extraordinary variety of public life and behavior and the wide variety of places used for those purposes. I began to read some about public life, and much of what I read seemed at odds with what I saw.

Teaching Again. In the late 1970s, I decided to teach design studio again after a 15-year layoff. I knew from my continued engagement with the other arts that each art did something no other could do, that each taught us something about ourselves, and that each particular work of art told two "stories," about itself and about its category. (As a child, my father said to me, as we looked at some wonderful Fragonard drawings together, that "every good drawing is both about what the drawing seems to be about but is also about *all* drawing.") I now began to think about architecture this way. And I began to think of building and landscape forms primarily as if they were ideas, carriers of meaning and feeling, as something like (although not actually) language, and operating at several levels.

Conservatively, I reentered design studios by teaching about content I knew, about innovative office buildings, about cold-region communities, about behaviorally complex situations. Around 1982 I decided to use my design studio to explore what I didn't know, the question of the origins of shared, strong feelings about places. As I put it to my students: "While most places don't, why do some places, like Stonehenge, the Acropolis, Macchu Picchu, the Piazza San Marco, the Taj Mahal, a lonely beach, and Niagara Falls, have the power to captivate so many people, from many cultures, in many eras? What is it in or of those places that could elicit common responses, across cultures and times?"

About Landscape. The vacations I enjoyed most were at beaches, but I'd never actually lived and worked at a beach. Starting in the summer of 1984, I rented a cottage facing Lake Erie's sand beach in Canada, 15 minutes from BOSTI, the University, and my home. I stayed longer each year, and now live there 6 months each year. The cottage is a bit small, unattractive, the interior poorly planned, and I love being there, for living and working are both enriched. I work at a tiny table in the bedroom's corner, in front of a window that opens onto the quiet beach. Although I am a near-classic "Type A" generally, I find myself calmed, tranquil, centered, really somehow becoming like that place, with its slow, insistent rhythms. I notice changes, small and large, on the beach, in the unkempt woods, in the water, and in the day and night sky. I meditate on these changes, their various rhythms, trying to understand them, and trying to understand the origin of the feelings I have about this place. I begin to notice such strong feelings in other landscapes, both natural and designed, and feel more kin to, more moved by landscape than I ever felt.

My Introduction to the Humanities. In parallel with these emerging feelings, questions, and changes, I was asked to serve on the New York Council for the Humanities, setting policy and evaluating proposals for humanities events and programs for the state. The council consisted largely of humanities scholars from history, ethics, anthropology, philosophy, cinema, sociology, and folklore. This was a new group to learn from, in an area of relative ignorance for me. Their focus was on interpretation; on exploring the questions of who we are; on *re*presenting ourselves to ourselves. Much of the work and the discussion was about how the varied surfaces of individual subcultures mask the similarities across them and how each finds its own interpretation of similar phenomena, ones often so dissimilar in presentation as to successfully obscure the common humanity at their base. Although there were very few proposals about places and place making, this experience reinforced my emerging feeling that places and place making could be understood, studied, taught, and perhaps practiced as a branch of the humanities.

EMPHASIZING DESIGN AS A BRANCH
OF THE HUMANITIES: PRESENT WORK

This third and current phase has lasted now for more than half a decade. Because it is current, I don't yet have a good point to view it from and am probably less certain of its shape than that of previous phases.

I now think architecture is, at its core, not explainable or knowable in terms other than itself, that it is a profound form of knowledge, providing us a means to dwell well on the earth, and to better understand "placeness," through the medium of particular places that embody meaning both about themselves and about all places. (It feels like what my father said about a very good drawing being about itself and about all drawing.)

I think architecture embodies this knowledge and is one of the things that provides us the possibility of a life filled with great meaning. Although it may appear that these meanings come through a formal language of culture-bound styles, I strongly suspect there is some deeper language, a natural language of symbolization unique to architecture, using the expressive repertoire unique to the medium.

I now meditate upon this natural language through a study of what I call "charged" places. These are made-places where people report experiencing strong feelings, where body and being seem affected; feelings of a sensory unity, of being enveloped in the place's sound, its smell, and the feel of its air; time slows to an all-time; you feel intensely real, profoundly human; in touch with something old and always. And Gaston Bachelard suggests very little of this passes through the "circuits of knowledge." The esthetics of some of these places may be pleasant, but some are awesome, and even forbidding. Examples of "charged" places are Stonehenge, the Taj Mahal, the Pantheon, Macchu Pichu, any garden by Luis Barragan, the Vietnam Memorial, Mesa Verde, Le Corbusier's chapel at Ronchamp, the caves at Lascaux and Altamira, Louis Kahn's Salk Center, the Zen garden of Ryoanji, Gaudi's chapel at Colonia Guell, Niagara Falls, a lonely beach, and a fairy ring of mushrooms in a clearing in the woods.

Perhaps as my antidote to today's trivial stylistic arguments in architecture and as an exploration of something that transcends (yet probably even underlies) style, I suggest there are common, powerful, and highly patterned responses to experiences of place, older and deeper than individual cultures and their specific styles, and our experiences in charged places are shaped by or resonate with "cosmic models" of places residing in each individual's still-active mythic consciousness, one shared with most others, or by "archetypes" of places in an analogy of Jung's "collective unconscious." Once again, I moved into an arena of thought in which I was largely ignorant. I didn't know what to read. Amos Rapoport sent his articles. I stumbled on Mircea Eliade and was stunned at his notion of the "eternal return" and the role of sacred place in it. I found Yi-Fu Tuan. Several EDRA colleagues were kind and helpful, sent me work and introduced me to Gaston Bachelard, William Lethaby, and Ernst Cassirer. With these as a base, I found much other work and found myself behaving, for me, in a peculiarly scholarly manner and read Joseph Campbell, Carl Jung, Karsten Harries, Mimi Lobell, Lord Raglan, Norman O. Brown, and others. I had not done so much reading since college, and it was not easy, and I wondered if I'd gotten out of the habit of reading hard things or that these were all simply harder. But I loved the mental exercise, and no longer needed a framework of in-the-world applications to act as spur to learning.

The combination of teaching about these matters, hard reading and thinking about them, and the discipline of presenting one or two pieces of work each year at conferences helped integrate it, and I began to see strong patterning and cohesion in this search, all revolving around the concept of *archetypes* of place.

Archetypes of Place and the Mythic Consciousness

I think that when we experience "charge" in a place, it happens primarily because that place springs from, or shares characteristics with, an archetype of place that resides in our minds and, somehow, resonates with it, creating the feeling of "charge."

An archetype seems to be, itself, an archetypal idea, a creation of our spirit. Plato and the Scholastic philosophers felt they sit behind much of our experience. Carl Jung spoke of them as "inherited" ideas, derived from the experience of the human species, and present in the unconscious of all individuals, a "collective unconscious." Joseph Campbell shows how they arise worldwide and spontaneously. Others have considered archetypes of place as important phenomena in our lives.

- Wolfgang Kohler posits "isomorphs," where, in the central nervous system of many animals (including humans) is an image of the "proper environment" for the species and that animals move inexorably toward environments that match this image.
- Yale's philosopher of architecture, Karsten Harries, speaks of a "natural language of form" related to our being embodied and mortal, on the earth, under a sky, vertical creatures, except when resting, sleeping, or dead, and about architecture which *re*presents itself to our senses.
- Amos Rapoport, the anthropologist–architect, talks of "cosmic models for sacred places" and how these models find expression even in lesser places, like the home.
- Mircea Eliade hypothesizes the "eternal return," a specieswide linkage where historic and mythic time and space overlap, so that, in ritual behavior and ritual places, we can experience always the beginnings

and argues that each sacred place embodies the myth of origin, of the first place, the world.

- Mimi Lobell suggests archetypes of a series of sequential civilizations, each paralleling a stage of human development, and that each civilization is a whole way of life; of knowing and being in the world, each complete, advanced, and fully satisfying, and that humans today contain and respond to archetypes from all the civilizations.
- Ernst Cassirer traces the role of the mythic consciousness in symbol formation, how myth is an original form of life, and is the genesis for all forms of cultural life, based in the mythic meaning of the fundamental experiences of space, time, and number.
- Gaston Bachelard conjures places for revery, "images of intimacy," the memories of real and dreamt places of our real and dreamt childhoods—the hut, the corner, the nook, the attic, the cellar, and the fantasy enclosures of the miniature and the seashell.

These scholars all supply concepts and support for my ideas about place archetypes: that they embody mythic themes, encoded into and transmitted through a place's form, using a natural language unique to places; that our responses to these are widely shared, transcultural, and perhaps specieswide, attesting to some form of imprinting during eons of human development; that our responses are unlearned, involuntary, and powerful; that these responses manifest themselves, largely, in bodily feelings; that we are conscious of the place as the source of, or the trigger for, these feelings; and that the feelings are ones that often include some or all of connectedness, rightness, perfection, delight, virtue, inspiration, wonder, terror, and awe.

Sacred places are the first places I thought about, for many mythically significant places are sacred places, places set apart, places reserved for matters of the spirit. However, not all sacred places are "charged," and not all "charged" places are sacred.

Scholars of sacred places suggest that their primary function is as the embodiment of, or carrier of, the first myth, of origins of place, of the gods' first creation of the first place, the world. Worldwide myths about the primordial act of creation all speak of the first creation of "difference" through an interruption of undifferentiated chaos and the birth of an order out of chaos; creating cosmos, an orderly and harmonious system; often patterned after our vision of celestial order; fixing a center from which orientations and the cardinal directions spring, as do verticalities, symmetries, boundaries, passage, rhythms, light and dark, and ordered materiality. All this is part of the natural language of places, each element of the language imbued with meaning, the meanings congruent with the tones the mythic consciousness originally gave each physicality.

A piece of work I enjoyed doing immensely was to test whether sacred places could be shaped solely by that myth of origins. After a goodly preparation, I imagined myself back in time, an archaic place maker making a sacred place. I used the creation myths as the "predesign program" for the place, with each successive design decision guided by the myths and embodying them in physical form. I did not design a place, but rather I developed a set of hierarchical "design guidelines" for sacred places. Completed, I was amazed at the congruence of these guidelines with sacred places in many of the world's cultures.

I speculate that there may be a small "original" set of place archetypes, each embodying a different myth and each serving a different fundamental human purpose. The set might include the sacred place; the settlement for "the people"; the space for the gathering (the dancing ground); the dwelling; the place to be alone with spirit; the land of the dead; and the garden of plenitude.

I believe design is the desire to give a good shape to how we live. Because they carry a myth in their form, place archetypes are, by definition, "best shapes," and because they are archetypes, they are themselves never seen. Because each built place is unique, so each place must be both about itself *and* about its archetype. This suggests that a good shape for a place is both a strong manifestation of the appropriate archetype *and* a good response to the situation's unique particulars of site, climate, materials, history, use, and context.

Archetypes of place is an entrancing subject for a place designer because it clearly links place making to humanities' basic questions: "Who are we?" "Where have we come from?" "Where should we go?" "What does it all mean?" It places the act of place making satisfyingly central to our humanness. In fact, it suggests that architecture and landscape architecture might be taught as a branch of the humanities, like ethics, philosophy, and history, one of the ways we *re*present ourselves to ourselves.

I teach this as an attitude, and not as a formula, a method, or a style, and it is not intended to supplant other ways of thinking about design, but to augment them, to enrich the designer's repertoire, the range of concerns, and the methods used in place making.

I have taught this material in both a seminar and in design studio. In both, the students do substantial reading and discuss the material. They describe their own experiences of charge places and interestingly, *all* have had them and have strong feelings about them. This both legitimates such experience and elevates their feelings to the status of "content," worthy of analysis.

We systematically analyze their sensations in these places, probe the meanings that flicker into consciousness, and try to understand what of the places' forms contributes most to these sensations. We speculate about what mythic themes might underlay, what the archetype might be, what the theme-form is of the deeper place "behind" a particular place.

The studio's final design juries have included architects and landscape architects, of course, and as well, poets, philosophers, psychologists, teachers of rhetoric, and of body movement. They have been gifted contributors, and this material seems to be naturally cross-disciplinary.

This teaching has taught me that you can teach about it, that it can become an attitude, and that students carry that attitude to other classes and out into practice. People do get comfortable with place actually being an idea, not just symbolizing one, and they do sense there is a "natural language" of form and explore it.

I found that design can, itself, be a mode of inquiry for the teaching has become, by accident and in retrospect, a source of research data for me. It occurred to me, after 4 years of such teaching that I had a kind of data base, of about 90 real places experienced by, and important to, people, and some 60 "unreal" places, their own designs, whose purpose was to communicate something of importance to its maker.

I looked at them, each and all, in a fairly systematic pattern analysis and was stunned to see a remarkable patterning of a large body of work, increasing my sense that there are basic themes of place embedded in the structure of the mind. Looking at the 90 actually experienced, important places, almost all could easily be seen as Bachelard's "images of intimacy," small single cells of space; held in great affection; none of them architecture but all humble and unprepossessing; frequently returned to for revery, solace, and contemplation; a special category of "charged" place I now call "embraced places." Although they took a variety of actual forms, they seem to have only two underlying forms: a *small clearing* in a natural setting and the small, quiet *hut*.

Examining the 60 design projects, almost all tend to be like, if I may use a peculiar phrase, "mainstream" sacred places. One quarter, both buildings and landscapes, could easily be characterized as "sacred mountains," one half as "walled gardens of paradise," and one quarter as "journeys through time." This last group puzzled me; they were places that encoded a journey, which you moved through in a kind of didactic retelling or reliving of a meaningful journey. It was not until I later read a wise book, by Elizabeth Munro, about the origins and meaning of pilgrimage that I understood the meaning of these.

The extraordinary contrast between the humble embraced places my students actually experienced and the far less humble architecture of those they designed have sparked additional explorations for me—there are intriguing questions raised, and I continue this work, and it is big fun in my life. I am attempting to develop and compile elements of this natural language with which I think places transmit meaning.

I have been struck by the prevalence and importance of landscapes for my students, and this in a school of architecture with almost no emphasis on landscape. As I continue this work, I find myself more and more drawn to ideas borne through landscape, and increasingly my preferred learning colleagues are landscape architects. Although this is the general shape and content of the work, I can also try to describe some of what I've learned/am learning:

- In exploring another form of knowing, I see how powerful Western ethnocentrism can be, for my culture and training have made it hard to accept other ways of knowing. Conversely, it is now hard to hold on to my culture and training as I appreciate other forms of knowing. I want to hold on to both together, to embrace disparate modes of knowing, for I feel that is how humans might best know. I have added to my reper-

toire, as legitimate windows into knowing—feelings, flickers of meaning, transcendent and spiritual experiences, and forms of empiricism
not generalizable other than by their commonness ("Yes, I feel that
too"). This shift reaches out to other knowing structures, like Feng
Shu'i, shamanic universes, and mythology, and suggests and legit-
imizes other knowing methods, like contemplation and meditation and
of "projecting" myself back in time, in order to in-dwell in a situation of
origin. I confess much affection for the lovely image of old Bachelard
gleaning, from the poetry of a people his special places, his "images of
intimacy," and I have enjoyed using my students' designs and experiences of place as data in a pattern recognition process.

- I've come to recognize how much of normal behavior is framed by
mythology as a still-living presence in our lives and not something lived
and enjoyed only by archaic peoples. I understand it as the first config-
uring, a way we make a world filled with meaning, and that this early
flower of the human spirit bonds configuration and meaning, a common
origin for science and art, linking them inexorably at their origin.

- I have begun to appreciate how beginnings continually shape and guide
the new, and how much knowing there was so early, and how much we
are in danger of forgetting so much we know.

- I believe archetypes, as a mythology of the unconscious, whose origins
and mechanisms can only be guessed at, flavor much of our individual,
very human experience. Archetypes of places link purpose to form, and
these purposes are often the contents of myth, embodied in a natural
language of physical forms that have their origins in human experience
and feelings about the body; landscape; space, time, number, and gravity; celestial cycles; and the imprints of both ordinary human experience
and extraordinary events. Although experienced by individuals in different cultures, it seems to be, at its core, a specieswide phenomenon. I
confess that the grandness of such a schema is entrancing for someone
delighted by patterns.

PUBLIC LIFE AND PUBLIC PLACE: ONTOLOGY AND TRANSFORMATION

A parallel interest in this current intellectual phase happened by accident,
although the work now feels much the same as that about archetypes—it has
become an attempt to understand phenomena by stripping away actual form to
"see" the archetypal form underneath. In 1987, I was asked to prepare a
keynote address about public place for a conference whose theme was about
public environments, not an area in which I had done work. Accepting it as an
assignment, I conceived of myself as a scout.

The most salient early knowledge in this was my own experience of public
life in many places, big and small, here and there, and my feelings about them.
I began by thinking more about public life than about public space, assuming
that a space where public life took place was, de facto, a form of public space. I
also thought about the assumptions Americans had about public life and place

and felt that images of a rich public life lived in the streets and squares of European countries dominated the American vision of what public life should be and that Americans were constantly taking themselves to task for lack of this public life. I wondered if that lack Americans felt was really true, or was an illusion, a form of nostalgia, and thought that there probably was a great deal of public life that went unrecognized because it didn't look like this European form of public life.

Trying to think about how public life differed from private life and the parochial life lived in neighborhoods and about how I'd classify certain behaviors as public life or not, led to the question of what public life really is—what it is for, how it happens, by whom it is desired, how it is shaped, and what it means.

A critical question seemed to be what is considered to be public life. If it were defined as something absent or waning, it would be felt as lack. If there were much public life not understood as public life, it would be felt as lack. And if both were true, then we'd be squandering public resources in search of a public life we don't have while overlooking the one we do have. At this point, as I always do, I structured a set of ideas and questions to guide my thinking about these matters, to help me be efficient in delving into the literature, and to enable me to talk with purpose to colleagues and friends as I sought their thoughts.

- We seem to have very strong images of a highly desirable public life. What are these images? Where do they come from? Why are they held in such affection or esteem?
- Why are they not consonant with the reality of public life today?
- What has happened to create this difference between image and reality—what is the nature of the transformation?
- What is the reality of today's public life?
- What problems might occur in having image and reality different?
- Is there a way to guide public life more toward its desirable image? Is it possible? Desirable? What would be the consequences of such action?
- Is there a way to more recognize and honor the real public life we do have?
- What would be a better way of thinking about public life?

My readings included Galen Cranz, C. S. Fischer, J. B. Jackson, Erv Zube on Jackson, Lyn Lofland, Richard Sennett, Camillo Sitte, and Peter Smithson. These included social histories of, and research about, European and American public life and place and about the classical forms of public space, streets and squares, and the newer parks. I began to sense there had been a long-term transformation of public life without much public recognition of that fact, that affection for the lost forms masks new public life, creates disdain for the new and nostalgia for the old, and that these feelings, when widely held, have powerful social consequences.

I made long lists of what I considered behavior events in public life, experiences I'd had interacting with strangers that had different norms of behavior than in life with family, friends, and colleagues and different than that with acquaintances in my neighborhood. Included were experiences from big cities and small towns, here and in other countries I'd visited. Playing with various classifying systems for these elements began to yield patterns, the most interesting being those where being with friends, family, or neighbors didn't much matter but being with *strangers* did, and where the interaction with or among strangers could alter the outcome of events, where what your co-strangers did mattered, and where you learned something from this interaction. I realized that I'd started to construct a pattern that could act like an ontology of public life and continue this work now, testing the ontology against my expanded vision of public life and public place.

I am still engaged in this work about archetypes, transformations, and ontology, am captivated by it and expect to keep at it, just for the pleasure. As well, I sustain my BOSTI-based practice in design/research, largely consulting to private-sector clients, although increasingly engaged in pro-bono work of various kinds. I have even started to design places again, often as part of a team, sometimes by myself, and find that I can now draw on an extended repertoire of knowledge in service of designing places filled with meaning, and that also serve, facilitate, and edify, and am exploring new ideas about esthetics.

A SUMMARY OF THE HISTORY

In constructing this history, I have seen three successive and somewhat distinct phases of thinking about place making. I have been, first, a designer of places, working in a traditional and received paradigm, whose concern was largely with place form as a producer of *esthetic delight*, although my own version of it had a decidedly functionalist character. Later, I saw place form largely as a producer of *psychosocial benefit*, and I participated in constructing a behavior/environment paradigm to learn better how to do this. Now I tend to see place making as a branch of the humanities, a producer of *humanistic understanding*, a profound way of representing ourselves to ourselves.

In examining how the mosaic of my thinking has changed in these three phases, I sense it has moved in the following general ways:

- The idea of what architecture's emphasis *is* has moved from a functional art to a social instrument, now to a conveyor of meaning.
- The idea of whom design is *for* moved from a designer's narcissistic focus (on me) *to* an altruistic one (on them), *to* a transcendent focus (on all of us, and always)
- A time frame that increases in breadth, from the no-time of timeless, ideal, and abstract esthetics *to* near-term concerns of good fit for people in specific places *to* longer term change, by using the process of place making as a social instrument, *to* a time that is always, a time of origins, to events and feelings that repeat themselves infinitely, Eliade's "eternal return."

- The set of interventions considered useful keeps extending *from* interceding in the design of places *to* that of rethinking their purpose, their management, their effects on organizations and individuals; their role in larger social systems; and now their role in human development, feeling, and thought.
- From a primarily visual appreciation of places to a more intellectual one, now to a more multisensory one, one that "does not pass through the circuits of knowledge," as Bachelard says, and to one, perhaps later that integrates mind and body and spirit
- From work that is done more in public, which is project and applications driven and embedded in institutions with missions and mandates *to* work that is more private, generic, scholarly, and speculative.
- Early on I deemphasized the unmeasurable by carefully excising art, spirit, and feeling from consideration in my largely quantifiable research; then I began to include it and now begin to see spirit as the origin of all making.
- From believing that there were fixed patterns or classification systems that were intrinsically meaningful *to* recognizing that selection of the categories or properties used to think about things is itself a creative act and that patterning is a creative process and subject to change.
- From a predilection for causal and deterministic ideas *to* ones about open systems, multiple pathways, ambiguity, evolution, growth, and change.
- From design empiricism, a reliance on my experience and observation, *to* research empiricism and reliance on experimental method *to* a search for that which is not observable, experienced, or experimentally explorable.
- From shorter term work and achievements (a building, a talk, a paper, a research project) *to* longer term ones, like really understanding something—a desire to live and work in what I call Chinese Time.
- From receiving a paradigm to constructing one, and hopefully to the integration of several of them.
- From being fairly sure that both what I knew and the ideology in which I used it were right *to* being far less sure of both and far more comfortable with being far less sure.

ABOUT THE MAKING OF THIS INTELLECTUAL HISTORY

The very idea of an intellectual history enhances mind–body separation, celebrates mentation over feeling, and thus is a questionable vehicle for someone who already suffers that skewed emphasis, the clinically diagnosed Narcissist, whose "I-ness" is centered in the mind, with its body and feelings relegated to a servant role. So this was not, for me, an altogether healthy assignment but had attractions enough: time set aside for self-analysis; the exercise of memory in one already worried about its loss; curiosity unleashed in searching for patterns that have a pleasing and useful form within a very messy context; and the staggering compliment of even having been asked to write such a history.

Having finished this, I now recognize this history as a fiction that happened in the sense that it is both real and retrospectively constructed. I never thought, in any rigorous sense, of even having an intellectual history until this book's editors suggested I'd had one. I hear tell that few people, when caught up in great events, realize they are experiencing history. It feels more like "just life." And compared to these great events, these minor events I write about, like an insight that changes a way of looking at something, seem even less like experiencing history.

Much of an intellectual history is not events at all but of slow and imperceptible changes, an idea received and played with over time; insights growing as ideas from disparate sources knit together; musing, daydreaming, and fantasizing; discarding thoughts that don't seem to lead anywhere only to find later that they do or still don't; or a chain of logic formed during years of projects. Although some external events (a new project or job) may act as markers of such slow changes, they are not the changes themselves. So even though it is as accurate a history in these terms as I know how, it is certainly paler, much more linear and organized, less messy, and surely bowdlerized, as compared to the life. It is a construct, a history of the making of a history.

Making an intellectual history turns out to be a fascinating exercise, and after original trepidation, I'd now truly recommend it to folks who think for a living *and* who have had a fair amount of living. (I couldn't, I think, have done it much earlier in my life and might well do it again 15 years from now, but for my own curiosity, thank you.)

We seldom think about the development of our own thinking. It is a peculiar idea, to separate out intellect, to make "figure" of it, against a "ground" of your other interlocking histories, your personal ecology of events in your life; bodily sensations; feeling and emotion; interacting with the thought of others, of paradigms, values, and ideology; and a lifetime of work, of learning, and teaching others in academic settings and in practice.

To offer an honest intellectual history in the lasting medium of print, in public, especially to friends, is a terror. (It is little consolation to assume only a few might actually buy this book, and fewer read it.) I've obviously gotten over the terror enough to do it. It recedes once you get fascinated by figuring out how you'd do it, by making it a project, and by conjuring the project's content and form. And it became easier once I realized the writing isn't, and shouldn't be, public psychoanalysis; nor a history of "I started public school in Brooklyn in . . . ."; nor polemic but rather a search for pattern that reveals something to me both in the process and in its product.

Writing the early part of the history was easier than the latter. I find I have less distance from and less perspective about more recent phenomenon and have a bit more difficulty in seeing their pattern, causes, and connections.

I thought, as I started this history, that I'd find an energetic dilettante's chaos because I've done such a variety of things, but on reflection, I do see a pattern, and it is a trajectory, not smooth, but a trajectory nevertheless. Making this history has helped clarify for me where I've been, lets me know some of the "why," and may even offer a glimpse of where I'm going. I have often worried about my frequent shift in interests. Now that I see a pattern, and a trajectory and one that feels largely all right, I am less worried. Thinking about how and what I've learned, and writing this, has made me feel a bit more peaceful and centered.

Acknowledgments

The following are people from whom I've learned much in conversation and in co-working and who have contributed to shifts in my thinking: Irwin Altman: environmental psychologist; William Breger: my professor and architect; David Bryan: kinesiologist, rhetorician, scholar; Kathleen Christensen: geographer of work and public thinker; Terry Collison: business entrepreneur and logician; Clare Cooper Marcus: landscape architect and explorer; Galen Cranz: sociologist and knower of bodies; Frances Downing: architect and imagery scholar; John Eberhard: public policy administrator and professional visionary; Harold Edelman: my professor and architect/artist; Karen Franck: environmental psychologist; Daniel Friedman: architect–scholar; David Gordon: choreographer; Sandra Howell: lifetime developmental psychologist; Al Katz: legal theorist and scholar; Setha Low: anthropologist; Ellen Konar-Goldband: statistician and psychologist; Stephen Margulis: psychologist; Michael Pittas: urban designer, arts administrator; Robert Riley: architect, landscape architect; Horst Rittel: systems analyst and theorist; Stanley Salzman: my professor and architect; Lynda Schneekloth: landscape architect, teaching colleague; Robert Shibley: educator and institutional theorist; Michael Tatum: industrial and interior designer; Margot Villecco: critic, analyst, and writer; and Sue Weideman: environmental psychologist of housing.

REFERENCES

Ackoff, R. (1960). Systems, organizations and interdisciplinary research. *General Systems Yearbook, 5,* 1–8.
Alexander, C. (1967). Systems generating systems. *Systemat, 7.*
Bachelard, G. (1969). *The poetics of space.* Boston: Beacon Press.
Bertallanffy, L. V. (1950). The theory of open systems in physics and biology. *Science, 111,* 23–29.
Brill, M. (1985a). *Sacred places and embraced places.* An address given to the Council of Educators in Landscape Architecture, September.
Brill, M. (1985b). *Using the place-creation myth to develop design guidelines for sacred space: A peculiar method.* An address given to the Council of Educators in Landscape Architecture, September.
Brill, M. (1989a). Transformation, nostalgia and illusion about public life and public environments. *Reflections,* No. 6, Spring, 48–60.
Brill, M. (1989b). An ontology for exploring public life today. *Places, 6*(1) (Fall), 24–31.

Brill, M. (1989c). Transformation, nostalgia and illusion in public life and public place. In I. Altman and E. Zube (Eds.), *Public places and spaces* (pp. 7–29). New York: Plenum Press.

Brill, M. (1989d). *Using archetypes in the design of "charged" places.* An address given as the Horace Cleveland Distinguished Fellow, Landscape Architecture Program, University of Minnesota, April.

Brill, M., & Parker, C. (1987). *Using office design to increase productivity for the small business.* Buffalo, NY: BOSTI, Inc.

Brill, M., with Margulis, S., Konar, E., & BOSTI (1984, 1985). *Using office design to increase productivity.* Buffalo, NY: Workplace Design and Productivity.

Brown, N. O. (1959). *Life against death: The psychoanalytical meaning of history.* Middletown, CT: Wesleyan University Press.

Campbell, J. (1959). *The masks of God.* London: Pitman Press Ltd.

Cassirer, E. (1955). *The philosophy of symbolic forms: Vol. 2. Mythical thought.* New Haven, CT: Yale Press. (Written in 1925).

Churchman, C. W. (1968). *The systems approach.* New York: Dell Publishing.

Cranz, G. (1982). *The politics of park design: A history of urban parks in America.* Cambridge: MIT Press.

Drury, C., with Brill, M. (1980). New methods of consumer product accident investigation. In *Human factors and industrial design in consumer products* (pp. 196–229). Medford, MA: Tufts University.

Eliade, M. (1954). *The myth of the eternal return.* Princeton: Princeton University Press.

Eliade, M. (1957). *The sacred and the profane.* New York: Harcourt, Brace & World.

Fischer, C. S. (1976). *The urban experience.* New York: Harcourt Brace Jovanovich.

Harries, K. (1982). Building and the terror of time. *Perspecta, 19,* 58–69.

Jackson, J. B. (1980). *The necessity for ruins, and other topics.* Amherst: University of Massachusetts Press.

Kuhn, T. (1962). *Structure of scientific revolutions.* Chicago: University of Chicago Press.

Lethaby, W. (1956). *Architecture, nature and magic.* London: Gerald Duckworth & Co., Ltd. (original 1892)

Lobell, M. (1983). Spatial archetypes. *Revision,* Fall, 69–82.

Lofland, L. (1985). *A world of strangers.* Prospect Heights, IL: Waveland Press.

Munro, E. (1987). *On glory roads: A pilgrim's book about pilgrimage.* New York: Thames and Hudson.

Raglan, F. R. S., IV, Baron (1936). *The hero.* London: Methuen & Co., Ltd.

Rapoport, A. (1982). Sacred places, sacred occasions and sacred environments. *Architectural Design* 52(9/10), 75–82.

Sennett, R. (1978). *The fall of public man.* New York: Vintage.

Sitte, C. (1965). *City planning according to artistic principles.* G. Collins & C. Collins Trans. New York: Random House. (Original work published 1889)

Smithson, P. (1981). Space is the American mediator, or the blocks of Ithaca: A speculation. *Harvard Architectural Review, 2,* 107–114.

Tuan, Y. F. (1977). *Spaces and places.* Minneapolis: University of Minnesota Press.

Villecco, M., with Brill, M. (1981). *Environmental/design research: Concepts, methods and values.* Washington, DC: Design Arts Program, National Endowment for the Arts.

Zube, E. H. (Ed.). (1970). *Landscapes: Selected writings of J. B. Jackson.* Amherst: University of Massachusetts Press.

9

Toward a Transactional Perspective

A PERSONAL JOURNEY

IRWIN ALTMAN

I WAS BORN ON JULY 16, 1930, in New York City. My parents, Ethel and Louis Altman, were first-generation Americans whose parents emigrated to this country in the late 1800s from the Soviet Union and Hungary, respectively. My wife Gloria and I were married in 1953 and have two children. Gloria was a primary-school teacher for several years but has worked in and managed a large travel agency in Salt Lake City for almost 20 years. Our older son, David, has a PhD in social ecology and is a senior research associate in the Center for Health Promotion, Stanford University. Our younger son, William, has a JD degree and a master's degree in public policy and works for the American Psychological Association, specializing in legislation and policy in the areas of health and aging.

I was educated in the public elementary and high schools of the Bronx, New York City, during the Depression and World War II. I did my undergraduate work at the University Heights campus of New York University, where I majored in psychology and minored in sociology and biology. I completed master's and PhD degrees in social psychology at the University of Maryland, under the direction of Elliott McGinnies. Beginning in 1957, and for the next 12 years, I worked in a variety of teaching, applied research, and basic research jobs in the Washington, DC area. These included teaching at American University (1957–1958), doing applied research at Human Sciences Research, Inc., on contract with the U.S. Air Force (1958–1960), working for the Special Operations Research Office at American University doing classified propaganda research for the U.S. Army (1960–1962), conducting basic research on social and environmental factors affecting adaptation to social isolation at the Naval Medical Research Institute. This position with the U.S. Navy spanned a 7-year period (1962–1969).

IRWIN ALTMAN • Department of Psychology, University of Utah, Salt Lake City, Utah 84112.

In 1969, I left the Washington DC area to become chair of the Department of Psychology at the University of Utah, a position I held for 7 years (1969–1976). Three years later I became dean of the College of Social and Behavioral Science (1979–1983) and subsequently was appointed vice president for academic affairs at the University of Utah (1983–1987). I presently am a distinguished professor of psychology and also have a faculty appointment in the Department of Family and Consumer Studies as well as an adjunct appointment in the Department of Communication, University of Utah.

I have served on a number of boards and committees in psychology and in the environment and behavior field and was president of the Society of Personality and Social Psychology (Division 8 of the American Psychological Association) and of the Division of Population and Environmental Psychology (Division 34, American Psychological Association). I have also been on the board of directors and was vice chair of the Environmental Design Research Association. I have received the Career Award of the Environmental Design Research Association, the Service Award of the Division of Population and Environmental Psychology of the American Psychological Association, and the Distinguished Research Award and Rosenblatt Prize for Excellence at the University of Utah.

I love my work and family and also enjoy skiing, tennis, hiking, gardening, and camping. And there is a very special place in my heart and mind for my first granddaughter, Rebecca Sarah, to whom this chapter is dedicated.

INTRODUCTION

Two metaphors portray the course of my three-decade career in social psychology and environment and behavior studies. The first is an ever widening spiral around a central core. The second metaphor is a main path with numerous side paths of unknown distances and directions, with the side paths always eventually leading back to the main path. These metaphors reflect the theme that my work over the years has addressed a common set of issues, even though I sometimes veered off into apparently tangential areas. It was often only later that I discovered why I had intuitively struck off in new directions and how I had unknowingly approached the same issue from a different perspective. On occasion I feared that the spiral or sidepath might take me too far afield, but I gradually learned to trust my intuition to pursue a particular topic and only later understand why I had been driven to do so. Indeed, I eventually learned that there was no possibility of my becoming lost intellectually because the recurrent issues of my scholarly work are also part and parcel of my personal life and struggle for self-understanding. That struggle traces back to my childhood and to an unpredictable and capricious family environment. My father, a bright, uneducated, and energetic man suffered from many personal frustrations and was alternately optimistic and pessimistic, elated and depressed, loving and rejecting. My mother, an older daughter of a poor immigrant family, worked in the sweat shops of New York from the time she was 12 in order to help support her many brothers and sisters who had been essentially abandoned by her father. An increasingly embittered woman, she did not comprehend my father's volatility and coped by creating a mechanically adequate but interpersonally cold home environment. All of this was confusing to me as a child, although I managed over the years to resolve personal problems that derived from my parental relationships and to understand their personal struggles with their own lives. I also have come to realize how I learned to track the unpredictable temporal flow of events in my family, pieced together an array of subtle cues to anticipate what would happen next, and adopted a holistic and contextual orientation to day-to-day life. So doing made a dizzying array of events more predictable, perhaps contributing to my lifelong interest in developing synthesizing frameworks to organize masses of information. For many years I have been genuinely grateful to have achieved an understanding of my parents and my own coping with many difficult early-life experiences. Those insights have made it possible for me to freely and constructively allow my work to reflect directly a personal view of the world that derived from my childhood. Thus my scholarly pursuits are autobiographical, and I cannot help but work on them.

The recurrent themes of my intellectual history include (1) a pervasive interest in interpersonal relationships, (2) a holistic perspective, (3) a focus on temporal aspects of phenomena, (4) an eclectic approach to research methods, and (5) a multidisciplinary orientation.

First, I have always been interested in the study of interpersonal relationships—how they form, grow, are managed, and deteriorate; how and why people achieve different degrees of intimacy, trust, and commitment. For example, Dalmas Taylor and I formulated social penetration theory, which examined the development of social relationships as a function of personal, interpersonal, and situational factors (Altman & Taylor, 1973). Later, I integrated a conceptual analysis of privacy regulation (Altman, 1975) with social penetration theory, yielding a more holistic framework of social relationships (Altman, Vinsel, & Brown, 1981).

Second, I have consistently adopted a holistic perspective in which social relationships and privacy are conceptualized as complex repertoires of verbal, nonverbal, paraverbal, and environmental behaviors (the latter including personal space, territory, proximity, and spatial practices). Another aspect of a holistic orientation involves molar units of analysis, for example natural "social units" of individuals, groups, families; place process units of homes, and so forth. As discussed later, such an orientation is at variance with some contemporary approaches, which tend to be analytic and dimensional. Finally, my holistic orientation includes sensitivity to the role of the physical and social environments in interpersonal relationships, especially home environments.

Third, I have always been interested in the temporal and changing qualities of social relationships. My doctoral dissertation examined group discussion over time; social penetration theory studied stages of relationship development; privacy regulation theory investigated the changing dialectic nature of openness and closedness to others; studies of homes considered the impact of relocation and seasonal factors.

Fourth, my work has always been methodologically eclectic. I concluded early that it is impossible to use a single method to study all aspects of a holistic phenomenon. Although I did my best to satisfy the methodological and philosophical dicta of my heritage in social psychology, many phenomena simply could not be studied using traditional methods, especially laboratory experiments. As a result, I gravitated over the years toward field-based and naturalistic approaches, surveys and interviews, and qualitative and conceptual analyses.

A final recurrent theme of my work is its multidisciplinary character. I have increasingly drawn on the ideas, values, content, and methodology of other disciplines, as I discovered their relevance to the study of social relationships and environment and behavior studies. My parent field of social psychology offers an important perspective, and it is my center of gravity. But its view is limited, and I have found it necessary to capitalize on the contributions of diverse social science fields, for example, sociology, social work, family studies, anthropology, history, and environmental design fields, for example, architecture, interior design, planning. At the same time I have tried to be sensitive to the dangers of using the knowledge, theories, and methods of other disciplines without having had rigorous training in them.

I must say, however, that I have only rarely collaborated directly in research with scholars from other disciplines. I have sought their advice, relied on their work, participated in multidisciplinary conferences and organizations, and co-edited the multidisciplinary series, *Human Behavior and Environment*. So, I have tuned into the approaches of many disciplines while working from the home base of my parent field of psychology.

A CONCEPTUAL FRAMEWORK

These five qualities—an interest in social relationships, a holistic perspective, a focus on temporal qualities of phenomena, an eclectic methodological strategy, and a multidisciplinary orientation—are the main path and recurring spiral of my career. Addressing these issues has also sensitized me to fundamental questions about units of analysis of psychological phenomena and philosophy of science and eventually culminated in a framework of "world views" or approaches to knowledge (Altman & Rogoff, 1987). As discussed later, we described four world views—trait, interactional, organismic, and transactional—based on a synthesis and extension of the writings of Dewey and Bentley (1949) and Pepper (1942, 1967). I will use aspects of that framework, especially the transactional world view, along with the five recurrent themes, to depict my intellectual history.

In describing the transactional approach to psychological units of analysis, Werner, Oxley, Altman, and Haggard (1987) stated:

> The essence of transactionalism is that psychological phenomena are best understood as holistic events composed of inseparable and mutually defining psychological processes, physical and social environments, and temporal qualities. There are no separate actors in an event; the actions of one person are understood in relation to the actions of other people and in relation to spatial, situa-

tional, and temporal circumstances in which the actors are embedded. These different aspects of an event are mutually defining and lend meaning to one another, and are so intermeshed that understanding one aspect requires simultaneous inclusion of other aspects in the analysis. (p. 244)

Altman and Rogoff (1987) summarized the transactional approach to temporal qualities of phenomena:

> The transactional world view incorporates temporal processes in the very definition of events. [It] shifts from analysis of the causes of change to the idea that change is inherent in the system . . . . Change is viewed more as an ongoing, intrinsic aspect of an event than as the outcome of the influence of separate elements on each other. (p. 25)

Figure 1 portrays five intellectual phases of my work, based on the transactional world view. I now realize that I have been pursuing one or another aspect of the transactional perspective throughout my career, often intuitively and without conscious planning. It is, therefore, a comfortable way to describe

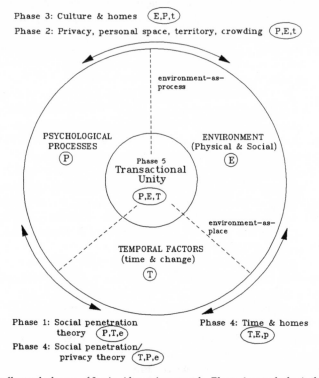

Figure 1. Intellectual phases of Irwin Altman's research. Phase 1: psychological processes as complex and holistic with dynamic temporal qualities (P,T,e); Phase 2: physical environment as an aspect of psychological processes (P,E,t); Phase 3: the unity of places and psychological processes (E,P,t); Phase 4: temporal qualities of places (T,E,p); temporal qualities of psychological processes (T,P,e); and Phase 5: the transactional unity of psychological processes, physical environments/places, and temporal factors (P,E,T).

my intellectual history. It is also gratifying to finally articulate a coherent rationale for what I have been doing for more than 30 years!

The dashed lines between the parts of Figure 1 symbolize the inseparability of physical and social environments, temporal factors, and psychological processes. The five career phases in the figure reflect my attention to various aspects of the holistic unity at different times, often returning to deal with issues again, but from a new perspective, and always implicitly dealing with all aspects of the whole. As a result, the career phases do not follow a strict chronological progression. The capital and lower-case P,E,T in the figure represent psychological processes, environments, and time, respectively, and illustrate the relative emphasis on these factors during a career phase.

PHASE I: PSYCHOLOGICAL PROCESSES AS COMPLEX AND HOLISTIC, WITH DYNAMIC TEMPORAL QUALITIES (P,T,e)

In this first phase I functioned primarily as a social psychologist, although aspects of my thinking departed from mainstream theorizing and research in the field. As indicated in Figure 1, my work focused on social relationships (P), with particular attention given to the temporal dynamics of relationship development (T). The physical environment was not centrally important, although it became increasingly so toward the end of the period.

Early on, my special interest in social psychology was small-group functioning, with my dissertation and other research addressing typical topics of the times—group performance, group member interaction, group composition, and the like. This interest culminated in an integration of the small-group literature (McGrath & Altman, 1966), giving me an opportunity to understand the field in a comprehensive way. During this period, I also conducted research for the U.S. Navy on the impact of social isolation on group processes, including self-disclosure, individual and group performance, stress and psychological symptomatology, group cohesion, and the like (Altman & Haythorn, 1965, 1967; Haythorn, Altman, & Myers, 1965; Haythorn & Altman, 1967; Altman, Taylor, & Wheeler, 1971; Taylor, Wheeler, & Altman, 1968, and others). With experience, I articulated a special interest in close relationships—self-disclosure, intimacy, interpersonal liking, conflict, trust, and relationship development and management (P in Figure 1).

I also now realize how much I always wanted to understand the temporal flow (T) of close relationships, partly on intellectual grounds and partly because of childhood experiences described earlier. This interest in temporal dynamics was a centerpiece of my dissertation (Altman & McGinnies, 1960), where I studied group discussions over time—charting who talked to whom, response rates and response lengths, and other measures—in order to see if groups composed of members with varying attitudes managed their discussions differently. It was my research on social isolation and social penetration, however, that highlighted temporal aspects of social interaction. Working with long-term socially isolated groups on a 24-hour-a-day schedule, for days at a time, made vivid the temporal dynamics of relationships, as people progressed from being total strangers to becoming friends (or enemies). This perspective became crystallized in social penetration theory (Altman & Taylor, 1973), wherein we conducted research and theorized about temporal stages of relationships, self-disclosure in superficial and intimate areas of the self at different stages of a relationship, psychological experiences associated with interpersonal exchange, and relationship conflict and dissolution. At the time, research on close relationships had not paid very much attention to temporal issues, making our studies of social isolation and social penetration somewhat unique.

Where does the physical environment (e in Figure 1) fit in this phase? Generally speaking, it was not at the forefront of my thinking and only began to emerge in importance during the latter part of this phase, largely as a result of the social isolation studies. It is true that the physical environment was a major independent variable in this work, for example, pairs were confined to small rooms, had little external stimulation, and shared or had their own rooms. But somehow, as discussed in Phase II, the physical environment only became salient when I saw it as an intrinsic aspect of behavior, that is, a dependent variable, in the form of territorial behavior, spacing, and other uses of the environment. Because of its less central role in Phase I, the environment is represented by a lower-case e in Figure 1.

The other recurrent themes of my career were also evident during this phase. A holistic approach to psychological phenomena emerged in my earliest exposure to psychology. As an undergraduate and graduate student, I intuitively resonated with the holistic approach of Gestalt psychology and its offshoots in the learning theory of Edward Tolman and the social psychological theorizing of Kurt Lewin. This proclivity was further strengthened in my own research. In social penetration and social isolation research, we emphasized the study of a "symphony" of behaviors that occur in social relationships, in the form of complex patterns of verbal, nonverbal, and environmental behaviors. Whereas social psychology had traditionally studied relationships in terms of single behaviors, we tracked shifting patterns of behavior from several domains.

During this phase, I also established a careerlong multidisciplinary perspective. I learned that the fields of clinical psychology, family relations, communications, social work, general systems theory, animal ecology, and sociology all offered valuable research and theory on one or another aspect of social relationships or related topics. From my narrow base in social psychology, I discovered whole new worlds of knowledge, theory, and method—a prospect that was both invigorating and scary. Although a bit overwhelmed by all there was to learn, I was excited and optimistic and convinced that from then on I had to be alert to work in other fields.

In this first phase, I also came to appreciate the value of an eclectic approach to research methodology. My experiences in graduate work, teaching, and several jobs in applied contract research, discussed later, as well as a holistic approach convinced me of the necessity of an eclectic methodological strategy and avoidance of sole reliance on the then highly valued laboratory experimental approach. I concluded early that research methods should be selected or tailored to the problem at hand; too often I had seen people decide that a particular problem was unworthy of study because it could not be researched by a particular method. Having a substantive research agenda dictated by methodology was unacceptable, and I was determined to first select a problem and then use whatever procedures were available, with appropriate recognition of the limitations of the method and findings. As a result, during this phase I conducted laboratory experiments, quasi-experimental designs, interview and questionnaire studies, field observations, and so on. I am pleased to have achieved this point of view so early in my career; it has enabled study of issues from which I might otherwise have shied away.

My proclivity toward a holistic, temporal, interdisciplinary, and eclectic methodological approach to social relationships was influenced and supported by colleagues and settings. My graduate education at the University of Maryland from 1951–1957 (which was interrupted by 2 years of duty in the U.S. Army) occurred in a small department of 7 faculty and 20 graduate students. With few exceptions, the faculty and fellow students (most of whom were World War II veterans and older than the few of us fresh out of undergraduate school) were interested in applied research. The fact that student stipends were primarily for work on military contracts legitimized an applied perspective and fostered a holistic, multidisciplinary, and methodologically pragmatic viewpoint. The recurring themes of my career were also nurtured by the small size of the program and its lack of specialization. For example, all students took the same classes, regardless of their interests; there was only one social psychologist on the faculty and only one other student in social psychology; I had only one graduate course in social psychology; the only specialized experiences were on my thesis, dissertation, and other research. Although my education in social psychology was minimal, which troubled me at the time, I now realize how my education in psychology was broadly based and how much it influenced me to look beyond my specialty for ideas and methods and to seek a holistic orientation.

My first postgraduate position was at American University, where I taught about 12 classes in the 1 year I was there. This included *seven* sections of introductory psychology, a year-long course in experimental psychology (including laboratories without TAs), and sections of social psychology and industrial psychology. I now appreciate how much I learned about the whole field during this then-horrendous teaching experience. Indeed, I don't think I have ever been as broadly knowledgeable about psychology as I was during my last years as a graduate student and my brief faculty stint.

My next two jobs, each lasting 2 years, were in applied research setting, where I was in frequent contact with military and government sponsors. In my first position at a so-called Washington "Beltway bandit" research and consulting firm, I had the good fortune to work with Joseph McGrath on a U.S.-Air-Force-sponsored project to integrate the then-burgeoning small-group research literature (McGrath & Altman, 1966). In this work, I was under the tutelage of a now 30-year friend and colleague who gave me much needed confidence in my ability to think and who fostered a multimethod, multidisciplinary, dynamically oriented, and holistic view of psychological phenomena. I also worked with former classmates who had formed the company and who were engaged in research on airport marking and lighting, command control systems in submarines, military training, transportation, and human engineering projects. In this position, I learned about the attitudes and values of government and military sponsors and their pragmatic problem-solving orientation. Similar experiences occurred in my next position in a U.S.-Army-sponsored research organization at American University, where I conducted classified research on propaganda under different military contingencies. Here I had contact with government officials, educators, missionaries, tourists, and others who served as informants and consultants, further adding to my holistic perspective, appreciation of a multidisciplinary approach, the necessity for tailoring methods to problems, and being sensitive to the pragmatic requirements of our military sponsors. More and more my natural proclivities were strengthened, and I could no longer comfortably think about psychological processes independent of their social and organizational contexts or in other than a holistic fashion.

My next position, a 7-year stint at the Naval Medical Research Institute, Bethesda, Maryland (I had now had affiliations with the U.S. Air Force, Army, Navy, and various governmental agencies) involved basic research on socially isolated groups. I blossomed intellectually during this period, as the themes of my career were solidified and as I eventually "discovered" the physical environment. The setting and people at NMRI were optimal. John Rasmussen, a U.S. Navy commander and PhD clinical psychologist, founded the laboratory and fostered our freedom. William Haythorn, a social psychologist and laboratory director was a nurturant leader and creative colleague. Everything was started anew—labs, offices, and research projects. Haythorn and I collaborated on the first isolation project and were compatible in our desire to implement a holistic and dynamic approach by tracking complex patterns of behavior over time. We struggled with massive data sets based on round-the-clock and up to 10-day isolation periods and identified temporally linked complex behavioral profiles that distinguished between successful and unsuccessful groups. And the process of relationship development in socially isolated groups was so vivid that Dalmas Taylor (at first a doctoral student, subsequently a postdoctoral fellow, and then a long-term colleague and friend) and I formulated and did research on social penetration theory, with its emphasis on the holistic and dynamic aspects of relationships.

In summary, the first phase of my career focused on social relationships (P), particularly intimacy, self-disclosure and interpersonal exchange processes, and the temporal development of social relationships (T). My tendencies toward a holistic approach also were established, as I sought to understand complex behavior patterns. My contacts with applied researchers, military and government sponsors, and forays into the work of other scholarly disciplines reinforced my interest in a multidisciplinary approach. And the complexity and breadth of the problems I wished to study made salient the importance of a flexible and pragmatic approach to research methodology. These formative years were a template for the future, and I am amazed to see how I have continued to practice an approach to research and theory that was largely unverbalized at the time.

PHASE II: PHYSICAL ENVIRONMENT AS AN ASPECT OF PSYCHOLOGICAL PROCESSES (P,E,t)

The importance of the physical environment (E) to psychological processes (P) came to the forefront of my thinking in Phase II, whereas issues of time and change (t) drifted somewhat to the background. And, I made a major commitment to environment and behavior studies and professional/institutional activities in this phase and curtailed to some extent my involvement in disciplinary affairs in social psychology.

Our research on territorial behavior, which charted the exclusive use of space and objects by socially isolated group members, symbolized the beginning of my immersion in environmental studies (Altman & Haythorn, 1967; Altman et al., 1971). Other environmental studies were done on territorial behavior in a boys' correlational facility (Sundstrom & Altman, 1974), privacy regulation and decorating in a college dormitory (Vinsel, Brown, Altman, & Foss, 1980), environmental and architectural factors associated with home burglaries (Brown & Altman, 1983), family use of home environments (Altman, Nelson, & Lett, 1972), and so on. I also engaged in exciting theoretical work on a dialectical model of privacy regulation that dramatically shaped subsequent phases of my career (Altman, 1975).

My blossoming interest in the physical environment was further fueled by multidisciplinary conferences and organizations that fostered collegial networks of social scientists from sociology, geography, psychology, and so forth and environmental designers from architecture, landscape architecture, interior design, planning. For example, the Environmental Design Research Association held its first meeting in 1969 (I attended the 1970 meeting and have rarely missed one since); Ray Studer, an architect, Aristide Esser, a psychiatrist, and I established the Association for the Study of Man–Environment Relationships, a research-oriented organization; the environmental psychology program at the City University of New York was established in the late 1960s; the journal *Environment and Behavior* was founded in 1970. Furthermore, I chaired a multidisciplinary Task Force on Environment and Behavior sponsored by the American Psychological Association. The task force, a 4-year effort (1973–1977), developed a newsletter, directory, panels and symposia at national and regional conventions, and work groups that enlisted the energies of a generation of young psychologists who subsequently became major contributors to environment and behavior studies (see White, 1979, for a summary of the work of the task force). Eventually, Division 34 of the APA (Division of Population and Environmental Psychology) became an institutional base for environmental psychology. Finally, beginning in 1976, Jack Wohlwill and I teamed up to edit a series of volumes, *Human Behavior and Environment: Advances in Theory and Research*. That series, in which the present volume is the eleventh, offers syntheses of research and theory on contemporary topics, with contributors drawn from a diversity of disciplines.

These were exciting and important years, as I joined a group of young and enthusiastic scholars and designers who essentially forged a new discipline. We were immersed in new opportunities and were stimulated by one another, but we also experienced some of the frustrations and difficulties of cross-disciplinary collaboration and communication. As the field of environment–behavior studies progressed, new institutional structures emerged—an international *Journal of Environmental Psychology*, other series of edited volumes, textbooks, educational programs, and, most recently, a *Handbook of Environmental Psychology* (Stokols & Altman, 1987).

The emergence of this new field was coincident with dramatic changes in my life. I left the Naval Medical Research Institute in 1969 to become chairperson of the Department of Psychology at the University of Utah. Along with the freedom of an academic setting, I enjoyed the stimulation of new colleagues and superb students, the latter including Barbara Brown, Mary Gauvain, George Keiser, Patricia Nelson, Eric Sundstrom, Anne Vinsel, and others. And I continued to be deeply involved in the aforementioned organizations, conferences, journals, and editorial work and developed strong networks with colleagues in psychology and other disciplines.

I also grew intellectually during this phase, as I discovered "my" way of doing research and theory. I became comfortable with and better able to articulate my personal intuitions and approach to scholarship and to feel less guilty that I didn't always resonate with the traditional value system of my training and discipline. Not that I rejected my heritage in psychology; I simply wanted to broaden its traditional "positivist" orientation and encourage alternative research philosophies. The changes in my thinking centered on two themes: (1) a conceptualization of environment as psychological process, with privacy regulation as a core idea, and (2) a philosophical perspective, that is, dialectics and its emphasis on wholism.

The idea of environment as an aspect of psychological processes became salient in our social isolation research, as group members actively used the physical environment as part of their behavioral repertoires, much as they used verbal and nonverbal behaviors. Whereas traditional psychological and environmental design studies had focused primarily on physical environments as independent variables or "causes" of behavioral change, we also viewed the environment as part of a complex pattern of behaviors that, taken together, formed a holistic unity. For example, we studied territorial behavior in socially isolated groups, observing that men used beds, chairs, and areas of their space in relatively exclusive ways. And groups who established exclusive territories early in isolation functioned better than those who did not. Similarly, team members who were in synchrony regarding time off and on beds, amount of time in various places, and the like also performed effectively. These data fit with other information on self-disclosure, stress, and performance, indicating that environmental behaviors were part of a holistic behavioral profile and that it is useful to examine environment as behavioral process.

As another example, Altman *et al.* (1972) identified two types of family living styles in homes—open and informal versus formal and closed. In the open style, bedroom doors were left open for recreation, leisure, sleeping and so forth, access by family members to one anothers' bedrooms was easy, eating and entertaining occurred in kitchens rather than dining rooms, at meal times fathers sat at one end of the table and mothers at the other end or amidst the children (in contrast with formal families, where mothers sat at the father's corner). Open-style families also engaged in more activities as a whole unit and had an informal system of job sharing. These two studies and other research on territoriality and privacy regulation described later illustrate how I viewed the physical environment as one aspect of a holistic pattern of psychological processes occurring in interpersonal relationships.

This phase was also significant on philosophical and conceptual grounds, as I formulated a framework anchored around a dialectical approach to the concept of privacy (Altman, 1975). Based on research and reading it became evident that crowding, personal space, territorial behavior, and privacy were very crucial. Yet different groups of scholars studied them separately. For example, crowding had long been the domain of urban sociologists and animal ecologists, and only in the 1970s did psychologists study it (and somewhat unsuccessfully in laboratory settings). Studies of personal spacing, stimulated by the anthropologist Edward Hall, mushroomed in psychology, perhaps because it was amenable to laboratory simulations. There were relatively few studies of human territorial behavior at the time, although animal territoriality had been researched by ecologists and biologists. Privacy was rarely studied empirically and was of particular interest to political scientists and legal experts. As I wrote separate syntheses of research on crowding, personal space, and territoriality and read about privacy, I gradually formulated a logic for integrating these concepts in a single framework, anchored around the concept of privacy. That analysis was one of the most challenging and rewarding projects of my career (Altman, 1975; Altman *et al.*, 1981).

The key to the framework was the articulation of privacy as a dialectic process. Traditional approaches viewed privacy as a "keep-out" process, whereby people hid information, avoided intrusion from others, and so on. In contrast, I described privacy as a boundary regulation process involving opening and closing of the self to others, exhibiting dynamic qualities, and incorporating a variety of behavioral processes that formed a holistic pattern.

I came to a dialectic way of thinking by virtue of being troubled by a seeming inconsistency across bodies of literature. On the one hand, research and theory on interpersonal relationships, including my work on social penetration, emphasized openness of people to one another. Yet, writings on privacy, personal space, territoriality, and crowding focused on interpersonal closedness, that is, how spatial intrusions were negative, how people spatially closed themselves off from others, and so forth. The concept of dialectics eventually became the logic for resolving these differences.

My interest in dialectics began with the provocative essays on interpersonal relationships by Georg Simmel (1950), a turn-of-the-century sociologist.

From there I found my way into ancient Chinese dialectic philosophy (Taoism and Yin Yang ideas) and thence to Greek and later dialectic thinking—Hegel, Marx, and others. In psychology I studied Russian and American developmental psychologists who adopted a dialectical perspective. Although I do not pretend to be a sophisticated dialectitian (it is said that there are as many approaches to dialectics as there are dialectitians!), I eventually induced some principles that were relevant to my interests. One set of ideas is that the opposites of openness and closedness are part of a holistic unity that exhibits change in various circumstances. Thus I conceptualized privacy as a boundary regulation process that involved varying degrees of openness and closedness as circumstances changed. So, a person or group may be more open and accessible at one time and more closed and inaccessible at another time. Openness and closedness are, therefore, aspects of unified self–other boundary regulation processes that include qualities of time and change. This way of thinking was wholly compatible with my career-long search for a holistic and dynamic approach to psychological phenomena.

The framework was also holistic in its description of privacy as a unified pattern of behavioral events. People were hypothesized to seek a desired momentary level of openness/closedness and then invoke a series of behavioral mechanisms to achieve their goal. These mechanisms include combinations of verbal and nonverbal behaviors and environmental behaviors of personal spacing, territoriality, and the like. Thus personal spacing and territorial behavior were conceptualized as functioning in the service of privacy regulation.

On occasion there is a discrepancy between desired and achieved levels of openness/closedness, that is, intrusion or crowding occurs when one has more contact with others than desired, and isolation or loneliness arises when one received less contact than desired. Each of these circumstances may trip off intensified or new combinations of behavioral mechanisms designed to achieve the desired condition. In summary, this framework was a valuable heuristic for integrating key concepts in the environment and behavior field and was also relevant to a holistic and time-oriented approach to interpersonal relationships.

In addition, I came to view privacy regulation as a fundamental social process that may be culturally universal (Altman, 1977). I hypothesized that all cultures provide their members with mechanisms for regulating openness/ closedness but that what differs among cultures is the particular configuration of mechanisms people may use. To document this idea I analyzed cases where there apparently was little privacy, as evidenced by communal living, easy access by outsiders to homes, constant scrutiny of people by one another. In spite of the frequent absence of environmental mechanisms for achieving closedness, ethnographic data indicated that people in such cultures had a variety of other mechanisms—verbal, nonverbal, cultural customs—for regulating their dealings with others. I also examined cultures where people apparently had minimal interpersonal contact and demonstrated that here too people had a variety of means for achieving access to one another. So, by adopting a dialectic, holistic orientation, I concluded that privacy regulation is a pervasive human phenomenon.

I further reasoned that the ability to regulate privacy successfully may be crucial to psychological viability. Specifically, I hypothesized, and found support in an array of literature (Altman, 1975), that the inability to achieve consistently a desired level of openness/closedness is often associated with poor psychological functioning. This idea was also confirmed in several studies. For example, we demonstrated that group members who established territories and synchronized their spatial behavior in social isolation were most viable and effective (Altman & Haythorn, 1967; Altman et al., 1971). Another study (Sundstrom & Altman, 1974) charted territoriality in a boys' detention center over a 10-day period. Under stable group composition, all boys had territories, with dominant boys controlling more desirable places, and very little group disruptive behavior. When group composition changed, however, the dominance hierarchy of the group was in contention, territorial controls broke down, and there was an increase in fighting, breaking rules, and disorderly behavior. In a third phase, the group began stabilizing, with a new configuration of territories slowly forming and disruptions declining. Thus group viability was associated, in part, with the presence of territories and, consequently, of mechanisms for regulating social interaction. A study of college freshman living in dormitories during their first quarter at a university examined more directly the relationship between privacy regulation and viability (Vinsel et al., 1980). We found that students who had fewer and less effective mechanisms for regulating their openness and closedness to others (especially the latter) eventually dropped out of school to a greater extent than students with more effective privacy regulation mechanisms. These results suggest again a linkage between the ability to regulate privacy and viability.

In another study, Brown and Altman (1983) examined the relationship between territorial marking of homes and incidence of burglary (where the absence of burglary reflects higher viability). In general, nonburglarized homes displayed stronger territorial controls than burglarized homes, in the form of *symbolic barriers* to access, for example, owners' names or addresses on signs in the yard or on the home; less indication of public accessibility to the street symbolized by stop signs; *actual barriers* such as fences and gates; *traces* or symbols of the presence of occupants, for example, toys in the yard, sprinklers operating; *detectability* or the visibility of the home to neighboring houses. Thus an effective privacy regulation system and specific territorial mechanisms were associated with enhanced social system viability.

In summary, during this second phase, my work focused on the physical environment as an aspect of psychological processes, with temporal factors being of somewhat less interest (P,E,t). True to the theme of a holistic orientation, I treated privacy as a complex unity of verbal, nonverbal, and environmental behaviors. This phase was also consistent with my interdisciplinary focus, as I drew on anthropology, history, philosophy, and religion in exploring dialectic and cross-cultural aspects of privacy. Although not salient during this phase, time and changes were included in the conceptualization of privacy regulation as a dynamic interplay of openness and closedness and in empirical studies of privacy regulation, territoriality, and related processes. Finally, the investigation of environment as psychological process relied on a broad spectrum of methodologies, including quasi-experimental studies, naturalistic observations of territorial behavior, qualitative ethnographic evidence, and so on.

All in all, this phase was most critical to my professional and scholarly development, as I came to appreciate the centrality of environmental factors to interpersonal relationships, and as I formulated a philosophical approach with which I was personally and professionally comfortable. I now had a much clearer sense of where I was heading.

PHASE III: THE UNITY OF PLACES
AND PSYCHOLOGICAL PROCESSES (E,P,t)

This phase was capstoned by my efforts to define a unique unit of analysis of psychological phenomena—a place-process unit. These efforts resulted from my observation that social science researchers and environmental designers had fundamental difficulties communicating and working with one another—which I eventually attributed to a divergence in their assumptions about units of analysis of phenomena. Specifically, after participating in innumerable discussions and debates about the gap between design and research orientations, I concluded that the issue was partly resolvable if we could treat environments as "places," as well as aspects of psychological processes. As a result, I began to articulate the nature of "place-process" units of psychological phenomena, a step that played a major role in my subsequent work and brought me closer to a transactional perspective. Thus in this phase I continued to emphasize the physical environment (E) and psychological processes (P), with somewhat less attention to temporal issues (t). But the focus was less on environment-as-process and more on environment-as-place.

What was the gap between social scientists and environmental designers? On the one side, environmental designers criticized behavioral scientists for doing irrelevant and nonapplicable research, hedging their findings with many qualifications, being unwilling to deal with budgetary and time realities of environmental design, and being insensitive to the "real" people and places with whom designers dealt on an everyday basis. On the other side, behavioral scientists chided environmental designers for being imprecise and nonanalytic, insensitive to the importance of theory, not doing research on the environments they designed, and seeking unduly simplistic answers to questions. Clearly, there was an intellectual gap between designers and researchers, and frequent debates occurred about how to bridge, eliminate, or circumvent the gap so that our distinctive talents could be combined.

To address the issue in substantive terms, I proposed a conceptual analysis of the differences in approach of researchers and designers (Altman, 1973). First, I portrayed environmental designers as criterion or dependent variable oriented, in the sense that they have a particular goal and design objective in mind, whereas basic researchers are independent variable oriented and have no particular level of behavior they wish to achieve. Second, environmental designers are synthesizers and holistic, integrating knowledge from a variety of sources to understand a specific holistic unity, for example, a building. In contrast, behavioral scientists analyze and dimensionalize phenomena and are less concerned with the immediate synthesis of findings from different domains. Third, I portrayed environmental designers as problem solvers and implementers, whereas basic researchers focus on knowing and understanding rather than immediate application. I also described how these distinctions often led to different questions and strategies, thereby contributing further to miscommunication and mutual frustration.

Superordinate to the preceding distinctions, I concluded that environmental designers are primarily interested in places, for example, hospitals, homes, neighborhoods, whereas social scientists are typically interested in psychological or other processes, such as cognition, privacy, territory. For social scientists, places are used to generalize findings or are sources of error. For environmental designers, however, places are primary, and they use knowledge about processes only insofar as it applies to a particular place. Therefore, it is no wonder, I stated, that a "gap" exists between researchers and designers.

My initial solution to these differences was rather pollyanish—let us understand our differences, try to think in one anothers' terms, and work toward mutual acceptance and respect, acknowledging the differences as probably unresolvable. I never was very satisfied with this wishy-washy resolution and now see how my subsequent work in Phase III was a more frontal attack on the problem. In essence, I sought a *place-process* unit of analysis of psychological phenomena, such that the qualities of places were unified with psychological processes. If accomplished, then the "gap" between social scientists and environmental designers would be reduced and another step taken toward a holistic orientation to psychological phenomena.

In this phase, my colleagues and I did cross-cultural analyses of home environments (Altman & Chemers, 1980; Altman & Gauvain, 1981; Gauvain, Altman, & Fahim, 1983; see also studies by Altman *et al.*, 1972, and Brown & Altman, 1983, in Phase II, and by Werner, Altman, & Oxley, 1985, in Phase IV). Why study homes? First, important human relationships occur in homes, including intimate social bonds and all manner of family relationships. In this sense, the study of homes fits nicely with my long-standing interest in interpersonal relationships. Second, almost all cultures have homes in which people live and perform various functions, and there is a vast data base in anthropology, history, and other disciplines. So, studying homes is an ideal way to explore place-process units of analysis.

In a crucial analysis that led to a place-process unit of analysis, Altman and Gauvain (1981) applied the dialectics of openness/closedness and individuality/communality to homes. Consistent with privacy regulation theory, we reasoned that people use their homes as a mechanism for being open or accessible and closed or inaccessible to others. Ethnographic and cross-cultural data illustrate how this is achieved by the siting of homes and management of territorial boundaries (e.g., facing communal areas with easy access of people to one another versus being set back and distant from public areas; use of fences, hedges, and gates versus easy access to dwellings, etc). Openness/closedness is also managed by front facade designs (e.g., open windows and easy visibility into homes versus blank walls) and by entranceways (e.g., open doors, welcome mats versus formal entranceways, closed doors). And interiors are often used to regulate openness/closedness by means of public and private areas.

A second dialectic—identity/communality—enables residents to exhibit simultaneously their distinctiveness and uniqueness versus affiliation and similarity with others. Cross-cultural data illustrate how identity/communality is reflected in home sites, (e.g., landscaping that fits with community norms but also displays uniqueness), front facades and entranceways decorated to reflect community values and individual tastes, and interiors (e.g., public rooms, shrines, and other settings) to portray communal religious and cultural values as well as unique family photographs, trophies, and so forth.

We "validated" the importance of the identity/communality and openness/closedness dialectics by examining different forms of cultural change (Gauvain et al., 1983). For example, the development of the Aswan Dam in 1963 required the relocation of 50,000 Nubian residents of Egypt, resulting in political, economic, and cultural upheaval, one aspect of which was a dramatic change in home and community environments. Hussein Fahim's extensive information about traditional Nubian homes confirmed our earlier analysis, that is, the Nubians traditionally decorated the exteriors and interiors of their homes, in part to regulate openness/closedness and identity/communality. We also concluded from his data that the new homes did not provide adequate means for maintaining these dialectic processes and that people attempted to restore the dialectics in an exact or modified form. For example, high windowless walls traditionally helped regulate closedness; in the new communities, one of the first building modifications was to heighten walls around homes and block off windows. And in traditional homes openness was achieved by people sitting on elevated platforms in front of homes, enabling contacts with neighbors. The relocation homes lacked seating areas, however; people used chairs and benches and built seating platforms whenever possible. Similar attempts were made to restore traditional identity/communality mechanisms.

By fusing places (homes) and psychological processes (identity/communality and openness/closedness) in an inseparable whole, these and related findings symbolize a major step toward a place-process unit of analysis. That is, homes were now *defined by* configurations of openness/closedness and identity/communality, making the home in essence a set of social and psychological processes. By the same token, psychological processes of identity/communality and openness/closedness were partly defined by the physical environment of homes. Thus homes and these dialectic processes are mutually defining and inseparable, yielding a place-process unit of study. Because places and processes were intrinsically joined in these analyses, I now saw a way of overcoming the traditional distinction between environmental designers as strictly place oriented and social scientists as strictly process oriented. Theoretically, there should be no schism because both parties could now employ the same unit of analysis. Coincidentally, I had an opportunity to test this line of thinking in the marketplace of environmental design. Gerald Davis, a research-oriented programmer–architect, invited me to consult on several office design projects. Although I had little prior design experience, our collaboration was productive, and we discovered that the place-process orientation described worked quite well. By shifting figure and ground, from process-oriented concepts, for example, openness/closedness and identity/communality, to particular office places, we communicated easily. More important, we developed effective relationships with administrators, workers, and environmental designers, in part because we could communicate about *their* physical places in terms of psychological processes that were part and parcel of those places—not processes that were remote, abstract, and situation free. Furthermore, although our previous work had been on homes, it was relatively easy to apply concepts such as openness/closedness to office settings, again because the concepts could be integrally linked to and partially defined by places and vice versa.

So, on philosophical and practical grounds I believe that the so-called "gap" between environmental designers and social scientists can be bridged if, along with traditional process-oriented and place-oriented approaches, we also work with place-process units of analysis. This shift in unit of analysis not only has a bearing on translating knowledge into practice, but it is important to our holistic understanding of phenomena.

In summary, in this career phase, I focused on environments as places and explored ways of integrating psychological processes and places into a holistic unit of analysis of environment–behavior phenomena. This was a dramatically different way of thinking for me and subsequently guided future work in a significant way. Also consistent with the holistic theme of my career, I treated the concepts of openness/closedness and identity/communality as complex, multifaceted behavioral repertoires that are displayed in different cultures in a variety of forms. And, similar to earlier phases, I delved into the resources of other disciplines, particularly anthropology. Finally, my research was methodologically eclectic, as I relied heavily on descriptive ethnographic material. Although time and change (t) were somewhat neglected during this phase, our efforts at formulating psychological process (P) and environmental place (E) units of analysis was another step toward a transactional perspective.

PHASE IV: TEMPORAL QUALITIES OF ENVIRONMENTAL PLACES (T,E,p) AND TEMPORAL QUALITIES OF PSYCHOLOGICAL PROCESSES (T,P,e)

In Phase IV, time and change became salient again, as they had been in the first phase of my career. Although temporal issues were addressed in every phase, they were usually secondary to my treatment of environment as an aspect of psychological processes (Phase II: P,E,t) and environment as part of place-process units of analysis (Phase III: E,P,t). In Phase IV, on the other hand, I deliberately set out to address two temporal issues: (1) the temporal qualities of places, thereby linking the environment-as-place orientation of Phase III with time and change; and (2) the integration of social penetration and privacy regulation theoretical frameworks. The first topic deals primarily with time and environmental places, with aspects of relationships subordinated (T,E,p); the second analysis highlights time and psychological process links, somewhat downplaying environmental issues (T,P,e). Although different in focus, both topics bring time and change to the forefront.

In a centerpiece paper, Werner *et al.* (1985) developed a conceptual framework of temporal qualities of home environments. We theorized that psychological meanings, displays, activities, and uses of homes incorporated overarching dimensions of *linear* and *cyclical* time, as well as other temporal dimensions. As in prior analyses, we worked with concepts that derived from and applied to homes in many cultures.

Linear time refers to the continuity and change of meanings and uses of homes from past to present to future. Thus homes reflect past ancestral, family, and personal life histories, contemporary aspects of family life, and future-oriented qualities, for example, house blessing ceremonies in many cultures call for the future well-being and prosperity of occupants and homes, and at the same time often link homes and occupants to their ancestors and heritage. So, an act, ritual, or object linked to one temporal referent, for example, the past, often blends into the present and even into the future, making the home a vehicle for expressing temporal continuity and change in the lives of people.

A second major dimension is *cyclical time,* or repetitive meanings and activities of homes, with cycles potentially recurring on daily, weekly, monthly, or other regular bases. Cyclical aspects of homes include day-to-day living, work, seasonal, agricultural, religious events. Many cyclical activities and meanings also reflect continuity and change. That is, although people repeat activities in homes from month to month or year to year, they also often alter their form or meaning from occasion to occasion.

Several other temporal qualities crosscut these dimensions. *Salience* refers to the predominant time orientation of activities, meanings, or objects in the past, present, or future. Temporal *scale* refers to the duration of a temporal event, for example, length of a celebration and the time interval between celebrations. Temporal *pace* refers to the relative rapidity or density of experiences, meanings or activities, for example, certain events occur at a slow, unhurried pace, whereas others involve rapid activities. Finally, temporal *rhythm* involves regularly occurring patterns and sequences of behaviors, feelings, and experiences.

We applied aspects of this framework to a variety of events and phenomena, including the annual house-blessing ceremonies of the Zuni Indians, the use of attics and cellars in rural France, annual Christmas celebrations in an urban neighborhood, and computer-mediated communication. Each application highlighted the integral temporal qualities of environmental settings, essentially "defining" environments in terms of psychologically relevant temporal processes. Similarly, our analyses illustrated how abstract temporal qualities can be imbued with psychological meanings associated with places.

Consider aspects of a comparison of the house-blessing ceremonies of the Zuni Indians (Werner *et al.*, 1985) and the annual celebration of Christmas Street (Oxley, Haggard, Werner, & Altman, 1986; Werner *et al.*, 1987; Werner, Haggard, Altman, & Oxley, 1988). The home is a sacred place in Zuni, and at the winter solstice several new homes are blessed during a 24-hour period, the culmination of an annual cycle of events. The cycle begins with the naming of households to be blessed a year hence and the appointment of young men to serve as impersonators of the Rain God Shalako. The impersonators participate in religious rituals at regular intervals during the year (temporal scale), learn about the history of the Zuni people (linear, past salience), take part in recurrent ceremonies (cycles and rhythms), and so on. As the main celebration approaches, the number and intensity of events increase (temporal scale, temporal pace). The 24-hour celebration is replete with a variety of cyclical activities at macro- and microtemporal scales and includes repetitive ritual prayers and recitation of the history of the people, dancing of the Rain God figures, and references to past history and religion, present lives of the occupants and the community, and the future well-being and prosperity of the residents of the dwelling. Thus the home has associated with it a variety of temporally based meanings and activities, yielding a time–place unity.

We also compared the Zuni house-blessing ceremonies with a neighborhood that celebrated Christmas as a communal event (Oxley *et al.*, 1986; Werner *et al.*, 1987; Werner *et al.*, 1988) (see Phase V for more details). The planning for Christmas Street also involved preliminary activities varying in scale, rhythm, and salience, with both celebrations culminating in increased pace as the celebrations approached. And they both involved recurrent events during the celebratory period itself, with the Christmas Street celebration involving extensive decorations of homes for a month, a party and parade during Christmas week, and related activities. Thus it was possible to describe and compare rituals associated with different places in terms of a common temporal framework.

We also applied the temporal framework to computer-based interpersonal communication (Hesse, Werner, & Altman, 1988). This new environment is dramatically different from the typical settings of everyday social exchange. Although computer communications eliminates many nonverbal cues, our thesis was that the computer environment also changed certain temporal aspects of social interaction. Thus we illustrated how temporal qualities of linear and cyclical time, and scale, pace, salience, and rhythm varied in face-to-face and computer settings. For example, the temporal scale of computer-mediated communication may become homogenized, as people become more similar in the duration of their communications with one another by virtue of the mechanics of interaction.

In summary, one aspect of Phase IV emphasized temporal aspects of physical environments (T,E,p), illustrating the intrinsic linkage between places and time/change. A second facet of this phase focused on temporal aspects of psychological processes (T,P,e). Specifically, Altman *et al.* (1981) synthesized earlier work on privacy regulation (Phase II) and social penetration theory (Phase I), providing a more comprehensive analysis than heretofore of temporal factors in relationship development. The integrated model hypothesized that relationship development involves recurrent cycles of openness and closedness as participants progress from strangership to closer bonds. The cycles of openness/closedness vary in amplitude, scale, and pace as a function of topical intimacy, relationship stage, conflict level, and other factors. We also theorized about the impact of mutual temporal synchrony or asynchrony of participants' cycles of openness/closedness on relationship viability.

This framework blended social penetration and privacy regulation, illustrating how seemingly separate areas of my work were actually aspects of the larger puzzle I had been pursuing throughout my career but had not connected precisely earlier. Thus I originally conceived of social penetration and privacy regulation theories as addressing different domains, even though they shared a holistic, multibehavioral approach. In the Altman et al. (1981) synthesis, we brought together the strengths of each perspective and overcame their individual limitations, yielding a unified framework. The key to the synthesis was the introduction of the openness/closedness dialectic into social penetration theory and the weaving in of temporal stages of relationship development into privacy regulation theory. One of the most difficult papers of my career to write yielded one of the most satisfying outcomes and a very rewarding association with my co-authors Anne Vinsel and Barbara Brown, then graduate students.

I also now saw how several studies linked to earlier phases complemented the temporal focus of the present phase. Thus the social isolation studies (Altman & Haythorn, 1967; Altman et al., 1971) analyzed the temporal development of territories; the study in a boys' detention home (Sundstrom & Altman, 1974) charted temporal changes in territorial behavior as group composition changed; the research on Nubian homes (Gauvain et al., 1983) tracked changes in home use from before to after relocation; the study of dormitory students (Vinsel et al., 1980) examined privacy regulation and decorating as predictors of later withdrawal from school. Although temporal factors were not always initially central to these studies, time and change eventually was addressed in order to interpret results. In that sense, these investigations supplement the work of Phase IV and illustrate how I always seemed to return to issues associated with the temporal dynamics of relationships.

Phase IV also incorporated the other central themes of my career. A holistic orientation prevailed, as I wove together psychological processes, the physical environment, and time in one or another configuration. An interdisciplinary orientation continued, as I drew on the findings of other fields. And, methodologically, I relied on a variety of approaches, this time emphasizing qualitative and conceptual analysis (including some fieldwork at the Pueblo of Zuni on house-blessing ceremonies). Most important, this phase highlighted time and change, thereby setting the stage for the present phase of my career— wherein I have begun to tackle explicitly the transactional unity of psychological processes, environments, and temporal factors.

PHASE V: THE TRANSACTIONAL UNITY OF PSYCHOLOGICAL
PROCESSES, PHYSICAL ENVIRONMENTS/PLACES,
AND TEMPORAL FACTORS (P,E,T)

This phase has just begun, as I strive to incorporate all aspects of the transactional perspective in every scholarly effort, thereby achieving the (P,E,T) core in Figure 1. In some ways the more than 30 years of my professional career have been preparatory, as I now finally see the opportunity to grasp some holistic qualities of psychological phenomena.

In Phase V, I have been exploring several facets of the transactional unity of psychological processes, environment, and time/change: (1) a philosophical analysis of "world views" or approaches to knowledge about psychological phenomena; (2) discussions of research methodology associated with the transactional world view; (3) sociological analyses of the history and present status of psychology, community psychology, and the field of culture and design according to a transactional perspective; (4) empirical research involving a case study of a neighborhood known as Christmas Street, and a field study of polygamous families.

Before discussing research, I wish to describe how the people and places of this phase played an important role in my work and life. During my fourth and fifth career phases I was dean of the College of Social and Behavioral Science (1979–1983) and vice president for academic affairs (1983–1987) at the University of Utah. These experiences were noteworthy for several reasons. They spanned several years of financial difficulty when I was directly responsible for budget cutting, reallocation, and program discontinuance—creating enormous administrative and personal challenges. Strange as it may seem, these often painful experiences contributed to my emerging transactional view. For example, I learned about the programs, budgets, people, space, and time-linked demands of the university as a whole. I saw firsthand the divergent values of different disciplines, including the strong pragmatic and monetary orientations of the professional schools and the technological disciplines, in contrast with the often pragmatically naive perspectives of the fine arts, humanities, and social sciences. I also experienced the fragmentation and centrifugal quality of the university and individual disciplines and sought to engender countervailing centripetal forces—sometimes successfully, often unsuccessfully. So, managing and attempting to grasp a sense of widely divergent fields and values and struggling to create some semblance of a unified institution reinforced my interest in (and also realism about) a holistic, process-oriented, and interdisciplinary approach to environment and behavior phenomena.

As a side benefit, I occasionally discussed theoretical and philosophical issues with a diversity of faculty colleagues (although intellectual discourse is not the everyday fare of administrators). I probed about philosophy of inquiry, current issues, values, and controversies in their fields and discovered that transactional issues are emerging in many disciplines, as are challenges to long-standing fundamental assumptions. For example, critical legal theorists, feminist scholars, writers, historians, economists, and others are exploring contextually oriented modes of inquiry; chemists and physicists continue to develop transactionally oriented quantum and relativity theories and so on.

My thinking was also influenced by Jack Wohlwill, a fine scholar and colleague, and our decade long co-editorship of the book series, *Human Behavior and Environment*, sponsored by Plenum Publishing Corporation. I also co-edited with Lawrence Wrightsman and Dan Stokols, two broad-gauged scholars and good friends, a multivolume monograph series on environment and behavior topics originally sponsored by Brooks/Cole Publishing Company and subsequently transferred to Cambridge University Press (and then edited by Stokols and me). Dan Stokols and I also co-edited the first *Handbook of Environment Psychology*, published by Wiley (Stokols & Altman, 1987). Editing is not always easy, but working with superb colleagues as co-editors (and there were others in some of these volumes) and with more than 200 authors from different disciplines contributed enormously to my personal and scholarly maturation and to my emerging transactional perspective.

I was also privileged to work with wonderful colleagues on crucial transactionally oriented projects. Barbara Rogoff and I co-authored a philosophical paper that compared transactional and other "world views" of psychological phenomena (Rogoff & Altman, 1987). Rogoff's broad knowledge of developmental psychology and her penetrating intellectual skills contributed significantly to my thinking. I am also especially pleased to have collaborated with Carol Werner, a longtime close friend and colleague, during the crucial fourth and fifth phases of my career. Our work on cross-cultural aspects of homes, Christmas Street and other projects, and our exploration of methodological and philosophical aspects of the transactional perspective benefited enormously from her quick and open approach to new ideas, and from her rigorous methodological orientation.

PHILOSOPHICAL ANALYSES OF WORLD VIEWS

The article by Altman and Rogoff (1987) and subsequent articles by Altman, Werner, Oxley, and Haggard (1987) and Werner *et al.* (1987, 1988) were major efforts to distinguish between alternative "world views" or approaches to the study of psychological phenomena. We described four world views—trait, interactional, organismic, and transactional—in terms of their unit of analysis of phenomena, treatment of time and change, and philosophy of science. For example, all but the transactional orientation assume that psychological processes are the primary units of analysis, with social and physical factors, and temporal variables treated as separate and independent entities. Even the organismic view, which argues that the whole possesses distinctive properties, treats elements as independently defined and separate entities. In contrast, the transactional world view assumes that psychological phenomena are composed of inseparable physical and social environments, temporal qualities, and psychological processes.

World views also differ in their approach to time and change. Trait perspectives assume stability or change based on predetermined internal timetables; interactional views consider change to result from the interaction of separate variables; organismic approaches assume that change is governed by underlying organic processes. In contrast, the transactional orientation treats temporal qualities and change as intrinsic aspects of psychological phenomena, which exhibit variable patterns of stability and change, are directed at short- and long-term goals, and are defined in terms of natural temporal units rather than artificially imposed chronological periods.

World views also differ in their underlying philosophy of science. Generally speaking, trait, interactional, and organismic approaches adopt a "positivist" philosophy of science, a view that has been shared by most social sciences during this century. They assume that observers can be separate from and objective about the phenomenon being studied, whereas the transactional perspective assumes that a phenomenon is partially defined by certain qualities of the observer, making the observer an aspect of the event and requiring multiple observers in different "locations."

World views also vary in their approach to Aristotle's fourfold schema of causation (Rychlak, 1977): the trait view emphasizes *material causation* (the cause is intrinsic to the phenomenon); interactional approaches adopt efficient causation (antecedent–consequent effects); organismic views rely primarily on *final cause* (phenomena are "pulled" in a particular direction by virtue of some teleologically based governing principle); the transactional view emphasizes *formal cause* (the coherent pattern, configuration, and flow of a phenomenon).

The first three perspectives seek to identify parsimonious universal laws, usually by means of analytic and parametric study of relationships between variables and with prediction and control as validation procedures. Thus the interactional approach (and the organismic to some extent) builds knowledge from the bottom up, so to speak, with relationships between variables cumulating to yield understanding of the whole. The organismic view also attempts to identify principles applying to the system as a whole. The transactional perspective seeks to understand a particular event—a time, people, and place-bounded occurrence—which may require application of one or more psychological principles, not necessarily universally applicable ones. This world view is not wholly idiosyncratic but is also open to the possibility that psychological principles may generalize across situations. So, the transactional approach encompasses aspects of the philosophy of science of other world views, although its starting point and goal is to describe and understand unique events that are temporally, spatially, and situationally bounded.

Research Methodology

Translating the transactional perspective into methodologically viable empirical research is a difficult challenge because research methods tend to be associated with world views and their goals and rules for studying phenomena. Because the interactional perspective and its associated methodology have prevailed for so many decades, implementing the transactional approach requires us to "break set" and either develop new methods or modify existing ones. We have proposed some general methodological strategies congruent with the transactional world view and also discussed external and internal validity, studying unique events, and other issues (Altman & Rogoff, 1987; Altman, 1988; Altman et al., 1987). One key principle is to develop laboratory and naturalistic methods for understanding social and physical contexts of psychological phenomena. This can be partially achieved by studying the meaning of an event to a variety of parties, not relying solely on the judgments of "objective" scientific observers or externally imposed measurement procedures. Another principle is to study time and change using natural units of behavior change rather than arbitrarily imposing chronological indicators. The methodology for so doing is presently available for certain types of research (Barker, 1968). In addition, understanding holistic unities requires charting multiple ongoing psychological processes. Here again, design, recording, and statistical procedures are presently available. We summarized a series of other methodological principles as follows:

> [Adopting a transactional approach] . . . is a challenging methodological task because it requires sensitivity to each situation and to each case, a strong linkage between theoretical constructs and measures, and an "artistic" ability to identify indicators that are embedded in situations. It also requires consideration of the function of any particular act in the setting in which it is observed, as well as the goals that the participants are attempting to meet. Ideally, therefore, a transactional approach does not unilaterally impose measures on an event, but it derives them from the event. What generalizes from study to study is not the measure, procedure, or technique but the construct and theory that underlies the research. (Altman & Rogoff, 1987, p. 35)

A capstone principle of the transactional approach is methodological eclecticism, with research designs, procedures, and measures ideally tailored to a particular configuration of psychological processes, settings, and temporal qualities. Laboratory experiments, field studies, and qualitative analyses are all acceptable methods, depending upon the problem being studied. Although easy to state as a principle, methodological eclectism requires willingness to become proficient in a variety of methods.

One by-product of my thinking about transactional methodology was a reformulation of the traditional distinction between basic and applied research and the highlighting of a heretofore neglected methodological approach (Altman, 1988, 1989). I argued that the rigid dichotomy between basic and applied research was based on superficial differences, such as purposes and goals of research (generation of knowledge and laws of human behavior by basic research and problem solving and amelioration of social problems by applied research), settings and contexts of research (laboratories for basic research and the "real world" for applied studies), researcher roles (client centered in applied research and discipline centered in basic research), and so forth.

Instead, I proposed that research strategies be linked to assumptions about *units of analysis* of phenomena. This resulted in a tripartite categorization of research methodologies, which I termed *process-oriented, outcome-oriented* and *transactional/contextual* approaches. Process-oriented studies focus on psychological processes as the fundamental unit of study, defined independently of situational and other factors. These studies adopt the goals and philosophy of science of trait, interactional, and organismic world views, for example, universal explanatory principles, prediction, and generalization, and the like. Process-oriented studies also systematically vary independent variables by experimentation or natural selection and permit dependent variables to vary freely. In contrast, *outcome-oriented research* attempts to assess, design, and determine the effectiveness of particular social units functioning in a bounded configuration of social and physical settings at a designated time. Analogous to traditional applied research and drawing on aspects of a transactional approach, these studies determine the extent to which some predetermined standard of functioning is or can be achieved by system design. Thus outcome studies are criterion oriented with respect to a specific configuration of people, places, and time.

A third approach, *transactional/contextual research*, largely neglected in psychological research, ideally adopts holistic psychological process-physical and social environment-temporal units of analysis. In reality, one usually needs to work with subsets of the whole, such as psychological process-physical place units, social units (individuals and groups) psychological processes, psychological process-time units, and the like. This approach provides a methodological strategy compatible with the transactional world view. Examples of such studies have been presented throughout this chapter.

This analysis strengthened my belief that the development of transactional research methodology is possible and that it must be closely linked to assumptions of that world view about units of analysis of phenomena (and, eventually, time and change).

Sociological Analyses

Along with philosophical and methodological discourses, I used a transactional approach to explore the sociology of community psychology, the new field of culture and design, and aspects of the history and current status of psychology.

In a commentary at a symposium celebrating the twentieth anniversary of community psychology, I remarked that the field seemed to have always aimed toward a transactional and/or organismic perspective (Altman, 1987b). Thus community psychology has been consistently holistic, calling for research and practice that treats psychological phenomena as embedded in social, cultural, and physical contexts. Moreover, the central concepts of process, prevention, intervention, and evaluation assume intrinsic properties of time and change. Although often implicit, community psychology also relies on a philosophy of science and methodology that is nonanalytic, focuses on patterns of relationships, is flexible about discovering universal principles, and is methodologically eclectic. I concluded with a call for community psychologists to be more introspective about philosophical assumptions and to develop and use research methodologies consistent with those assumptions. I did a similar analysis of the newly emerging field of culture and design (Altman, 1986).

In a somewhat presumptuous paper presented at the National Conference on Graduate Education in Psychology, I used dialectic and transactional ideas to describe the 100-year history of modern psychology (Altman, 1987a). I characterized the field as transactionally congruent with the sociocultural milieus of higher education and American society within which it is embedded. And I described how dialectic centripetal and centrifugal trends in psychology, higher education, and American society exhibited properties of opposition, unity, and change over the decades. Thus I portrayed psychology as primarily centrifugal and not unified in its formative years (1870–1900) but unified and centripetal during the period 1900–1960, as was higher education and American society at large. Then in the 1960–present era, American society, higher education, and psychology have been centrifugal, exhibiting disunity and fragmentation. Finally, I reiterated the transactional theme that plans and assessments about the future of the field need to consider the trajectory of events in its larger contexts.

EMPIRICAL RESEARCH

I also tried to achieve a comprehensive transactional perspective in a study of an urban neighborhood and in an investigation of polygamous families. My colleagues and I investigated "Christmas Street," a cul-de-sac of 31 single-family dwellings where Christmas has been celebrated as a community event for more than 40 years (Altman et al., 1987; Oxley et al., 1986; Werner et al., 1987, 1988). During the holiday season, homes are richly decorated with lights and displays, a large red and green neon sign reading "Christmas Street" arches over the entrance to the street, and a decorated tree is in the circle at the end of the street. The street, visited by thousands of people during the holiday season, holds a variety of coordinated activities, including planning meetings, a children's party, parade, and Santa Claus in residence. In accordance with a transactional strategy, we collected a variety of information at different times of year, using a range of methodologies. We collected information about social relations and social networks, psychological attachments to the street and community, environmental behaviors and decorating, and ethnographic information about customs, norms, and history of the celebration. Our methodology included interviews, questionnaires, observations, and photographic analyses, with data collected during the summer and holiday season, and also tracking the yearly cycle of planning and activities.

Although complex, the results illustrated the value of a guiding transactional perspective. For example, social networks shifted somewhat from summer to winter, although core members of networks maintained their associations throughout the year, reflecting both stability and change of social bonds. Social affiliations were also related to decorating and community attachment, primarily during the Christmas season, when those in close social networks expressed greater attachment to the street and put more energy into decorating their homes. Similarly, during the summer, social bonds and community attachment were related, although environmental behaviors were primarily associated with individual characteristics. Taken together, there was both continuity and change on Christmas Street, with a consistent profile of involved and uninvolved people reflected in social attachments, attitudes, behavior, and environmental activities, with some shifts in these associations from season to season.

A project recently begun in collaboration with Joseph Ginat, an anthropologist, is exploring social relationships in polygamous families in the western United States (Altman & Ginat, 1989a,b). We are collecting information about husband–wife and wife–wife relationships at various stages of the family life cycle, for example, decisions about adding another wife, courtship, weddings, adjustment of and to new wives, ongoing relationships between wives and husbands and between wives, management of privacy and territories, place attachment, observance of holidays, birthdays and anniversaries, living arrangements, home management and decorating practices, and the like. We are attempting to satisfy a transactional approach by collecting interview, observational, and archival data that are sensitive to temporal stages of relationships and to psychological and environmental aspects of relationships.

The philosophical, conceptual, methodological, sociological, and empirical work of this phase reflects again the consistent themes of my professional life. First and foremost, I am consciously striving to include all aspects of the transactional world view in each project, that is, psychological processes, physical environments as places and/or processes, and time/change. Although not always done to perfection, I sense coming closer than heretofore to the holistic perspective I have always sought. In addition, I continue to maintain a long-standing interest in the dynamic, process-oriented qualities of interpersonal relationships. Furthermore, the multidisciplinary and methodologically eclectic perspectives of earlier stages continue to prevail, as I draw on ideas and knowledge from philosophy, history, anthropology, sociology, and other disciplines, and as I rely on a variety of methodological strategies. This phase feels like it has just begun, and I look forward to its continuation with enthusiasm and optimism.

RETROSPECTIVE AND PROSPECTIVE

I began this essay by portraying my career as a main path with many side trails or as a spiral circling around a core set of issues. I now know that the path and spiral are unending and that each career phase has been both a culmination and a beginning. The present phase is a culmination in several respects. I now feel more prepared than ever before to adopt a transactional perspective in which psychological processes and physical and social contexts are woven together into a changing and flowing holistic unity. And I am now quite comfortable drawing on other disciplines while maintaining my perspective as a psychologist. Furthermore, I am confident of the importance of an eclectic approach to research methodology and of my capacity to learn about and employ a variety of procedures.

But my career is also just beginning! After three decades of preparatory work, I feel that I am now ready to tackle some important transactional questions. Indeed, I have a sense of beginning and possibility that is no less than that I felt in the first days of my professional life.

I also feel fortunate in more than an intellectual sense. The holistic, dynamic, multimethod, and multidisciplinary approach that has pervaded my career is not just a professional and scholarly stance. Some years ago I realized that I have always personally viewed my own and others' social relationships in a flowing, holistic sort of way, as well as being sensitive to their contexts. I can also now trace the personal quality of my scholarship to my childhood and family life-style, which made it necessary for me to be tuned into complex, changing, and contextually linked social dynamics. The natural congruence of my work and life is very gratifying because the research contributes to my personal growth, and my personal life often brings new dimensions to my scholarship.

As for the future, I will continue to veer off the main path and around the endless spiral of my career, but with the complete confidence that I will always return to the central core of my work and personal being. It cannot be otherwise.

Acknowledgments

I appreciate the comments of several people on an earlier draft of this chapter: Gloria Altman, William Altman, Michael Brill, M. Brewster Smith, Carol M. Werner, Lawrence Wrightsman. I also thank Judith Jerome Altman for her work on Figure 1.

REFERENCES

Altman, I. (1973). Some perspectives on the study of man-environment phenomena. *Representative Research in Social Psychology, 4,* 109–126.

Altman, I. (1975). *Environment and social behavior: Privacy, personal space, territory and crowding.* Monterey, CA: Brooks/Cole (reprinted by Irvington Press, 1981).

Altman, I. (1977). Privacy regulation: Culturally universal or culturally specific? *Journal of Social Issues, 3,* 79–109.

Altman, I. (1986). A perspective on the study of culture and homes. In D. G. Saile (Ed.), *Architecture in cultural change: Essays in built form and culture research* (pp. 5–16) Lawrence: University of Kansas.

Altman, I. (1987a). Centripetal and centrifugal trends in psychology. *American Psychologist, 42,* 1058–1069.

Altman, I. (1987b). Community psychology twenty years later: Still another crisis in psychology? *American Journal of Community Psychology, 15,* 613–627.

Altman, I. (1988). Process, transactional/contextual, and outcome research: An alternative to the traditional distinction between basic and applied research. *Social Behavior: International Journal of Applied Social Psychology, 3,* 259–280.

Altman, I. (1989). Further commentary on the transactional world view. *Social Behavior: International Journal of Applied Social Psychology, 4,* 57–62.

Altman, I., & Chemers, M. M. (1980). *Culture and environment.* Monterey, CA: Brooks/Cole (Reprinted by Cambridge University Press, 1984).

Altman, I., & Gauvain, M. (1981). A cross-cultural and dialectic analysis of homes. In L. S. Liben, A. H. Patterson, & N. Newcombe (Eds.), *Spatial representation and behavior across the life span.* (pp. 283–320). New York: Academic Press.

Altman, I., & Ginat, J. (1989a). *Social relationships in polygamous families.* Invited address at the Second Iowa Conference on Personal Relationships. Spring. University of Iowa, Iowa City, Iowa.

Altman, I., & Ginat, J. (1989b). *The ecology of polygamous families.* Invited address at the joint meeting of the Rocky Mountain Psychological Association and the Western Psychological Association. Spring. Reno, Nevada.

Altman, I., & Haythorn, W. W. (1965). Interpersonal exchange in isolation. *Sociometry, 23,* 411–426.

Altman, I., & Haythorn, W. W. (1967). The ecology of isolated groups. *Behavioral Science, 12,* 169–182.

Altman, I., & McGinnies, E. M. (1960). Interpersonal perception and communication in discussion groups of varied attitudinal composition. *Journal of Abnormal and Social Psychology,* 390–395.

Altman, I., & Rogoff, B. (1987). World views in psychology: Trait, interactional, organismic, and transactional perspectives. In D. Stokols & I. Altman (Eds.), *Handbook of environmental psychology. Volume 1* (pp. 1–40) New York: Wiley.

Altman, I., & Taylor, D. A. (1973). *Social penetration: The development of interpersonal relationships.* New York: Holt, Rinehart & Winston.

Altman, I., Taylor, D. A., & Wheeler, L. (1971). Ecological aspects of group behavior in isolation. *Journal of Applied Social Psychology, 1,* 76–100.

Altman, I., Nelson, P., & Lett, E. E. (1972). The ecology of home environments. *Catalog of Selected Documents in Psychology,* Spring.

Altman, I., Vinsel, A., & Brown, B. B. (1981). Dialectic conceptions in social psychology: An application to social penetration and privacy regulation. In L. Berkowitz (Ed.), *Advances in experimental social psychology. Volume 14* (pp. 107–160) New York: Academic Press.

Altman, I., Werner, C. M., Oxley, D., & Haggard, L. M. (1987). "Christmas Street" as an example of transactionally oriented research. *Environment and Behavior, 19,* 501–524.

Barker, R. G. (1968). *Ecological psychology: Concepts and methods for studying the environment of human behavior.* Stanford, CA: Stanford University Press.

Brown, B. B., & Altman, I. (1983). Territoriality, defensible space and residential burglary: An environmental analysis. *Journal of Environmental Psychology, 3,* 203–220.

Dewey, J., & Bentley, A. F. (1949). *Knowing and the known.* Boston: Beacon.

Gauvain, M., Altman, I., & Fahim, H. (1983). Homes and social change: A cross-cultural analysis. In N. R. Feimer & E. S. Geller (Eds.), *Environmental psychology: Directions and perspectives* (pp. 80–118) New York: Praeger.

Haythorn, W. W., & Altman, I. (1967). Personality factors in isolated environments. In M. Appley & R. Trumbull (Eds.), *Psychological stress* (pp. 363–386). New York: Appleton-Century-Crofts.

Haythorn, W. W., Altman, I., & Meyers, T. I. (1965). Emotional symptomatology and subjective stress in isolated pairs of men. *Journal of Experimental Research in Personality, 1,* 290–306.

Hesse, B. W., Werner, C. M., & Altman, I. (1988). Temporal aspects of computer-mediated communication. *Computers in Human Behavior, 4,* 147–165.

McGrath, J. E., & Altman, I. (1966). *Small group research: synthesis and critique of the field.* New York: Holt, Rinehart, & Winston.

Oxley, D., Haggard, L. M., Werner, C. M., & Altman, I. (1986). Transactional qualities of neighborhood social networks: A case study of "Christmas Street." *Environment and Behavior, 18,* 640–677.

Pepper, S. C. (1942). *World hypotheses: A study in evidence.* Berkeley: University of California Press.

Pepper, S. C. (1967). *Concept and quality: A world hypothesis.* La Salle, IL: Open Court.

Rychlak, J. (1977). *The psychology of rigorous humanism.* New York: Wiley.

Simmel, G. (1950). *The sociology of Georg Simmel.* Trans. by K. H. Wolff. New York: Free Press.

Stokols, D., & Altman, I. (Eds.). (1987). *Handbook of environmental psychology.* New York: Wiley.

Sundstrom, E., & Altman, I. (1974). Relationships between dominance and territorial behavior: A field study in a youth rehabilitation setting. *Journal of Personality and Social Psychology, 30,* 115–125.

Taylor, D. A., Wheeler, L., & Altman, I. (1968). Stress reactions in socially isolated groups. *Journal of Personality and Social Psychology, 9,* 369–376.

Vinsel, A., Brown, B. B., Altman, I., & Foss, C. (1980). Privacy regulation, territorial displays, and effectiveness of individual functioning. *Journal of Personality and Social Psychology, 39,* 1104–1115.

Werner, C. M., Altman, I., & Oxley, D. (1985). Temporal aspects of homes: A transactional perspective. In I. Altman & C. M. Werner (Eds.), *Home environments. Volume 8. Human Behavior and environment* (pp. 1–32) New York: Plenum Press.

Werner, C. M., Altman, I., Oxley, D., & Haggard, L. M. (1987). People, place and time: A transactional analysis of neighborhoods. In W. H. Jones & D. Perlman (Eds.), *Advances in personal relationships* (pp. 243–275). New York: JAI Press.

Werner, C. M., Haggard, L. M., Altman, I., & Oxley, D. (1988). Temporal qualities of rituals and celebrations: A comparison of Christmas Street and Zuni Shalako. In J. E. McGrath (Ed.), *The social psychology of time: New Perspectives* (pp. 203–232) Beverly Hills, CA: Sage.

White, W. (Ed.). (1979). *Resource book on environment and behavior.* Washington, DC: American Psychological Association.

10

One Person-in-His-Environments

SEYMOUR WAPNER

Born on November 20, 1917, in Brooklyn, New York, I received my AB degree from University College, New York University (1939) with a major in psychology and biology and my MA (1940) and PhD (1943) in psychology from the University of Michigan. My first job was technical assistant (1943–1945) and later director (1945–1946) of the University of Rochester Office of the Committee on Selection and Training of Aircraft Pilots, National Research Council. In 1946, I moved to Brooklyn College as assistant professor of psychology and then served as acting chair of the psychology department during the academic year 1947–1948. In 1948, I accepted a position at Clark University in Worcester, Massachusetts, where I remain today.

In the ensuing years I served as associate professor, professor, and G. Stanley Hall Professor of Genetic Psychology. From 1960 to 1986 I chaired the Department of Psychology, with a year (1969–1970) as the first provost of the university. I have held visiting professorships at Nihon University (October 1978), Japan, and the University of Puerto Rico (February/March 1979), and was a Foreign Research Fellow of the International Association of Traffic Safety Sciences (August 1982) in Japan. A member of the board of directors of the Heinz Werner Institute for Developmental Analysis (formerly the Institute of Human Development and Heinz Werner Institute of Developmental Psychology) since its inception in 1956, I am currently chair of the executive committee (since 1965) of that institute, now a part of the newly founded Frances L. Hiatt School of Psychology at Clark University.

Initially my work dealt with problems at the biological level of organization/integration (e.g., effect of brain injury on *what* a rat learns; effects of high pressure oxygen on learning; and abnormal behavior in the rat). It then shifted to the psychological level (e.g., space perception; sensory-tonic field theory of perception; cognitive, including perceptual development; cognitive style). More recently the work has encompassed the

SEYMOUR WAPNER • Heinz Werner Institute for Developmental Analysis, Frances L. Hiatt School of Psychology, Clark University, Worcester, Massachusetts 01610-1477.

impact of the sociocultural level on experience and action (e.g., cross-cultural differences in values; migration; relations between sociocultural change and individual action). These problems are being addressed currently in a research program dealing with critical person-in-environment transitions through the life span. The research focuses on environmental psychology from a holistic, developmental, systems-oriented perspective and analyzes experience (cognition, affect, value) and action with respect to a broad diversity of physical, social, and cultural objects of the macroenvironment.

Just before leaving Rochester in 1946, I married the former Lorraine E. Gallant, who, beside her extraordinary attributes as person, as dancer, as writer, as culinary artist and more puts a gentle but firm creative editorial hand to my problematic formulations and changes them into readable English. Our son Jeffrey Gallant Wapner is a Fordham PhD working as a school and clinical psychologist in the Bronx, NY. Our daughter Amy, a dance therapist trained at Hunter College, is married to Zachary Studenroth, historic preservationist, who was trained at Columbia University. The Studenroths have three children—Jacob, Jenny, Noah—whom we grandparents, *atypically*, regard as the most beautiful, most intelligent, most caring, most sensitive children in all the world.

PRECURSORS

My serious concern with research problems involving relations between experience/action and the environment was triggered by 1 year of service as provost of Clark University. That year, 1969–1970, was the peak of student unrest nationally, and my involvement was totally with their world and that of people more generally in their everyday life situations. Under these conditions, the "world-out-there" as a potentially fruitful laboratory for study of theoretical and practical problems of significance became more figural, and I began to move away from, but by no means abandon, the laboratory with its highly controlled conditions. Work on such problems as the development of experience (cognition, affect, value) and orientation in a microenvironment (e.g., the university) replaced work involving use of the darkroom laboratory with its luminous rods and tilting chairs to study space perception.

Although I feel certain that this 1-year experience with the real world played a significant role in deepening my concerns for the study of environmental psychology, I also recognize that general factors, including childhood influences and many contacts with different people in different universities and other environments, prepared me for responding to the precipitating condition in the way that I did.

GENERAL FACTORS

What were those general factors? Though my focus here shall be on the origins and background for adopting the general assumptions and methodologies of my approach to environmental psychology, a brief diversion to very general childhood influences seems worthy of inclusion because they speak to reasons for some pervasive general attitudes and interests that shaped my vocational choice as well as my concerns with environmental psychology.

The earliest antecedents of my current academic and avocational activities were deeply intertwined with two events involving two very important people in my interpersonal environment. One event involved my father—an excellent craftsman, upholsterer by trade, and owner of a furniture and decorating business. I still clearly recall that when I exhibited great reluctance to enter the kindergarten of the Brooklyn Model School, my father arranged for a uniformed, strong-armed motorcycle policeman friend of his to "order" me to go. From a stubborn balk, my body muscle tone acquired a dynamic that quickly brought me to school with my father trailing behind. I usually claim that this event had a powerful effect on my vocational choice, insofar as it resulted in my remaining at school ever since. More than that, the aesthetic, furniture building, home-oriented context in which I lived shaped my early desire to become an architect and my interest in the physical environment and sculpture. Architecture and sculpture were largely short-lived interests. My interest in architecture led me to enroll in the Brooklyn Technical High School. However, when I learned that one was restricted to instruction in only *one* foreign language during their 4-year program oriented toward engineering, I left after 2 days and enrolled in Boys High School, which was more academically oriented.

I also claim that another event, involving my mother—a warm, loving, growth-fostering, good humored, tender person—aborted or at least made latent my interest in sculpture. Given the Depression of the 1930s and especially because the household breadwinner, my father, had passed away, my mother had no choice but to use my Ivory soap carving of Abraham Lincoln for the family bath. Though my aesthetic interests remained over the years, as a consequence of that event, I did not return to sculpture as a hobby for some decades.

These specific events involving my parents were couched in the particular pervasive, nourishing attitude they conveyed by their acts and decisions and by the permissions they granted and withheld. The determining posture was that of warmth, of love, of fostering and taking joy in my individual development, of a strong respect for creative work and its pleasures, and for doing the job well.

Let us turn now to the central concern here, namely the general factors that moved me into environmental psychology in the early 1970s. These general factors are grounded in the broader sociocultural context and the Clark University context along with my particular academic history. We shall consider these in turn.

THE SOCIOCULTURAL CONTEXT

The character of the broader sociocultural context relevant to the study of environment and behavior is briefly described by Canter and Craik (1987) in their special Clark University issue of the *Journal of Environmental Psychology*

(December, 1987). They noted the importance of the political climate of the early 1970s, the national atmosphere of debate, the "need for reassessment of the role of the U.S. on the world map" (p. 283) as well as the *Zeitgeist* fostering interdisciplinary work as contextual factors spurring on the growth of environmental psychology.

THE CLARK UNIVERSITY CONTEXT

In addition, Canter and Craik (1987) note how at Clark University, with its strong tradition in geography and psychology, with federal funding (NSF Department Science Development Grants held by both departments), and with strong institutional support, the general milieu was ripe for interdisciplinary study of problems of the environment and behavior, including team research and teaching, by both geographers and psychologists.[1]

As can be gathered from my description of the situation (Wapner, 1987b), it was in this general ebullient local and national context that my own involvement began. Saul Cohen, who had an interest in extending behavioral analysis in geography, Bernard Kaplan, who was thinking about links between architecture and psychology, and I, who was thinking about persons-in-environments as a unit of analysis, wrote a piece on transactions of persons-in-environments that set the stage for a long-term research program on critical person-in-environment transitions or more generally transactions (experience and action) of persons-in-environments (Wapner, Kaplan, & Cohen, 1973). This program, with the collaboration of many colleagues (currently with the creative contributions of Jack Demick) and students from here and abroad[2] continues to develop both empirically and theoretically (cf. Wapner, 1978, 1981, 1987a, 1987b, in press; Wapner & Demick, in press).

ACADEMIC BACKGROUND

Although the two events described may have served to have a limiting influence on my vocational and avocational interests, the general factors that underpin the origins and development of my particular perspective to environmental psychology are grounded in my academic history. How shall I proceed to get a picture of those influences? Perhaps the most direct way of uncovering

[1] A fuller description of the context, both nationally and at Clark University, is given by the various contributors—J. Anderson, J. M. Blunt, A. Buttimer, D. Canter, K. H. Craik, R. A. Hart, R. W. Kates, D. Leventhal, G. F. McCleary, Jr., G. D. Rowles, D. Seamon, D. Stea, S. Wapner, J. F. Wohlwill, D. Wood, E. H. Zube—to this issue. Other critical people in the Clark scene at the time were R. Beck, M. Bowden, S. B. Cohen, B. Kaplan, R. Kasperson, G. Moore, T. O'Riordan, and H. Prince.

[2] Others who were deeply involved in our research program on the Clark scene were Bob Ciottone, Mark Quirk, Gail Hornstein, Ogretta McNeil, and numerous graduate and undergraduate students. Three groups of colleagues abroad currently involved include in Hiroshima, T. Yamamoto, S. Ishii, K. Asakawa, W. Inoue, H. Minami, and T. Toshima; in Tokyo, M. Asai and I. Souma; in Puerto Rico, A. Pacheco and N. Lucca-Irizarry.

them is, as a first step, to state the central assumptions and methodologies ingredient in my general approach to environment psychology. Then in conjunction with each assumption, I will tooth-comb my past research involvements in a variety of domains, with the goal of uncovering primordial conceptualizations that were consonant with or forerunners of current conceptualization, methodology, and issues regarding relations between environment, experience, and action. This will be followed by a description of research on critical person-in-environment transitions and finally by a brief treatment of issues, open problems, and challenges for the future.

THE GENERAL APPROACH

The perspective taken to the study of this problem of the transactions (experience and action) of persons-in-environments is characterized as holistic, developmental, and systems oriented (e.g., Kaplan, Cohen, & Wapner, 1976; Wapner, 1977, 1981, 1986, 1987a,b; Wapner, Ciottone, Hornstein, McNeil, & Pacheco, 1983; Wapner & Demick, 1988, in press; Wapner, Kaplan, & Cohen, 1973). Its assumptions and methodologies as well as the basis for their adoption are diverse and general.

ASSUMPTIONS OF THE PERSPECTIVE[3]

Theoretical

The major assumptions of the approach, which are linked to its embeddedness in both an organismic and a transactionalist (contextualist) world hypothesis (Pepper, 1942; cf. Altman & Rogoff, 1987), are as follows:

- The person-in-environment system is the unit to be analyzed (*transactionalism*).
- The person-in-environment system, including its *operations at different levels of organization/integration* (i.e., including biological, psychological, and sociocultural functioning) operates as a unified whole so that change or disturbance in one part affects other parts and the totality (*holism*).
- The person-in-environment system is analyzed formally and comparatively with respect to *structure* (part–whole relations; e.g., more or less differentiated parts) and to *dynamics* (means–ends relations; e.g., changing or maintaining a structure).

---

[3] The approach is an extension—elaborated conceptualization and increased range of empirical study—of the organismic–developmental perspective (Werner, 1957) that penetrated Werner's (1948) classic work on comparative mental development, Werner and Kaplan's (1963) work on symbol formation, and my work with Werner and others on the sensory-tonic field theory of perception (Werner & Wapner, 1949, 1952, 1956; Wapner, Cirillo, & Baker, 1969, 1971) and on perceptual development (Wapner & Werner, 1957).

- The transactions (experience and action) of the person-in-environment system includes *cognitive* (sensorimotor, perceptual, conceptual), *affective*, and *valuative* processes.
- The transactions (experience and action) of the person-in-environment system are characterized by *teleological directedness*, coupled with its corollary *planning*, a representation for moving the person-in-environment system through use of specified instrumentalities from some initial state of dynamic equilibrium to some end state.
- The experiencing person in the system actively structures and organizes the environment and its objects (*constructivism*) and has the capacity to adopt different intentions (*multiple intentionality*) with respect to self–world relations.
- The *physical environment* (e.g., geographic) is distinguished from the *experienced environment* (e.g., behavioral), which is the effective basis for individual functioning.
- Persons live in different, yet related, experiential worlds (the *multiple worlds* of Schutz, 1971).
- Transactions (experience and action) of the focal person, including his/her *physical/biological, psychological,* and *sociocultural* features, take place with respect to *physical objects* (e.g., things), *interpersonal objects* (e.g., people), and *sociocultural objects* (e.g., laws and rules).
- Ideal progressive *development* is viewed as movement of the person-in-environment system from an undifferentiated to a differentiated and highly integrated system state (*orthogenetic principle*) with capacity for freedom, self-mastery, and the flexibility to shift from one person-in-environment state to another as required by goals, by the demands of a situation, and by the instrumentalities available. Such progressive development is complemented by regressive development, which, for example, may occur with perturbation to any part or function of the ongoing person-in-environment system state. A central question is under what *conditions* developmental transformation is reversed, arrested, or advanced? This "how" question brings us closer to causal analysis so that inquiry may involve prediction as well as explication.

Methodological

Intimately tied to these general assumptions are some general and more specific features of the methodologies admissible by this perspective. Most generally, a number of dicta regarding empirical study are accepted. These include Werner's (1937) insistence on the importance of "process" in contrast to achievement analysis, on Maslow's (1946) stress on shaping problem-oriented as opposed to means-oriented empirical studies, on the links between the stance of our perspective on the "natural science" versus "human science" controversy, and on the nature of acceptable methodology. With respect to the focus on process, we seek to understand the means whereby a given person-in-environment end state is achieved and a careful examination of the activities that lead to that achievement. This general principle and Maslow's (1946) concern that method, means, or instrumentalities are subordinate to research problems has led us to use very diverse methods, for example, topographic maps with inquiry, psychological distance maps that focus on experience, activity logs, reconstructions, ecologically oriented observations, retrospective reports, debriefing techniques, rating scales, rank ordering of values, phenomenologically oriented, open-ended interviews, followed by structured interviews, and so forth (cf. Wapner, 1978). In opposition to those who demand that psychology must model itself after *either* "natural science" *or* "human science" (cf. Giorgi, 1970), our perspective takes the position that methodologies tied to both of those viewpoints are appropriate, but this depends on the nature of the problem and the level of organization/integration to which the analysis is directed. Hence, hermeneutic phenomenologically oriented investigations are appropriate when dealing with research problems at complex levels of organization/integration in everyday life situations where controls are difficult to achieve and when the focus is on explication rather than prediction; in complementary fashion, controlled experimentation is appropriate when the research problems are directed toward lower, less complex levels of organization/integration and toward understanding of process or mechanisms. Important values are involved in the decision to focus on explication or controlled experimentation. For example, whereas the former sacrifices precision for "relevance to everyday life," the latter sacrifices relevance for precision.

PREDISPOSITIONS TOWARD ASSUMPTIONS: PEOPLE AND PLACES

HOLISM: LEVELS OF ORGANIZATION/INTEGRATION

The focus on holism and levels of organization/integration in my approach to psychology in general and environmental psychology in particular was deeply rooted in my undergraduate experience at University College, New York University. Against a broad background, my early focus was on biology and later changed to psychology. My concentration in biology and special interest in its developmental aspects penetrated my general orientation toward psychology. As a junior, the open problems exposed in my first year-long course in psychology with E. R. Henry revealed a superb match with my facility to shape them into experimental study and a more general correspondence with my interests in people and my intellectual strengths. I took enough psychology courses in my senior year to graduate with the equivalent of both a major in psychology as well as biology. Three year-long courses included physiological psychology with Louis William Max, social psychology with Malcolm Campbell, and tests and measurements with Edwin Henry.

A central interest was the linkage between the biological and psychological aspects of functioning. This general interest in the levels of organization/integration notion was supported further by contact with Max's (1935) fascinating work with normals and deaf-mutes on the motor theory of consciousness and the laboratory experience connected with his course. Max's discoveries—muscle action currents occurred in body parts that would ordinarily be involved in carrying out an imagined act; action currents were recorded from arm muscles when deaf-mutes were dreaming or solving abstract problems, but little activity was recorded from those muscles when normal subjects imagined the acts—reinforced my latent view that relations among levels of organization/integration is a critical contemporary problem. This theme reasserts itself again and again in my research (cf. Wapner, Cirillo, & Baker, 1969; Wapner & Demick, in press) and remains as a basic research problem for me today (cf. Wapner, 1987a,b).

Another stage in this focus on "levels" thinking was hatched by a laboratory experience in Max's physiological psychology class that involved analyzing abnormal behavior in the rat. The model for this laboratory experiment was Norman R. F. Maier's research at the University of Michigan on abnormal behavior in the rat for which he received the AAAS award in 1938 (Maier, 1939) and Calvin Hall's (1934) observations of the rat's emotional behavior while exploring an open field. The route of analyzing abnormal behavior in the rat by studying animals in paradigmatic situations involving conflict and frustration resonated with my then-dual concern for analysis of important psychological problems through biologically oriented, experimental approaches. The decision was clean and clear. I wanted to work with N. R. F. Maier on this problem. I applied and was accepted to the PhD program at the University of Michigan.

Before long I was working with Maier and his students Nathan Glazer and James B. Klee on problems of abnormal behavior in the rat and involved in my PhD thesis that dealt with the effect of brain injury on equivalence reactions in the rat (Wapner, 1944). This move to a problem in psychobiology brought me in contact with some very special biologists like Elizabeth Crosby (cf. Ariens Kappers, Huber, & Crosby, 1936), and in particular, Charles Judson Herrick (1949), who made important contributions to the conceptualization of levels of organization/integration. Concurrently, I became involved in research on physiology and behavior with J. W. Bean of the University of Michigan Medical School. We studied the effects of exposure to oxygen of high barometric pressure on higher functions of the CNS, in particular, maze learning and retention (Bean & Wapner, 1943; Bean, Wapner, & Siegfried, 1945). Furthermore, other people in the exciting Ann Arbor environment played a striking role. In addition to my contemporary fellow students in psychology,[4] others from related fields[5] fertilized the seed of focusing on levels of organization/integration and on multiple perspectives in both shaping a research problem and utilizing multiple, diversely grounded methodologies.

---

[4] Including Jim Klee, Jane Shohl, Irwin Berg, Urie Bronfenbrenner, Harold Guetzkow, Raoul Weisman, Estefania Aldaba, and Tooi Xoomsai.
[5]Ted Berlin and Bill Sleator (physics/chemistry), Esther Sleator (medicine), Julie Youngner and Herman Lichtstein (bacteriology), William Dusenberry (economics), Leonard "Jimmy" Savage and Sammy Eilenberg (mathematics), and Jane Savage (anthropology).

Another person in Ann Arbor, who ultimately played a very powerful role in my thinking and my future, was Heinz Werner. After an illustrious career (cf. Barten & Franklin, 1978; Kaplan & Wapner, 1960; Wapner & Kaplan, 1966; Werner & Kaplan, 1963; Witkin, 1965) as professor at Hamburg, with his classic *Einführung in die Entwicklungspsychologie* published in 1926, he left Germany at the time of the demise of the Hamburg Institute at the hands of the Nazis. During the period 1938–1944, he was located at Harvard, Michigan, and the Wayne County Training School. At the training school, Werner was involved in his ground-breaking work on mental retardation (see Kaplan & Wapner, 1960; Witkin, 1965; and Barten & Franklin, 1978, for references on this work by Werner and his collaborators).

My contact with Werner did not come from the classroom. Our first contact was in a departmental colloquium, during the academic year 1940–1941. He presented some of the ideas that later appeared in his article on a vicarious relationship between motion and motion perception (Werner, 1945) that utilized Rorschach's analysis of responses to ink blots. It was in the attempt to account for the interchangeability of the experience of motion on the one hand and motor activity on the other that Werner used the vicariousness concept. This concept was later incorporated in the "sensory–tonic" field theory of perception (e.g., Werner & Wapner, 1949, 1952) to be discussed later. Werner's conceptualization reminded me of the work Max (1935) had done linking motor activity and mental processes and thereby raised my consciousness about the importance of the problem of a relationship between levels of organization/integration.

My first postdoctoral job—research in aviation psychology during World War II with the Committee on Selection of Aircraft Pilots of the Civil Aeronautics Division in liaison with the Army, Air Force, and Navy—also pointed to the importance and value of an holistic as compared with elementalistic analysis. For example, in an attempt to cope with the critical problem of assessing reliability and validity of the flight instructor's ratings of the student pilot's performance, a motion picture was made of the performance on a second set of instruments during a student's test flight. An elementaristic analysis of the changes in altimeter, banking, and other flight instruments turned out to be both difficult and worthless. A holistic assessment by the flight inspector that could take into account the entire context of a flight test—including, for example, responsivity to sudden changes in up–down air currents—was more meaningful, more valid, more reliable (cf. Walker, Wapner, Bakan, & Ewart, 1946).

The press toward a more holistic analysis took further shape when I accepted my first teaching position at Brooklyn College. The levels of integration notion, so clearly and sharply characterized by Novikoff (1945a,b), a member of the biology department, and work with Hy Witkin in psychology had a significant impact on my thinking. Earlier, I had brief contact with Witkin's work on spatial orientation in relation to selection and training of aircraft pilots, which we analyzed at Rochester. At Brooklyn College, I collaborated with him and others on the related research that eventuated in the 1954 publication of *Person-*

ality through Perception (Witkin, Lewis, Hertzman, Machover, Meissner, & Wapner, 1954). The three-word title tells the story. The approach was holistic in the sense that personality characteristics penetrated and were manifest in all operations of the organism, including perception as well as other cognitive and affective processes.

Another research direction impacting the holistic assumption had its origins in some beginning talks with Heinz Werner at Brooklyn College in 1946–1947. During that year we began thinking about a program of research linked to the then-developing "new look" in perception, which focused on bringing in subjective factors along with autochthonous factors as determinants of perception (cf. Bruner & Klein, 1960; Zener, 1949a,b; Blake & Ramsey, 1951). Our approach, which became more fully formed, developed, and indeed flourished[6] as the sensory-tonic field theory of perception was organismic and holistic. The central point of the theory was that organismic factors are part and parcel of every percept. More specifically, perception was conceived as a function of, or better, a reflection of a relationship (stable vs. unstable) between stimuli from objects out there (objective) and the ongoing state of the organism (subjective), which was formed and defined by affective, valuative along with neuromuscular states or more generally sensory-tonic states (cf. Werner & Wapner, 1949, 1952, 1956; Wapner, Cirillo, & Baker, 1969, 1971).

One significant factor in thinking more holistically was a review of this work by Kurt Goldstein in the Festschrift for Heinz Werner (Kaplan & Wapner, 1960). Goldstein said:

> I welcome the opportunity of presenting this viewpoint in a volume in honor of Heinz Werner. I would like my article to be considered an expression of my affirmation of the principle of sensoritonic basis of perception; but I merely would like to add a hint that sensoritonic theory may need expansion in the direction of the organismic theory of behavior. (Goldstein, 1960, p. 122)

That this constructive criticism was taken seriously is evident in such later work as Wapner, Cirillo, and Baker's (1969) attempt to advance the theory holistically by first linking it more systematically to Werner's comparative developmental perspective (Werner, 1926, 1948) and later on by the approach to environmental psychology—the holistic, developmental systems-oriented perspective—that has been shaped over the last 15 years with my colleagues and students (for example, see Demick & Wapner, 1988a,b, in press; Wapner, 1986, 1987a,b; Wapner & Demick, 1988; Wapner, Ciottone, Hornstein, McNeil, & Pacheco, 1983; Wapner, Kaplan, & Cohen, 1973).

CONSTRUCTIVISM

The epistemological position of constructivism with its assumption that the person actively structures and organizes the environment and its objects

[6]Our extensive program of research, supported by NIMH Research Grant MH #00348 for 23 years, resulted in more than 100 publications, approximately 40 PhD theses, 50 MA theses, and 150 papers presented at professional meetings.

coupled with multiple intentionality, already evident in the description of sensory–tonic theory, was early ingrained. It was perhaps first manifest in my PhD thesis (Wapner, 1944), where von Uexküll's (1957) notion of Umwelt underpinned my study of learning in the partially decorticated rat. The concern was not with the reinforcement history required to learn but rather with "what" the animal learns. First, a discrimination between a large black circle on a gray ground (unlocked, rewarded) and a small black circle on a gray ground (locked, punished) was learned, using the Lashley jumping stand; then, in keeping with Klüver's (1942) method of equivalent stimuli, the rat was presented with a number of pairs of unlocked cards systematically varying the properties of size, brightness, and figure–ground relations, so that his/her "free" choice could be assessed. On the basis of the "free choice" series, the cards regarded as "equivalent" to the training pair was established. The rat responded to "darker than" rather than to "bigger than," and this increased following removal of parts of the cortex.

This focus on the organism's experience or mode of structuring stimulation is an ingredient in the work on field dependence/independence cognitive style, in the work on sensory-tonic theory, and on the developmental analysis of perception (Wapner & Werner, 1957). It remains a central notion in our approach to environmental psychology as evidenced by Wapner, Kaplan, and Cohen's (1973) stress on Kuntz's (1968) notion of "rage for order," on acceptance of Koffka's (1935) distinction between geographic (physical) and behavioral (experienced) environment, on our current working definition of critical person-in-environment transitions that are experientially defined, and on our fostering of Schutz's (1971) notion of *multiple worlds*, for example, in our studies of retirement where the structure of work, home, recreation, and other worlds are analyzed with respect to retirement from work (Hornstein & Wapner, 1984, 1985).

MULTIPLE INTENTIONALITY

Special attention should be given to the assumption of multiple intentionality, which refers to the person's capacity to intend and shift such intention on what is figural with respect to an aspect of the environment (e.g., the beautiful building is figural), an aspect of self (e.g., one's body qua object as in the experience "I am short and fat"), or an aspect of self–environment relations (e.g., I feel very comfortable in my office at Clark). This assumption that has a central role in our current systems-oriented extension of organismic-developmental theory played a very significant part in our earlier program of research guided by the sensory-tonic field theory of perception.

In that research program, we not only treated perception of things out there but became involved in systematic studies of body perception and the relation between body and object perception. Initially, studies were conducted that demonstrated that articulation of the boundary of the head (by touching cheekbones) made for a shrinkage in apparent width of the head (Wapner, Werner, & Comalli, 1958). This held for other body parts. For example, it was found that apparent extension of the outstretched arm (1) decreased when the fingertip was touched (Humphries, 1959) and (2) was judged to be shorter in a close-confined environmental context than in an open-extended context (Wapner, McFarland, & Werner, 1963)—a finding, by the way, that has significance for environmental psychology and environmental design insofar as body experience is in part dependent on the spatial context. These results were interpreted to indicate that experience of the boundary of the body was made more distinct by touching it or by being in a confined environmental context (namely facing a wall). Such increased articulation of the boundary presumably made for (1) an experience of increased separation of the body from context and (2) a decrease in perceived size of the body part (Wapner, 1969; Werner, 1948; see also Wapner, Werner, & Comalli, 1958; Wapner & Werner, 1965). More recently, it was shown that the stress of relocation makes for a change in apparent head width, with differential effects dependent on psychopathological status, namely with impending relocation schizophrenics overestimated apparent head width more, and antisocial patients overestimated head width less (Demick & Wapner, 1980).

The work on body perception was reinterpreted following the discovery of seemingly contradictory findings when the attitude of "being touched" versus "touching" was not controlled. The findings were reinterpreted in terms of the speculative analysis of Merleau-Ponty (1962) who discusses "being touched" as a passive experience and "touching" as an active experience (i.e., "being impinged upon" and "projecting one's self upon the environment," respectively). This interpretation, which brings the assumption of intentionality into focus, is grounded in the distinction between active versus passive touch (cf. Fuhrer & Cowan, 1967; Gibson, 1962; Gordon, 1978). It was supported in two experiments that tested the hypothesis that apparent length of the partially outstretched arm (1) shrinks when the fingertips of the passive hand are touched by an object and (2) increases when the fingertips of the active hand touch an external stationary object (Schlater, Baker, & Wapner, 1981). This series of studies is an interesting example of the way in which experimentation and theoretical conceptualization go hand in hand; but more than that, the studies show how two sets of findings that are seemingly contradictory can, and indeed must be, superceded by constructs and consonant methodology—here multiple intentionality and its control by instructions—that encompass both.

Our current concern with relations between self and environment were foreshadowed by studies that deal with the relations between body space and object space (cf. Wapner, 1968; Wapner & Werner, 1965). More specifically, the earlier studies treated the relation between experienced location of one's own body (adjustment of a luminous rod to the longitudinal axis of the body) and of objects out there (adjustment of a luminous rod to vertical) under different conditions of body tilt. This relationship exhibited systematic age changes (7 to 17 years). Under 30° left and right body tilt, it was found that (1) with increase in age the position of apparent vertical shifts from the side of body tilt to the side opposite body tilt; (2) although apparent location of the longitudinal body axis deviates beyond true body tilt in all age groups, after 7 years there is a slight decrease in deviation followed by an accelerated increase after 13 years of age. Thus the angular disparity between apparent vertical and apparent body axis position is relatively small for 7- to 13-year-olds compared with 15- to 17-year-olds. These findings were interpreted as a reflection of an ontogenetic shift toward increasing differentiation between the body spatial reference system and the external reference system. They thereby are examples that show how the self–world concept, which is so significant for our contemporary work in environmental psychology, was operationalized in earlier studies restricted to object perception (Wapner & Werner, 1957). Moreover, they together with earlier studies on development of space perception point to my current interests in the intersection between developmental and environmental psychology from our holistic, developmental, systems-oriented perspective (e.g., Wapner, 1981, 1987a,b; Wapner & Demick, 1987, in press).

Definition of Environment/of Person

That it was important to define the environment broadly to include *interpersonal, sociocultural,* as well as *physical* objects goes back to or at the least was emphasized for me by Heider's (1957) distinction between inanimate and animate objects, noting that only the latter "acted back on" a person. Moreover, in an early study (Wapner & Alper, 1952) evidence was accumulated to show that the nature of the audience or experimenter (interpersonal context) played a significant role in a choice situation. Werner (1948), of course, had early noted that the child more frequently experienced inanimate things as animate. This distinction between things and people, coupled with a holistic viewpoint, meant that one must take into account all three levels of environmental features, namely the physical, the interpersonal, and the sociocultural. Although for purposes of analysis many investigators in environmental psychology focus on the physical object, from our own holistic, developmental, systems-oriented perspective, this is a double-edged sword: While restricting the focus of investigation *only* to physical aspects simplifies analysis, at the same time it may serve to lose the essence of the complex phenomenon being studied (cf. Rapoport, 1972). To understand the human being in all the complexity of the everyday life situation, it may be necessary to sacrifice some of the precision that comes with simplification. The concern for, yet the fear of, simplification was early embedded in my thinking as a graduate student at the University of Michigan, where John Shepard and Norman Maier instilled strong respect for Lloyd Morgan's canon, on the one hand, and concern for the grave errors that potentially come from assuming simple phylogenetic continuity, on the other hand (cf. Maier & Schneirla, 1935).

The definition of the person, like the environment, is linked to the levels of organization/integration notion. The levels concept suggested analysis of three aspects of the person parallel to those of the environment, namely the biological (e.g., physiological status), psychological (e.g., self-concept), and sociocultural (e.g., role as parent).

PERSON-IN-ENVIRONMENT AS A UNIT OF ANALYSIS

What are the people–place antecedents for our assumption that the person-in-environment system is the unit to be analyzed? I trace this notion most generally back to an acceptance of the gestalt position that the whole differs from the sum of its parts (Koffka, 1935; Köhler, 1929); to the general appreciation of the part–whole relationship and the focus on structural analysis in Werner's (1948) comparative psychology, where, for example, he speaks of *pars pro toto*, the part standing for the whole in the cognition of the young child; to Piaget's (1952) contention that the problem of relationship of parts to whole is relevant to all levels beginning with the living cell and including organism, species, society, and so forth; to the rejection by von Bertalanffy (1968) and others of the reactive, robot model of the human together with acceptance of an active organism; to a constructivist position (Lavine, 1950) that speaks to cognitive development as a consequence of the active operation of given biological equipment (Sameroff, 1983); to Dobzhansky's (1951) treatment of the environment as an essential feature of genetics; to resonating with the transactionalist position as defined by Dewey and Bentley (1949) and advanced by Cantril (1960) and Ittelson (1973); and to its consonance with Prigonine's revised theory of thermodynamics that speaks to the "inseparability between the structure and the environment at the lowest levels of chemical organization" (Sameroff, 1983, p. 265).

More specifically, there is a powerful, more immediate link of person-in-environment as unit of analysis to the work by Werner and myself (e.g., Werner & Wapner, 1949, 1952, 1956) on the sensory-tonic field theory of perception. According to this theory "there is a field consisting of two parts: body (psychophysical) and object (psychophysical). The perceptual properties of an object depend on the way in which stimuli from a physical object affect the organism and on the subsequent specific and active manner in which the organism reacts to it" (Werner & Wapner, 1952, p. 325). In sensory-tonic theory, our basic assumption was that perception is a reflection of a relationship (R) between stimuli from an object out there (s) and the state of the organism (o), namely $P = f(oRs)$. The state of the organism is presumed to be influenced by any kind of stimulation whether it comes through extero-, proprio-, or interoceptors. For example, a rod is perceived as vertical when there is a stable relationship, that is, perception of rod is vertical: (1) with organismic vectorial counteractive force (induced by a broad variety of stimuli applied asymmetrically) to left and luminous rod physically tilted left ($o-Rs-$); (2) with counteractive force to right and rod physically tilted right ($o+ R s+$); and (3) with body erect and rod physically upright (o R so). In one sense, this description of mechanism is a more specific application of the person-in-environment as the unit of analysis. The relationship described depends invariably on *both* stimuli from environmental objects out there and the ongoing neuromuscular state of the person, including stimuli from sources other than the object perceived. Because person and environment are constituent parts in the analysis of the whole system, it is clear how the part–whole relationship enters, that is, how change in one part (any aspect of the environment—e.g., Demick, Hoffman, & Wapner, 1985—or any aspect of the person—e.g., Rand & Wapner, 1967) can make for change in the total relationship.

Cognition, Affection, Valuation

Moreover, in sensory-tonic field theory, a significant step was taken in keeping with our current assumption that the transactions (experience and action) of the person-in-environment system includes *cognitive* (sensorimotor, perceptual, conceptual), *affective*, and *valuative* processes, which are related to one another in the living organism. For example, studies were conducted under the aegis of sensory-tonic theory on the effect of danger (affect) on space perception (Wapner, Werner, & Krus, 1957; Werner & Wapner, 1955), on perception of time (Langer, Wapner, & Werner, 1961), and on perception of speed (Langer, Werner, & Wapner, 1965). (See Wapner & Demick, 1987, August, for a review.) This conceptualization, as noted earlier, was directly linked to the "new look" in perception (e.g., Bruner & Klein, 1960; Erdelyi, 1974; Zener, 1949a,b), which stressed the role of subjective as well as objective factors.

Developmental Analysis

The focus on developmental analysis is, of course, deeply ingrained in my long-term association with Heinz Werner, Bernard Kaplan, and many other colleagues and students who were part of the Clark University atmosphere over the 40 years that I have spent at this institution. But, more specifically, my contact with Werner in relation to developmental conceptualization dates back more than 45 years ago to my PhD dissertation at the University of Michigan. One aspect of the dissertation (Wapner, 1944) showed that with cortical injury in rats there is an increase in the *relational* responses (e.g., jumping to a card "darker than") made by the rat. In contradiction to those who regarded response to relationship as a sign of a higher mental process, the fact that brain injury increases these responses was evidence for me in keeping with Werner's (1948) contention in *Comparative Psychology of Mental Development* that there were "levels" of generalization ranging from "primitive" to developmentally advanced. This position was consonant with the position of Lashley (1942), who distinguished between levels of generalization and who considered "responses to brighter than or darker than relations" as an early, relatively primitive form of discrimination. It also fit with the perspective of Goldstein and his associates (Goldstein, 1939, 1940; Goldstein & Scheerer, 1941) who, in their analysis of the effects of brain injury, distinguished between concrete and abstract behaviors. When I presented a paper based on my dissertation at the Michigan Academy of Science, Werner reiterated the importance of my developmental interpretations in his contributions to the discussion that followed. In that and later meetings there was rapidly manifest a commonality of interests with the broad view of development, which is the striking, creative characteristic of Werner's (1948) work.

Although my collaboration with Werner—which had its beginnings at Michigan, its further development at Brooklyn College, and came to fruition at Clark University—was initially largely restricted to our organismic theory of perception, my movement into a more formal, systematic involvement in developmental analysis was initiated in the early 1950s when we carried out our study on perceptual development (Wapner & Werner, 1957). Complementing this study on age changes were others on psychopathology (Carini, 1955) and effects of such primitivizing drugs as Lysergic acid diethylamide-25 (Krus & Wapner, 1959, 1962; Liebert, Wapner, & Werner, 1957; Liebert, Werner, & Wapner, 1958). Although both points of view—sensory-tonic field theory and comparative–developmental theory—guided the research during this period, they were largely left as parallel frameworks with the relations between them unarticulated. Kaplan (1966, 1967) played a powerful role with Werner (e.g., Werner & Kaplan, 1956, 1963) in systematizing organismic–developmental theory.

With that background, these two viewpoints were integrated, especially with the efforts of Leonard Cirillo (Wapner, Cirillo, & Baker, 1969), as an exemplar of the *organismic–developmental approach* (Wapner & Werner, 1957; Werner, 1957; Werner & Kaplan, 1963). From the organismic–developmental viewpoint, organisms in their environmental settings constitute systems that may be analyzed and compared with one another in formal terms. In such a formal, comparative analysis, a system is treated as having a characteristic structure that is maintained or transformed by specifiable dynamic processes. Focusing on the characteristic structure of the system entails the analysis of the system into more or less differentiated parts or subsystems that are more or less integrated with one another in specifiable ways. Focusing on the dynamics of the system entails the determination of the means by which a characteristic structure is achieved or maintained. The *structural* or *part–whole analysis* of a system and the *dynamic* or *means–ends analysis* of a system are two complementary aspects of the formal description of the system.

Because the orthogenetic principle refers to such formal, organizational features of transactions when it speaks to the development of the person-in-environment system from an undifferentiated to a differentiated and highly integrated state, it has broad applicability. This includes (1) *temporal change* as in (a) *ontogenesis*, that is, changes from conception to maturity (e.g., Wapner, 1968; Wapner & Werner, 1965) and old age (e.g., Comalli, Wapner, & Werner, 1959; Wapner, Cirillo, & Baker, 1971) and in (b) *microgenesis*, that is, the formation of a percept, a thought, a judgment, a spatial organization (e.g., Schouela *et al.*, 1980), and so forth; (2) *group differences* including (a) *phylogenesis*, that is, comparison and contrast of activities and adaptation manifest by typical members of different species (Wapner & Demick, in press; Werner, 1948); (b) *pathogenesis*, i.e., organic and functional pathology (e.g., Carini, 1955, Demick & Wapner, 1980) on the basis of a corollary of progression, namely regression; and (3) *conditions* of functioning, that is, drugs/placebo (e.g., Krus & Wapner, 1959), stress/optimal (e.g., Demick & Wapner, 1980, on relocation), which represent extremes varying respectively from less to more advanced as defined by the orthogenetic principle.

Teleological Directedness

Compatibility with the assumption of *teleological directedness* of the person-in-environment system dates back to my days as a senior at University Heights, New York University, where Malcolm Campbell introduced us to Lewinian field theory through a thorough examination of J. F. Brown's (1936) *Psychology and the Social Order*. This experience had profound effects. Relevant to my present concern is the vectorial analysis of the individual directed toward goals, a conceptualization that is very close to considering the person-in-environment system as goal directed and accomplishing those goals through use of a variety of instrumentalities.[7]

Planning

The focus on directedness and means–ends relationships of the organismic–developmental theoretical orientation, the classic volume by Miller, Galanter, and Pribram (1960), Murray's (1959) provocative comment on the need for cognitive psychologists to study planning as well as my concern to treat problems central in everyday life served as general background factors for becoming empirically and theoretically involved with the problem of planning and its development. The theoretical trigger to get me involved was the particular description of the orthogenetic principle given by Werner in Harris's volume (Werner, 1957) and Kaplan's (1967) statement on the teleological determination of behavior.

Werner (1957) pointed to

> increasing subject-object differentiation [which] involves the corollary that the organism becomes increasingly less dominated by the immediate situation; the

---

[7] There are, of course, other linkages of Lewinian field theory to the approach described here; witness, for example, the linkage between the notion of person-in-environment as the unit of analysis and the concepts of *membership character*, the analysis of individual perception, motor activity, and emotional activity in terms of decreasing reality that is essentially based on a levels of organization conceptualization, the distinction between genotype and phenotype that parallels Werner's (1937) distinction between process and achievement, the structural and dynamic analyses undertaken in field theory of personality genesis and its relation to structural (part–whole) and dynamic (means–ends) analysis of organismic–developmental theory, and the like. The compatibility with field theory was further fostered in my collaborative work with Leon Festinger on decision processes (Festinger & Wapner, 1945) and on the effect of success and failure on level of aspiration. Finally, of marked significance in the links to field theory has been the presence at Clark since 1953 of Tamara Dembo, whose field theoretical view of problems of rehabilitation (Dembo, 1960) and focus on analysis of behavior in the everyday life situation and study of values bear directly on the perspective described.

person is less stimulus bound and less impelled by his own affective states. A consequence of this freedom is the clearer understanding of goals, the possibility of employing substitutive means and ends. There is hence a greater capacity for delay and *planned action* [italics mine]. (p. 127)

Kaplan (1967) pointed to behavior

as teleologically determined, that is, comprised of functions and functionally regulated structures and processes. Immanent and uncognized in the primordial form of organic activity, such directiveness and "normic regulation" becomes transcendent at the highest levels in the shape of plans and projects, and in the formulation of novel means to execute these plans and projects. (p. 78)

The empirical studies on planning were initiated in an undergraduate class, which was part of the undergraduate research apprenticeship program I developed in 1971 following my return to the psychology department after my year as provost. The first study on planning involved young (7 years) and adult (20 years) male and female subjects learning a sequence of lights of various colors, with half the group requested to verbalize plans ("planners") before beginning the task and the other half given an extraneous task during this time ("nonplanners"). Among the children, planners took significantly less trials, made fewer errors, and used more developmentally advanced strategies than did "nonplanners" (Shapiro, Rierdan, & Wapner, 1973).

Following this and the completion of other pilot studies, Leonard Cirillo and I prepared and submitted in July 1973 a grant application for a research program on development of planning, which sadly enough was not funded (Wapner & Cirillo, 1973). As I see the current situation, with the burgeoning of research on planning and such happenings as two volumes published on planning (Forbes & Greenberg, 1982; Friedman, Scholnick, & Cocking, 1987) and RFAs (Request for Applications) distributed in July 1988 by the National Institute on Child Health and Human Development and the National Institute on Aging, Cirillo and I were ahead of our time.

In part, the lack of funds to conduct the planning research, but most important, the rapid development of our program of research on critical person-in-environment transitions largely put the work on planning in a secondary position,[8] namely as a variable impacting how we experience and act in an environment we are about to leave or to enter. For example, the existence and formulation of plans to leave a university environment in which seniors were currently located significantly affected how the person experiences—for example, by greater self–world distancing from—the environment (Wofsey, Rierdan, & Wapner, 1979) and how the person copes, for example, by constructive criticism, with the conflict between expectation and actual happenings in an environment (Apter, 1976).

The role of planning has already been and will continue to be built into as many of the studies on critical transitions of person-in-environments that is

---

[8]Nevertheless, PhD theses have been recently completed (Neuhaus, 1988) and are still being conducted in this area of research.

possible. I have discussed (Wapner, 1987a), for example, the introduction of planning in studies on environmental relocation, radical disruption (e.g., by tornado, earthquake) of the person-in-environment system, the freshman's first year in college, and deterioration of an urban environment. Although these and other aspects of planning point toward change from present to future person-in-environment system states, they force giving further consideration to the nature of the present, where our everyday is characterized by an ongoing flow of activities.

An ordinary day consists of spatiotemporal change of activities that occur in different places—an office, a restaurant, a tennis court, a meeting room—with different or with the same people. From one moment to the next, spatially organized objects (things, people, animals) are changing with respect to other spatially organized objects. This totality of spatiotemporal change is differentiated into parts. As people-in-environments, we structure changes into meaningful units (Wapner & Lebensfeld-Schwartz, 1976). This ongoing flow of activities that we structure into discrete units or events is separated from preceding and from subsequent units by temporal boundaries. Thus from the primordial condition of spatiotemporal change, we may abstract or intend temporally bounded units (e.g., duration), independent of spatiality, or we may abstract or intend spatially bounded units (e.g., a room, a building), independent of temporality. Ongoing experience is structured into "spatiotemporal figures" or events, which have a beginning and an end. There is differentiation of the given event from the rest of experience; moreover, there is differentiation of a given event into parts. Further, there evolves a hierarchic relation between the parts, where, for example, the temporal aspect can be subordinated to the spatial aspect and vice versa.

The heuristic value of focusing on temporal as well as spatial features of experience is exemplified by studies completed in the Clark laboratories some 30 years ago dealing with shrinkage of space and time under danger. Werner and Wapner (1955) found that space shrunk for blindfolded subjects while walking toward danger (precipitous edge of a theatre stage). A parallel finding for temporality occurred, where subjects moving toward a precipitous edge of a staircase overestimated the time that elapsed (Langer, Wapner, & Werner, 1961). Langer, Werner, and Wapner (1965) obtained parallel findings for speed of walking toward danger.

This early conceptualization and experimentation underpinned some more recent interest in the study of spatial and temporal change under danger in the context of a macrospace, for example, a city. How do we act in an environment that we experience as becoming more dangerous? What is the relation between the experience of such environmental change and the initiation of environmental action? Bill Ittelson and I formulated this problem in a paper we presented at the 1980 Japan/U.S.A. Seminar on Environment and Behavior (Wapner & Ittelson, 1982). The problem of the relations between perceived environmental change, environmental action, and the nature of the person-in-environment state has important practical implications for intervention as well as for theory relevant to environmental psychology. For example, given a perceived environmental change (e.g., increasing urban crime), action taken can involve a change in the person (e.g., I will carry a gun), a change in the environment (e.g., I will board up my windows), or a change in the relation between them (e.g., I will move to a less dangerous neighborhood). Understanding of the conditions under which these various alternatives occur has both practical and theoretical significance.

This analysis touches on my current concern with the problem of relations between experience and action that resonated with my earlier contact with the Lewinian focus on action research (cf. Chein, Cook, & Harding, 1948) and parallels my own concern for action in the real-life situation generated during my 1969–1970 stint as provost at Clark.

RELATIONS BETWEEN EXPERIENCE AND ACTION

The theoretical focus on the relations between experience (cognitive, affective, valuative) and action has its origins in a number of sources. First, Werner's (1948) *Comparative Psychology of Mental Development* described a developmental aspect of this relationship, which recognized sensorimotor functioning as prior to perceptual and conceptual functioning. He provided extensive evidence that things-of-action, expressed in affective, sensorimotor patterns, characterize the world of the very young infant and that sensorimotor action shifts to become a basis for knowing objects. With development, there is movement toward utilization of other cognitive processes, namely perception followed by conceptual and symbolic processes, with the less highly developed forms not lost but rather becoming integrated with more highly developed forms.

Such a relationship is based on the levels of organization principle. That the complexity of organization of a system as a whole increases with the emergence of higher levels was more concretely described by Wapner, Cirillo, and Baker (1969) for relations among three levels: (1) sensorimotor action in maintaining balance; (2) perceptual objectification in localization of an object (namely perception of verticality); and (3) experienced relations between percepts (namely one's own body and objects out there). At the first level, *maintaining the body erect and balanced*, asymmetrical stimulation is directly expressed in the action of imbalance. At the second level, *perceptual objectification*, asymmetrical stimulation and organismic state are differentiated; organismic state is a context against which stimulation from a "to-be-constructed object" is related. At the third level, the body qua object is differentiated from the thing out there, and a variety of phenomenal *relations between body and objects* is possible, a body part, a finger may be used instrumentally to point to some object out there.

The importance of the relation between perception and action became more figural in a concrete way some long time ago when Werner and I began formulating the sensory-tonic field theory of perception (Werner & Wapner, 1949). We began to study vicarious relations between motor activity and perceived movement, such that with decrease (increase) of motor expression, perceived movement increases (decreases) (cf. Goldman, 1953; Korchin, Melt-zoff, & Singer, 1951; Krus, Werner, & Wapner, 1953).

Further shaping of this interest in the relation between experience and action was advanced by contact with Ittelson's (1951, 1960) analysis of perception, which was grounded in Dewey and Bentley's (1949) transactionalist position (cf. Ames, 1955; Ittelson, 1952; Ittelson & Cantril, 1954). Ittelson (1960) rejected the separation of perception and action as independent entities and pointed to the reciprocal relation between them that comprises the event to be studied. In describing such an event, he speaks of: "thing" significance (world of objects and people described as entities apart from the observer); "sequential" significances (the world of objects continuously changes); "action" significances (in addition to passive observance of an event, we act and make assumptions about what follows the action; and "evaluative" significances ("what-for" and "how-to-do" evaluations are made when operating as an active participant in any concrete situation).

This general approach to perception and action and our own work on transactions of persons-in-environments led to speculation (Wapner & Ittelson, 1982) about the relationship between the experience of environmental change and the initiation or acceptance of environmentally oriented action from a union of both of our perspectives (cf. Wapner, 1988). At least three assumptions were of importance in the analysis: (1) the transactional assumption common to our approaches that the person-in-environment is the unit to be analyzed; (2) the general recognition that perception and action are related—"for example, for Gibson (1979) actions represent plans for perception while for others perceptions are seen as plans for action, as in Ames's assertion that perceptions are 'directives for action'" (Wapner & Ittelson, 1982, p. 191); and (3) the interdependence of change and stability. Our constructivist analysis also involved linkage to the symbolic interactionist position of Schutz (1971) who points to the purposiveness of action, how it may be overt or covert, and how it may involve choice so that "no simple one-to-one relation between perceived environmental change and environmental action should be expected" (Wapner & Ittelson, 1982, p. 192).

RESEARCH PROGRAM ON CRITICAL PERSON-IN-ENVIRONMENT TRANSITIONS

As alluded to earlier, the general assumptions described were formulated with relevance to environmental psychology in the context of a research program utilizing a central empirical paradigm, that of critical or dramatic person-in-environment transitions. This research program conducted with many colleagues and students was initiated in 1970 (Wapner, Kaplan, & Cohen, 1973) and has continued for almost two decades (cf. Wapner, 1987b). During that time, our general assumptions were sharpened and shaped in the context of our findings and the problems posed. Critical transitions of the person-in-environment system are linked to changes in the person, changes in the environment, and changes in the relation between them, which occur throughout the life cycle.

Although every moment of our lives involves change, the main concern has been for those transitions where the perturbation to the person-in-environment system is experienced as so potent that the ongoing modes of transacting with the physical, interpersonal, and sociocultural features of the environment no longer suffice. Such transitions are of great significance because they may represent the occasion for regressive change or progressive development. As already noted, the holistic aspect of the approach implies that functioning of part processes at the psychological level (e.g., cognizing including sensorimotor acting, perceiving, thinking, symbolizing, imagining; feeling; and valuing) are integrated with functioning at other levels of organization (biological, sociocultural); because the organism operates as a unified whole, a disturbance in one part affects the entire person-in-environment system. Following perturbation of the person-in-environment system, which in keeping with the orthogenetic principle, may induce regression, there is reestablishment of a new dynamic equilibrium (progression) or of an ongoing person-in-environment state that is directed toward accomplishment of short- and long-term goals.

We have carried out many studies based on the critical transitions paradigm. Sites of possible perturbations to the person-in-environment system, which may initiate critical transitions are, somewhat arbitrarily, listed in Table 1. This table gives examples of problems open for study as well as work already initiated or completed (shown in italics). Studies involving a perturbation to *physical* aspects of the environment include (1) an assessment of the role of cherished possessions in adaptation of the elderly to a nursing home (Demick & Wapner, 1986; Redondo, Demick, Collazo, Inoue, & Wapner, 1986); (2) a developmental analysis of an unanticipated powerful system shock induced by tornado, earthquake, atomic bomb, and technological catastrophe (Wapner, 1983); (3) an assessment of transactions of antisocial and schizophrenic patients prior to and following relocation of a psychiatric community (Demick & Wapner, 1980); (4) transfer to a new college (Lauderback, Demick, & Wapner, 1987); (5) migration and return migration of adolescents between Puerto Rico and U.S. mainland (Lucca-Irizarry, Wapner, & Pacheco, 1981; Pacheco, Lucca-Irizarry, & Wapner, 1979; Pacheco, Lucca-Irizarry, & Wapner, 1984; Pacheco, Lucca, & Wapner, 1985; Redondo, Pacheco, Cohen, Kaplan, & Wapner, 1981; Wapner, Ciottone, Hornstein, McNeil, & Pacheco, 1983); (6) the impact of urban renewal on cognitive and affective experience of a city by people who live in high and low socioeconomic neighborhoods (Demick, Hoffman, & Wapner, 1985); (7) an analysis of alcoholics over a period of 5 weeks from entrance to time of leaving a hospital setting (Demick & Wapner, 1986).

With respect to the *interpersonal* aspects of the environment, studies have been conducted on (1) the development of friendships following entry into the university (Thomason, 1986) and (2) the development of personal networks following entrance into a new environment (Minami, 1985).

With respect to *sociocultural aspects* of the environment, studies have been conducted on (1) entering a nursery school (Ellefsen, 1987; Wapner, Ciottone, Hornstein, McNeil, & Pacheco, 1983; Wells, 1987); (2) entering and leaving college (Apter, 1976; Schouela, Steinberg, Leveton, & Wapner, 1980; Wofsey, Rierdan, & Wapner, 1979); (3) entering and adapting to medical education (Quirk, Ciottone, Letendre, & Wapner, 1987); (4) the impact of introducing legislation regarding use of automobile seat belts (Demick, Inoue, Wapner, Ishii, Minami, Yamamoto, & Nishiyama, 1986; Rioux & Wapner, 1986).

A few comments on the last of these studies is relevant because of its bearing on the problem of the relation between a group or sociocultural change and individual experience and action, a topic of concern mentioned earlier. Parallel studies were conducted in Hiroshima, Japan, and Massachusetts. Whereas observed seat-belt usage increased in both countries following the law, it reached a higher level (99% on highway) in one Japanese sample than in a Massachusetts sample (46%); further, in Massachusetts, soon after passage of the law, enough people signed a petition to put it to test, and 54% voted the law out of existence. Here, we have an important example of how the introduction of sociocultural change may make for differential personal action and in turn how personal action may make for changes at the sociocultural level. This work on use of seat belts sharpened our interest in the general problem of individual differences with respect to the relation between experience and action. As shown by Rioux and Wapner (1986), "There is a considerable different effect on action [use of automobile seat belts] when the potential hazard is experienced as 'damage to the automobile' (non-user) than when the potential hazard is experienced as 'personal injury' (committed user)" (p. 27).

Only some beginnings have been made on studies concerned with the person as the site for perturbations to the person-in-environment system (Table 1). At the *physical* level, studies have been initiated on the impact of the onset of diabetes (Collazo, 1985). At the *sociocultural* level, most studies have dealt with change in role. For example, Clark (1989) is initiating an investigation on the impact of becoming a parent on working women. The most extensive series of studies in this category are on the transition from work to retirement (Hornstein & Wapner, 1984, 1985).

The problem area of critical transitions provides many possibilities for empirical investigation. A more comprehensive understanding of the nature of critical person-in-environment transitions and the course of subsequent recovery and/or developmental advance of the person-in-environment system requires empirical study of the impact of perturbations to many of the sites listed in Table 1. Steps will be taken in future years to obtain a more complete sampling of studies where perturbations are introduced at all levels of the environment and of the person, where there is a challenge to person-in-environment reorganization by (1) *addition* of worlds (e.g., from being at home to being in home plus nursery school); (2) *substitution* (e.g., migration, relocation where one world is replaced by another); and (3) *elimination* of worlds (e.g., retirement where the work world is removed).

TABLE 1. SITES AND EXAMPLES OF PERTURBATIONS TO PERSON-IN-ENVIRONMENTS SYSTEMS THAT MAY INITIATE CRITICAL TRANSITIONS[a]

Person (× environment)	Environment (× person)
Physical (biological)[b]	Physical[b]
Age (e.g., onset of puberty, menopause, death)	Objects (e.g., acquisition or loss of cherished possessions)
Pregnancy	Disaster (e.g., onset of flood, earthquake, tornado, volcanic eruption, nuclear war)
Disability	Relocation (e.g., psychiatric community, nursing home, rural, urban, transfer to new college, migration)
Illness	Urban change (e.g., decline, renewal)
Addiction (e.g., onset and termination of alcoholism, obesity, drug addiction)	Rural change (e.g., industrialization)
Chronic (e.g., onset of diabetes, rheumatoid arthritis)	Interpersonal
Acute (e.g., onset and treatment of cancer, AIDS)	Peer relations (e.g., making or dissolving a friendship or social network, falling in or out of love)
Psychological	Family (e.g., change in extended family, immediate family, parents, relatives)
Body-experience (e.g., increase or decrease in size of body, onset of experience of positive or negative body evaluation, acquisition or loss of cherished possessions)	Neighbors
Self-experience (e.g., self-concept and experience of control, dignity, identity, power, security as in onset of or recovery from mental illness, changing role in social networks)	Co-workers
	Roommates
	Teachers

Sociocultural
  Role
    Work (e.g., becoming employed, temporarily employed, unemployed, *retired*)
    Financial (e.g., becoming rich as in winning lottery, becoming poor as in stock market crash)
    Educational (e.g., professor, student, administrator)
    Marital (e.g., being married, divorced, widowed, *parenthood, adoption*)
    Religious (e.g., becoming priest, minister, rabbi, nun, Jesuit, "Born Again" Christian, conversion)
    Political (e.g., becoming a refugee, undercover agent, war veteran, Holocaust survivor, survivor of terrorism, elected official)
    Cultural (e.g., becoming a celebrity, member of youth cult group)
  Ethnicity (e.g., becoming aware, proud of, ashamed of background)
  Gender (e.g., changing sexual orientation, from justice to caring orientation)

Sociocultural
  Economics (e.g., new technology, job opportunity)
  Educational (e.g., *nursery school*, kindergarten, elementary school, high school, *college*, graduate, or *professional school*)
  Legal (e.g., abortion, legislation, driving age, *automobile seat belt legislation*, child abuse, retirement legislation, euthanasia)
  Mores (e.g., attitude toward sex)
  Political (e.g., social, country, prison, defection)
  Religious (e.g., oppression, change in policy re female ministers and rabbis, celibacy of priests)

[a] Adapted from Wapner (1986, November). Italicized items indicate published studies or studies in progress.
[b] Though listed in one category, some perturbations involve simultaneous changes in other categories.

Such work in the future on critical person-in-environment transitions will be integrated with studies utilizing other paradigms that treat transactions (experience—including cognition, affection, valuation—and action) of persons-in-environments more generally. The form taken by such investigations depends on how one construes issues, open problems and challenges.

ISSUES AND CHALLENGES FOR THE FUTURE

What constitutes a central issue, an open problem, and a challenge for the future is, of course, a personal matter deeply ingrained in and indeed colored by one's orientation to psychology in general and to environmental psychology in particular. Such issues, problems and challenges—which represent directions for work in the future—have surely been covertly implied if not mentioned focally in the description of my orientation, its roots, and the research programs on critical person-in-environment transitions. In another context (Wapner, 1987b), I have described a number of open problems or issues: whether one adopts a transactional perspective and its corollary person-in-environment as unit of analysis or takes on an interactional perspective; whether adaptation is regarded as a one-way street with the person changing in keeping with the environment or whether adaptation implies change in both person and environment; whether the environment should be defined narrowly, for example, physically, or whether it should be defined broadly to encompass sociocultural, interpersonal, as well as physical aspects; whether one should conduct a holistic or a partitive analysis; whether an agenetic or a developmental analysis is more appropriate and inclusive.

I also described a number of challenges, including finding ways of linking environmental psychology with other areas of psychology and with the social sciences; finding ways of conceptualizing that encompass general relationships as well as problems of individuality; uncovering conditions that make for supportive, antagonistic, or substitutive relations between operations at different levels of integration; and developing overarching theoretical orientations that encompass theory and practice and provide linkages between environmental psychology and the environmental professions, other areas of psychology as well as the social and biological sciences more generally.

I close by emphasizing this last point, namely the importance of developing an overarching theory for psychology more generally. In other contexts, for example, the 1987 National Conference on Graduate Education in Psychology (Wapner, 1987c) and a presentation at the 52nd annual convention of the Japanese Psychological Association (Wapner, 1988, 1989), I have pointed to the large variety of signs that psychology is splintering into divisive units: the resignation of academic psychologists from the American Psychological Association and their election to be associated with the newly spawned American Psychological Society; the growing identification of psychologists with subspecialties; the rigid adherence to one mode of inquiry (either the "natural science" perspective *or* the "human science" perspective); specialty oriented graduate training; and the growing isolation between subfields and the isolated treatment of part processes, for example, cognitive processes, emotion. For a more comprehensive discussion of this disunity, see Altman (1987) who has placed it in a historical context by describing the pre-1900 period in psychology as primarily centrifugal (oppositional, emerging), the 1900–1960 period as centripetal (consolidating and unifying), and the post-1960 period as centrifugal. As I see it, one of the most important challenges for the future of environmental psychology as well as psychology more generally is the need to develop strategies and theories for moving toward a psychology that can be characterized as "integrated as well as differentiated" (cf. Wapner, 1987b, 1988).

APOLOGIA

Although I have mentioned a number of my experiences with people-in-places who have influenced my work in environmental psychology, I recognize that these influences most frequently proceed on cat's feet. For example, I have found that very frequently, it is only many years after an experiment has been completed or idea formulated that I become aware of the ramifications and linkages of the thinking processes that went into that particular effort. I am certain that I have left out of this review important people-in-places. I hope not only that they will forgive me for this omission, but also I hope they will be assured that the influence of such people-in-places will manifest themselves at another time in another place.

Acknowledgments

I express my appreciation to L. Cirillo, J. Demick, and L. G. Wapner for their constructive comments on an early draft of this chapter.

REFERENCES

Altman, I. (1987). Centripetal and centrifugal trends in psychology. *American Psychologist, 42*, 1058–1069.

Altman, I., & Rogoff, B. (1987). World views in psychology: Trait, interactional organismic and transactional perspectives. In D. Stokols & I. Altman (Eds.), *Handbook of environmental psychology* (pp. 1433–1465). New York: Wiley.

Ames, A., Jr. (1951). Visual perception and the rotating trapezoidal window. *Psychological Monographs, 65*(7) (Whole No. 324).

Apter, D. (1976). *Changes in mode of responding to conflict in an environment as plans develop for moving to another environment.* Unpublished master's thesis, Clark University, Worcester, MA.

Ariens Kappers, C. U., Huber, G. C., & Crosby, E. C. (1936). *The comparative anatomy of the nervous system of vertebrates, including man.* New York: Macmillan.

Barten, S. S., & Franklin, M. B. (Eds.). (1978). *Developmental processes. Heinz Werner's Selected Writings* (Vols. 1–2). New York: International Universities Press.

Bean, J. W., & Wapner, S. (1943). Effects of exposure to oxygen of high barometric pressure on higher functions of the CNS. *Proceedings of the Society of Experimental Biology and Medicine, 54*, 134–135.

Bean, J. W., Wapner, S., & Siegfried, E. C. (1945). Residual disturbance in the higher functions of the CNS induced by oxygen at high pressure. *American Journal of Physiology, 143*, 206–213.

Bertalanffy, von., L. (1968). *Organismic psychology and systems theory.* Worcester, MA: Clark University Press.

Blake, R. R., & Ramsey, G. V. (1951). *Perception: An approach to personality.* New York: Ronald.

Brown, J. F. (1936). *Psychology and the social order.* New York: McGraw-Hill.

Bruner, J. S., & Klein, G. (1960). The function of perceiving: New look retrospect. In B. Kaplan & S. Wapner (Eds.), *Perspectives in psychological theory* (pp. 161–177). New York: International Universities Press.

Canter, D., & Craik, K. H. (1987). Special Clark University Issue, Environmental Psychology at Clark University: Circa 1970–72. *Journal of Environmental Psychology, 7*, 281–288.

Cantril, H. (Ed.). (1960). *The morning notes of Adelbert Ames, Jr.* New Brunswick, NJ: Rutgers University Press.

Carini, L. P. (1955). *An experimental investigation of perceptual behavior in schizophrenics.* Doctoral dissertation (Clark University Microfilm No. 13009).

Chein, I., Cook, S. W., & Harding, J. (1948). The field of action research. *American Psychologist, 3*, 43–50.

Clark, W. (1989). *Transition to parenthood: An organismic-developmental analysis of the transactions of dual career couples.* PhD thesis (in progress), Clark University, Worcester, MA.

Collazo, J. A. (1985, March). *Transition from illness to health: Experiential changes following the onset of diabetes.* Paper presented at annual meeting of the Eastern Psychological Association, Boston, MA.

Comalli, P. E., Wapner, S., & Werner, H. (1959). Perception of verticality in old age. *Journal of Psychology, 47*, 259–260.

Dembo, T. (1960). A theoretical and experimental inquiry into concrete values and value systems. In B. Kaplan & S. Wapner (Eds.), *Perspectives in psychological theory. Essays in honor of Heinz Werner* (pp. 78–114). New York: International Universities Press.

Demick, J., & Wapner, S. (1980). Effect of environmental relocation upon members of a psychiatric therapeutic community. *Journal of Abnormal Psychology, 89*, 444–452.

Demick, J., & Wapner, S. (1986, July). *Entering, living in, and leaving the psychiatric setting.* Paper presented at the 21st International IAAP Congress, Jerusalem, Israel.

Demick, J., & Wapner, S. (1987, November). *A holistic, developmental approach to body experience.* Paper presented at "Body experience and literature: An interdisciplinary conference" at SUNY–Buffalo, Buffalo, NY.

Demick, J., & Wapner, S. (1988a). Open and closed adoption: A developmental conceptualization. *Family Process, 27*(2), 229–249.

Demick, J., & Wapner, S. (1988b). Children-in-environments: Physical, interpersonal, and sociocultural aspects. *Children's Environments Quarterly, 5*(3), 54–62.

Demick, J., Hoffman, A., & Wapner, S. (1985). Residential context and environmental change as determinants of urban experience. *Children's Environments Quarterly, 2*(3), 44–54.

Demick, J., Inoue, W., Wapner, S., Ishii, S., Minami, H., Yamamoto, T., & Nishiyama, S. (1986, August). *Experience and action of automobile seat belt usage: U.S. and Japan.* Paper presented at a symposium on "Psychological-Legal-Ethical Aspects of Automobile Seat Belt Usage" at the American Psychological Association Meetings, Washington, DC.

Dewey, J., & Bentley, A. F. (1949). *Knowing and the known.* Boston, MA: Beacon.

Dobzhansky, T. (1951). *Genetics and the origin of species* (3rd ed. rev). New York: Columbia University Press.

Ellefsen, K. F. (1987). *Entry into nursery school: Children's transactions as a function of experience and age*. Unpublished master's thesis, Clark University, Worcester, MA.

Erdelyi, M. H. (1974). A new look at the new look: Perceptual defense and vigilance. *Psychological Review, 81*, 1–25.

Festinger, L., & Wapner, S. (1945). *A test of decision time: Reliability and generality* (Report No. 48). Washington, DC: C.A.A. Division of Research.

Forbes, D. L., & Greenberg, M. T. (Eds.). (1982). Children's planning strategies. *New directions for child development*. San Francisco: Jossey-Bass.

Friedman, S., Scholnick, E. K., & Cocking, R. R. (Eds.). (1987). *Blueprints for thinking: The role of planning in cognitive development*. Cambridge: Cambridge University Press.

Fuhrer, M. J., & Cowan, C. O. (1967). Influence of active movements, illumination, and sex on estimates of body part size. *Perceptual and Motor Skills, 24*, 979–985.

Gibson, J. J. (1962). Observations on active touch. *Psychological Review, 69*, 477–490.

Gibson, J. J. (1979). *Ecological theory of visual perception*. New York: Houghton Mifflin.

Giorgi, A. (1970). Towards phenomenologically based research in psychology. *Journal of Phenomenological Psychology, 1*, 75–98.

Glick, J., & Wapner, S. (1968). Development of transitivity: Some findings and problems of analysis. *Child Development, 39*, 622–638.

Goldman, A. E. (1953). Studies in vicariousness: Degree of motor activity and the autokinetic phenomenon. *American Journal of Psychology, 66*, 613–617.

Goldstein, K. (1939). *The organism*. New York: American Book Co.

Goldstein, K. (1940). *Human nature in the light of psychopathology*. New York: Schocken Books.

Goldstein, K. (1960). Sensoritonic theory and the concept of self-realization. In B. Kaplan & S. Wapner (Eds.), *Perspectives in psychological theory. Essays in honor of Heinz Werner* (pp. 115–123). New York: International Universities Press.

Goldstein, K., & Scheerer, N. (1941). Abstract and concrete behavior: An experimental study with special tests. *Psychological Monographs, 57*(4).

Gordon, G. (Ed.). (1978). *Active touch: The mechanism of recognition of objects by manipulation*. Oxford: Pergamon Press.

Hall, C. S. (1934). Emotional behavior in the rat. I. Defecation and urination as measures of individual differences in emotionality. *Journal of Comparative Psychology, 18*, 385–403.

Heider, F. (1957). Perceiving the other person. In R. Taguiri & L. Petrullo (Eds.), *Person perception and interpersonal behavior* (pp. 22–26). Stanford, CA: Stanford University Press.

Herrick, C. J. (1949). A biological survey of integrative levels. In R. W. Sellars, V. J. McGill, & M. Farber (Eds.), *Philosophy for the future* (pp. 222–242). New York: Macmillan.

Hornstein, G. A., & Wapner, S. (1984). The experience of the retiree's social network during the transition to retirement. In C. M. Aanstoos (ED.), *Exploring the lived world: Readings in phenomenological psychology* (pp. 119–136). Carrollton, GA: West Georgia College Press.

Hornstein, G. A., & Wapner, S. (1985). Modes of experiencing and adapting to retirement. *International Journal of Aging & Human Development, 21*(4), 291–315.

Humphries, O. (1959). *Effect of articulation of fingertip through touch on apparent length of outstretched arm*. Unpublished master's thesis, Clark University, Worcester, MA.

Ittelson, W. H. (1951). The constancies in perceptual theory. *The Psychological Review, 58*, 285–294.

Ittelson, W. H. (1952). *The Ames demonstrations in perception*. Princeton, NJ: Princeton University Press.

Ittelson, W. H. (1960). *Visual space perception*. New York: Springer.

Ittelson, W. H. (1973). Environmental perception and contemporary perceptual theory. In W. H. Ittelson (Ed.), *Environment and cognition* (pp. 1–19). New York: Seminar Press.

Ittelson, W. H., & Cantril, H. (1954). *Perception as a transactional approach*. New York: Random House.

Kaplan, B. (1966). The comparative developmental approach and its application to symbolization and languages in psychopathology. In S. Arieti (Ed.), *American handbook of psychiatry* (Vol. 3; pp. 659–688). New York: Basic Books.

Kaplan, B. (1967). Meditation on genesis. *Human Development, 10,* 65–87.

Kaplan, B., & Wapner, S. (Eds.). (1960). *Perspectives in psychological theory. Essays in honor of Heinz Werner.* New York: International Universities Press.

Kaplan, B., Wapner, S., & Cohen, S. B. (1976). Exploratory application of the organismic-developmental approach to man-in-environment transactions. In S. Wapner, S. B. Cohen, & B. Kaplan (Eds.), *Exploring the environment* (pp. 207–233). New York: Plenum.

Klüver, H. (1942). Functional significance of the geniculostriate system. *Biological Symposia, Visual Mechanisms, 7,* 253–299.

Koffka, K. (1935). *Principles of gestalt psychology.* New York: Harcourt Brace.

Köhler, W. (1929). *Gestalt psychology.* New York: Liverwright.

Korchin, S., Meltzoff, J., & Singer, J. L. (1951). Motor inhibition and Rorschach movement responses. *American Psychologist, 6,* 344–345.

Krus, D. M., & Wapner, S. (1959). Effect of lysergic acid diethylamide (LSD-25) on the perception of part-whole relationships. *Journal of Psychology, 48,* 87–95.

Krus, D. M., & Wapner, S. (1962). Effect of LSD on pace of performing a variety of tasks. *Perceptual and Motor Skills, 14,* 255–259.

Krus, D. M., Werner, H., & Wapner, S. (1953). Studies in vicariousness: Motor activity and perceived movement. *American Journal of Psychology, 66,* 603–608.

Kuntz, P. G. (1968). *The concept of order.* Seattle: University of Washington Press.

Langer, J., Wapner, S., & Werner, H. (1961). The effect of danger upon the experience of time. *American Journal of Psychology, 74*(1), 94–97.

Langer, J., Werner, H., & Wapner, S. (1965). Apparent speed of walking under conditions of danger. *Journal of General Psychology, 73,* 291–298.

Lashley, K. S. (1942). The problem of cerebral organization in vision. *Biological Symposia, Visual Mechanisms, 7,* 301–322.

Lauderback, A., Demick, J., & Wapner, S. (1987, April). *Planning and coping with conflict: Transfer vs. non-transfer college students.* Paper presented at the annual meeting of the Eastern Psychological Association, Arlington, VA.

Lavine, T. (1950). Knowledge as interpretation: An historical survey. *Philosophy and Phenomenological Research, 10,* 526–540; *11,* 80–103.

Liebert, R. S., Wapner, S., & Werner, H. (1957). Studies in the effects of lysergic acid diethylamide (LSD-25): Visual perception of verticality in schizophrenic and normal adults. *A.M.A. Archives of Neurology and Psychiatry, 77,* 193–201.

Liebert, R. S., Werner, H., & Wapner, S. (1958). Studies in the effects of lysergic acid diethylamide (LSD-25): Self and object size perception in schizophrenic and normal adults. *A.M.A. Archives of Neurology and Psychiatry, 79,* 580–584.

Lucca-Irizarry, N., Wapner, S., & Pacheco, A. M. (1981). Adolescent return migration to Puerto Rico: Self-identity and bilingualism. *Agenda: A Journal of Hispanic Issues, 11,* 15–17, 33.

Maier, N. R. F. (1939). *Studies of abnormal behavior in the rat.* New York: Harper.

Maier, N. R. F., & Schneirla, T. C. (1935). *Principles of animal psychology.* New York: McGraw-Hill.

Maslow, A. H. (1946). Problem-centering versus means-centering in science. *Philosophy of Science, 13,* 326–341.

Max, L. W. (1935). An experimental study of the motor theory of consciousness. III. Action-current responses in deaf-mutes during sleep, sensory stimulation and dreams. *Journal of Comparative Psychology, 19,* 469–486.

Merleau-Ponty, M. (1962). *Phenomenology of perception.* London: Routledge & Kegan Paul.

Miller, G. A., Galanter, E., & Pribram, K. H. (1960). *Plans and the structure of behavior.* New York: Rinehart and Winston.

Minami, H. (1985). *Establishment and transformation of personal networks during the first year of college: A developmental analysis.* Unpublished doctoral dissertation, Clark University, Worcester, MA.

Murray, H. A. (1959). Preparation for the scaffold of a comprehensive system. In S. Koch (Ed.), *Psychology: A study of a science* (Vol. 3; pp. 7–54). New York: McGraw-Hill.

Neuhaus, E. C. (1988). *A developmental approach to children's planning.* Unpublished doctoral dissertation, Clark University, Worcester, MA.

Novikoff, A. B. (1945a). The concept of integrative levels and biology. *Science, 101,* 209–215.

Novikoff, A. B. (1945b). Continuity and discontinuity in evolution. *Science, 101,* 405–406.

Pacheco, A. M., Lucca, N., & Wapner, S. (1979). Migration as a critical person-in-environment transition: An organismic-developmental interpretation. *Revista de Ciencias sociales [Social Sciences Journal], 21,* 123–157.

Pacheco, A. M., Lucca-Irizarry, N., & Wapner, S. (1984). El estudio de la migracion: Retos para la psicologia social y la psicologia ambiental. [The study of migration: Challenges for social and environmental psychology]. *Revista Latinoamericana de Psicologia, 16*(2), 253–276.

Pacheco, A. M., Lucca, N., & Wapner, S. (1985). The assessment of interpersonal relations among Puerto Rican migrant adolescents. In R. Diaz-Guerrero (Ed.), *Cross-Cultural and national studies in social psychology* (pp. 169–176). North Holland: Elsevier Science Publishers B.V.

Pepper, S. C. (1942). *World hypotheses: A study in evidence.* Berkeley, CA: University of California Press.

Piaget, J. (1952). Autobiography. In E. G. Boring, H. S. Langfeld, R. M. Yerkes, & H. Werner (Eds.), *A history of psychology in autobiography* (pp. 237–256). Worcester, MA: Clark University Press.

Quirk, M., Ciottone, R., Letendre, D., & Wapner, S. (1987). Critical person-in-environment transitions in medical education. *Medical Teacher, 9*(4), 415–423.

Rand, G., & Wapner, S. (1967). Postural status as a factor in memory. *Journal of Verbal Learning and Verbal Behavior, 6,* 268–271.

Rand, G., & Wapner, S. (1969). Ontogenetic changes in the identification of simple forms in complex contexts. *Human Development, 12,* 155–169.

Rapoport, A. (1972). The search for simplicity. *Main Currents in Modern Thought, 28,* 79–84.

Redondo, J. P., Pacheco, A. M., Cohen, S. B., Kaplan, B., & Wapner, S. (1981). Issues and methods in environmental transition: Exemplar from Puerto Rican migration. *Revista/Review Interamericana,* Vol. XI, 3, 376–386.

Redondo, J. P., Demick, J., Collazo, J. A., Inoue, W., & Wapner, S. (1986). *Role of cherished possessions in adaptation to the nursing home.* Paper presented at the annual meetings of the American Psychological Association, Washington, DC.

Rioux, S., & Wapner, S. (1986). Commitment to use of automobile seat belts: An experiential analysis. *Journal of Environmental Psychology, 6,* 189–204.

Sameroff, A. S. (1983). Developmental systems: Context and evolution. In W. Kessen (Ed.), *History, theories, methods* (pp. 237–294). Vol. 1 of P. H. Mussen (Ed.), *Handbook of child psychology.* New York: Wiley.

Schlater, J. A., Baker, A. H., & Wapner, S. (1981). Apparent arm length with active versus passive touch. *Bulletin of the Psychonomic Society, 18*(3), 151–154.

Schouela, D. A., Steinberg, L. M., Leveton, L. B., & Wapner, S. (1980). Development of the cognitive organization of an environment. *Canadian Journal of Behavioural Science, 12,* 1–16.

Schutz, A. (1971). *Collected papers.* The Hague: Martinus Nijhoff.

Shapiro, E., Rierdan, J., & Wapner, S. (1973). *Effect of planning by children and adults on serial learning.* Unpublished manuscript, Clark University, Worcester, MA.

Thomason, D. (1986, April). *Growing friendships: A developmental analysis.* Paper presented at the annual meeting of the Eastern Psychological Association, New York City.

Von Uexküll, J. (1957). A stroll through the world of animals and men. In C. H. Schiller (Ed.), *Instinctive behavior* (pp. 5–80). New York: International Universities Press.

Walker, R. Y., Wapner, S., Bakan, D., & Ewart, E. S. (1946, October). The agreement between inspectors' observations as recorded on the Ohio State Flight Inventory and instrument readings obtained from photographic records. Washington, DC: C.A.A. *Division of Research, Report No. 67.*

Wapner, S. (1944). The differential effects of cortical injury and retesting on equivalence reactions in the rat. *Psychological Monograph, 57.*

Wapner, S. (1968). Age changes in perception of verticality and of the longitudinal body axis under body tilt. *Journal of Experimental Child Psychology, 6,* 543–555.

Wapner, S. (1969). Organismic-developmental theory: Some applications to cognition. In P. H. Mussen, J. Langer, & M. Covington (Eds.), *Trends and issues in developmental psychology* (pp. 38–67). New York: Holt, Rinehart & Winston.

Wapner, S. (1977). Environmental transition: A research paradigm deriving from the organismic-developmental systems approach. In L. van Ryzin (Ed.), *Wisconsin Conference on Research Methods in Behavior Environment Studies. Proceedings* (pp. 1–9). Madison: University of Wisconsin.

Wapner, S. (1978). Some critical person-environment transitions. *Hiroshima Forum for Psychology, 5,* 3–20.

Wapner, S. (1981). Transactions of persons-in-environments: Some critical transitions. *Journal of Environmental Psychology, 1,* 223–239.

Wapner, S. (1983). Living with radical disruptions of person-in-environment systems. *IATSS Review, 9*(2), June, 133–148. (In Japanese. English translation available.)

Wapner, S. (1986, November). *An organismic-developmental systems approach to the analysis of experience and action.* Paper presented at a conference on "Holistic approaches to analysis of experience and action," at the University of Catania, Sicily.

Wapner, S. (1987a). A holistic, developmental, systems-oriented environmental psychology: Some beginnings. In D. Stokols and I. Altman (Eds.), *Handbook of environmental psychology* (pp. 1433–1465). New York: Wiley & Sons.

Wapner, S. (1987b). 1970–72: Years of transition. *Journal of Environmental Psychology, 7,* 389–408.

Wapner, S. (1987c). Special focus limits creativity. *The APA Monitor, 18,*(2), 10.

Wapner, S. (1988). The experience of environmental change in relation to action. *The Journal of Architectural and Planning Research, 5,* 237–256.

Wapner, S. (in press). Unifying psychology: Strategies from a holistic, developmental, systems perspective. *Hiroshima Forum.*

Wapner, S., & Alper, T. G. (1952). The effect of an audience on behavior in a choice situation. *Journal of Abnormal and Social Psychology, 47,* 222–229.

Wapner, S., & Cirillo, L. (1973). *Development of planning.* Public Health Service Grant Application.

Wapner, S., & Demick, J. (1987, August). *Some relations among cognition, emotion, and action: A holistic, developmental, systems approach.* Paper presented at International Society for Research on Emotions Annual Meeting, Worcester, MA.

Wapner, S., & Demick, J. (1988, October). *Some relations between developmental and environmental psychology: An organismic-developmental systems perspective.* Paper presented at a conference "Vision of Development, the Environment, and Aesthetics: The Legacy of Joachim Wohlwill," at The Pennsylvania State University, 25–27 October.

Wapner, S., & Demick, J. (in press). Development of experience and action: Levels of integration in human functioning. In G. Greenberg & E. Tobach (Eds.), *Scientific methodology in the study of mind: Evolutionary epistemology.* Fourth Biennial T. C. Schneirla Conference Series. Hillsdale, NJ: Erlbaum.

Wapner, S., & Ittelson, W. H. (1982). Environmental perception and action. In G. Hagino and W. H. Ittelson (Eds.), *Interaction processes between human behavior and environment: Proceedings of the Japan-United States Seminar, Tokyo, Japan, Sept. 24–27, 1980* (pp. 189–200). Tokyo: Bunsei Printing Company.

Wapner, S., & Kaplan, B. (Eds.). (1966). *Heinz Werner: 1890–1964.* Worcester, MA: Clark University Press.

Wapner, S., & Lebensfeld-Schwartz, P. (1976). Toward a structural analysis of event experience. *Acta Psychologica, 41,* 397–401.

Wapner, S., & Werner, H. (1957). *Perceptual development.* Worcester, MA: Clark University Press.

Wapner, S., & Werner, H. (1965). An experimental approach to body perception from the organismic-developmental point of view. In S. Wapner and H. Werner (Eds.), *The body percept* (pp. 9–25). New York: Random House.

Wapner, S., Werner, H., & Krus, D. M. (1957). The effect of success and failure on space localization. *Journal of Personality, 25,* 752–756.

Wapner, S., Werner, H., & Comalli, P. E., Jr. (1958). Effect of enhancement of head boundary on head size and shape. *Perceptual and Motor Skills, 8,* 319–325.

Wapner, S., McFarland, J. H., & Werner, H. (1963). Effect of visual spatial context on perception of one's own body. *British Journal of Psychology, 54,* 41–49.

Wapner, S., Cirillo, L., & Baker, A. H. (1969). Sensory-tonic theory: Toward a reformulation. *Archivio Di Psicologia Neurologia E Psichiatria, 30,* 493–512.

Wapner, S., Cirillo, L., & Baker, A. H. (1971). Some aspects of the development of space perception. In J. P. Hill (Ed.), *Minnesota Symposia on Child Psychology* (Vol. 5; pp. 162–204). Minneapolis: University of Minnesota Press.

Wapner, S., Kaplan, B., & Cohen, S. (1973). An organismic-developmental perspective for understanding transactions of men in environments. *Environment and Behavior, 5,* 255–289.

Wapner, S., Ciottone, R., Hornstein, G., McNeil, O., & Pacheco, A. M. (1983). Critical transitions through the life cycle. In S. Wapner & B. Kaplan (Eds.), *Toward a holistic developmental psychology* (pp. 111–132). Hillsdale, NJ: Erlbaum.

Wells, C. A. (1987). *The child's entrance into nursery school: A family life cycle transition.* Unpublished doctoral dissertation, Clark University, Worcester, MA.

Werner, H. (1926). *Einführung in die Entwicklungspsychologie.* Leipsig: Barth (2nd ed., 1933; 3rd ed.; 1953; 4th ed., 1959).

Werner, H. (1937). Process and achievement: A basic problem of education and developmental psychology. *Harvard Educational Review, 7,* 353–368.

Werner, H. (1945). Motion and motion perception: A study in vicarious functioning. *Journal of Psychology, 19,* 317–327.

Werner, H. (1948). *Comparative psychology of mental development* (revised ed.). New York: International Universities Press. (First copyright 1940).

Werner, H. (1957). The concept of development from a comparative and organismic point of view. In D. Harris (Ed.), *The concept of development* (pp. 125–148). Minneapolis: University of Minnesota Press.

Werner, H., & Kaplan, B. (1956). The developmental approach to cognition: Its relevance to the psychological interpretation of anthropological and ethnolinguistic data. *American Anthropologist, 58,* 866–880.

Werner, H., & Kaplan, B. (1963). *Symbol formation.* New York: Wiley.

Werner, H., & Wapner, S. (1949). Sensory-tonic field theory of perception. *Journal of Personality, 18,* 88–107.

Werner, H., & Wapner, S. (1952). Toward a general theory of perception. *Psychological Review, 59,* 324–338.

Werner, H., & Wapner, S. (1955). Changes in psychological distance under conditions of danger. *Journal of Personality, 24,* 153–167.

Werner, H., & Wapner, S. (1956). Sensory-tonic field theory of perception: Basic concepts and experiments. *Revista di Psicologia, 50,* 315–337.

Witkin, H. A. (1965). Heinz Werner: 1890–1964. *Child Development, 30,* 308–328.

Witkin, H. A., Lewis, H. B., Hertzman, M. Machover, K., Meisner, P. B., & Wapner, S. (1954). *Personality through perception.* New York: Harper & Brothers.

Wofsey, E., Rierdan, J., & Wapner, S. (1979). Planning to move: Effects on representing currently inhabited environment. *Environment and Behavior, 11,* 3–32.

Zener, K. (Ed.). (1949a). Interrelations between perception and personality: A symposium (special issue). Part I. *Journal of Personality, 18*(1).

Zener, K. (Ed.). (1949b). Interrelations between perception and personality: A symposium (special issue). Part II. *Journal of Personality, 18*(2).

11

Landscape Research

PLANNED AND SERENDIPITOUS

ERVIN H. ZUBE

I AM A MIDWESTERNER BY BIRTH, born in Milwaukee, Wisconsin, in 1931—during the Great Depression. I have many pleasant memories from the 1930s when times were tough, memories of simple kinds of family activities—most often long walks with my sister Lorraine and my mother and father. My parents both came from large families, my mother, Germaine, had five brothers and sisters, and my dad, Ervin L., had six. There was no shortage of family support nor of cousins. The European roots were predominantly German; however, my mother's maiden name was Petersen, providing one-quarter Scandinavian heritage.

After completing elementary and secondary school in Milwaukee and before entering the University of Wisconsin, I worked for a couple of months for the New Orleans Recreation Department making floats for the Mardi Gras. That was followed by a season of work in blister-rust control and fire fighting for the U.S. Forest Service on the Panhandle National Forest. Upon my return from Idaho, I enrolled at the University of Wisconsin in Madison and majored in landscape design. During my undergraduate years, I worked as a waiter in a sorority house where I met Margaret Pew. We were married in 1954. Following graduation, which also included a commission as a Second Lieutenant in the Air Force, I worked part-time as assistant dean of men and also pursued graduate study in soil science. Before finishing my MS I was called to active duty.

Following 2 years in the Air Force, study at the Graduate School of Design at Harvard University led to a master of landscape architecture degree. I then was awarded the Rome Prize in landscape architecture and spent the next 2 years at the American Academy in Rome. We left for Rome with an infant son, Eric, born on April 21, 1959. Rick is now an aerospace engineer living in Seattle and working for the Boeing Aircraft Company.

My academic career as of this writing spans 28 years and includes positions at the Universities of Wisconsin–Madison (1961–1964), California–Berkeley (1964–1965), Mas-

ERVIN H. ZUBE • School of Renewable Natural Resources, University of Arizona, Tucson, Arizona 85721.

sachusetts–Amherst (1965–1977), and Arizona (1977–). Of those 28 years, 22 were in administration (1965–1987). My academic career has always been combined with liberal portions of professional practice, consulting, or public service activities.

During the years we were at the University of Massachusetts, Margaret and I both returned to school for doctorates—she at the University of Massachusetts in anthropology with an emphasis in gerontology and I in geography at Clark University with a parallel interest in environmental psychology. Since our arrival in Tucson, Margaret has been responsible for building and coordinating an interdisciplinary graduate Gerontology Certificate Program. I currently teach in landscape architecture, geography, and the interdisciplinary graduate program in Renewable Natural Resources Studies. This is enlivened with a liberal dose of research in diverse aspects of landscapes and serving on several nonprofit museum and service organizations' boards of directors.

INTRODUCTION

How does one select and organize salient ideas and events that span two decades of research? The options are many and include chronologically, by the influences of mentors, peers, colleagues, and graduate students, by major projects, or by conceptual or theoretical orientations. All of these organizing strategies are employed in different sections of this chapter, albeit not consistently.

This chapter is introduced with a conceptual schema utilizing four paradigms of landscape perception/assessment research that I published with two graduate students in 1982. This schema provides a useful framework for discussing the changing directions and emphases in my research and also for the career shifts that I made from teacher–practitioner, to teacher–administrator–practitioner, to teacher–administrator–researcher, and most recently to teacher–researcher.

A FEW CAVEATS

A few words of warning seem appropriate before undertaking this retrospective account of research. What is presented in the following paragraphs may convey a sense of orderliness and sequential evolution that is not always the case. Serendipity and opportunism have at various times figured prominently in my career. Also, hindsight frequently infers that one had 20–20 foresight and that one was consistently deliberate and planful. This can be an exaggeration of the actual level of acuity for either hindsight or foresight.

With very few exceptions, interactions between humans and landscapes have been the consistent object of my research. Stilgoe (1982) has suggested that *landscape* is a slippery word. He substantiated his suggestion with a revealing discussion of the changing definitions and meanings that have been associated with the word over the last four centuries, including "land modified for permanent human occupation," paintings of rural scenes, views and vistas, and the gardens of country houses. Meinig (1979) discusses 10 different perceptions of landscape, depending on "the organizing ideas we use to make sense out of what we see." He describes landscape as nature, habitat, artifact, system, problem, wealth, ideology, history, place, and aesthetic.

In one way or another, and to a greater or lesser extent, most of these meanings have been encountered in my research during the past 20 years. The landscapes of my research have been and continue to be places and spaces where humans and outdoor environments interact. They range from built to natural landscapes and include designed and vernacular places from the past and the present. They do not exist without human occupancy and use. They span a wide range of geographic scales, from regions and river basins to urban plazas. And they encompass different degrees and kinds of interactions ranging from high intensity on-site physical and social experiences to low intensity off-site solitary, contemplative experiences.

THE PARADIGMS

During the fall semester of the 1979–1980 academic year, Jonathan Taylor and James Sell, then PhD students in renewable natural resources studies and geography, respectively, stopped in my office to ask about the possibility of undertaking a readings course in landscape perception. After some deliberation, we concluded that we ought to pursue the topic collectively with a definite objective in mind. A quick review of several journals readily reinforced our suspicions that a substantial body of research had been undertaken and published in the preceding 15 years. Our objective became the writing and publication of a major review of the literature. Two years later, the task was completed, our efforts appeared in print (Zube, Sell, & Taylor, 1982) and, for our efforts, we received one of two research honor awards given by the American Society of Landscape Architects that year.

The review identified over 160 articles published in 20 journals between 1965 and 1980 plus several major conference proceedings and resource agency technical reports. A process model in which landscape perception was considered as a function of the interactions of humans with landscapes was adopted as a basis for analyzing the reported research. The model consisted of three components: the human, the landscape, and the human–landscape interaction.

> The human component encompasses past experience, knowledge, expectations, and the socio-cultural context of individuals and groups. The landscape component includes both individual elements and landscapes as entities. The interaction results in outcomes which in turn affect both the human and the landscape components. (Zube, Sell, & Taylor, 1982)

The application of this model to the 160 published papers resulted in the identification of the four previously mentioned general paradigms of landscape perception research (see Table 1):

> 1. *The expert paradigm.* This involves evaluation of landscape quality by skilled and trained observers. Skills evolve from training in art and design, ecology, or

TABLE 1. RELATIONSHIPS OF MODEL COMPONENTS AND PARADIGMS[a]

	Components		
Paradigm	Human	Landscape properties	Interaction outcomes
Expert	Highly skilled trained observers	From principles of art, ecology, and resource management	Statements of landscape qualities
Psychophysical	Observer as respondent	Specific landscape elements and properties manipulatable through management and design	Numerical/statistical expression of perceived values
Cognitive	Observer as processor of information	Associated with obtaining information and meanings	Meanings, ratings of satisfactions and preferences
Experiential	Active participant	World of everyday experiences	Habitual behavior, understanding of human, and landscape development

[a] Adapted from Zube, Sell, and Taylor, 1982.

in management fields where wise resource management techniques may be assumed to have intrinsic aesthetic effects.

2. *The psychophysical paradigm*. This involves assessment through testing general public or selected populations' evaluations of landscape aesthetic qualities or of specific landscape properties. The external landscape properties are assumed to bear a correlational or stimulus–response relationship to observer evaluations and behavior.

3. *The cognitive paradigm*. This involves a search for human meaning associated with landscape or landscape properties. Information is received by the human observer and, in conjunction with past experience, future expectation, and sociocultural conditioning, lends meaning to landscape.

4. *The experiential paradigm*. This considers landscape values to be based on the experience of the human–landscape interaction, whereby both are shaping and being shaped in the interactive process. (Zube, Sell, & Taylor, 1982, p. 8)

A major conclusion emanating from this exercise was the atheoretical nature of much of the research done to that date and the diversity of theoretical orientations associated with the balance. As a step in the direction of an integrating theoretical framework, we borrowed from Ittelson's 1973 transactional discussion of the "minimum considerations" for the study of environmental perception. Ittelson called for recognition that the environment (or landscape) surrounds the perceiver, is multimodal, provides peripheral as well as central information, provides more information than can be used, provides symbolic meanings and motivational messages, always has an ambience, and provides opportunities for action, control, and manipulation.

That review, including the exercise of analyzing and categorizing the published research literature and addressing the issue of an integrating theoretical framework now provides a partial framework for this review of my research. The paradigms help explain changes in research objectives and methods. The next section provides a brief review of activities and events that were influential in shaping my interest in and concept of landscape and my early research.

20–20 HINDSIGHT

With 20–20 hindsight, I can now identify a number of experiences that were influential in stimulating interest in landscapes, broadly defined. My first introduction to large-scale landscapes was via training and experience as a photo-radar intelligence officer in the Strategic Air Command of the U.S. Air Force in the mid-1950s. Reading intelligence reports and interview records from individuals who had escaped through the Iron Curtain and viewing unfamiliar landscapes through a stereoscope provided new perspectives on physical landscapes and relationships between human developments and the works of nature. Being confronted with responsibility to assess large geographic areas for intelligence information provided a perspective that differed profoundly from the site-scale orientation I had developed as an undergraduate student in landscape design courses at the University of Wisconsin in Madison.

A stint at Harvard University, Graduate School of Design, followed my discharge from active duty in the Air Force. Within the required curriculum for the master of landscape architecture degree, I encountered the subjects of landscape history with Norman Newton and systematic analysis of landscapes for design and planning purposes with Walter Chambers and Hideo Sasaki, two topics that would resurface in my research at varying times in the future. The Harvard experience also provided exposure to some of the early literature in a field that is now called "environment, behavior, and design." Notable to me at that time (and volumes that are still in my library) were Festinger, Schachter, and Back's (1950) study of the relationships of the design of a student housing complex at MIT with social behaviors within the complex, and William H. Whyte's (1957) study of social behavior in a Chicago commuter suburb. And the year I completed my degree, Lynch and Rivkin (1959) published "A Walk around the Block," a precursor to Lynch's (1960) seminal publication 1 year later, *The Image of the City.*

After Harvard, 2 years at the American Academy in Rome greatly enhanced my fascination with historic landscapes, both vernacular and designed. The attraction to vernacular landscapes was reinforced several years later when, on the faculty at the University of California in Berkeley, I was assigned to co-teach a graduate seminar with J. B. Jackson. What this really meant was that I made sure the classroom door was unlocked and that a slide projector was ready for his use. He was the founder of *Landscape*, a magazine that introduced American scholars to the writings of individuals such as Jean Gottman and Constantino Doxiadis before their names became commonplace among designers and geographers. His writings on the American landscape have influenced the thoughts and activities of landscape scholars for more than three decades. I sat in awe of his knowledge of designed and vernacular landscapes and his remarkable ability to effectively share this knowledge. Contact with "Brinck" Jackson was maintained when he became a frequent visiting lecturer in the Department of Landscape Architecture and Regional Planning that I headed at the University of Massachusetts from 1965 to 1972 and also when I edited a collection of his writings (Zube, 1970a).

FROM TEACHER–PRACTITIONER TO TEACHER–RESEARCHER

My goal upon returning to the United States from Europe was to develop a combined career as a university teacher and a practicing landscape architect, and that is what I did for nearly 10 years while at the Universities of Wisconsin–Madison, California–Berkeley, and Massachusetts–Amherst. The nature of the practice tended more and more toward the planning of large landscapes. These included schemes for the reclamation of potential taconite mines in northern Wisconsin, a landscape analysis of the south shore of Lake Superior, landscape resources studies for the Island of Nantucket and the U.S. Virgin Islands, planning for a national park on the Island of Jamaica, and a number of large area federally funded water resources planning projects in the New England and Mid-Atlantic regions. It was one of these projects that cast the die and precipitated a turn in my career from that of teacher–practitioner to teacher–researcher. Actually, in taking on the duties of a department head at the University of Massachusetts in 1965, administration had also become a major activity.

Shortly after arriving in Amherst, I joined forces with Julius Gy Fabos and several other faculty members from the Department of Landscape Architecture and Regional Planning to create the firm of Research, Planning and Design Associates, Inc. (RPD). All of the principals in RPD were faculty members, and the only employees in the firm were graduate students. Primary objectives of the firm were to work on large-scale landscape planning and design projects, to have opportunities to explore new approaches to planning in real-world situations, and to provide opportunities for graduate students in landscape architecture and regional planning to gain professional experience while completing their degrees. This involvement of graduate students in practice became a standard procedure in future years as I turned to research and consulting activities.

In the spring of 1968, RPD was invited to participate in the North Atlantic Regional Water Resources Planning Project (NAR). Our task was to assess the visual and cultural resource values of the planning region and to relate them to environmental quality and national economic efficiency planning objectives as part of a 17-agency planning team (Zube, 1970b). The NAR planning area encompassed 167,000 square miles, all or parts of 1ᴗ states extending from the

Virginia–North Carolina border to Canada and including approximately 25% of the national population. A landscape inventory, classification, and evaluation system encompassing physical and cultural landscape components was designed, applied, and acknowledged by other planning team participants and the National Planning Advisory Committee for the project as innovative and a singularly important contribution.

The evaluation system was predicated solely on our professional judgments about visual and cultural values, it represented what we would identify nearly two decades later as the "expert paradigm." Realizing that we had identified and represented those values on behalf of 25% of the U.S. population based solely on our professional education and experience, and that recommendations based on those data had influenced potentially important resource allocation decisions that were projected to extend into the twenty-first century was a very heady and sobering experience. This one project was instrumental in changing the course of my career. I felt a compelling need to know more about the broad field of landscape values and to explore other approaches to the systematic study of the field. By 1969, together with graduate students, I was involved in landscape perception research projects designed to assess some of our NAR assumptions about landscape values. I had also started working part-time on a doctoral degree in geography.

A PARADIGM SHIFT

Among the few publications we found during the course of our literature search for the NAR landscape assessment project that addressed issues of qualitative environmental values were the edited issue of the *Journal of Social Issues* by Kates and Wohlwill (1966) and a paper by Robert Kates, "The Pursuit of Beauty in the Environment" (1966–1967). Kates's paper was one of the earliest of what would soon become many that addressed the problems identified in the 1965 White House Conference on Natural Beauty (*Beauty for America*, 1965). Not only was his paper provocative and helpful in conceptualizing the NAR project, but when I started thinking about pursuing a PhD, Bob Kates seemed like the logical person to consult. That turned out to be one of my better decisions. And, the Graduate School of Geography at Clark University was not only a logical place to go, it was an excellent place. The stimulating intellectual environment in environment–behavior, behavioral geography, environmental perception, or environmental psychology at Clark in the early 1970s—call it what one will—was another heady experience for a middle-aged doctoral student and has been documented in a special issue of the *Journal of Environmental Psychology* (1987a; cf. Canter & Craik, 1987).

In addition to the privilege of working with Bob Kates, Clark University also provided the setting for a fortuitous meeting with Kenneth Craik. In 1970–1971, Ken was there as a senior postdoctoral fellow in psychology, the same year that I was on a leave of absence from the University of Massachusetts to work full-time on my degree. From that meeting grew a continuing professional relationship and personal friendship. In addition, Ken's early paper, on "The Comprehension of the Everyday Physical Environment" (1968), in which he outlined a schema for environment perception research, served as an important methodological foundation for my venture into research.

My dissertation focused on assessing the efficacy of the assumptions we had made in the NAR study about the physical attributes of visual quality in the northeastern U.S. landscape; the validity of using aerial photography and topographic maps as basic data sources for inventorying and classifying the visual attributes of regional and subregional landscapes; and the values and meanings residents of the region associated with these landscapes. The research design embraced both psychophysical and cognitive paradigms—although I didn't recognize them as such at the time. Although strongly tied to pragmatic planning concerns, the research also explored theoretical issues that were to play a larger role in my research in the future.

AN EMPHASIS ON RESEARCH

A fortuitous and seemingly serendipitous event occurred before my dissertation had been completed; I was offered a position as dean of a school of design at another university. The University of Massachusetts made a counteroffer to me to assume the position of director and develop active research and service programs in what was a somewhat moribund environmental institute. The challenge was intellectually enticing and emotionally appealing as my wife was about 1 year away from completing her PhD in anthropology at the University of Massachusetts. Accepting the director's position would provide me with a new challenge and allow Margaret to finish her degree. Included with the offer were several staff positions and a modest operating budget. With the most meager of research credentials, I accepted a position that turned out to be very important in the development of my career and in gaining a better understanding of the public policy process. First, I was able to continue the landscape values research that had been triggered by the NAR study and pursued in dissertation research. Second, the Institute for Man and Environment (IME) provided an environment that required development of the ability to communicate with individuals from very diverse disciplines. Third, it was a stimulus to expand the domain of my landscape research to encompass urban places and spaces. And fourth, it provided an opportunity to become involved in state government.

For a period of time between 1973 and 1975 and while serving as the institute director, I also commuted weekly between Amherst and Boston and served as director of the Coastal Review Center in the Executive Office of Environmental Affairs of the Commonwealth of Massachusetts. This position was fortuitous, not only for the governmental experience it provided but also for facilitating the involvement of the institute in the review of coastal zone management policies and as the agency responsible for basic resource inventory and assessment studies required for the state's Coastal Zone Management

Plan. A primary responsibility in Boston had to do with designing policies and procedures for reviewing proposals for developing in the coastal zone while planning was still in process.

Three research and/or service centers were created within the IME in the areas of environmental policy, environment and behavior, and community development. A fourth unit, a Cooperative Park Studies Unit (CPSU), was a research arm of the National Park Service. The CPSU was responsible for coastal ecological and geomorphological research in Mid- and North Atlantic coastal parks. The lessons learned in RPD about the value of providing opportunities for graduate students were immediately transferred to IME and a policy adopted that required every project undertaken to include student support. The institute involved as many as 40 graduate students per year in projects administered through the three centers and the CPSU. Among those who played major roles in the Environment and Behavior Research Center (EBRC) were Joseph Crystal, Gary Evans, James F. Palmer, David Pitt, and Craig Zimring, each of whom is still involved in the active generation and/or utilization of environment and behavior research.

The early 1970s was a period of great activity in the promulgation of environmental policies at the national, state, and local levels of government. Among the issues being addressed in these policies were visual, sonic, air, and water quality. An important distinction among these qualitative concerns was the unit of measure employed in assessing quality. For air and water, the unit of measure was based on physical properties, whereas for visual and sonic, the unit of measure was based on perceptual properties. For many environmental managers, the notion of defining values on the basis of publics' perceptions rather than on expert opinions was alien. For such information to be credible with these managers, it was necessary to demonstrate convincingly that the perceptions of quality were broadly shared among the affected populations and that they could be related to environmental/landscape attributes and elements that could be modified by management, planning, or design decisions. In other words, there was an intellectual environment within agencies that challenged and fostered the aggressive development of the psychophysical paradigm.

Ken Craik spent a sabbatical leave in the IME during the 1974–1975 academic year. Prior to his arrival and with his initiative, we successfully submitted a proposal to the National Science Foundation to explore the concept of Perceived Environmental Quality Indices (PEQI). This proposal was responsive to the concerns already expressed, but equally important, it reflected our conviction that any reasonable assessment of the quality of the environment had to take into account the perceptions and experiences of the users of that environment. Our intent was to explore the state of the art and science of environmental perception and to assess the efficacy of using the human as a measuring instrument of the quality of the environment.

Through a series of commissioned review papers and small workshops, a state of the art assessment of research in environmental perception was produced (Craik & Zube, 1976). The environment was conceptualized in three broad categories: scenic and recreational; residential and institutional; and the media of air, water, and sound. Nine review papers were commissioned to address specific aspects of each of the three categories, including assessment methods and procedures and existing policies. Methodological and procedural issues included demonstrating the reliability and generality of PEQIs; distinguishing between personal preferential judgments and comparative appraisals that invoke some implicit or explicit standard of comparison; and identifying the properties of the person as an instrument for measuring the perceived and experienced quality of the environment. These properties included social class, degrees of agreement between experts and laypersons, consensus among individuals and groups, and relationships between observer-based appraisals and attributes of the physical environment.

In addition to the authors of the commissioned papers, the workshops included representatives of federal and state environmental and resource management agencies who had policy and management responsibilities. Clearly, the methodological and procedural issues referred to here have bearing on the utility of PEQIs for decision making and policy. The workshops focused on the practicality of the idea and the potential consequences of its adoption and use. The product of the project was a publication that included the review papers and discussions about research needs and strategies that addressed the identified methodological, policy, and procedural issues (Craik & Zube, 1976). Little did I realize that this endeavor would play an influential role on the direction of my research after I assumed the position of director of the School of Renewable Natural Resources at the University of Arizona in Tucson.

Landscape research carried on while at IME included continuation of work on the relationships of physical measures with perceived visual values and meanings of landscapes and perceptually based classification systems for landscapes. Underlying most of this work was a continuing interest in the planning and policy implications of the findings. Much of my research in this area and of the graduate students I worked with at the institute has been reported in a chapter in Volume 1 of this series (Altman & Wohlwill, 1976) and will not be covered here. A few points do merit mention, however, because they represent important benchmarks for work that was continued in the 1980s.

A question we have raised repeatedly, for both practical and theoretical reasons, is what is the extent of agreement among individuals and/or groups about the visual quality of landscapes? As suggested the practical implications are, if there is high agreement, that planners and managers can effectively refute that tired old adage, "beauty is in the eye of the beholder" and strive through participatory processes to plan and manage in concordance with normative public values. If there is substantial disagreement, it is important for planners and managers to know who disagrees, to understand why, and to recognize that the development of plans is likely to involve a series of negotiating sessions to resolve disagreements among concerned interests. The theoretical reason lies in the desire to unravel some of the factors that might explain why differences exist and the salience of the underlying values.

A visual landscape study undertaken in 1973 to develop a predictive model of scenic values for a public utility company in southern New England and using physical landscape dimensions triggered a continuing series of studies that explored the question of degrees of variability in perceptions of visual quality. The electric utility company was interested in being able to systematically inventory and evaluate visual qualities of landscapes so as to be more responsive to public values and avoid, or at least minimize, perceptions of insensitive siting of new power plants and transmission lines. The study demonstrated the feasibility of using physical measures of the landscape to predict scenic values in rural Connecticut River Valley landscapes. The study also demonstrated the validity of using color photographic prints for assessing perceived scenic values.

In the design and conduct of the study, we identified different participant groups that varied by place of residence, occupation, age, and ethnicity (Zube, Pitt, & Anderson, 1975). An important finding from that study was that the majority of our study participants who were white middle class, predominantly young adults to middle aged, and residents of suburbia and small towns, were in strong agreement, whereas a small sample of black urban residents differed significantly from the white participants in their ratings of visual landscape values. They did not share the orientations of other groups that placed highest value on landscapes that showed minimum signs of human intervention. Human-made structures in the landscapes were perceived more favorably by the black participants than by any other group. Intergroup correlations on the scenic rating of 56 landscapes depicted in colored photographs ranged between .75 and .96, with the majority being over .92. Correlations of the black group with all other groups on the same rating task ranged from .19 to .50, with the majority being below .33. These differences sparked a continuing interest in both intra- and cross-cultural differences in various landscape contexts. They also led to a developmental study some years later in which we found that perceptions of the white, young, and middle-aged adults differed significantly from those of young children and older adults (Zube, Pitt, & Evans, 1983).

Important lessons about the utility of my early landscape assessment research for planning and policy applications emerged a number of years later. In 1978, I was invited to meet with representatives of the Nuclear Regulatory Commission in Washington, DC, to discuss the siting of nuclear power plants in the northeastern United States. To my great surprise, they showed me how our Connecticut River Valley research findings had been employed to assess a nuclear power plant site in the state of New York (U.S. Nuclear Regulatory Commission, 1979, pp. m-44–m-64).

One year later, 1979, a major national conference on the American landscape was held at Lake Tahoe where approximately 100 papers were presented by researchers, planners, and managers and subsequently published in conference proceedings (Elsner & Smardon, 1979). Following the conference, an evaluation of the citations listed in the proceedings was conducted (Priestly,

1983). Only 20 references were cited more than 5 times each in the proceedings. Of that group, which totaled 147 citations, our work represented 26%, or 37 citations. The influence on policy, planning, management, and subsequent research of the 5 publications that made up the 37 citations is difficult to assess, but the analysis suggests that they were probably among the more influential of the citations. In a more recent bibliographic survey conducted by the Delphi technique, our work was again among the most frequently referred to by participants in the process (Cats-Baril & Gibson, 1986). An important lesson learned from these experiences is that I often did not and probably still do not know how my work was and is being used and applied.

CROSS-CULTURAL STUDIES

In the following years, cross-cultural studies became one of several continuing themes in my research. Involvement in coastal zone planning as a consultant to the Governor's Office of the U.S. Virgin Islands between 1974 and 1977 provided an opportunity to collect data on native West Indians' and immigrant Anglos' perceptions of Carribean coastal landscapes. This consulting project not only provided important information about public values that was subsequently used in the development of the coastal zone management plan and policies but was also designed to explore cross-cultural perception questions. A master of regional planning thesis (Hathaway, 1976) utilized the Connecticut River Valley images to replicate part of that study and to assess the perceptions and meanings of those landscapes to immigrant Italian-Americans and their American-born children. Association with an American graduate student working in coastal-zone planning in Lorne, Australia, provided an opportunity to compare U.S. and Australian responses to the Lorne coastal landscape. And, in the spring of 1979, while teaching at the University of Ljubljana in Yugoslavia, I exploited that serendipitous opportunity and used the photographic images from the Connecticut River Valley and the Virgin Islands to study Slovenian university students' landscape perceptions.

Findings from these cross-cultural studies reinforced our interpretation of the data from the black center-city residents in the Connecticut River Valley study (Zube & Pitt, 1981). Significant differences were found in visual quality ratings between immigrant Italian-Americans and other groups and between black West Indians and other groups. Between-group correlations for the perceived scenic quality of the Virgin Islands coastal zone depicted on two photographic panels, for example, ranged from .46 to .57 for West Indians with Slovanian students and University of Massachusetts personnel. In contrast, the correlations between the Slovanian students and University of Massachusetts personnel on the two photographic panels were .92 and .96. Nor were significant differences found between Australians and white Americans. Whether the differences can be attributed to ethnicity or some other set of variables is conjectural. The primary point of difference between these groups, however, is response to landscapes containing indications of human interventions. For example, black West Indians (BWI) did not perceive the presence of hotels on beaches as diminishing visual quality. Their responses to structures in the landscape were similar to those of the black urban dwellers (BUD) in the Connecticut River Valley study. And, the immigrant Italian-Americans (IIA) responses paralleled those of the black participants.

Do these findings reflect differences that can be explained by race and nationality, or do they reflect differences that can be better explained by different landscape contexts and transactions including life-style, environmental experience, personal values, and education? Two of the three groups, BUD and IIA, have strong urban ties and life-styles associated with densely populated urban landscapes. The majority of the West Indian survey sample were also urban dwellers, in contrast with the others who tended to be residents of suburbia and small rural towns. In addition, the two major islands, St. Thomas and St. Croix, are predominately humanized landscapes with few vestiges of seemingly undisturbed natural landscapes remaining. It seems likely that the differences are attributable to multiple factors including environmental context and experience, education, and personal values.

The interest in cross-cultural research continued following my move to Arizona. Serving as chairman of a faculty advisory committee for a large arid-lands, instructional, and research development project at King Abdulaziz University in Jeddah, Saudi Arabia, led to a comparative study of Saudi Arabian and American perceptions of the environmental quality of two desert cities, Jeddah and Tucson—with an emphasis on the sonic environment. The study was precipitated by a proposal for the City of Jeddah to adapt U.S. or Great Britain noise standards. As a reviewer of the proposal, I questioned the validity of such an action in the absence of data indicating comparability of Saudi Arabian and American or British perceptions of urban sounds. Serendipity again played an important role when I was asked to redesign the proposed research and to become an active participant in it. The study was designed to address cross-cultural differences in perceptions, to assess the validity of audiovisual simulations, and to assess a concept discussed in the PEQI workshops—the validity of using touring panels for purposes of assessing environmental quality (Craik & Zube, 1976).

Both cities were presented in audiovisual simulations (Zube, Vining, Law, & Bechtel, 1985). On-site visits were also made to four locations in Tucson by touring panels of American and recently arrived Saudi Arabian graduate students. The same environmental quality assessments were obtained from residents of the four study neighborhoods in Tucson. Significant between-culture differences were found in perceptions of environmental quality. Low correlations, ranging from +.29 to −.57 on six environmental quality scales, were found between each of the student groups and the residents. Modest support for the validity of the audiovisual simulation was obtained in the form of correlations between residents and the American students but not between residents and the Saudi Arabians. The study demonstrated clear differences between Saudi Arabian and American perceptions of urban environmental quality and provided additional evidence of the need to consider cultural differences in the assessment of perceived and experienced landscape qualities.

EXPERIENCING A NEW LANDSCAPE

The move to Arizona in 1977 involved not only a change in jobs but also a profound change in natural and cultural landscapes. Within 60 miles of my home, I have experienced natural landscapes as diverse as the Lower Sonoran Desert with its very distinctive flora including saguaro cactus and palo verde trees that have green-chlorophyll-producing bark (which compensates for miniscule, water-conserving leaves), to a sub-Alpine forest at 10,000 feet elevation—and all of the life zones that lie between. Within this same distance are diverse cultural landscapes including Indian Reservations, Mexican and American border communities, cattle ranches, centers of mining and irrigated farming, elaborate destination resorts, and one of the fastest growing cities in the country. This is a far cry from the rolling farmlands of the Connecticut River Valley, frequent small towns and cities, and forest-clad hills of western Massachusetts. Furthermore, Arizona is an urban state with nearly 60% of its population living in two metropolitan areas, Phoenix and Tucson. In addition, it has been and continues to be one of the fastest growing states in the nation. It is a magnificent and challenging complex of landscapes for someone who is interested in the relationships of humans and landscapes. It had a profound effect upon my life-style and world view and upon my research.

Shortly after the move to Arizona, Ken Craik and I were at work on a research proposal to be submitted to the National Science Foundation to continue work in PEQIs. In spite of very good reviews, we were turned down. Funding priorities were changing—as they have in the past and will again in the future—and the environmental projects were no longer high on the national agenda. A proposal to the University of Arizona Agricultural Experiment Station did provide funds, however, to adapt some of our ideas from the PEQI project and explore landscape values of Arizona residents. With a little more hindsight now, I can see that my research had been rapidly evolving from emphases on the psychophysical and cognitive paradigms to the cognitive and experiential paradigms.

The first experiment station study was designed to assess residents' perceptions of and attitudes toward the Arizona landscape. Prior to designing the instrument for a mail survey of 1,500 households and to help define salient issues, open-ended exploratory interviews in the humanistic manner of the experiential paradigm were conducted with approximately 90 Arizonans representing different interests and geographic areas across the state. Among the issues identified in the interviews and that were included in the mail survey were attitudes toward growth and change, perceptions of valued landscapes and valued landscape experiences, attitudes toward expenditure of public funds for different landscape management purposes, and the relationships of these issues with places of residence. A significant departure from the design of most mail survey formats was made with the inclusion of multiitem semantic differential and landscape rating scales. A 65% response rate was obtained from the 1,303 deliverable questionnaires.

Literature review for this project turned up several unexpected historical documents that raised provocative questions about the perceptions of early white visitors to and settlers in the area. They triggered a long-time but somewhat dormant interest in history that pointed me in a new direction and called for a different research approach, one that was included under the experiential paradigm in our 1982 review paper. A parallel study was initiated to try to understand the historic nature and evolution of landscape values in the arid and semiarid Southwest and, in particular, Arizona. This curiosity took me to interesting community libraries around the state searching out diaries, journals, travel logs, and other historic documents that might shed light on first perceptions and ensuing changes. These excursions revealed that early visitors and settlers, during the post-Civil War years of 1865 to 1895, were very much aware of the beauties of the landscape. They saw in it opportunities for economic gain in mining and agriculture and were also aware of the dangers and hazards associated with the landscape, dangers associated with limited water, Apache Indian raids, and poisonous reptiles and insects. They were also supportive of change because it meant more people, increased economic opportunities, and greater security in a very sparsely settled territory (Zube, 1982).

Popular literature of the time that was available to the Eastern population in magazines such as *The Atlantic Monthly* tended to emphasize the negative attributes of the territory. To counteract these images, the territorial legislature established the office of the Commissioner of Immigration in 1881. The responsibility of the commissioner was to promote the territory and to attract immigrants and capital for investments. This would also enhance chances for statehood. Over time the promotional literature provided by territorial and county offices began to project images of nondesert landscapes, of tree-lined city streets and Victorian houses, of lush, green, flood-irrigated fields. One promotional brochure produced in Maricopa County after the turn of the century started with the bold statement, "Phoenix is not in a desert" (Zube & Kennedy, 1990). In many respects, this was probably a self-fulfilling prophesy. Phoenix is today a much greener city than Tucson; the average daily per-capita water consumption in Phoenix is approximately 40% greater than in Tucson. A study of Tucsonan and Phoenician attitudes toward urban and regional parks lends support to the continuing perception that "Phoenix is not in a desert" but rather is in a human-engineered oasis (Zube, Simcox, & Law, 1986). Tucsonans expressed stronger preferences for desert landscape parks, whereas Phoenicians expressed stronger preferences for green irrigated parks. The transactions between Tucsonans and Phoenicians and their environments have resulted in different urban landscapes.

RIPARIAN LANDSCAPES

A wealth of data was obtained from the statewide survey but most important were two findings that shaped a major portion of the research that followed. The first was not particularly surprising but did provide substantiation for developing a specific focus on riparian landscapes. When asked which landscapes provided the most valued outdoor experiences, an overwhelming majority of respondents identified mountains and valleys. With 83% of the land in the state in public ownership or held as trust lands, most, if not all of the mountainous areas are publicly owned. In contrast, most of the valley and desert riparian landscapes are in private ownership. These are valued landscapes that have been desired and fought over for hundreds of years. They are the areas where water is found in the desert, and they currently represent less than 0.4% of the surface area of the state. The primary focus of this project was on exploring and understanding potential differences in value orientations and human interactions with these landscapes.

The upper part of the San Pedro River Basin was selected as one of the initial study sites. The San Pedro River in southeastern Arizona has its headwaters in Mexico and flows northward to its confluence with the Gila River. The upper portion, for about 40 miles north of the international border, is a perennial stream—one of the very few remaining streams in the southern half of the state that has a continuous year-round flow. It is also recognized as a landscape of significant floral and faunal diversity and was declared a National Conservation Riparian Area by Act of Congress in 1988. At the time our study was initiated, however, it was owned by a large land-holding and development corporation.

Shortly after the project was initiated, serendipity again intervened, and a friend who was the head of a nongovernmental conservation organization informed me confidentially that a large land trade was imminent, that approximately 44,000 acres of prime, corporately owned upper San Pedro riparian landscape would be transferred to the U.S. Bureau of Land Management in exchange for equal-value land elsewhere in the state. Our plans to follow the same procedure that was employed in the statewide survey, of interviews followed by a mail survey, were immediately revised in an attempt to beat the public announcement about the land trade. A mail survey was rapidly designed. Fortunately, a graduate student, Dave Simcox, and I had just published a bibliography of more than 380 publications on Southwestern riparian research and had a good command of the major resource issues (Simcox & Zube, 1985). Data from the statewide survey were used to define the attitudinal and perceptual issues. The survey was designed, mailed, and returned (75% response rate from 461 deliverable questionnaires) prior to public announcement of the land transfer. The race was won.

The questionnaire was designed to explore perceptions of landscape values, appropriate land uses, and changes in and adjacent to the riparian area; descriptions of the riparian landscape; and attitudes toward the adequacy of planning in the riparian area and the adjacent city of Sierra Vista. The survey sample was designed to include, in addition to a sample of the general public, six special interest groups: the local water resources association, farmers and ranchers, real estate agents, elected and appointed governmental officials, members of a local conservation group, and resource managers having responsibility within the riparian landscape.

There was considerable agreement among all groups and the public sample about riparian resource values. Discriminant analysis revealed some important differences, however, in how some groups described the landscape, in their perceptions of change, and in their attitudes about appropriate land uses in the riparian area and the adequacy of existing planning. Perhaps most notable was the extreme positions exhibited by the resource managers on three of the four discriminant functions, on the description of the riparian area and on the perception of change in the area—both of which were addressed using bipolar scales—and on attitudes about the adequacy of planning in the area. Although a study by Culhane (1981) indicated that public agency resource managers in the southwest are successful in balancing multiple-use management objectives and conflicts between commodity and noncommodity interests, the managers on the San Pedro River represented the extreme resource preservation position among all groups surveyed. These data suggested that the managers perceived the riparian landscape as not appropriate for multiple uses but as an area to be preserved and with very limited access.

This position is reflected in the way the managers revealed more detailed and specific knowledge about riparian conditions in their use of semantic scales to describe the riparian area and in their more strongly stated attitudes about the inadequacy of existing planning to protect this landscape resource. Real estate interests reflected the opposite end of the spectrum on the adequacy of planning, considering it very adequate. The managers were also more aware of change than most other groups, except the conservationists. Conservationists' perceptions of change and appropriate land use for the area also closely paralleled the managers. These two groups supported designation of the area as a nature preserve. Real estate interests were reflected in strong support of using the area for flood control and thus enhancing development potential on adjacent lands. Farmers and ranchers supported continued use of the area for agricultural activities, and local officials supported using the area for public recreation. On most issues, the public sample and the water resources association occupied positions that were supportive of conservation uses for the riparian area but that also provided opportunities for recreational use.

The second finding from the statewide survey that shaped future research was a surprise. In spite of the much heralded progrowth image that was being projected of the state, there existed a very substantial antigrowth sentiment among the population. There was substantial agreement among respondents about least and most preferred land uses within a radius of 20 miles of where they lived. The least preferred included second home areas, subdivisions, and commercial uses. The most preferred uses, including farming, can be categorized generally as open space. Following this finding, James Sell, currently occupying a postdoctoral position in landscape architecture, and I (1986; Sell, Zube, & Kennedy, 1988) initiated a series of studies exploring public perception of and response to major environmental change. The focus of these studies was a number of large development projects in and around metropolitan Tucson, ranging in area from approximately 325 to 485 hectares (800 to 1,200 acres).

PERCEIVING LANDSCAPE CHANGE

Following the statewide survey, we undertook a broad-scaled review of the perception of change literature and found it to be sadly lacking in reference to understanding human perceptions of and responses to environmental changes associated with large-scale environmental planning and design projects (Sell & Zube, 1986). Based on the literature review and a subsequent case study of a controversial project in metropolitan Tucson, we proposed a general model of the perception and response process (Zube & Sell, 1986). This model is similar to that suggested by Aldwin and Stokols (1988) and posits that perceptions are influenced by characteristics of the change such as the kind of change, existing environmental context, obtrusiveness of the proposed change, proximity to the observer, and length of time to complete the change. Other factors include the observers' personal values, perceived locus of control, access to information, and social status. Potential responses include: to deny its existence, ignore it, attempt to change it, attempt to halt it, or to relocate away from it.

The case study provided a limited validation of the model. A follow-up telephone survey of residents proximate to five large-scale developments in the Tucson metropolitan area focused on the perceptual dimensions of the model and provided further validation (Sell, Zube, & Kennedy, 1988).

As noted, we also addressed perceptions of change in the San Pedro riparian study, focusing on change in both the riparian landscape and the respondents' proximate residential environment of Sierra Vista, a city adjacent to the San Pedro River (Zube, Friedman, & Simcox, 1988). Although there was widespread recognition of change in the riparian landscape, there were significant differences in the perceptions of the amount of change. Those individuals who made frequent use of the riparian landscape for recreational or occupational activities were aware of greater change than those who reported lesser use.

Responses indicated that residents were aware of change in their proximate environment as well as the general magnitude of change as indicated by measures of increase in hectares of developed land and in kilometers of new roads. The amount of change was impressive; the developed area increased from 4,535 to 8,330 hectares between 1973 and 1987, and the kilometers of roads increased from 106 to 294 in the same time period, increases of 84% and 177%, respectively.

The notable difference in responses to change between Tucsonans and residents of Sierra Vista was that there was a generally negative response to change associated with the large multiuse development projects in metropolitan Tucson, whereas there was a generally positive response to the change from grazing lands and farm fields around Sierra Vista to more subdivisions and small commercial centers. The relatively few Tucsonans who perceived the change as positive tended to be newcomers to Tucson and believed that their own property had increased in value as a result of the adjacent change. However, the majority of the respondents tended to see personal costs associated with the changes, costs such as loss of open space, increased traffic, and air pollution. On the other hand, Sierra Vista residents believed that they had a better place to live because of the growth and change. In contrast with the Tucson metropolitan area changes, growth in the Sierra Vista area created more low-density landscapes that were an extension of the existing built landscape. These new landscapes were not perceived as obtrusive. A new kind of land use was not introduced. Not only was the new landscape a familiar one, but those who inhabited it were of the same socioeconomic status and were, in a general way, also familiar.

LOOKING BACKWARD AND FORWARD

The research that I have reported here started more than 20 years ago with a primary emphasis on providing answers to questions associated with landscape policy and planning. It had its genesis, at least in part, in landscapes experienced through a stereoscope, through design and planning problems, the pages of history, and in just being there—in various places around the world. Over time, encountering questions of why as well as how, and through associations with many individuals, some mentioned in this chapter and others not, theoretical questions began to surface and play an equal or greater role in shaping the research. That is not to say, however, that concerns with potential applications in policy and planning are now absent. Rather, I would like to believe that some reasonable balance has been struck. The conceptual underpinnings of my work have shifted in significant ways during this period, initially from the expert paradigm to the psychophysical and cognitive and then to the cognitive and the experiential. Now all figure in my research, depending upon the question or questions being addressed, but the emphasis is clearly on the latter two.

The transactional approach to research as advanced by Ittelson (1973) and by Altman and Rogoff (1987) has become a guiding force. It encompasses historical and contemporary perspectives. It has aided and abetted the expansion of my outlook on landscape assessment as noted, from the expert paradigm and the psychophysical and cognitive to include the experiential. It recognizes that one should not consider individuals or groups independent of the culture of which they are a part and the landscape in which they exist (Zube, 1984a). It provides an appropriate framework for conceptualizing and pursuing the kinds of research I have described in this chapter.

My research has not been a solitary venture; I have been very fortunate in having outstanding professional and academic colleagues and exceptionally bright graduate students who rapidly became colleagues. Education is truly a two-way street. As much of the satisfaction in my research has come from sharing the activity as from the actual discovery.

Several enduring research themes can be traced through the 20-plus years of the research discussed in this chapter, including the relationships of landscape assessment research findings with public policy, planning, and management; searching for the human and physical dimensions of scenic beauty and other landscape values; and exploring intra and cross-cultural differences in human–landscape interactions. Research in these thematic areas has been conducted in a variety of landscape contexts—natural, rural, suburban, and urban. Most of the work reported here has been in rural and suburban areas; however there is a body of research that I have either not included here or have only mentioned in passing and that focuses on natural landscapes, notably on national parks. It includes research on the social carrying capacity of Yosemite Valley (Frissell, Lee, Stankey, & Zube, 1980); public assessments of visitor centers in national parks (Zube, Palmer, & Crystal, 1976); a proposed wildlife park in Upper Egypt (Zube, 1984b); visitor satisfactions with selected national monuments (Zube, Kennedy, & Simcox, 1987); park–local population interactions in developed and lesser developed nations around the world (Zube, 1986; Zube & Busch, 1988); and a current study that addresses the quality of the built environment in U.S. National Parks. A similar pattern could be traced of urban-oriented research.

Serendipity in different forms also entered in from time to time. For example, returning to the San Pedro River riparian project, we had no specific applied target in mind when the study was initiated; we were searching for understanding of the values and interactions of individuals and groups with a landscape that was nationally recognized because of its diverse flora and fauna. Nevertheless, the land transfer resulted in the need for the Bureau of Land Management (BLM) to consider alternative management plans. Our data base on public and special interest groups' perceptions and attitudes concerning the riparian landscape was relevant to the question of probable public responses to the alternatives. At the request of the BLM, a technical report was prepared that focused on attitudes and values related to alternative management plans for the riparian area, alternatives that ranged from continuation of commodity and noncommodity uses to strict preservation and minimal human use.

Current research includes continued studies of the transactions of humans and special value landscapes, such as desert riparian areas, great gardens of the world, and national parks. A project is underway that explores differences in value orientations, meanings, perceptions of change, and preferred patterns of use associated with ephemeral streams and their related riparian landscapes. These are streams that rarely have surface water in their channels, only after intermittent desert rains. Nevertheless, they have great resource significance in desert environments. The intention is to replicate the San Pedro study in an ephemeral stream watershed and to compare human responses to and interactions with perennial and ephemeral desert streams. In another project we are exploring the meanings and values associated with gardens from around the world, gardens that were built between the fifteenth and twentieth centuries and that are still in existence.

The second major research focus is also a continuation of current interest in the interactions of local populations with national parks and equivalent reserves. This project has been supported by the U.S. Man and the Biosphere Program and is of international interest. The nineteenth- and early twentieth-century concept of national parks devoid of human habitation that developed in the United States and that has been exported around the world is no longer feasible in many countries. In many places where it has been attempted, problems of great magnitude have been encountered that involve resistance of the local population. Our work to date has focused on identifying strategies that are being employed to try to facilitate more positive relationships and that recognize the needs and rights of populations that have been deprived of access to subsistence resources by the creation of a park or reserve. Future research will attempt to define new models of parks that are emerging and the kinds of park–people interactions that have potential for applications in different landscape and cultural contexts.

But the role of serendipity in the future cannot be overlooked. One never knows when an opportunity may be presented that merits putting current projects on temporary hold so that a new but related avenue of inquiry can be explored. As indicated in the preceding pages, I have experienced a number of such delightful and rewarding surprises in my career. Others can be added to those already mentioned, including the opportunities to study urban residents' perceptions of the sky (Zube & Law, 1984) and their responses to varying wind patterns in an urban central business district (Zube, 1979).

Finally, there is no shortage of provocative and significant issues and questions to be pursued concerning human–landscape interactions. There is only a shortage of time in which to pursue them.

REFERENCES

Aldwin, C., & Stokols, D. (1988). The effects of environmental change on individuals and groups: Some neglected issues in stress research. *Journal of Environmental Psychology. 8,* 57–75.

Altman, I., & Rogoff, B. (1987). World views in psychology: Trait, interactional, organismic, and transactional perspectives. In D. Stokols and I. Altman (Eds.), *Handbook of environmental psychology* (pp. 7–40). New York: John Wiley & Sons.

Altman, I., & Wohlwill, J. F. (Eds.). (1976). *Human behavior and environment: Advances in theory and research.* New York: Plenum Press.

Beauty for America. (1965). Proceedings of the White House Conference on Natural Beauty. Washington, DC: U.S. Government Printing Office.

Canter, D., & Craik, K. H. (Eds.). (1987). Special Clark University issue. *Journal of Environmental Psychology, 7.*

Cats-Baril, W. L., & Gibson, L. (1986). Evaluating aesthetics: Major issues and a bibliography. *Landscape Journal, 5,* 93–102.

Craik, K. H. (1968). The comprehension of the everyday physical environment. *Journal of the American Institute of Planners, 34*, 29–37.

Craik, K. H., & Zube, E. H. (Eds.). (1976). *Perceiving environmental quality.* New York: Plenum Press.

Culhane, P. J. (1981). *Public lands politics.* Baltimore: Johns Hopkins University Press.

Elsner, G. H., & Smardon, R. C. (Eds.). (1979). *Our national landscape* (General technical report PSW-35). Berkeley, CA: U.S. Department of Agriculture, Pacific Southwest Forest and Range Experiment Station.

Festinger, L., Schachter, S., & Back, K. (1950). *Social pressures in informal groups.* New York: Harper and Brothers.

Frissell, S. S., Lee, R. G., Stankey, G. H., & Zube, E. H. (1980). A framework for estimating the consequences of alternative carrying capacity levels in Yosemite Valley. *Landscape Planning, 7*, 151–170.

Hathaway, S. M. (1976). *The view from the North End: A study of landscape attitudes.* Unpublished master of regional planning degree thesis. Amherst: University of Massachusetts.

Ittelson, W. (1973). *Cognition and environment.* New York: Seminar Press.

Kates, R. W. (1966–1967). The pursuit of beauty in the environment. *Landscape, 16*, 21–24.

Kates, R. W., & Wohwill, J. F. (Eds.). (1966). *The Journal of Social Issues, 22.*

Lynch, K. (1960). *The image of the city.* Cambridge: MIT Press.

Lynch, K., & Rivkin, R. (1959). A walk around the block. *Landscape, 8*, 24–34.

Meinig, D. W. (1979). The beholding eye. In D. Meinig (Ed.), *The interpretation of ordinary landscapes* (pp. 33–48). New York: Oxford University Press.

Priestly, T. (1983). The field of visual analysis and resource management: A bibliographic analysis and perspective. *Landscape Journal, 2*, 52–59.

Sell, J. L., & Zube, E. H. (1986). Perception of and response to environmental change. *Journal of Architectural and Planning Research, 3*, 33–54.

Sell, J. L., Zube, E. H., & Kennedy, C. L. (1988). Perception of land use change in a desert city. *Journal of Architectural and Planning Research, 5*, 145–162.

Simcox, D. E., & Zube, E. H. (1985). *Arizona riparian areas: A bibliography.* Tucson: School of Renewable Natural Resources, University of Arizona.

Stilgoe, J. R. (1982). *Common landscapes of America.* New Haven: Yale University Press.

U.S. Nuclear Regulatory Commission. (1979). *Final environmental statement related to construction of Greene County Nuclear Power Authority.* Washington, DC: Office of Nuclear Reactor Regulation.

Whyte, W. H. (1957). *The organization man.* New York: Simon and Schuster.

Zube, E. H. (Ed.). (1970a). *Landscapes: Collected writings of J. B. Jackson.* Amherst: University of Massachusetts Press.

Zube, E. H. (1970b). Evaluating the visual and cultural landscape. *Journal of Soil and Water Conservation, 25*, 137–141.

Zube, E. H. (1976). Perception of landscape and land use. In I. Altman & J. F. Wohlwill (Eds.), *Human behavior and environment: Advances in theory and research* (Vol. 1; pp. 87–121) New York: Plenum Press.

Zube, E. H. (1979). Pedestrians and wind. In J. Wagner (Ed.), *Images of information* (pp. 69–83). Beverly Hills, CA: Sage Publications.

Zube, E. H. (1982). An exploration of southwestern landscape images. *Landscape Journal, 1*, 31–40.

Zube, E. H. (1984a). Themes in landscape assessment theory. *Landscape Journal, 3*, 104–110.

Zube, E. H. (1984b). Developing and maintaining support for national parks and ecological preserves. *Egyptian Journal of Wildlife and Natural Resources, 5*, 64–68.

Zube, E. H. (1986). Local and extra-local perceptions of national parks and protected areas. *Landscape and Urban Planning, 13*, 11–18.

Zube, E. H. (1987a). From synthesis to analysis and back again. *Journal of Environmental Psychology, 7,* 425–433.

Zube, E. H. (1987b). Perceived land use patterns and landscape values. *Landscape Ecology, 1,* 37–45.

Zube, E. H., & Busch, M. (1990). Park-local population interactions: An international perspective. *Landscape and Urban Planning.*

Zube, E. H., & Kennedy, C. B. (1990). Changing images of the Arizona Territory. In L. Zonn (Ed.), *Place images in the media.* New York: Rowan and Littlefield.

Zube, E. H., & Law, C. S. (1984). Perceptions of the sky in five metropolitan areas. *Urban Ecology, 8,* 199–208.

Zube, E. H. & Pitt, D. G. (1981). Cross-cultural perception of scenic and heritage landscapes. *Landscape Planning, 15,* 107–117.

Zube, E. H., & Sell, J. L. (1986). Human dimensions of environmental change. *Journal of Planning Literature, 1,* 162–176.

Zube, E. H., Pitt, D. G., & Anderson, T. W. (1975). Perception and prediction of scenic resource values of the Northeast. In E. H. Zube, R. O. Brush, & J. G. Fabos (Eds.), *Landscape assessment: Values, perceptions and resources* (pp. 151–167) Stroudsburg, PA: Dowden, Hutchinson and Ross.

Zube, E. H., Palmer, J. F., & Crystal, J. (1976). Design quality in the national parks. *Design and Environment, 7,* 34–37.

Zube, E. H., Sell, J. L., & Taylor, J. G. (1982). Landscape perception: Research, application and theory. *Landscape Planning, 9,* 1–33.

Zube, E. H., Pitt, D. G., & Evans, G. W. (1983). A lifespan developmental study of landscape assessment. *Journal of Environmental Psychology, 3,* 115–128.

Zube, E. H., Vining, J., Law, C. S., & Bechtel, R. B. (1985). Perceived urban residential quality: A cross-cultural bimodal study. *Environment and behavior, 17,* 327–350.

Zube, E. H., Simcox, D. E., & Law, C. S. (1986). The oasis image in two desert cities. *Landscape Research, 11,* 7–11.

Zube, E. H., Kennedy, C., & Simcox, D. E. (1987). *Chiricahua National Monument and Fort Bowie National Historic site visitor survey.* Tucson: Cooperative National Park Service Studies Unit, University of Arizona.

Zube, E. H., Friedman, S., & Simcox, D. E. (1988). *Landscape change: Perceptual and physical measures.* Unpublished paper. Tucson: University of Arizona.

12

In Search of Objectives

DAVID CANTER

WHEN THERE WERE RIOTS IN LIVERPOOL'S Toxteth district in the early 1980s, they led to the closure of the bank I and my father before me had used for over 30 years. This brought to an end the last remaining contact I had with a small area of Liverpool in which I had been born on January 5, 1944, where I had gone to the Hebrew Primary School and the Collegiate Grammar school. The same square mile also housed Liverpool University, where I had obtained my undergraduate degree in psychology in 1964 and my doctorate in 1968.

Like many Jews in Liverpool, my father had arrived there around the time of World War I, escaping from the pogroms in Lithuania, with every intention of going on to the United States. His painful life, including the death of all his close relatives in concentration camps, culminated in his marrying my mother who had been born in Liverpool, but whose father had come from Russia.

My Liverpudlian roots being so shallow, it is not surprising that in 1966, I took the opportunity to join the psychology department at Strathclyde University, in Glasgow, and the year after to move to the School of Architecture in the same university, as a member of the Building Performance Research Unit. In Glasgow, I was joined by Sandra, who had been doing psychology with me at Liverpool (she did rather more than I did because I spent so much time in the university dramatic society).

Sandra had completed an outstanding MSc in clinical psychology at Queens University in Ontario before coming to Glasgow. She went on to do a PhD at Glasgow University on schizophrenic thought disorder, while working as a clinical psychologist. Over a 10-year period, she developed her career as a clinical psychologist as well as giving birth to our three children. She is now responsible for psychological services in a health district in South London.

Our first child, Hana, was just 6 months old when we went to Japan in 1970 on a Leverhulme Fellowship. On our return we spent a year in Glasgow, where Daniel was born. Then we moved to Guildford, where I took up a lectureship in the psychology department at Surrey University in 1972. We managed a sabbatical in University of

DAVID CANTER • Department of Psychology, University of Surrey, Guildford, Surrey GU2 5XH, England.

California–Berkeley in 1980 a few months after Lily was born, which makes her virtually the same age as the *Journal of Environmental Psychology*, which Ken Craik and I got moving while I was on sabbatical.

The lack of movement in the British university system has kept me in Surrey for as long as I lived in Liverpool, being appointed as a professor of psychology and then head of the department a couple of years ago. Being less than 1-hour's journey from the center of London has undoubtedly contributed to the very many research opportunities I have had over the last 15 years, from government departments, industry, commerce, charitable bodies, and research councils.

I enjoy horse riding, and a few years ago started to learn the clarinet. A great delight last year was to have an exhibition of my collages in the University of Surrey gallery. Exposing my self to that kind of public scrutiny was a good preparation for writing the present chapter.

EARLY DAYS

Any account of a natural process must be a simplification. The written word can only sketch the variety that is integral to growth and change. This is true whether it is a garden that is being described or a human career. But for a career there is a further distortion. The sequence of activities that intertwine to make a period in a person's life when written as a history has far more shape and direction to it than it ever had at the time, when it is being experienced.

Certainly, for me, setting out to produce an intellectual history of myself, I am aware that the history I am about to describe, as confused as it may be presented, will appear far less haphazard than it felt at the time. The arbitrariness of the emerging story line may be gauged by considering the research contracts for which I am currently responsible. These range from studies of the experience of homeopathy to examination of the behavior of serial murderers and rapists and include studies of safety in the steel industry and the design of psychogeriatric facilities. All these current studies have roots in my earlier work in environmental psychology, even though those roots may be confusingly entangled in a disordered undergrowth. The present chapter, therefore, is in part at least a personal exploration through this undergrowth. I want to see if I can discover how I got to where I am. I hope that this will help me to understand more fully the nature of my current location and the possibilities it gives me for future ventures. It is to be hoped too that any such personal discoveries will also benefit you—the reader.

OFFICE SIZE

The profligate diversity of my current activities all started from an unambitious PhD on the effects of office size on worker performance. What the PhD had in common with nearly all my later work and all my current research is a determination to use field-based methodologies to develop psychological theories about environmental actions and experience. A predilection for using multivariate statistics as an aid to the development of these theories was also present from my earliest studies.

Curiously, though, I had found my way into the study of office size from an undergraduate degree in psychology at Liverpool University. The psychology department at Liverpool was steeped in the experimental tradition of British psychology, but through the guidance of its head, L. S. Hearnshaw (cf. his history of psychology 1987) and other members of staff, notably D. B. Bromley (as revealed clearly in his book on case study methodology, 1986), there was a productively eclectic debate about the nature of psychology and appropriate directions for its growth. I had wished to follow my personal interests in art to study empirical aesthetics for a doctorate, but the only opportunity available to me was to join the Pilkington Research Unit in Liverpool University's Department of Building Science. This multidisciplinary team was led by an architect, Peter Manning, who had written on architectural education and systematic design procedures. His objective was to develop appraisals of all aspects of a building's environment. He brought a geographer and a physicist on to the team as well as a psychologist, Brian Wells, who was studying the psychological implications of open plan offices (Manning, 1965). In effect, Brian Wells supervised my PhD, which was nonetheless registered in the Department of Psychology. Thus my existence with feet in more than one university discipline was presaged from my earliest days as a researcher.

The Pilkington Research Unit encouraged me to move away from a focus on aesthetics and look directly at the implications of office size for worker performance. At times I feel that my subsequent research has been a struggle to return to my original interest in how the physical phenomena that are artistic productions can have such a significant emotional impact. But the office research convinced me that field research explores a different class of phenomena to those that are studied within the confines of the experimental psychology laboratory. So, although there can be fruitful interactions between laboratory and field studies, they should not be misconstrued as studying the same thing.

My own interests have always been in what people do in their daily lives rather than in what they can do if a psychologist asks them. I think that this perhaps also has some roots in my experiences in student drama when I was an undergraduate. It became very clear to me that people have a huge flexibility for generating actions under training and instruction. The laboratory experiment really examines the range and limits of this flexibility.

The study of offices taught me this because I had set off to examine directly the impact of office size on the performance of clerical workers. The results showed that people in their own small offices were performing better than people in their own large offices but that this effect disappeared when people were tested in other people's large or small offices. This was difficult to understand as a direct effect of office size on performance. But when I stopped looking at the results as revealing the effects of the office size on the workforce and started looking at them as an indication of the type of person who would accept, or stay in, a job in an office of a particular size, they made much more sense.

Looking on the subjects of the research as actively part of their context, selecting where they would work (or at least being selected), rather than passively being influenced by the room made the results quite comprehensible (Canter, 1968). Better, more committed clerical workers were more likely to be found in the preferable smaller offices.

Yet this active, context-specific interpretation could never have been gleaned by asking people to rate slides unless they were asked to say if they would be prepared to work in such a room. That question, though, touches on the wider significance of the design. Its meaning to the respondent as part of their lives, rather than as a "stimulus."

ROOM MEANING

My experimental, mechanical origins in psychology did not fade away too rapidly. After the office research, I thought (as many researchers still do) that I could study the meanings, implied by the differences between the people found in different rooms, in a systematic, controlled way. So that when Roger Wools, an architect joined me to do a PhD under my supervision, together we continued with simple laboratory studies. We wanted to look at which aspects of buildings held particular meanings for people and used a classical, factorial experimental design in which types of furniture, ceiling angles, and window sizes were modified in drawings and photographs of models (Canter & Wools, 1970).

These studies showed very clearly that people did associate sloping ceilings and easy chairs with room friendliness. But although a few doctoral students attempted to follow this idea directly, they found that it was not really possible to establish a vocabulary of forms, whereby certain physical constituents could be linked to particular responses. One reason was a methodological one. The experimental design quickly becomes very complicated and unmanageable if a large number of aspects of form are explored.

Yet the need to explore interactions between aspects of form mean that a series of simple experiments are likely to prove inconclusive. The other reason was more closely tied to the psychological processes revealed by later studies. The meaning of the forms is probably specific to context and culture as well as relating closely to respondents' reasons for judging meaning. In other words, just as office workers' responses are a function of their position in the organization, so the ratings of pictures relate to the particular type of experimental/subject role that the rater is taking.

This continues to be a challenging area of environmental research, but it is noteworthy that most of the people who have started to explore this avenue have moved on to quite other research questions, usually more distinctly field-based. Even those who set up major laboratories to create simulations of environments to study have changed the way these simulations have been used and distanced themselves from the mechanical stimulus/response examination inherent in looking at which architectural variables "cause" which semantic differential responses.

It was about 15 years after I supervised Roger Wools's thesis that I was able to work with Linda Groat, who, having a design training initially, asked very similar questions to Roger but who was able to benefit from the work that had been going in the interim. In supervising her MSc (published in part in Groat, 1982) and PhD thesis (Groat, 1985), it was possible to work on nonexperimental approaches to architectural meaning. Indeed the work helped to establish an approach very different from the semantic differential and the factorial designed models that Roger Wools had worked with (Canter *et al.*, 1985) and gave rise to work that was published in *Progressive Architecture* (Groat & Canter, 1979), a rare acceptance by the architectural profession of findings from an uncompromising piece of environmental psychology.

The study of environmental "meaning" as it has been called has continued to be a recurrent theme in my research. As an undergraduate, I had been very interested in empirical aesthetics. At that time, in the mid-1960s there was virtually no literature on the topic, and what there was appeared to be mainly the discursive writing of retired professors, it not being a fit subject around which to build a career. But I had carried out my own undergraduate projects on Christmas card selection and the judgments of paintings. These studies, cast in a quite strong experimental tradition had been unsatisfying, but I had wanted to take these studies further; the opportunity to join the Pilkington Research Unit had therefore been seen as a way of approaching aesthetic issues through the architectural context.

But, in preparing this chapter, I have also had occasion to think about roots that might have been even deeper than an interest in the arts. It dawned on me that the search for significance beyond mere signs, attempting to reach for more symbolic aspects of the environment, may well have been laid in my study from the age of 10 or so of Talmudic interpretations of the Bible. To be introduced to the possibility, at such an early age, that words can have layers of meaning that can be peeled back, or like a Swiss Army knife, have hidden within them an unfolding range of tools and applications, did, I think, prepare a way of thinking that has remained with me ever since. Indeed the facet approach that I came to much later can be seen as a scientific procedure for generating hermeneutic frameworks.

THE ARCHITECTURAL CONTEXT

We are all conduits for the ideas and actions of others. So that one of the illusions my personal intellectual history could create is that my actions in some way can be clearly distinguished from the actions of others. This, of course, is far from the truth. Peter Manning and Brian Wells both set the agenda for my PhD work, and although I was supervising Roger Wools, he taught me much of what an architect strives for in psychological research. The research that was my main activity at the time that I was working with Roger was also shaped by the perspectives of others. This was the development of building evaluation procedures and their use in the evaluation of comprehensive schools.

My work on offices was conducted as part of the "total environment" evaluations of the Pilkington Research Unit at the University of Liverpool. That unit had pioneered the use of building appraisals as a contribution to design. Following on directly from it, Tom Markus established at Strathclyde University, in Glasgow, the Building Performance Research Unit. It was as a member of that unit that I found myself supervising Roger Wools. In 1967, it did not seem as strange as it might today for a psychologist to join a research team in a school of architecture. The quest for interdisciplinarity was still strong, and Tom Markus brought together a team with very varied backgrounds.

Tom Markus brought a rare combination of expertise to lead the Building Performance Research Unit (which published a book, BPRU, 1972). Trained as an architect, he had completed higher degrees in both architectural history and building science. We were joined throughout the 5 years of the team by Tom Maver, who had a degree in mechanical engineering with postgraduate research in service engineering, and Peter Whyman, an architect with a particular interest in modular design. Tom Markus brought the team together to develop evaluation, or performance, procedures that could be widely used. Once the team was together, we all soon agreed that we had to know what was being evaluated before evaluation procedures could be developed. Thus began the continuing debate on how to conceptualize buildings and where to find the appropriate criteria for their assessment.

I had published a couple of papers while still a student with the Pilkington Research Unit; one pointed out that building appraisal procedures could learn a lot from psychometric concerns about reliability and validity (Canter, 1966). The other was a first sketchy attempt to outline a theory of what the function of a building was (Canter, 1970). It should be remembered that in the late 1960s when these papers were written, the architectural slogans of "form follows function" in praise of the International Style was still the dominant fashion. Postmodernism and the associated discussions of architectural meaning were unheard of. So to suggest, as I did, that one of the functions of a building was to provide meaning was treated as fairly radical.

The burden of my earlier arguments had been that the central function of buildings was to provide appropriate contexts for people, an idea that has certainly not been totally accepted within architecture and one that was challenged in the late 1960s. But the work of the BPRU gave me a chance to take that idea a step further by asking what it meant to evaluate a building when its function was seen in human terms. The answer to this question required some view on the nature of people, and this was where my perspective on the active, context-specific use of the environment had its influence. Drawing on my office research, I took a broadly organizational view on building use and proposed that evaluation was an indication of the extent to which an environment enabled people to achieve their objectives.

It was a number of years later that this idea was developed into the model of purposive evaluation (Canter, 1983), partly because at this stage I was still reliant on statistical models that constrained solutions as distinct, orthogonal dimensions; yet what I was studying was a system of interrelated components. So the list of variables produced from factor analysis has really been absorbed into more complex later models. But one particular aspect of the BPRU work did encourage me to take the more active models of human experience of place even more seriously.

Peter Whyman and I had noted how many of the new school buildings had undergone changes to their fabric and use in the few years since they had been first occupied. He had called these modifications *improvizations* and had noted for a number of school buildings that the changes varied from major alterations, such as the addition of new classrooms, to minor changes, such as the redesignation of room allocation, with sealing up doors or moving walls as more intermediary levels of change. We wondered what the consequence of all this improvization was. A simple environmental effect hypothesis would suggest people were reacting to poor conditions. A more active hypothesis would suggest that they were positively making sense of their buildings.

It was possible to test these opposing hypotheses because we had building evaluations of the schools and we were able to derive scores for the amount of improvization that had been carried out. The result was very clear: a significant positive correlation between degree of satisfaction and degree of improvization. I took this to support the active hypothesis. Unfortunately, no one has been able to replicate this study. It takes a dedicated architect and a large-scale survey to make it possible, but if the result could be reproduced, it would have enormous implications both for environmental psychology and for approaches to design.

Looking back, toward the end of my time at the School of Architecture at Strathclyde University, my research activity had provided me with some basic principles that my subsequent research struggled to make sense of. These may be summarized as follows:

1. Environmental psychology had to be carried out in existing environments. Too much is left unsaid and unstudied if it is moved into the abstractions of the laboratory.

2. The environment is not just a useful base for research with complex variables. It provides a context for examination that has to be studied in its own terms.

3. The environmental context cannot be approached devoid of any world view or metatheory. A perspective that searches for the role of human agency is more likely to be fruitful.

4. But human agency itself implies that people have some understanding of their environment and its significance. Examination of people's experience of environments must therefore include exploration of what is signified by them as well as how people evaluate their contribution to their own actions.

PSYCHOLOGY FOR ARCHITECTS

By 1970, I had become convinced that psychology had much to offer architecture, especially architectural education. As part of my job in the school of architecture I had set up a variety of courses, so that students studied various aspects of psychology in every one of their 5 years. Increasingly, I had found that as the architectural psychology literature had been developing, architecture students needed some background in psychology in order to understand the advancing field of research. But none of the existing psychology texts answered their needs. I therefore set about writing *Psychology for Architects* (Canter, 1974). I mention this because, although I now regard it as being very dated in its account of psychology, it has continued to sell a few copies each year for the almost 20 years it has been in print. It therefore must continue to answer some sort of need, serving to show that psychologists can be too ambitious in what they aspire to give to designers. This book contains virtually no "environmental psychology," just an account of psychological ideas with architecturally relevant examples.

THE JAPANESE EXPERIENCE

I suppose, in all honesty, I was rather bemused toward the end of the BPRU work as to what direction was appropriate for my research, although with hindsight, the seeds of my current work can be seen in the principles and emphases of *Building Performance* (BPRU, 1972) and other publications from the late 1960s and very early 1970s. Certainly, if in those days, I'd been asked if 20 years later I'd be working with the Salvation Army on hostel design, I'd have said I hope so. But behavior in fires and emergencies would have been more difficult to foresee, and the current involvement with the police on offender profiling would have seemed beyond the scope of our theories and methods.

Two nascent themes already present in the late 1960s, but the significance of which I had not recognized then, can now be seen as directly pertinent to later directions that my work took. One of these themes was the drift from an individualistic to a social psychological context for considering environmental experience and meaning. The other was the need for methods for constructing theories and the associated analysis systems that would help in finding patterns in data harvested from "the field."

So that when the opportunity arose of spending a year in Japan, I was, now I think, already primed to be sensitive to a number of possibilities that later dominated my research. The undemanding fellowship to Japan was of particular significance in that it virtually shocked me into seeing the power of culture on all aspects of behavior, especially the way people deal with each other and make use of their surroundings. By living in such a different culture it became clear to me that the significance of a place was not some reflection of the external physical parameters that characterize that place but derives from the cultural framework within which a person experiences a place. These are reflections of the way they see the world and think about it.

ETHNOSCAPES

Like so many influences of that kind, it was a number of years before they really surfaced openly in my publications. It was certainly one of the reasons why I was so keen to include regional reviews in the *Journal of Environmental Psychology,* a development that was clearly seen to be of value because the distinguished editors of the *Handbook of Environmental Psychology* later emulated the practice.

Even more directly, the recent series of books I have established with David Stea, *Ethnoscapes: Current Challenges in the Environmental Social Sciences* (Canter *et al.,* 1988), make explicit the need for environmental research to embrace cultural diversity. This is not just a matter of including cross-cultural comparisons on the research agenda but of integrating studies in different national and subcultural contexts within the framework of research activities. One important example of this approach is allowing research questions, for example, to be defined by local, cultural imperatives, rather than by some reference to the current intellectual fashion in North America.

This series had truly transnational roots, evolving out of meetings I had with David Stea in Indonesia and Venezuela and Martin Krampen in Germany. All three of us were aware that there was a changing mood in environment and behavior studies being reflected in conferences around the world. Yet the old vocabulary of *environment, behavior, architecture, psychology,* and so on was masking these changes. We therefore deliberately set out to coin a new term that would reflect the new sensitivities of researchers in many countries and to launch a series of books that could act as a vehicle for publishing this research. We defined *Ethnoscapes* as:

> scholarly and/or scientific explorations of the relations between people, their activities and the places they create and/or inhabit; historical, psychological or sociological studies of the experience of places, attitudes toward them, or the processes of shaping, managing or designing them. (Canter *et al.,* 1988, p. xi)

To some extent, the growth of our field beyond the North Atlantic Basin has naturally lead to a greater cultural diversity in the studies being carried out, with, I think, enormous long-term benefits to the field. But I was also made aware, in Japan, that the cultural divide could be bridged in some ways by the written word. I was really surprised to find copies of my early papers already known and translated in Japan, being quoted and drawn on, even if inappropriately. An intellectual imperialism can be rife without really intending it.

The experience of living in an unfamiliar large city also alerted me to environmental psychology issues at a planning scale, which I had never really explored before. In particular I was aware that Tokyo was such a complex city to find my way around that I became interested in how that was possible. Route finding appeared an inappropriately simple-minded, and practically extremely difficult way of exploring the basis of urban navigation. I therefore started asking people to estimate "crow flight" distances (although in one study that I supervised in Japanese this got lost in the translation and the respondents ended up giving me shortest walking route distances!).

I had begun some similar, tentative explorations in Glasgow before going to Japan, but I was surprised by how accurate people could be in a city as complex as Tokyo. On my return to Glasgow, I worked with Stephen Tagg and others to explore this further (Canter & Tagg, 1975) and became aware of the power of dominant features such as the "circle line" of Tokyo's underground system and the Thames and underground train network in London. Clearly, people form some sort of composite conceptualization of a city that they use to act on. This is more pragmatic and individualistic than Lynch's "image," although it clearly relates to it. But it was not until my return to Britain and my move to Surrey University in Guildford, near London, that I was able to develop these ideas much further. I also needed the opportunity to get to know a strange building in depth in the way I had got to know Tokyo.

EMERGING CONCEPTUALIZATIONS OF PLACE

On my return from Japan, I had a unique opportunity to study the Royal Hospital for Sick Children at Yorkhill in Glasgow. I was able to spend a great deal of time over 6 months, with assistance from students and colleagues in examining the new building at the request of the *Architects' Journal*. The editor had requested the study because he felt that a children's hospital should not look like a multistorey office block and he wanted, I think, a psychologist to confirm this.

The intensive study I was able to do (Canter, 1972) was close to an ethnographic account of the building and quite unconstrained by any limitations as to how it should be done. I interviewed whomever I could, carried out behavioral mapping studies, and got people to complete repertory grids and questionnaires. Probably the most valuable aspect of the work for me was the training it gave me in what a building is and how it is shaped by many forces. I certainly learned more about the real world or architecture in that study than I had in the previous 5 years in a school of architecture. The study helped me to develop a number of ideas for which I had been reaching. Three in particular are worth noting at this stage.

First, how a building is created, the social, political, and economic processes, as well as the design intentions, is very important in influencing what results. This will seem obvious to any practicing architect, but it is a point that is still virtually ignored in the environmental psychology literature.

Second, by being able to explore in detail, with a number of people, their views and experience of the building, it became very clear what large differences there were between them in what they saw the building as being and, as a consequence, how they evaluated it. The major difference appeared to be a function of what they wanted to do in the building, what they were in the building for. This I summarized as "role differences in conceptualizations."

The third idea to emerge more strongly from the Yorkhill study had been presaged a few years earlier in a paper entitled "Should We Treat Building Users as Subjects or Objects?" (Canter, 1969) in which I argued that, to get a full picture of the psychological implications of a building, we needed to combine observation of buildings in use with explorations of the significance of those uses to the users. The intensive Yorkhill study, using a mixture of very different methods of data collection, also forced me to accept that the experience of the building was reflected in the combination of actions and conceptualizations.

By carrying out behaviorally oriented studies following Barker's ecological perspective, in combination with personal construct studies following Kelly, it was clear that both had something to offer and any future development must find ways of combining these two very different perspectives. Barker had ignored the interpretations of the people being studied, and Kelly's intense clinical perspective seemed inappropriate for the essentially public and social qualities of a building. Taken together they could leaven each other's weaknesses.

A STUDENT QUEST

Soon after the Yorkhill study I moved from Glasgow to Surrey. (In fact, I think the final draft was written in the greenhouse of my new Surrey residence because there was still no furniture in the house.) At Surrey I joined a new, rapidly developing psychology department. So there was something of a culture change as I rediscovered my psychological roots and also came to terms with the difference between the south of England and Scotland. Yet, with the foolhardyness of youth, being in my mid-20s, I quickly (possibly too quickly) established the graduate program in environmental psychology, the first entry of which was in 1972. In those days, there were almost no books in the field, and most teaching was done from photocopies of articles. Therefore one of the first major tasks was to write a text book for the course.

This text I put together with Peter Stringer. It was called *Environmental Interaction* (Canter & Stringer, 1975) in order to emphasize the significance of what people brought to their surroundings as well as what consequences the environment had for people. In order to organize the course and the book, a simple framework was needed that would capture the range of material that we wanted to cover. It seemed reasonable to choose environmental scale as the structuring component because this also provided increasingly complex phenomena to deal with, starting with heating and noise through to building use and on to the urban scale and landscape. In retrospect, this appears far more of a theoretical statement about the psychological processes involved than it did at the time.

By eschewing the psychologist's approach of dealing with supposedly "fundamental" issues such as perception and learning, before moving on to matters like social processes, we made a stand on the integrated nature of environmental experience, showing that differences of the scale of variable dealt with may change the complexity of the interactions under study but do not necessarily change fundamentally the psychological processes involved. This idea was to see light in a much stronger, more theoretically articulate form in my book published a couple of years later, *The Psychology of Place* (Canter, 1977).

The postgraduate program, especially the dominant 12-months' master's course, had a direct impact on the development of my thinking. The challenge from students to put ideas into a more coherent framework, as well as the rapid evolution of ideas brought about by postgraduate dissertations being produced by a cohort of 10 or so students every 12 months has meant that I am now constantly chasing in written work ideas that have been superceded by subsequent student activities. Some scale of this problem can be gauged by the fact that there are now over 100 MSc dissertations and more than 20 PhD dissertations that have been completed by environmental psychology graduate students at the Surrey university. At least one in four of these contains material well worthy of publication, but so far only five or six have had some component that has seen the light of day in formal publication.

This very poor rate of publication against a background of a full library of theses has the strange consequence that master's and doctoral students at the University of Surrey have access to a rapidly evolving body of knowledge. They can learn a great deal from work completed only a few months earlier, but unfortunately this creates a sort of hidden school of environmental psychology that the outside world catches curious glimpses of. It is like a medieval monastery with its illustrated scrolls available to its residents.

I have been told that other graduate schools in our field suffer in similar ways. It is partly a function of the employability of our graduates. They are so quickly taken off into practical jobs that they have no time or inclination to write up their dissertations for a journal. It also serves to show why productive new developments in our field can take so long to spread. They really have to wait their turn in the queue before time can be found to give a public account of them.

THE THEORY OF PLACE

By the mid-1970s, students on the MSc course were pressing for some coherent, theoretical account of where I stood in relation to environmental psychology. It was probably more clear to them than to me that the type of research I had done and the context within which I had done it made it rather different from the essentially U.S.-based texts they were reading.

These differences were not characterized by a total repudiation of U.S.-based empirical research, but it was possibly confusing to students that I found such a mixture of good and bad in apparently different traditions in U.S. research. For example, with hindsight, I wonder what they made of my strong criticisms of the behavioral tradition in U.S. research and its associated S-R models of environmental impact, yet my obvious interest in the general value of Barker's ecological approach (Barker, 1965) that so self-consciously focuses on behavior. They were possibly confused further by my arguments that Kelly's personal construct theory (Kelly, 1955), with the importance given to individual interpretations of experience, was not only of great potential significance to environmental psychology but actually complemented Barker's approach.

The pressure from students for me to organize my ideas in a way they could grasp, together with the Japanese experience, the Yorkhill study, and the distance estimation studies became the basis for an attempt at an outline of an environmental psychology theory, which became my book *The Psychology of Place* (Canter, 1977).

However, my predilection for field research and the growing dawning of the need for a systemic rather than mechanical approach to the environment was tempered by my experience with the BPRU and the Strathclyde School of Architecture. The book therefore still looked at how the complex process that shapes our surroundings could be influenced by a psychological perspective. Further, the need to deal with different environmental scales, made clear to me in producing *Environmental Interaction*, was a further specification for designing the book.

The need to take human objectives into account was implicit in much of the book, stemming from my office studies and the BPRU work, but because the book was written very much with students, rather than researchers in mind (remembering the apparent value of *Psychology for Architects*), it became more of a descriptive text than an articulated theory. Nonetheless, looking back on it, *The Psychology of Place* does sketch out the beginnings of a model of environmental experience with which I am still reasonably comfortable.

The writing of that book was the most personally valuable course of study I have ever undertaken. Indeed, in planning a second edition of it, I realized how much the personal development that I experienced when writing the book is reflected in the unfolding story line of the chapters. It is the final chapter that reveals the nub of the book because it was only really at that point in writing it that I began to become clear in my own mind what the book was aiming at, although this is not really the best place to put the most significant part of any book.

In writing the book, it became clear to me there were two fundamental difficulties with which environmental psychology has to struggle. One is the empirical fact that the physical environment can only be shown to have any strong impact at the margins of physiological tolerance. Any other significance of variations in the environment can be readily swamped by social processes and motivation. Yet a great deal of effort and resource goes into shaping our surroundings. One task for environmental psychology is to resolve this paradox of why resources are spent on something that does not seem to produce direct measurable effects on behavior or performance.

The second difficulty stems from the first. How can psychological involvement contribute to the improvement of our surroundings? If social processes and personal expectations are so much more important than any direct impact of the surroundings, how can we make recommendations about the form, shape, or characteristics that those surroundings can take? Talking in general terms about design flexibility, individual variation and social constraints do not really give an architect anything very specific, or concrete, to go on.

In considering these issues, they seemed to me to be so fundamentally difficult to resolve that the questions themselves must have some basic illogicality in them. It was out of these reflections that I began to think that taking the environment as an entity distinct from behavior was the flaw. A unit of focus for research was needed that adjusted the emphasis. The idea of a place as that unit seemed worth exploring. This "place" became a system that integrated physical and psychological aspects of experience. Research therefore needed to discover the structure of places. Contribution to design became participation in the shaping of these structured systems.

When *The Psychology of Place* was published, there were very many loose ends to the model sketched there and some fairly fundamental ambiguities in what was being proposed, but it took a variety of further studies to identify these clearly and begin to tidy them up. In doing so, certain aspects of the model that were not emphasized in the book turned out to be very fruitful and have taken on much more significance in later writing, especially role differences and associated rules of environmental use, but I think it took a very different research domain to draw my attention to the power of these particular concepts.

THE JOURNAL OF ENVIRONMENTAL PSYCHOLOGY

Writing *The Psychology of Place* and the associated reading and discussion with students had alerted me to the fact that there was a strange hiatus in publications in our field. The only major journal, *Environment and Behavior,* deliberately had the important objectives of communicating across disciplines and making direct contact with policy issues. Furthermore, because so many researchers carrying out applied studies, in effect, published mostly for the nonspecialist who might act on their results, there were very few opportunities for researchers to present to other researchers intensive, academic accounts of their work.

I believe it is essential that we debate with each other at the most demanding intellectual levels the theories, methods, and results out of which our discipline is evolving. After all, it is such internal debate that gives science its strength. But by the late 1970s, although there was a reasonably sized, scholarly community in environmental psychology, the pressures to communicate with those who fund our activities tended to mask the equally important communication among ourselves.

I therefore proposed to Academic Press that we launch *The Journal of Environmental Psychology.* A sabbatical in 1980, at UC–Berkeley with Ken Craik enabled us to launch the journal by 1981. In launching it, though, we were determined that it should not ossify the field but contribute to its evolution. We therefore have been eclectic in what we take environmental psychology to be and have deliberately cherished many forms of communication besides the report of empirical studies. As the journal enters its tenth year, it is curious to ponder why we did not start it 20 years ago.

FIRE RESEARCH

My directly applicable research activities were also given a fillip in Japan when I came across a small study carried out by Masao Inui and his colleagues, which as far as I know was never published. They had interviewed people who had been in buildings on fire. I was struck by the possibility that these Japanese building science researchers had discovered of getting people to answer questions about a threatening and traumatic situation. As an undergraduate, I had been introduced to the work of Quarantelli (1957) on disasters and learned from his studies that patterns could be found to seemingly bizarre and random behavior, but I had not appreciated the potential significance of these studies for building design.

In the context of the Japanese Building Research Institute, I began to see that the fire regulations governing the design of buildings were based upon assumptions of what people would do in a fire. Yet these assumptions were all derived from major enquiries of very unusual incidents. Very little systematic research had been done. On my return from Japan, I approached the British Fire Research Station and discovered that they, themselves, were developing an interest in human behavior in fires and so started to support our own endeavors.

This research on fires has provided me with one of the strongest themes to my work over the last 10 years. Yet often when I am reviewing my research, I forget, initially, to mention it. I think that this is because it is unlike my other research activities in very many ways. It is field research in the most extreme form, in that the only really effective way to carry it out is to follow up incidents that have already happened.

What emerged as quite remarkable from studies of 20 or so incidents, including some very large-scale ones that my colleagues John Breaux and Jonathan Sime and I examined, was the consistency in the overall pattern of actions that occur in fatal building fires (Canter et al., 1980). In order to explain these consistencies, it was necessary to ask what are mechanisms that maintain human actions in these very unusual circumstances? The answer that I propose draws heavily on the idea of place rules and environmental roles (Canter, 1986).

The work also revealed that the early stages in any emergency are potentially very confused. The time it takes to make sense of the rapidly changing events can be what turns an emergency into a disaster. The importance of these findings was recognized by the Fire Research Station, especially because they acknowledged the widely experienced problem that alarm bells are not, usually, taken seriously. A series of studies were therefore commissioned on what we called Informative Fire Warning systems (Canter et al., 1987). Out of this work, prototype computer-based warning systems have been developed and installed, which could eventually have a large impact on approaches to fire safety in buildings.

It is interesting that this work, with its roots in a fixed engineering view of provision for escape, should have matured into yet another context in which

the interpretations that people make of their surroundings and the opportunities or threats they pose are paramount. The design developments therefore directly address ways of facilitating effective understanding and consequently more effective plans of action in threatening circumstances. This
approach to design for active understanding and control doubtless has applications to many other aspects of the environment.

BUILDING EVALUATIONS

The studies of human behavior in fires was one strand of the contract
research that I was carrying out during the mid-1970s to the mid-1980s. In
parallel, my earlier involvement in building evaluations was continuing
through a series of studies of housing satisfaction and evaluations of acute
wards in hospitals and prison buildings (Canter, 1986; Canter & Rees, 1982;
Kenny & Canter, 1981).

These were all studies that were defined in terms of the methodology most
appropriate for them. I found this increasingly unsatisfying for three reasons.
One, it was difficult to see any accumulation of approach or knowledge. Each
study seemed to exist on its own, in a sort of theoretical limbo. Second, the
questionnaire methodology sometimes seemed to so structure people's responses that many of the insights apparent in the pilot work were lost by the
time that the main study was completed. Third, the implications for action
from the evaluation studies were not always apparent.

These three problems led me to use the evaluation studies, increasingly, as a
vehicle for developing new methodologies and a general theory of evaluation.
The multiple sorting task (Canter et al., 1985) and the purposive evaluation
model (Canter, 1983) were the result of that. Curiously, these rather academic
developments opened the way to a much more direct, yet rather distinct, mode
of involvement in the design process. These developments required a much
more flexible methodology, more subtle in how it could be used to uncover
interacting systems. Facet theory increasingly provided the vehicle for this.

FACET THEORY

One of the other coincidences about my stay in Tokyo was that during my
time there Louis Guttman visited for a month. I had been interested in the
unusualness of the approach to attitude scaling that is named after Guttman
and wished to explore possible developments of it with him. To my amaze-
ment, I discovered that the principles inherent in Guttman scaling had evolved
into a major new approach to doing scientific research.

When I met Louis Guttman in Tokyo, he had probably not met anyone for
a few weeks who spoke fluent English and was prepared to listen at length to
his thoughts. I was therefore given the privilege of a lengthy disquisition on his
theory about how science should be carried out, which he called facet theory. It
took me a number of years to digest and understand the implications of what I

was told that morning (Canter, 1985). Indeed, looking through my diary and notes for my year in Japan, I can find no reference to that meeting, although I remember it clearly, and Louis Guttman also mentioned it when I met him again a few years later.

What attracted me to his approach was that it did away with arbitrary levels of acceptability for "findings" and put the creation of a lucid account of the system being studied at the forefront of scientific activity. My methodological interests and the search for some sort of theoretical perspective that would capture the essence of an ongoing system had pushed me further and further away from the experimental models in which I had been schooled, but I did not feel comfortable with a retreat into a type of journalistic, purely qualitative account rendering. As I worked within the facet framework, it became clearer to me that it would provide a sound methodological framework for the type of theoretical accounts I was trying to give.

Facet Theory enables me to generate models that describe initially complex phenomena in quite simple, clearly structured ways. Probably the two most fruitful uses this has been put to so far are first in the development of the purposive model of evaluation (Canter, 1983) and second in the analysis of multiple sorting procedures (Canter et al., 1985). In both these cases, a system of interrelationships is revealed upon which future elaboration is possible without having to start from scratch.

Purposive Evaluation

One particular contribution of the facet approach was to enable us to start building a model of environmental evaluation that would evolve from one study to the next. The first large data set we had to work with was drawn from an evaluation of hospital wards (Kenny & Canter, 1981). Initial factor analysis gave us a very patchy picture of the reactions to these wards, but when we carried out nonmetric multidimensional scaling, with a faceted framework for interpretation, it became clear that the provision of care at the bedside was the metaphorical as well as the literal focus of ward evaluation. Furthermore, a clear level of interaction facet, showing the different scales of the place, from the bedside to the whole ward, was also found in the results.

This provided a testable system of relationships that was consistent with studies of attitudes in other very diverse fields. We were therefore encouraged to look for evidence for this framework in other data. The housing satisfaction data we had collected yielded a similar structure (Canter & Rees, 1982), and Donald (1985) found evidence for the same model in office evaluation. However, because each of these studies used different questionnaires, they were able to identify quite different foci for the places being studied. Such foci were the central purposes of those places as conceptualized by the respondents.

Place Goals

Other studies conducted since, as part of graduate dissertations, have found the model fruitful when applied to places as varied as neighborhoods, city parks, and training centers. This range of applications has enabled us to consider whether there are places in which there is a mixture of purposes that may be in conflict. Such an idea had already been presaged in the work Sandra Canter, a clinical psychologist, and I had done on therapeutic environments. This was summarized in the book we edited, *Designing for Therapeutic Environments* (Canter & Canter, 1979). In the introduction to that book, we outlined the various goals for therapeutic environments, ranging from custodial to personal enhancement.

More recent student research has shown that different groups within a hospital will have different goals and, as a consequence, will differ in the designs that they consider appropriate. Some of these goals may also be in conflict. Our research is therefore beginning to use the purposive model of place as a way of establishing the emphases in place goals and how conflicts between them may be resolved by approaches to management and design.

A DEVELOPING THEORY OF ENVIRONMENTAL (SOCIAL) PSYCHOLOGY

The use of the facet approach, to help develop the model of place, has also served to show that some of the directions in which such unfolding was productive related to social and conceptual processes, rather than perceptual or formal architectural ones. This has helped to move beyond some of the weaknesses of the earlier frameworks.

Indeed, once *The Psychology of Place* had been published, it became clear in discussions with students that there was a productive, but fundamental, ambiguity in the model sketched out in the book. In striving to develop a research focus that bridged the environment/behavior divide, I had left it unclear as to where the "places" being studied were. It was argued that they were not simply physical locations but shaped by the actions and experiences of people, but it was also argued that they were not merely mental representations of environments. They clearly have physical components that are integral constituents. So, if they are not just a part of an individual's psyche and they are not simply a physical location, the question emerges as to what they actually are.

To provide any confident answer to this would be to imply that 2,000 years of philosophical debate had been resolved, but some interesting possibilities can be gleaned from taking a social psychological perspective (or even a sociological one, depending where you draw the boundaries between the disciplines) on our experience of our surroundings. Within this framework, especially as elaborated by Moscovici (Farr & Moscovici, 1984), it is recognized that many phenomena experienced as having an independent existence, whether they are for example, "health," "psychoanalysis," or "unemployment," all are socially constructed so that their existence is more than the agglomeration of attitudes or perceptions held by a number of separate individuals.

My development of this view has been spurred on by the shift in the audiences that have asked me to write for them or make presentations to them.

In the 1970s and early 1980s I would guess that the majority of invitations came from architectural sources, but this has given way to far more invitations from psychologists, especially social psychologists. Of course, this shift could be entirely due to what I might be able to comment on with any skill, but I think it is more a reflection of changes in the disciplines themselves. As architects have moved away from a concern with their users to a concern with form and image, so social psychology has become more environmental.

I became most strongly aware of this when Michael Argyle asked me to talk at a seminar on "situations," which eventually emerged as a book edited by Furnham (1986). Here, at last (I thought) were social psychologists examining the context in which behavior occurred. Unfortunately, I soon found that their experimental traditions soon destroyed this interesting exploration, treating "situations" as independent variables to be manipulated and thereby losing the significance of the context to which Barker had drawn attention 30 years earlier.

From this experience, I began to look at how the notion of place could be linked to the situational debate in psychology. My paper, "Putting Situations in Their Place" (Canter, 1986) was a result of this exploration. The conclusion I came to was that the search for situations and the associated attempt to classify them and systematize their impact was really at too fine a level of detail to reveal any general structures. The concept of place, which could house a number of characteristic situations, was more likely to prove fruitful. Part of the reason for this view was that a variety of studies of place use had produced consistent, eminently interpretable multivariate structures. In studies of domestic contexts at least, the activities in Glasgow, Tokyo, and Lagos appeared to have a similar form to them, although cultural differences were also apparent, especially among tribal groups in Nigeria (Omotayo, 1988).

As I presented these results at a number of conferences, where their self-evident nature was challenged by the difficulty of explaining them to an audience that had not been through the history of my thought processes, I was increasingly concerned to try and understand what it was that these consistencies were consistencies of. We had found that certain clusters of activities were found in certain rooms. Bedrooms, dining rooms, kitchens, and so on can be characterized by what goes on within them, even though the words used to describe these rooms in different languages do not necessarily encapsulate their function as it does in English.

That people should sleep in bedrooms, eat in the room with a dining table in it, should not be too surprising. But that there are a whole range of other activities and expectations that also coalesce around these actions is a clear example of the existence of "place" systems. The questions that reveal these most strongly, though, deal with who is responsible for the furniture or activities in a room and what is allowed or not allowed in a room. In other words, the rules that structure that place.

This awareness that the interpretable structures we were finding were reflections of place rules took much longer to emerge than might be apparent from a reading of *The Psychology of Place*, written 10 years before "putting situations in their place." What might be called the anthropological shift took some accepting.

From the writing of "putting situations in their place," my attention had been drawn to the actions that are central to the definition of places, but in that paper I was uncomfortable with the apparently static qualities that this model had. Places appeared as givens, yet there are many reasons why they should not be expected to be static. Perhaps the most fundamental is the dynamic conflict between the active nature of human agency in making sense of the environment and the implied coercive qualities of places that structure human experience. Furthermore, our daily experience shows change and modification as characteristic of place experience, just as "improvization" was so prevalent in the Scottish comprehensive schools. I was therefore puzzled by the need to find a balance between the consistency of place use and experience, necessary for a social sharing, and the dynamic qualities that are part of life as it is lived.

The opportunity to chase these ideas further came from being asked to give a keynote address at the Berlin IAPS conference (Canter, 1985). For that presentation, I explored the possibility that it is the interplay between the static quality of places and the dynamic, purposive nature of human action that provides the process out of which both places and actions evolve and change. I suppose this is a model of person/environment interaction shifted to a higher level of complexity. But in moving to this level I am finding that there is much more real possibility of the application of environmental psychology ideas without diluting their subtlety.

THE FEASIBILITY OF APPLICATION

The fire research was the first set of studies in which I have been involved that led clearly and directly into some aspect of policy formulation. It had the consequence of my being invited to join two government-established enquiries into major fires, one for the Bradford City Football Ground fire, the other set up to examine the Kings Cross Station Underground fire. These experiences have caused me to examine closely what it is that we have to contribute. Increasingly, I am coming to the conclusion that it is not some specific facts or findings but ways of thinking about a problem. This parallels closely the oft-quoted remark by Kurt Lewin that "there is nothing so applicable as a good theory." But there is nothing so difficult to develop and then communicate as "a good theory."

This attempt to communicate a way of thinking about an environmental problem domain has been followed through in my most recent book, written as a result of the work on the Football Ground fire, *Football in Its Place* (Canter *et al.*, 1989). The book quite deliberately is used as a vehicle to develop a popular account of the relevance of environmental psychology and had as its subtitle, *An Environmental Psychology of Football Grounds*. As chance would have it, the book was planned to be published in the late spring of 1989, so it was published shortly after the Hillsborough football ground disaster in which 95 people were killed.

Embracing the "Media"

The Hillsborough tragedy brought home to me how inevitable is contact with journalism and the "mass media" for an applied field like ours, if we really do have anything to contribute. For, although over the last few years my research activities have increasingly become of interest to television, radio, and the newspapers, it has been easy, from an academic position within a university, to dismiss all this interest as trivial or to see my involvement as merely significant as a form of advertising or self-enhancement.

Yet, when our work may contribute toward the saving of lives, we have to consider seriously how our findings can be communicated to those many important audiences who do not read academic journals or attend professional conferences. We should weigh carefully the implications of media coverage. After all, our research activities are unashamedly aimed at changing environmentally relevant actions and decisions.

The applied orientation of person/environment studies has never been in doubt. As Robert Sommer (1988), for instance, has been at pains to point out, the people outside of the academic community whom we wish not only to communicate with but also to influence do not read articles in the *Journal of Environmental Psychology* or *Environment and Behavior*. They read newspapers and watch television. In Great Britain, they also listen to national radio.

The problem this raises is that once we do have something to say that is of general public interest, there is a temptation to shape research in relation to the questions journalists ask. This is wrong. The role of the research community is to formulate ways of thinking about the world that are shaped by empirical scientific processes, not by populist or political ends. I have found the need to constantly examine what the objectives are for my research in the same way that my research has led me to try and unravel the role of the objectives of others. This search for objectives is the central scientific quest. This is not an easy point to make to journalists who want immediate discoveries to quote for tomorrow's publication deadlines.

Beyond Applicability

So, although my research since its earliest days in the study of school buildings and offices had applicability as a major objective, the building satisfaction surveys did not, of themselves, appear to have any impact or even clear consequences for design decision making. Yet the ways of thinking about buildings that emerged from those studies could have radical consequences for architecture and the design process. This consequence stems from two related perspectives. One is that the form of any design is evaluated in terms of its potential contribution to what a person is trying to achieve in any given context. The second is that the social/organizational rules that structure place use have to be incorporated into design considerations.

The consequence of this approach has been to reconsider design participation. Drawing heavily on the techniques developed by Arie Peled (Peled & Ayalon, 1988), we have found it possible to get people to develop design proposals that incorporate views of how the building is to be used. From this, principles can be drawn out that give direct, clear guidelines to the design team. The attractive quality of this is that it is open to use with groups that are not usually considered amenable to such investigations. Currently, for instance, we are working with the Salvation Army on the design of facilities for the homeless in London using purpose-oriented design participation exercises.

BROADENING HORIZONS

In writing a personal intellectual history, it becomes apparent to me that recent and current research is too close to see in perspective. Its roots can be traced with some confidence, but in all honesty, the long-term directions in which it is leading are far from clear. Looking back, I did not think at the time and could not have guessed that my PhD research on offices would have taken me so far away from examining the effects of the environment on behavior. At the time of the Yorkhill Hospital study, I did not think that it would have led me to put such store by role differences. Nor was I aware for at least another 10 years that in-depth evaluation of a building in use could provide the basis for a participative design procedure.

The studies of behavior in fires were aimed at the building regulations, so I had not appreciated how they would lead me into considerations of the management of safety in industry (Powell & Canter, 1985). Although that organizational perspective on emergencies and accidents is completely consonant with the social perspective on building design, the emphasis that the safety research has given with regard to place rules was especially unexpected.

So, given all the vagaries of previous research, in which personal discoveries have overtaken initial hypotheses, the directions in which current activities will lead are difficult to predict. Nonetheless, they all reflect a drift even further away from the experimental, perceptual tradition in which I was schooled to a much more transactional, social psychological framework. Of particular delight is the discovery that the problems of environmental research are so difficult that if some handle can be got on them, then this is likely to be of value in other field-based studies as well.

As a direct result of the perspectives and methodologies I have mentioned, I have become involved in looking at criminal behavior, with a direct contribution to ongoing police investigations, in some cases even making a contribution to the apprehension of a person who has murdered a number of strangers (Canter, 1989). Thinking about how a criminal may structure his or her objectives, in relation to the understanding he or she has of the environment in which he or she operates, turns out to be a fruitful basis for the application of the facet approach.

Even less obviously related are the studies I have been conducting on the experience of alternative medicine, most notably homoeopathy (Canter, 1987). Yet here again it is the understanding and direct experience of the user that is the focus, rather than the medical impact of any particular drug. Not unlike an effective environment, it is also emerging that alternative medicine seems to be attractive because of the control over their illness it gives patients. In other words, how it helps them to be more successful in achieving their daily objectives. It may seem a long way from studies of the effect of office size on worker performance to the experience of homoeopathic medicine, but the strands tying them together are unbroken. The search for active, human agency interacting with the world of physical experiences is the problem of why art exists that I was curious about as an undergraduate. Seeing these 20 years of research in this light makes me feel that, at last, I am ready to begin.

REFERENCES

Barker, R. G. (1965). Explorations in ecological psychology. *American Psychologist, 20*, 1–14.

BPRU. (1972). *Building performance*. London: Applied Science Publishers.

Bromley, D. B. (1986). *Case study method in psychology and related disciplines*. Chichester, England: Wiley.

Canter, D. (1966). On appraising building appraisals. *Architects' Journal*, December 21, 881–888.

Canter, D. (1968). Office size: An example of psychological research in architecture. *Architects' Journal*, April 24, 881–888.

Canter, D. (1969). Should we treat building users as subjects or objects? In D. Canter (Ed.), *Architectural psychology*, London: RIBA Publications. (pp. 11–17).

Canter, D. (1970). Need for a theory of function in architecture. *Architects' Journal*, February 4, 299–302.

Canter, D. (1972). A psychological analysis of The Royal Hospital for Sick Children: Yorkhill, Glasgow. *Architects' Journal*, September 6, 525–564.

Canter, D. (1974). *Psychology for architects*. London: Applied Science Publishers.

Canter, D. (1977). *The psychology of place*. London: Architectural Press.

Canter, D. (1983). The purposive evaluation of places: A facet approach. *Environment and Behaviour, 15*(6), 659–698.

Canter, D. (1985). (Ed.). *Facet theory*. New York: Springer-Verlag.

Canter, D. (1986). Putting situations in their place. In A. Furnham (Ed.), *Social behaviour in context* (pp. 208–239). Boston: Allyn & Bacon.

Canter, D. (1987). Research agenda for therapy studies that consider the whole patient. *Complementary Medicine Research, 2*, 101–113.

Canter, D. (1988). Action and place: An existential dialectic. In D. Canter, M. Krampen, & D. Stea (Eds.), *Environmental perspectives* (pp. 1–17). Aldershot, England: Avebury.

Canter, D. (1989). Offender profiles. *The Psychologist, 21*(1), 12–16.

Canter, D., & Canter S. (1979). (Eds.). *Designing for therapeutic environments* Chichester, England: Wiley.

Canter, D., & Rees, K. (1982). A multivariate model of housing satisfaction. *International Review of Applied Psychology, 31*, 185–208.

Canter, D., & Stringer, P. (1975). *Environmental interaction* New York: International Universities Press.

Canter, D., & Tagg, S. (1975). Distance estimation in cities. *Environment and Behaviour, 7*(1), 59–80.

Canter, D., & Wools, R. (1970). A technique for the subjective appraisal of buildings. *Building Science, 5,* 187–198.

Canter, D., Breaux, J., & Sime, J. (1980). Domestic, multiple occupancy and hospital fires. In D. Canter (Ed.), *Fires and human behaviour* (pp. 117–136). Chichester: England: Wiley.

Canter, D., Brown, J., & Groat, L. (1985). A multiple sorting procedure for studying conceptual systems. In M. Brenner, J. Brown, & D. Canter (Eds.), *The research interview* (pp. 79–114) London: Academic Press.

Canter, D., Powell, J., & Booker, K. (1987). *Psychological aspects of informative fire warning systems.* Borehamwood, England: Building Research Establishment.

Canter, D., Krampen, M., & Stea, D. (Eds.). (1988). *Environmental perspectives.* Aldershot, England: Avebury.

Canter, D., Comber, M., & Uzzell, D. (1989). *Football in its place: An environmental psychology of football grounds.* London: Routledge.

Donald, I. (1985). The cylindrex of place evaluation. In D. Canter (Ed.), *Facet theory* (pp. 173–201). New York: Springer-Verlag.

Farr, R. M., and Moscovici, S. (Eds.). (1984). *Social representations.* Cambridge: Cambridge University Press.

Furnham, A. (Ed.). (1986). *Social behavior in context.* Boston: Allyn & Baker.

Groat, L. (1982). Meaning in post-modern architecture: An examination using the multiple sorting task. *Journal of Environmental Psychology, 2*(1), 3–23.

Groat, L. (1985). *Psychological aspects of contextual compatibility in architecture: A study of environmental meaning.* Unpublished doctoral dissertation, University of Surrey, England.

Groat, L., & Canter, D. (1979). Does post-modernism communicate? *Progressive Architecture, 12,* 84–87.

Hearnshaw, L. S. (1987). *The shaping of modern psychology.* London: Routledge.

Kelly, G. A. (1955). *The psychology of personal constructs.* New York: Norton.

Kenny, C., & Canter, D. (1981). A facet structure for nurses' evaluations of wards designs. *Journal of Occupational Psychology, 54,* 93–108.

Manning, P. (Ed.). (1965). *Office design: A study of environment.* Liverpool, England: Department of Building Science.

Omotayo, F. B. (1988). *A cross-cultural comparison of space use in the Hausa, Ibo and Yoruba families of Nigeria.* Unpublished doctoral dissertation, University of Surrey, England.

Peled, A., & Ayalon, O. (1988). The role of the spatial organisation in family therapy: Case study. *Journal of Environmental Psychology, 8*(2), 87–107.

Powell, J., & Canter, D. (1985). Quantifying the human contribution to losses in the chemical industry. *Journal of Environmental Psychology, 5,* 37–53.

Quarantelli, E. L. (1957). The behavior of panic participants. *Sociology and Social Research, 41,* 187–194.

Sommer, R. (1988). A better world not utopia. In D. Canter, M. Krampen, & D. Stea (Eds.), *New directions in environmental participation* (pp. 144–152). Aldershot, England: Avebury.

13

An Environmental Psychologist Ages

M. POWELL LAWTON

I WAS BORN IN ATLANTA IN 1923 and raised as a partial Southerner, despite having gone to public school in Aliquippa, Pennsylvania, where my father worked in the steel industry as an engineer. Although my parents were staunch "Rebels," that characteristic was expressed in other ways most unusual for their milieu. For example, my mother would typically insist on sitting in the back of buses long before the Civil Rights movement and did her best to persuade blacks not to create a new color line behind her. At age 87, she decided it would be nice to see us more often, and she moved from Atlanta to an apartment near us, doing all her own packing.

I went to Haverford College before and after World War II, which I spent as a conscientious objector working variously in a mental hospital, as a guinea pig in an infectious hepatitis experiment, and as a cowboy escorting animals to Europe right after the war. Psychology came after returning to college, happily requiring me to attend Bryn Mawr College because at the time Haverford had a minimal department.

After serving as a VA trainee in New York while attending Teachers College, Columbia, I went to the Providence VA Hospital in 1952 and then to Norristown State Hospital for a total of about 10 years as a clinical psychologist.

As noted in my chapter, my career change to geropsychology came in 1963, and I've been at the Philadelphia Geriatric Center ever since. Any latent plans for retirement were shattered by the receipt of a MERIT grant award from the National Institute on Aging when I was age 64. This award can be renewed for up to 10 years.

Division 20 (Adult Development and Aging) of the American Psychological Association, the Gerontology Society of America, and EDRA have provided me with a superb convoy of stimulating scientists and warm, supportive friends. I have done stints as president of Division 20 and president of the Gerontological Society and have been the fortunate recipient of the Distinguished Contribution Award (Division 20), the Kleemeier Award (Gerontological Society), the Career Award (EDRA), and the Ollie Randall

M. POWELL LAWTON • Philadelphia Geriatric Center, 5301 Old York Road, Philadelphia, Pennsylvania 19141.

Award (Northeastern Gerontological Society). I was founding editor of *Psychology and Aging*, the APA journal.

My wife Fay is a remedial reading specialist at Greene Street Friends School and Bryn Mawr College's Child Study Institute. She and I both might rather have been musicians, writers, or something in that category. Our children have obliged us by living out our fantasies. Tom is a professional jazz pianist, Jenny an art photographer (panoramic photography), and Pamela a painter. Grandparenthood is great, too, thanks to Isabel and Leo.

INTRODUCTION

Writing an intellectual autobiography tempts one to smooth the edges, fit in pieces that began disparately, and tailor a retrospective philosophy that encompasses all. The present chapter will try to avoid such a leveling process. The best guarantee of preserving the complexity of one's field and assuring that wicked problems remain wicked is to utilize the dialectical perspective, which among other attributes, construes all scholarship as a continuous process of problem definition and redefinition, with apparent solutions being either temporary or illusory. At the outset then, a particular debt is due the genius of the late life-span psychologist–theoretician Klaus Riegel (1977) and the senior editor of this series, who brought and elaborated the dialectic perspective into person–environment relations (Altman & Gauvain, 1981; Altman & Rogoff, 1987).

The dialectic perspective will be used (discursively, as befits the tone of this volume) to examine dilemmas that are very general but that do not necessarily always have a confluence in the work of any one career. The dilemma of knowledge in the service of people versus knowledge as a scholarly goal in its own right, or applied versus basic science, was my first dilemma in a chronological sense and perhaps in overall importance. A second source of tension in the practice of research is the degree to which theory directs scientific work versus the degree to which empirical approaches predominate. Third, environmental psychology's intrinsic dilemma is to define what is person and what is environment, or are they? These three dilemmas constitute parallel threads that bind this writer's intellectual career, but to some extent, the order in which they have been named here is both their chronological order and their order of increasing differentiation. In shorthand form, they will be characterized as the basic versus applied dilemma; the theoretical versus empirical dilemma; and the person versus environment dilemma.

BASIC VERSUS APPLIED: LOVE OF HUMANITY
AND LOVE OF KNOWLEDGE

Haverford College was the nurturing environment for many young men who would spend lifetimes in the service of society. My own interest in social causes was stimulated by the strong Quaker milieu at Haverford, and I have continued to be an active Quaker. Haverford has also been one of the small colleges with highest academic standards. Thus as an undergraduate, the pull between the ideals of humanitarian service and the scholarly career were very evident. An early rush of sentiment occasioned abandoning a major in chemistry for a major in psychology—certainly a good decision in retrospect but one made at the time under some internal compulsion to do good and therefore suspect. That motive is still alive and still suspect.

The redirection of career goals found a natural home in clinical psychology, which in the immediate postwar years was an extraordinarily flourishing, intellectually euphoric activity. It is difficult to describe adequately the optimism, the conviction that the answers were at hand, and the sense of social mission among the early postwar clinicians.

Fortunately what had to precede clinical training was a strenuous undergraduate program whose results affirmed the principles of primacy in learning and of early experience in psychological development for long-term outcome. Although this first exposure to psychology came during my early 20s, the nervous tissue or brain areas specific to psychology must have a very late period of maximum receptivity to external input because the intellectual background of my first two courses in psychology has remained to this day a major component of my approach.

Introductory psychology (most of the psychology taught at that time was at Bryn Mawr College rather than Haverford) was taught by Donald MacKinnon, one of the illustrious group of students of Henry Murray at Harvard. MacKinnon managed to get his undergraduates to read Murray's *Explorations in Personality* (1938) and Lewin's *Dynamic Theory of Personality* (1935) and at the same time to respect Freudian psychology. By contrast, the central course for the psychology major was Harry Helson's experimental psychology. Helson had played a major role in introducing Gestalt psychology to the United States before the stream of population displacements brought Köhler and Koffka themselves to our country (Helson, 1925). My time with Helson came during the phase of his early development of adaptation level theory (Helson, 1964). As a student and also a subject in some of his experiments on brightness matching (I once had the misfortune of producing an outlier response for which I was chastised as an ungrateful apprentice) the real impact of adaptation level (AL) escaped me. Helson was a classical psychophysicist and at the time had little interest in the social and subjective aspects of psychology. His major theoretical contribution was in specifying the way sensory stimulation becomes perceived psychologically. His own research demonstrated an extraordinary variety of ways in which the three components of the stimulus situation—the focal stimulus, the contemporary context of the stimulus, and the anchoring framework of earlier experiences with similar stimuli—determined the transformation of the physical energy of the stimulus into the psychological perception. For example, the judged brightness of a stimulus patch varied depending, of course, on the physical light properties of the patch but also on the lighting of the ground, the presence of other stimuli in the visual field, and the recent history of exposure to other patches and the order in which a series of patches of differing brightness had been introduced.

Helson regretted the soft direction in which my interest led. On leaving Haverford, it was the field theory, personology, and psychodynamic conceptions so well taught by MacKinnon that formed the bridge to graduate study at Teachers College, Columbia, and a clinical internship in the early days of the Veterans Administration clinical psychology program. Adaptation level theory was easy to leave behind. Learning how to perform psychological assessment and psychotherapy was totally consistent with the need to use knowledge for humanitarian purposes. The philosophical approach of Carl Rogers was represented at Teachers College by Nicholas Hobbs. "Nondirective" or "client-centered" therapy (Rogers, 1942, 1951) was extraordinarily consistent with the Quaker philosophy in its respect for the person and his or her potential for growth. Research was valued in this system, but, not surprisingly, a distinctly negative value judgment was attached to using the statistical norm as a basis for assessment, treatment planning, or judging therapeutic success. Indeed, "ipsative measurement" (that is, quantification of attributes in terms of their relative salience within an individual) was the research methodology of choice in the client-centered approach of the day. Stephenson's (1953) Q-methodology of factor analysis was borrowed for purposes such as studying an individual's ranking of life goals or self-concept before and after counseling. Client-centered research was also highly empirical. The system as a whole was a loose philosophy more than a theory. Theory in the traditional sense was viewed as a possible barrier to the growth of self-determination. Client-centered research thus tended to seek through the exhaustive study of recorded therapy sessions details of therapist–client interchange that might be associated with client outcomes such as expressions of self-determination, self-regard, and self-discovery. With the self being seen as the core of both problems and growth, the nonself was part of the picture only in phenomenological terms. This same situation of obliviousness to the environment characterized many approaches to clinical treatment of the time. A famous analyst (the source has slipped from my memory at this point) once noted that good psychotherapy could take place in a pigpen.

Thus within late-1940s clinical psychology, the application of empirically directed research based on the individual as a unit was the usual state of affairs. Projective techniques were the assessment tools of choice, again with the uniqueness of the individual as the focus. In projective tests, the stimulus configuration was made as ambiguous as possible in order to maximize the amount of idiosyncratic material elicited. I remember a fellow student's discovery of a new graded ambiguous stimulus test: typed nonsense sentences in multiple onionskin carbon copies, where the fourteenth carbon (the smudge of type was barely differentiated from the white paper) produced the perfect stimulus for personal preoccupations to emerge as one attempted to read!

The problem with the ambiguous stimulus was that responses to it inevitably were interpreted normatively as well as ipsatively. Thus, on the Rorschach test, responses where the form of the percept was poorly delineated or the percept itself was formless ("a blob of blood") were pathological indicators regardless of which card or portion of a card elicited them. The application of this oversimplified interpretive approach to an assessment technique whose strength should reside in the justice it does to the individual bothered me. It led to my dissertation, which dealt with person–environment interaction, a fact that I discovered only some years later.

The study was based on the hypothesis that the quality of a person's projective response to a stimulus is a function both of the psychopathology of the responding individual and the gestalt quality of the stimulus. I constructed a series of two-dimensional figures (cut out of black paper and applied to a white background, eliminating the variations in color and shading that add to the complexity of the Rorschach stimuli) and asked a panel of judges to rate each of the 60 figures in terms of the ease with which something was suggested by each form. This process resulted in five figures that consensus established as "highly structured," five figures that were very "poorly structured" (almost everyone found it difficult to think of anything they were reminded of by the figure), and five that were of medium structure. Several indicators of response quality commonly used in Rorschach interpretation were applied to the responses given by subjects who were asked to tell what each figure looked like. These indicators (the most important of which were form quality and congruousness of the percept with reality) were those whose negative aspects were associated with the diagnosis of psychopathology. Three subject groups were recruited from patients in VA facilities: psychoneurotics, outpatient borderline schizophrenics, and hospitalized overt schizophrenics. The results were very clear in showing main effects of stimulus structure and psychopathology on response quality. An interaction effect was also seen such that the maximum differences among the groups came when the stimuli were most ambiguous. Yet, these very ambiguous stimuli elicited pathological responses from people of all those degrees of pathology, which the most highly structured figures were unlikely to do.

I take space in this chapter to describe such a long-forgotten study (Lawton, 1952, 1956) because it represented at the time an idiosyncracy. My faculty committee liked the neatness of the design but found the content uninteresting because the intrapsychic phenomenon under study was diluted in significance by its combination with the mundane concept of stimulus structure. Had I recognized it at the time, I should have framed the study within the framework of person–environment interaction. As it was done, the research was meant to moderate the claims of psychodiagnosticians that intrapsychic productions could be interpreted in an absolute sense without regard to the context in which the production was elicited. The approach was totally empirical, designed to affect practice, not theory.

Ten years of clinical practice followed completion of the doctorate. It was the opportunity to do occasional clinical research that gave spice to that period and finally to the decision in 1963 to seek a full-time research job. Such a job happened to become available at the Philadelphia Geriatric Center, a high-quality service institution that had decided to build a research effort in the still first-generation scientific area of gerontology. This chapter is not about chance as a facet of the environment, but it certainly was a chance phenomenon to have run across a heretofore unknown institution with a creative executive, Arthur Waldman, who was willing to take a chance on me despite my total lack of background, knowledge and, initially, even motivation, for aging research. I think the last and determining aleatory event was the comment of my sociologist friend Paul Hare that at age 40 I'd better accept this job offer because "aging is the coming thing."

GERONTOLOGY: APPLIED AND EMPIRICAL

The clinical years had left Lewin, Murray, and Helson distant memories. The path that led eventually toward environmental psychology began independently of this background. The first years in a new field, almost a new career, revealed a nascent subdiscipline characterized by enthusiastic research and service experimentation. As it happened, one of the hot areas of service development during the early 1960s was housing for the elderly. The first federal program of housing designed explicitly for older people (Section 202 nonprofit construction program) had been authorized in 1959, about the time when age-segregated public housing began to be developed. In 1960, Arthur Waldman and the Philadelphia Geriatric Center had initiated one of its many innovative services, the first low-cost housing for older people that set out explicitly to provide supportive services as a part of the shelter package. This housing was intended for a segment of the noninstitutional population who were less independent than the usual tenants of housing for the elderly. This model eventually became known as "congregate housing." A companion building, York House South, opened after I arrived at the geriatric center and seemed to offer a natural opportunity for a traditional research evaluation, which was done with little environmental content.

The intervening event that set the form for later evaluation strategies and for long-term development of the rest of my research career was the publication of the *Journal of Social Issues* monograph on the physical environment, edited by Kates and Wohlwill (1966). The seminal article by Wohlwill (1966) that related knowledge about the psychology of stimulation to environmental transactions reawakened the latent adaptation level in me, whereas Sommer's (1966) article illustrated to me how research designed to better the lot of people could be better applied research if driven by theoretically meaningful concepts. To my mind the publication of this monograph dates the beginning of environmental psychology. The same year saw Roger Barker's integrative award lecture to the American Psychological Association on ecological psychology (Barker, 1965).

The design of new research to follow the evaluation of York House South afforded the opportunity to add some environmental elements to the usual evaluation scheme. In particular I found some of the research techniques central to behavior setting analysis (Barker, 1968) and others detailed by Ittelson, Rivlin, and Proshansky (1970) to have direct applicability for our research with older people. These approaches involved the systematic observation of how people distributed themselves among the spaces in the housing. Housing for the elderly was built with hallways, floor lounges, a lobby, social rooms, activity rooms, laundry, physician's office, and so on. At the time, however, no one had bothered to ask how much such spaces were used, by whom, or for what purposes. Picking up on the clinical orientation toward observing behavior and developing empirical knowledge for use in solving a problem of the moment, it was easy to see the benefits of simply finding out whether the spaces that were so expensively produced were being used enough to justify their cost. Through systematic, replicated behavior mapping it was easy to determine, for example, that the roomy 12- × 40-foot lounges at the end of one hallway on each of the 10 floors of York House had mean population counts that approached zero over about 400 instances of observation. The usefulness of this information to sponsors and architects is obvious. Producing the information required little theory, only the time and patience to do the counting.

The continuation of the research yielded anther small finding, rather insignificant in its own right, but one that led me back from empirics to theory. One aspect of the evaluation of the building was a sociometric survey of all 250 tenants 12 months after occupancy (Lawton & Simon, 1968). All tenants had also received a physical examination by our own physicians, information that was used to make an overall health rating. We found the expected propinquity effect in naming friends; that is, people's friends tended to be neighbors on the same floor rather than on other floors, and even within the same floor, the probability of being named as a friend was a linear function of the distance between apartments. What was more interesting, however, was that the propinquity effect was moderated by the health of the person making the friendship choices. Tenants in better health ranged more widely throughout the building in making their choices, whereas those in poorest health were likely to name only their closest neighbors. It was clear that the environmental barrier of distance (defined physically but clearly experienced in psychological "life space," Lewin, 1951) became more salient for those of reduced physical ability. The healthier people, with a larger pool from which to choose, thus had a higher probability of finding people who shared values, interests, and sympathetic personality traits rather than simple proximity.

The generalization derived from this finding was more like a hypothesis than a principle. I framed the "environmental docility hypothesis" to suggest that decreased personal competence led to a greater likelihood that one's behavior or subjective state would be controlled by environmental factors, or alternatively, that a greater proportion of explanation for personal outcomes was due to environmental influence for less competent people. Later on, I reviewed other gerontological literature, for example, research on cognitive functioning and environmental relocation, to conclude that the environmental docility hypothesis was upheld by other types of evidence for the selective effect of environment on the more impaired (Lawton, 1982).

Before moving on to the next chronological phase, let me pause to note explicitly where the core dilemmas fit into this early experience in gerontology.

The occasion for there being a job opportunity at a center providing services to older people was the demand for applied research. The aged were just beginning to be recognized as a priority group for planned services. There was no Medicare, no Older Americans Act, and perhaps 1,000 units of housing in federal programs—programs that in 1989 account for well over 1 million older people. But all of these innovative programs already existed in the minds of foresighted planners, some of whom saw the need for evaluation as a component of the planning process. Basic research was never in this picture at all. Theory in gerontology would slowly develop, but it was a latecomer. Chronologically earlier and totally consistent with the applied thrust of the research, an atheoretical empirical approach to housing research was extraordinarily well-suited to produce information that could be consumed by a waiting audience. Planners wanted to know the kinds of services potential clients would want. Administrators wanted to know how satisfied clients were with different design features. Architects wanted to know what features would be used most frequently or what would be associated with better outcomes. These applied issues addressed in this research demanded a head-counting, empirical approach, but its results led to the docility hypothesis, a theoretically relevant contribution. The final dilemma, person or environment, ended with a somewhat greater degree of synthesis than did the other two. After a highly person-oriented clinical phase, the early gerontology phase produced the sociometric research finding whose formal characteristics were exactly in the mold of the stimulus structure and psychopathology research: Person (older people in good and poor health) and environment (unrestricted versus constricted geographic range) interact in determining an evaluatable outcome (wide versus narrow choice of friends, the wider choice presumably eventuating in greater satisfaction). The appealing aspect of this finding was the position of relatively equal importance given person and environment.

As the gerontology phase matured, good fortune with grant funding and a highly supportive environment of administrators, professionals, and a growing body of research colleagues made possible a succession of research projects that dealt with specialized housing, unplanned housing, institutions, and alternative supportive environments.

The executive of the Philadelphia Geriatric Center, Arthur Waldman, not only created the first research institute located in a nonprofit home for the aged, but the housing study described was only one of several research endeavors built around Arthur's visionary ideas. He foresaw by 20 years the need to be concerned with providing a positive quality of life for Alzheimer's-disease patients. A 5-year planning process was devoted to the social and physical concept of the Weiss Institute, a building designed explicitly for this subject group. This process included assistance from person–environment researchers such as Robert Sommer, Humphrey Osmond, Kyoshi Izumi, Robert Kleemeier, Louis Gelwicks, Edward Hall, and Joseph Esherick. Alton DeLong spent a summer doing valuable behavior observation. Another innovation of Waldman was the remodeling of a dozen inexpensive houses near the Center for the use of relatively independent older people. My colleague Elaine Brody evaluated this alternative housing effort, and I had the good fortune of participating in it. Arthur Waldman and Elaine Brody were only the first of an extraordinary succession of people at the Philadelphia Geriatric Center attracted to early work with older people. They knew a great deal more than I—Arthur with his lightning-quick ability to diagnose a need and Elaine with in-depth knowledge of how real people think and act in situations that researchers tend to over-abstract. Over the years, in similar fashion, I had as collaborators Mort Kleban from whom to learn better statistics; Sandra Howell for iconoclastic thinking about person and environment; Lucille Nahemow for fortifying the social psychological aspects of our research; and Tom Byerts and Bob Newcomer as longer distance collaborators and co-authors.

Collective collaboration was just as important, the prime example of which is the Environmental Design Research Association (EDRA), which I discovered at EDRA 2 in Pittsburgh. EDRA is the annual meeting that it is possible to love totally because its fun and stimulation are not, like those of larger organizations, adulterated with overload and the primacy of politics. Tom Byerts and I, plus colleagues that spanned both person–environment and gerontology (Howell, Nahemow, Pastalan, Regnier, Windley, and others), enlivened our inner lives by thinking of ourselves as the gerontological Mafia of EDRA. In fact, this effort was an environmental project of the Gerontological Society that did affect the programming of EDRA for years and in return attracted a number of EDRA people to gerontology. One of these subprojects on theory (Lawton, Windley, & Byerts, 1982) successfully promoted major contributions by nongerontologists like Ittelson, Rapoport, and Archea.

MIDCAREER GERONTOLOGY: INTERACTION

The years from 1970 through 1985 produced a number of large-scale research endeavors. There was a national study of federally assisted housing (Lawton, Nahemow, & Teaff, 1975, for example), the Weiss Institute evaluation (Lawton, Fulcomer, & Kleban, 1984), a follow-up of the national assisted housing sample (Nahemow, Lawton, & Howell, 1977, for example), the analysis of the early years' data on the older population from the *Annual Housing Survey* (Lawton & Hoover, 1979), Brody's evaluation of alternative housing (Brody, 1978; Lawton, Brody, & Turner-Massey, 1978), and a qualitative study of impaired older people receiving in-home services and the ways they used their homes (Saperstein, Moleski, & Lawton, 1985).

Throughout this time, not only the service-providing sector but the policymaking sector (Congressional committees, the Department of Housing and Urban Development—HUD—the Administration on Aging, the Farmers Home Administration, and even the White House) provided opportunities for our research results to become visible. The work described has continued to influence such areas as national policy in congregate housing, design standards for housing, and the design of institutions.

The design of our research and the analysis of the data developed a style whereby we typically defined psychological and social outcomes (for example, psychological well-being, housing satisfaction, or amount of social interaction) and sought environmental correlates of these outcomes that remained significant after controlling for the usual background and other personal factors that might be associated with outcome. In this manner, we showed that such external environmental features as high neighborhood age concentration (Lawton, Moss, & Moles, 1984), low neighborhood crime rate (Lawton, Nahemow, & Yeh, 1980), and the presence of tenant-controllable heat (Lawton & Nahemow, 1979) were associated with favorable outcomes, whereas project size was not (Lawton, Nahemow, & Teaff, 1975). Such empirical findings from our research were in demand by the gerontological services community.

This style of research spoke to the third dilemma, person and environment. Most of our work, in showing that some environmental feature did contribute to the outcome, provided repeated confirmation that environment counts. Much environmental research has had that same intent, without having gone further to establish rules to predict when that effect will be observed and when it will not. Thus it seems evident that new environmental features will continue to be evaluated by asking the same simple question: Does the feature contribute prediction to a desired outcome over and above that predicted by personal and social factors?

The theory-relevant product from this phase, unlike that represented by the dissertation and the sociometric survey, did not come from a particular finding, however. Rather, a more encompassing theory development came about because Lucille Nahemow and I had to write a chapter for an American Psychological Association monograph on aging (Eisdorfer & Lawton, 1973). Although by then many other geropsychologists had addressed environmental issues, our chapter was to be the first integrative review of the new field that we called "ecology and aging" (Lawton & Nahemow, 1973). She and I discussed for hours and days how best to conceptualize the field and in desperation tried to draw what we were talking. Our diagram of "the ecological model" (Figure 1) put together the environmental docility hypothesis, adaptation level, and the psychology of stimulation and withdrawal into an interactional model where the person was represented by "competence" (White, 1959) and environment by "press" (Murray, 1938). Because the purpose of this chapter is not to rehash this now very old model, it is appropriate only to make reference to later attempts to develop these ideas further (Lawton, 1982, 1989). For the present, the important points to make are, first, that despite the applied, empirical focus of much of the housing and institutional research, a contribution to theory somehow fell out of it. Second, person and environment in our conception were clearly separated and found to interact nicely, as good P–E researchers would expect.

The next three sections will turn to more extended discussions of the three dilemmas.

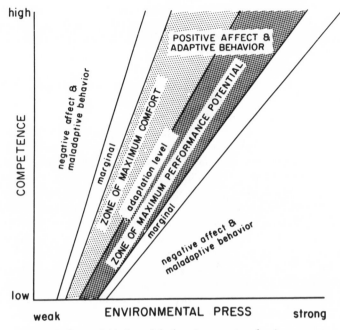

Figure 1. An ecological model of environment and aging.

BASIC RESEARCH, APPLIED RESEARCH, AND DISSEMINATION

One may well begin the discussion of the basic-applied dilemma with the reasonable question—Is there any research in environmental psychology whose results do not have some application in practice?" Of course, it is partly a matter of degree. Yet, the mere fact that most research of this kind has perforce represented the environmental aspect of the research with variations that are, or could be, components of real living environments automatically makes easier a translation from laboratory to life—compare environmental research with research on the structure of affect, for example, in terms of lesser possibility for immediate application.

Ideally basic and applied aspects merge and mutually reinforce one another. It is worthwhile citing at length one of the first and still one of the most influential major research endeavors in housing for the elderly, performed by the sociologist Irving Rosow (1967). Rosow's research was performed in a number of apartment buildings in Cleveland that represented a broad range of age concentrations, from totally age-segregated to those with just a scattering of older people. Although this research produced an immense amount of new knowledge, the findings for which the research is best remembered dealt with the relationship between the age concentration in an apartment building and the social involvement and integration of its older residents. Briefly, Rosow's data showed clearly that the amount of social integration was a direct function of the number of age peers living in one's building. Although social interchange between people in different age cohorts did occur, overall amount of social interchange involving older tenants was restricted in direct proportion to the excess of younger residents in a given building.

Coming as it did when the first age-segregated purpose-built federal housing was being produced, the impact of this research on later policy and practice was major. Age segregation was, and to some extent still is, an emotionally unpalatable idea to many. The continued production of this form of housing in the 30 years that have followed was aided tremendously by these research findings.

Yet, Rosow himself has steadfastly insisted (personal communication) that he *never* performed housing research! Rather, housing was the context for his testing a very carefully reasoned theory that our society did not provide a structure that facilitated socialization to old age. The result was that rolelessness, strain, and isolation were risks for older people but risks that were lessened where the social context could foster age-specific socialization opportunities.

Most research does not achieve such a perfect blend of goals as that of Rosow. I shall propose two strategies for good, but not perfect, achievement of defensible goals for the person–environment researcher. Both begin with a social need and thus are more likely to serve applied goals particularly well. The first is post-hoc basic research, where research is formulated to answer a question relevant to a social need but the design is determined in such a way as to add to the knowledge base in a form generalizable beyond the present social need. A classic example is the research Lewin (1952) performed on the then-cogent environmental problem of getting people to accept offbeat types of meat rather than traditional steak and roast varieties during the wartime meat shortage. The results were useful in achieving the applied goal but also helped develop the larger system that became the theory of "group dynamics."

On a much more modest level, research I performed to evaluate the impact of congregate, or service-rich, housing on older people produced results that helped understand better some of the personality dynamics of old age. Whether supportive services such as on-site meals, homemaker, or physician services should be a part of housing planned for older people who are clearly able to live outside an institution was a persistent issue in the early days of the national housing programs. Our research program first identified some of the complexities in this question. People were clearly sorting themselves nonrandomly into this type of housing. That is, the people who chose congregate housing were more impaired in a number of ways than those who chose noncongregate, or independent, housing (Lawton, 1969). After a year, the impact on tenants in the two types of housing was, indeed, different (Lawton, 1976), even after accounting for the initial differences between tenants in the two housing types. However, the difference was not as hypothesized; that is, favorable effects were not a function of the "correct" initial matching of tenants with most appropriate housing (i.e., most-competent people in independent housing and least-competent in congregate housing). Rather, there were differ-

ent main effects: Independent housing showed enhanced outgoing social behavior and continuation of interaction in the local neighborhood but no favorable effect on psychological well-being. Congregate housing appeared to
produce a relative improvement in subjective well-being as compared to independent housing but a relative restriction of social space. Thus we were able to
inform sponsors about some possible effects of the two types of housing. On a
theoretical level, the pattern of findings portrayed both the self-directive process of matching one's needs with an appropriate environment and the existence of a possible trade-off between contentment and excitement. Let me be
the first to point out both the post-hoc nature of this latter finding and at the
same time the legitimacy of making the most out of such unexpected results.

The second practice-directed research strategy is simply design-problem
research done to provide guidance to those responsible for decisions regarding
the person-made environment. This type of research is so familiar that examples seem unnecessary. What does deserve comment is the intrinsic tension in
the milieu composed of researcher and consumers of research information.
This confluence best illustrates the wicked nature of the relationship between
basic knowledge and practice. Synthesis is rarely a feasible goal in reaching an
informed design solution because the demand for practical solutions always
outstrips the resources of basic science to deliver them. Thus the researcher
faces the dilemma of communicating unsatisfyingly small amounts of knowledge derived from research that meets acceptable methodological standards or,
on the other hand, going significantly beyond the data so as to provide concrete design assistance. Either way someone loses, the practitioner in frustration over the limited amount of guidance available from the academic, or the
researcher in risking a loss of integrity in going beyond the data.

Since I began to do research in environment and aging, a significant portion of my professional life has been spent in translating knowledge regarding
person–environment relationships to other professionals. This 25-year-long
lecture tour has often been directed to multidisciplinary audiences but has also
included specialized groups of architects, urban planners, social workers, occupational therapists, nutritionists, administrators of long-term care, and
many other professionals. The clamor for knowledge is deafening. One always
flirts with the temptation to make the rules sound simple, the applications
general, the alternatives definitive. My conviction is that one should be willing
to risk giving informed advice that is consistent with research- or theory-based
knowledge but goes beyond what has been clearly demonstrated. One can find
in every group discussing a design problem someone much less informed than
oneself who is ready to assert an armchair opinion as scientific fact. Therefore,
assuming that one has an edge on people of that type who purvey misinforma-
tion, the greater social good is clearly served by judiciously going beyond the
available data in order to speak relevantly to the design issue. There are several
roles that the researcher with a social mission can play—the sensitizer, the
advisor, and the facilitator.

The *sensitizer* has a very rewarding function. Most practitioners, particularly those outside the design professions, have never thought of the idea that

the environment can influence well-being and that they are in a position to affect the way the environment functions. Naive people are thus ripe and enthusiastic consumers of some of the basic principles of behavioral design. "My lecture" has been given hundreds of times by now. I introduce the basic rationale for including the environment as a "member of the treatment team" and the special reasons for the salience of environment in serving old people (i.e., the environmental docility hypothesis). When I anticipate some modicum of sophistication in the prospective audience, I display the ecological model. The meat of the lecture is a series of slides illustrating the potential effects of good and bad design features on the functional, social, and psychological well-being of the older user. The moral is that many of these useful aids to adaptive behavior represent the results of applying common sense, once the otherwise design-naive service worker becomes sensitized. Enhancing sensitization is a level of generality of dissemination where I function most effectively.

The *advisory* role might be seen as similar to that of a performing chef. Whatever the area of application of knowledge, scientists tend to be suspicious of the cookbook approach. Yet 35 years ago Meehl (1956) effectively corrected the course of clinical psychology by just the right amount when he argued that what we need is a better cookbook, not subjective, clinical, artistry. A really effective cookbook for behavioral design has not yet been written because our experts are just beginning to organize the kind of knowledge that comes only from repetitive observation of thousands of success and failures made by others in the design process. A beginning of this type of compendium was made in two publications by Zeisel and associates (Zeisel, Epp, & Demos, 1978; Zeisel, Welch, Epp, & Demos, 1983), which collected the germinal knowledge and observations of people who were mostly researchers in the person–environment area. I feel that such an advisory role is best performed by someone with credentials in one of the design fields, provided they have enough behavioral science in their training to reinforce the necessary skepticism and respect for evidence that such a background confers. In any case, there are a few people in this field who go far beyond the sensitization function as they lecture or consult with clients on the nitty-gritty elements of design. The sensitizer is not suited to work by the drawing board with the architect. The behaviorally trained architect in an advisory role is.

Finally, the *facilitator* combines the technical expertise of the advisor with rare human relations skills to function as a member of a multidisciplinary team working in a dynamic design process. All good design is the result of such a process to some extent, but the facilitator is there to insure that all the people with a stake in the product, in addition to the client and the architect, have a chance to interact and be heard. This early involvement clearly has long-term consequences in motivating staff to make a structure work during the postconstruction phase.

The use of knowledge derived from basic research is decreasingly visible as one moves from the sensitizing to the advisory to the facilitating role. It is important to recognize the limits of one's consumer group's tolerance for material that sounds academic. There is often an undertone of hostility when a consumer group perceives that the knowledge being disseminated goes too far from their everyday concrete problems of giving service. Thus the usual succession of knowledge moves from the researcher toward the trend setters, the vanguard of people in the practice arena who approach their own work conceptually and who in turn translate these concepts into the how-to terms of the practitioners who work for them. The sensitizer works best with the practitioner trend setter, often being perceived by line-level practitioners as speaking over their heads. The advisor and the facilitator are usually not the primary producers of research knowledge but have training in the methods that produce such knowledge and therefore bridge well the research and practice arenas.

To conclude this section, I repeat my conviction that basic and applied research feed one another and that dissemination of the knowledge gained from both is a responsibility of the researcher. At the same time, it is a long chain beginning with basic research that moves on toward everyday practice. The most effective dissemination efforts span only a few links in the chain, not the entire chain.

THEORY AND EMPIRICS

Basic research is likely to be theory driven. Thus much that might be said about theory has been covered in discussing basic and applied research. In this section, I shall acknowledge once more the power of good theory to direct basic research and ultimately practice but go on to argue that descriptive, atheoretical research in environment and behavior is also necessary.

The subdiscipline of person–environment relations has woefully neglected the task of establishing the basic parameters that characterize the way people relate to their environments. Despite the genius of Roger Barker and his students, his major accomplishments have not been fully integrated into the thinking of our subdiscipline. In recent years, it is the theoretical aspects of Barker's work that have caught our attention, for example, undermanning theory (Barker, 1968). Few researchers have continued the task of specifying the yardsticks by which person–environment transactions are measured by performing behavior-setting analyses and the other descriptive tasks advocated by Barker. The comparison of Yoredale and Midwest (Barker & Schoggen, 1973) is not easily replicated on a large scale. Yet it amazes me that no one in all the time since that study or since the one report from the study that dealt with age (Barker & Barker, 1961) has made any attempt to elaborate on that methodology to help understand how age affects the everyday life of both the aged and of everyone else in a community.

Most fields recognize better than do psychology the necessity for defining the usual as a beginning point for understanding variability and deviation. Perhaps because description is the first phase of developing a science, there is a compulsion to prove one's sophistication by moving quickly beyond description toward explanation and control. Neither botany nor chemistry would ever have gone far, however, without the Linnaean classification or the periodic table. Granted that Linnaeus and Mendeleev were theoreticians of the highest order, an immense amount of description led to the major conceptual breakthroughs afforded by these taxonomic schemes. Of course the changing quality of people, societies, and environments makes our field quite different from the field of chemistry. Nonetheless it would seem that if we only had data on the means and variances of some of the Barkerian attributes of behavior settings we should understand geographic, cross-national, or age differences much better.

A neglected resource in what we might call person–environment demography is the American Housing Survey (formerly the Annual Housing Survey, Office of Policy Development and Research, 1983). The fourteenth such national survey of the housing of samples of about 60,000 Americans is now under way, containing an immense amount of information regarding housing, neighborhoods, and the demographic characteristics of its occupants. Perhaps because these data sets are short on psychological variables, interest in these data has generally been limited to economists and the housing development sector, with some exceptions (Lawton, 1980b; Newman, 1985; Struyk & Soldo, 1980).

Such large descriptive surveys have often been the basis for monitoring national programs and ultimately for the development of policy. In the case of the American Housing Survey, for example, it was possible to identify the combination of rural residence in the South and being old and black as circumstances defining a level of housing deficiencies about seven times greater than that experienced by Americans 65 and over in general (Lawton & Hoover, 1971).

Were there more interest in such data it might be possible to mobilize pressure on HUD or the Bureau of the Census to augment future housing surveys with more social or psychological data items. Existing archives in fact contain more data sets with both environmental and social psychological content than is commonly recognized. Other opportunities to collect such parametric data have been systematically lost by agencies like HUD, who ought to be taking the responsibility for archiving data like those obtained in large-scale studies of public housing management, older homeowner's repair activity, and congregate housing. Instead, these data have disappeared.

I have written a detailed review of existing and lost data sets in housing of the elderly (Lawton, 1989). That chapter concludes with the recommendation that a task force be established by organizations concerned with aging and environmental services for the aging to derive a "minimum data set" on the housing of older people. The purpose of defining the components of a short set of data items would be, first to insure that future surveys gather the most important items of housing information; second, that they do so in standard form; and, third, to make it easy to attach the most basic housing items to surveys that focus on other content, such as health, income, or work. The chance that research on the explanatory level may be possible with any data set depends particularly on having some items that enable the cross-disciplinary analysis of data.

I confess to a real enjoyment in counting. Stimulated by Barker and Barker's (1961) and Ittelson *et al.*'s (1970) work, one component of my first multiple-site housing research compared 12 housing sites by means of replicated behavior maps covering all their public spaces (Lawton, 1970). That is, without distinguishing which people were observed, counts were made that identified where people were at time-sampled intervals. Among other findings, these data underlined the importance of common spaces for the less-mobile older tenant: Housing sites with less healthy tenant populations were found to have a greater proportion of their populations visible in public areas than was true for the sites with healthier tenants. One concluded that such on-site spaces were thus more salient to the quality of life of frail, older tenants than for the more independent. In all cases, the lobbies were the heavily used areas, even where they were restricted in space or tenants' use of them was hampered by administrative decree. The sites where open apartment doors were more frequently counted were those with higher levels of social life as determined by sociometric survey. Further, those tenants with open doors were themselves more socially integrated by other criteria. We thus concluded that the open door was an active environmental manipulation performed by people who wished to make a social invitation. In sum, one can learn a great deal about the dynamics of person–environment relations from the right kind of head-counting data. The time budget is another type of descriptive research from which the returns have been great (Altergott, 1988; Lawton & Moss, 1986–1987; Michelson, 1977; Szalai, 1972), although the potential for linking behavioral data with environmental data (i.e., the location of the behavior) has been infrequently recognized.

Along with this confession of love for counting, I acknowledge an even greater transgression, that of having failed to publish some head-counting data because it seemed inconsistent at the time with the greater glory to be derived from doing more theoretically relevant research. The housing research done with Nahemow represented the only research ever done that was able to study from a psychosocial perspective a nationally representative probability sample of the two major planned housing programs for older people, 100 public housing sites and 50 Section 202 sites (Lawton & Nahemow, 1975). A nested sample of 2,000 older tenants in these environments furnished a small set of basic data, and about half of them received an extended interview. Thus we had the wherewithal to produce an enlightening description of these important behavior settings as they existed in 1971. We chose not to put the time into such a report because, echoing the judgment of many of our scientific peers, we undervalued the worth of purely descriptive data. As an illustration of the potential value of such description, however, we did pull out a small piece of our descriptive data to contrast the extent to which the public housing program served black elderly (well) with comparable data for the 202 program (infinitesimally). This paper, published in an obscure journal (Lawton & Krassen,

1973), nevertheless came to the attention of HUD officials and occasioned a total review of how the federal programs reported their minority populations and ultimately contributed to strengthening the affirmative marketing requirements for the 202 program.

In conclusion, descriptive data contribute greatly to scientific knowledge as well as to the monitoring of social programs and development of policy. As mentioned earlier in the case of applied research, post-hoc analyses of the right kind of descriptive data may utilize or lead to theoretically meaningful concepts. The best way to increase the probability that one's descriptive data are of "the right kind" is to establish, through multidisciplinary consensus, a short list of necessary environmental components that should be used in standard form in environmental research and used to link environmental concepts to other concepts in research whose major purpose is in some area other than person–environment relations.

PERSON, ENVIRONMENT, AND TRANSACTION

In the beginning phase of environmental psychology, it was simply accepted that person and environment were the dual foci of attention and that the neglected feature of psychological research was the interaction between the two. Partitioning the amount of variance in some outcome (for example, social behavior) that was attributable to environment and that attributable to person was the favorite research strategy of the time. An exemplary research project was reported by Moos (1968), who found that behavioral responses to different psychiatric settings were significantly predicted by differences among subjects, differences among settings, and by the differential effects of particular settings on particular people (i.e., the interaction between person and environment).

As mentioned earlier, this P, E, P × E structure characterized my dissertation research, where the ordered severity of psychopathology was the person aspect and the ordered degree of stimulus structure the environmental aspect. Similarly, the environmental docility hypothesis and its elaboration into the ecological model began with a study of the relationship between the personal characteristic of health and the environmental characteristic of location and distance between residences. It seems like stretching things very little to say that virtually all empirical research in environmental psychology that has related person and environment to some outcome has utilized the interaction paradigm.

Put this fact together with another attribute of person–environment science, that is, that the greatest minds in this field deny that environment can be distinguished from the person, for example, Ittelson (1973):

> The environment involves the active participation of all aspects. Man is never concretely encountered independent of the situation through which he acts nor is the environment ever encountered independent of the encountering individual. It is meaningless to speak of either as existing apart from the situation in

which it is encountered. The word "transaction" has been used to label such a situation, for the word carries a double implication: One, all parts of the situation enter into it as active participants; and two, these parts owe their very existence as encountered in a situation to such active participation—they do not appear as already existing entities which merely interact with each other without affecting their own identity. (pp. 18–19)

Elsewhere Ittelson says, "the environment is an artifact created in man's own image" (1973, p. 18).

More recently, Wapner (1987) stated that "the treatment of the person and his or her environment as separable, independent parts, which influence one another, represents a partitive, elementaristic, and interactional analysis that is rejected" (p. 1440).

The views of Altman and Rogoff (1987) on transaction, rather than interaction, as the appropriate form for understanding person and environment may be portrayed by a few of the section headings of their treatment of "world views" in P–E relations: "Transactional research takes settings and contexts into account" (p. 33); "transactional research seeks to understand the perspective of the participants in an event" (p. 34); and "transactional research emphasizes the study of process and change" (p. 34).

Transaction thus moves beyond interaction to view person and environment as inseparable and therefore must find a unit of analysis that subsumes both. For Barker (1968), this metaunit was the behavior setting and for Altman and Rogoff (1987) the event.

These and other writers have found exciting ways to demonstrate the interrelatedness, mutual causal patterns, and the hierarchical nature of different scales of human action. I have found the greatest contribution of the transactional world view to be the emphasis on the consistency among levels of meaning of phenomena of differing levels of complexity. Along with this multiple layering of person–environment transaction has come the strong case for qualitative research and analysis as the mode most appropriate to the study of transaction.

The last environmental research I have done was inspired directly by the transactional model (Lawton, 1985; Saperstein, Moleski, & Lawton, 1985). Philadelphia's local area agency on aging sought our team to take a look at the way highly impaired older people were managing to continue to live alone in their community residences. The origin of this project lay in the wish to learn about deficiencies in the physical quality of the home and the way people coped with them. Thus once again an applied-research goal was the beginning point.

The team that visited 50 homes consisted of a social worker, an architect, a psychologist, and an occupational therapist. Three products resulted from this research. The first was a checklist of home deficiencies, which resulted in an ability to tally the most prevalent ones. For example, the hazardous rug and extension cord were ubiquitous. The second was an inventory of interesting environmental solutions that the older people in collaboration with their families had managed in order to compensate for their disabilities and vulnerabilities. As an example, one of the most prevalent measures taken was to use the dining table as a surface on which the display of objects would serve either as a reminder of things to be done or as a way of making their retrieval easier (medicines; bills to pay; dishes, glasses, and pans). The third product of the research was on a different level. The entire person-in-context constellation of some of these people, through our qualitative observations, suddenly yielded a generalization describing this arrangement: the "control center." A number of the least-mobile people had established an area of the living room where a great deal of their day was spent. From their position in the chair, their "surveillance zone" (Rowles, 1984) included the front door and a view through the living room windows of the exterior entrance and varying portions of the sidewalk and street. Control over other types of incoming information was afforded by having the telephone, radio, and television in easy reach. Other instrumental and affective stimulation was managed by the objects laid on surfaces within arm's reach: medicine, food, letters, photographs, reading material, and whatever else.

These three products illustrate well the significance and the limitations of our methods for studying person–environment relations. The purely descriptive checklist, if we had a larger and more representative sample, could provide a guide to the local home maintenance and repair agency and the in-home social services agency regarding the major problems to be looked for in their areas. Similarly, good ideas on the types of home adaptations that might be possible for older clients and their families to make were yielded by the case examples observed in these homes. The observations that led to formulating the concept of the control center were useful at the theoretical level of understanding the transactions that linked the person and his or her personal environment. That is, one could discern the parallels among differing needs at different levels that were being served by the control center. Poor health and reduced mobility shrunk the relevant physical space for the people. The remaining relevant space assumed greater salience. Their sensory and cognitive functions, being focused on this reduced surveillance zone, achieved a higher density of control over what went on in that zone. Social space, also restricted, was fortified in compensatory fashion by heightened attentiveness to proxy means of social integration such as watching street behavior, watching television, and using the telephone. One could spin out this picture of impaired people doing the best they could, given their disabilities, by adapting to, and at the same time creating, a new living environment.

The point of describing the control center in such detail is to illustrate some attributes of the transactional approach. The method best suited to P–E transactional study is qualitative. There was no focus on outcomes and their determination by causally prior events. In transactional research, multiple features of person and context require attention. The two results of this part of the study were, first, better understanding of the meaning of environment and self to the impaired person, and second, an illustration of the syntony among different levels (person, environment) and scale (aspects of proximal visual stimuli, the room, the neighborhood, the world) as person and environment exchanged and changed one another.

Without the intellectual encouragement in the writing of Altman, Wapner, and Ittelson, my receptiveness to the control center phenomenon would probably have remained subthreshold. In going back to the seminal literature in person–environment relations while writing this chapter, it became increasingly clear to me that 25 years of research in this area has made some of the gaps in the science wider, rather than bridging them. On transactionalism, where has this approach led? The answer is mainly toward theory development, through qualitative observation and conceptual creativity. This approach has fed every stream of application in the design professions because the levels of generality of transactional concepts are the same level of art practiced by planners and architects as they strive to operationalize means toward the achievement of human goals—that is, highly generalized and conceptual. The other side of this question is that transactionalism has not led us to much traditional social scientific research. To understand personal meaning and *psychophysical parallelism* (Köhler's early term to account for the ability of person and external world to relate to one another) are knowledge-extending goals, but their ability to lead toward the solution of concrete problems is not direct.

Although one can argue about the overall efficiency of yield of linearly conceived attempts to determine the contributions of single or multiple environmental attributes to personal well-being, the fact is that practically all quantitative empirical P–E research has been of this type. I argue further that the planning and design process requires such linear, interactional research every bit as much as it does the grander concepts of transactionalism. To name a few types of such interactional research, demography, social area analysis, time budget study, human factors research, and program evaluation cannot be performed without the concept of a desired outcome that can be affected by attention to some manipulable quality of the physical environment. Thus, I come down squarely in the camp of the Society for Preservation of Person and Environment as Interacting Elements (sometimes) of a Causal Sequence.

PRESENT AND FUTURE RESEARCH

Recent years have seen me return to more traditionally psychological research, dealing variously with the quality of the last year of life (Lawton, Moss, & Glicksman, 1989), care-giving stress (Lawton, Brody, & Saperstein, 1989), and depression (Parmelee, Katz, & Lawton, 1989). At present I am still working in each of these areas but also in a new area for me, and one relatively neglected in gerontology—emotions in adult development. The grant from the National Institute of Aging can potentially support a program of research over a 10-year period and allows interesting new ideas to be developed as they arise.

Early results from this research appear to affirm the idea that increasing age involves some constraining of affective experience in both positive and negative directions. That is, our older people report that they are, thankfully, free of the mood swings of earlier years. They also may experience fewer "highs." Although the latter may be regrettable, the trade-off for fewer "lows" is totally desirable. Further, many are very firm in seeing themselves to be the creators of this new maturity.

So far the research has not dealt with environmental issues. However, within the next 2 years I plan to go back to some of the stimulating research on the meaning of home by Altman and Werner (1985), Rowles (1984), and Rubinstein (1989) to explore further how affect becomes invested in the home by some and not by others. It is particularly interesting to wonder how those who relocate into retirement communities and other positively chosen new contexts deal with such processes as attachment to and identification with home. Does age-related constriction of affective experience make the change easier, or do some people reinvest affect in a new home so readily that the relocation is not even bothersome?

In this turn back to environmental research there will no longer be Arthur Waldman, who died, nor Elaine and Steve Brody, who are about to retire. Fortunately, my convoy of people who know more than I do continues in a younger cohort: Robert Rubinstein, Mark Luborsky, and Steven Albert, creative anthropologists with real interest in environment; Pat Parmelee, a student of Irwin Altman, Rachel Pruchno with a lineage to Jack Wohlwill and Martin Faletti, and even younger people from Irvine (Paul Thuras) and City University environmental psychology (Chris Hoffman and Doris Hunt). This future looks fantastically stimulating!

CONCLUSION

The two threads of this chapter link basic research, theory, and transactionalism, on the one hand, and applied research, descriptive research, and interactionism on the other. It is clear that most contributors to the science of person–environment relations have their personal preferences for one or the other of these lines. My conclusion about the gaps that separate the basic from the applied researcher, the theoretician from the empiricist, and the transactionalist from the interactionist is that they are real, representing dialectic forces whose tension perhaps provides continuing motivation to seek new knowledge. In conclusion, my own major mission is to help in the solution of society's problems. Translating this goal into the arena of P–E, it is something of a revelation for me to recognize belatedly that the practice of environmental design is spoken to by both of these streams. The one characterized by transactionalism deals best in purposes, goals, and innovations. The one characterized by interactionism deals best with the mechanics of design.

REFERENCES

Altergott, K. (1988). *Daily life in later life: Comparative perspectives.* Newbury Park, CA: Sage Publications.

Altman, I., & Gauvain, M. (1981). A cross-cultural and dialectic analysis of homes. In L. S. Liben, A. H. Patterson, & N. Newcombe (Eds.), *Spatial representation and behavior across the life span* (pp. 283–320). New York: Academic Press.

Altman, I., & Rogoff, B. (1987). World views in psychology: Trait, interactional, organismic, and transactional perspectives. In D. Stokols & I. Altman (Eds.), *Handbook of environmental psychology* (Vol. 1, pp. 7–40). New York: John Wiley.

Altman, I., & Werner, C. M. (1985). *Home environments (Vol. 8). Human behavior and environment.* New York: Plenum Press.

Barker, R. G. (1965). Explorations in ecological psychology. *American Psychologist, 20,* 1–4.

Barker, R. G. (1968). *Ecological psychology.* Stanford: Stanford University Press.

Barker, R. G., & Barker, L. S. (1961). The psychological ecology of old people in Midwest, Kansas, and Yoredale, Yorkshire. *Journal of Gerontology, 16,* 231–239.

Barker, R. G., & Schoggen, P. (1973). *Qualities of community life.* San Francisco: Jossey-Bass.

Brody, E. M. (1978). Community housing for the elderly. *The Gerontologist, 18,* 121–128.

Eisdorfer, C., & Lawton, M. P. (Eds.). (1973). *The psychology of adult development and aging.* Washington, DC: American Psychological Association.

Helson, H. (1925). The psychology of Gestalt. *American Journal of Psychology, 36,* 342–370.

Helson, H. (1964). *Adaptation level theory.* New York: Harper & Row.

Ittelson, W. H. (1973). *Environment and cognition.* New York: Seminar Press.

Ittelson, W. H. (1976). Some issues facing a theory of environment and behavior. In H. M. Proshansky, W. H. Ittelson, & L. G. Rivlin (Eds.), *Environmental psychology* (2nd ed. pp. 51–59). New York: Holt, Rinehart & Winston.

Ittelson, W. H., Rivlin, L. G., & Proshansky, H. M. (1970). The use of behavioral maps in environmental psychology. In H. M. Proshansky, W. H. Ittelson, & L. G. Rivlin (Eds.), *Environmental psychology: Man and his physical setting* (pp. 658–668). New York: Holt, Rinehart & Winston.

Kates, R. W., & Wohlwill, J. F. (Eds.). (1966). Man's response to the physical environment. *Journal of Social Issues, 22* (Whole No. 4).

Lawton, M. P. (1952). *Stimulus structure and psychopathology as determinants of the perceptual response.* Unpublished doctoral dissertation. Columbia University.

Lawton, M. P. (1956). Stimulus structure as a determinant of the perceptual response. *Journal of Consulting Psychology, 20,* 351–355.

Lawton, M. P. (1969). Supportive services in the context of the housing environment. *The Gerontologist, 9,* 15–19.

Lawton, M. P. (1970). Public behavior of older people in congregate housing. In J. Archea & C. Eastman (Eds.), *Environmental Design Research Association II* (pp. 372–380). Stroudsburg, PA: Dowden, Hutchinson & Ross.

Lawton, M. P. (1976). The relative impact of congregate and traditional housing on elderly tenants. *The Gerontologist, 16,* 237–242.

Lawton, M. P. (1980a). Environmental change: The older person as initiator and responder. In N. Datan & N. Lohmann (Eds.), *Transitions of aging* (pp. 171–193). New York: Academic Press.

Lawton, M. P. (1980b). Residential quality and residential satisfaction among the elderly. *Research on Aging, 2,* 309–328.

Lawton, M. P. (1982). Competence, environmental press, and the adaptation of older people. In M. P. Lawton, P. G. Windley, & T. O. Byerts (Eds.), *Aging and the environment: Theoretical approaches* (pp. 33–59). New York: Springer.

Lawton, M. P. (1985). The elderly in context: Perspectives from environmental psychology and gerontology. *Environment and Behavior, 17,* 501–519.

Lawton, M. P. (1989). Behavior-relevant ecological factors. In K. W. Schaie & C. Schooler (Eds.), *Social structure and the psychological aging processes* (pp. 57–78). Hillside, NJ: Lawrence Erlbaum.

Lawton, M. P. (1989). Knowledge resources and gaps in housing for the aged. In D. Tillson (Ed.), *Aging in place.* Glenview, IL: Scott Foresman.

Lawton, M. P., & Hoover, S. L. (1979). *Annual Housing Survey: 1973. Housing characteristics of older persons in the United States.* (Publication No. HUD-501-1-PDR). Washington, DC: U.S. Government Printing Office.

Lawton, M. P., & Krassen, E. (1973). Federally subsidized housing not for the elderly black. *Journal of Social and Behavioral Sciences, 19*, 65–78.

Lawton, M. P., & Moss, M. (1986–1987). Objective and subjective uses of time by older people. *International Journal of Aging and Human Development, 24*, 171–188.

Lawton, M. P., & Nahemow, L. (1973). Ecology and the aging process. In C. Eisdorfer & M. P. Lawton (Eds.) *Psychology of adult development and aging* (pp. 619–674). Washington, DC: American Psychological Association.

Lawton, M. P., & Nahemow, L. (1975). *Cost, structure, and social aspects of housing for the aged.* Final report to Administration on aging, DHEW. Philadelphia Geriatric Center.

Lawton, M. P., & Nahemow, L. (1979). Social science methods for evaluating the quality of housing for the elderly. *Journal of Architectural Research, 7*, 5–11.

Lawton, M. P., & Simon, B. (1968). The ecology of social relationships in housing for the elderly. *The Gerontologist, 8*, 108–115.

Lawton, M. P., & Yaffee, S. (1980). Victimization and fear of crime in elderly public housing tenants. *Journal of Gerontology, 35*, 768–779.

Lawton, M. P., Nahemow, L., & Teaff, J. (1975). Housing characteristics and the wellbeing of elderly tenants in federally-assisted housing. *Journal of Gerontology, 30*, 601–607.

Lawton, M. P., Brody, E. M., & Turner-Massey, P. (1978). The relationship of environmental factors to changes in well-being. *The Gerontologist, 18*, 133–137.

Lawton, M. P., Nahemow, L., & Yeh, T. M. (1980). Neighborhood environment and the wellbeing of older tenants in planned housing. *International Journal of Aging and Human Development, 11*, 211–227.

Lawton, M. P., Windley, P. G., & Byerts, T. P. (Eds.), (1982). *Aging and the environment: Theoretical approaches.* New York: Springer.

Lawton, M. P., Fulcomer, M., & Kleban, M. H. (1984). Architecture for the mentally impaired elderly. *Environment and Behavior, 16*, 730–757.

Lawton, M. P., Moss, M. S., & Moles, E. (1984). The suprapersonal neighborhood context of older people. *Environment and Behavior, 16*, 84–109.

Lawton, M. P., Brody, E. M., & Saperstein, A. R. (1989). A controlled study of respite service for caregivers of Alzheimers disease patients. *The Gerontologist, 29*, 8–16.

Lawton, M. P., Moss, M., & Glicksman, A. (1989). *The quality of the last year of life of older persons.* Duplicated report, Philadelphia Geriatric Center.

Lewin, K. (1935). *Dynamic theory of personality.* New York: McGraw-Hill.

Lewin, K. (1951). *Field theory in social science.* New York: Harper & Row.

Lewin, K. (1952). Group decision and social change. In G. E. Swanson, T. M. Newcomb, & E. L. Hartley (Eds.), *Readings in social psychology* (2nd ed., pp. 330–344). New York: Holt.

Meehl, P. E. (1956). Wanted—A good cookbook. *American Psychologist, 11*, 263–272.

Michelson, W. (1977). *Environmental choice, human behavior, and residential satisfaction.* New York: Oxford University Press.

Moos, R. H. (1968). Situational analysis of a therapeutic community milieu. *Journal of Abnormal Psychology, 73*, 49–61.

Murray, H. A. (1938). *Explorations in personality.* New York: Oxford.

Nahemow, L., Lawton, M. P., & Howell, S. C. (1977). Elderly people in tall buildings. In D. Conway (Ed.), *Human responses to tall buildings* (pp. 175–181). Stroudsburg, PA: Dowden, Hutchinson and Ross.

Newman, S. J. (1985). Housing and longterm care: The suitability of the elderly's housing to the provision of in-home services. *The Gerontologist, 25*, 35–40.

Office of Policy Development and Research. (1983). *Annual housing survey, 1981.* Washington, DC: U.S. Department of Housing and Urban Development.

Osmond, H. (1957). Function as the basis of psychiatric ward design. *Mental Hospitals, 8*, 23–30.

Parmelee, P. A., Katz, I. D., & Lawton, M. P. (1989). Depression among institutionalized aged: Assessment and prevalence estimation. *Journal of Gerontology: Medical Sciences, 44*, M22–M29.

Riegel, K. F. (1977). The dialectics of time. In N. Datan & H. W. Reese (Eds.), *Life-span development psychology: Dialectical perspectives of experimental research* (pp. 3–45). New York: Academic Press.

Rogers, C. (1942). *Counseling and psychotherapy.* Boston: Houghton-Mifflin.

Rogers, C. R. (Ed.). (1951). *Client-centered therapy.* New York: Houghton-Mifflin.

Rosow, I. (1967). *Social integration of the aged.* New York: Free Press.

Rowles, R. L. (1984). Aging in rural environments. In I. Altman, M. P. Lawton, & J. F. Wohlwill (Eds.), *Elderly people and the environment* (pp. 129–157). New York: Plenum Press.

Rubinstein, R. L. (1989). The home environments of older people: Psychosocial processes relating person to place. *Journal of Gerontology: Social Sciences, 44,* S45–S53.

Saperstein, A., Moleski, W. H., & Lawton, M. P. (1985). Determining housing quality: A guide for home-health care. *Pride Institute Journal, 4,* 41–51.

Sommer, R. (1966). Man's proximate environment. *Journal of Social Issues, 22,* 59–70.

Stephenson, W. (1953). *The study of behavior.* Chicago: University of Chicago Press.

Struyk, R. J., & Soldo, B. J. (1980). *Improving the elderly's housing.* Cambridge, MA: Ballinger.

Szalai, A. (Ed.). (1972). *The use of time.* The Hague: Mouton.

Wapner, S. (1987). A holistic, developmental, systems-oriented environmental psychology: Some beginnings. In D. Stokols & I. Altman (Eds.), *Handbook of environmental psychology* (Vol. 2, pp. 1433–13466). New York: John Wiley.

White, R. W. (1959). Motivation reconsidered: The concept of competence. *Psychological Review, 66,* 297–333.

Wohlwill, J. F. (1966). The physical environment: A problem for a psychology of stimulation. *Journal of Social Issues, 22,* 29–38.

Zeisel, J., Epp, G., & Demos, S. (1978). *Low-rise housing for older people: Behavioral criteria for design.* Washington, DC: Office of Policy Development and Research, U.S. Department of Housing and Urban Development.

Zeisel, J., Wech, P., Epp, G., & Demos, S. (1983). *Midrise elevator housing for older people.* Cambridge, MA: Building Diagnostics.

Index